Instructor's Resource Manual and Test Bank

for

Theory and Practice of Counseling and Psychotherapy

Textbook and Student Manual

Seventh Edition

Case Approach to Counseling and Psychotherapy

Sixth Edition

The Art of Integrative Counseling

CD-ROM for Integrative Counseling

Instructor's Resource Manual and Test Bank

for

Theory and Practice of Counseling and Psychotherapy

Textbook and Student Manual

Seventh Edition

Case Approach to Counseling and Psychotherapy

Sixth Edition

The Art of Integrative Counseling

CD-ROM for Integrative Counseling

Gerald Corey

California State University, Fullerton

THOMSON

BROOKS/COLE

Australia • Canada • Mexico • Singapore • Spain • United Kingdom • United States

Printed in the United States of America

1 2 3 4 5 6 7   07 06 05 04

Printer: West

0-534-53610-7

For more information about our products, contact us at:
Thomson Learning Academic Resource Center
1-800-423-0563

For permission to use material from this text or product, submit a request online at
http://www.thomsonrights.com
Any additional questions about permissions can be submitted by email to
thomsonrights@thomson.com

Brooks/Cole Thomson Learning
10 Davis Drive
Belmont, CA 94002-3098
USA

Asia
Thomson Learning
5 Shenton Way #01-01
UIC Building
Singapore 068808

Australia/New Zealand
Thomson Learning
102 Dodds Street
Southbank, Victoria 3006
Australia

Canada
Nelson
1120 Birchmount Road
Toronto, Ontario M1K 5G4
Canada

Europe/Middle East/South Africa
Thomson Learning
High Holborn House
50/51 Bedford Row
London WC1R 4LR
United Kingdom

Latin America
Thomson Learning
Seneca, 53
Colonia Polanco
11560 Mexico D.F.
Mexico

Spain/Portugal
Paraninfo
Calle/Magallanes, 25
28015 Madrid, Spain

CONTENTS

PREFACE

This *Instructor's Resource Manual* is designed to accompany an integrated learning package:

- *Theory and Practice of Counseling and Psychotherapy* (7th ed., 2005)

- *Student Manual for Theory and Practice of Counseling and Psychotherapy* (7th ed., 2005)

- *Case Approach to Counseling and Psychotherapy* (6th ed., 2005)

- *The Art of Integrative Counseling* (2001)

- *CD –ROM for Integrative Counseling* (2005)

My aim is to share with you some ideas that I've found useful in teaching my own counseling courses, on both an undergraduate and graduate level. In this *Instructor's Resource Manual*, I present many ideas and suggestions concerning the content and structure of the counseling theory courses, materials, and teaching aids, and I share some of the problems and experiences I've had in these courses. I offer questions, exercises, activities, lecture guides, objective quizzes and test items for each theory chapter, short essay questions, final examination, and other materials that I hope will be of use to you in designing your courses.

I've prepared this *Instructor's Resource Manual* to provide suggestions for an integrated package of learning materials: *Theory and Practice of Counseling and Psychotherapy*, the *Student Manual for Theory and Practice of Counseling and Psychotherapy, Case Approach to Counseling and Psychotherapy,* and *The Art of Integrative Counseling*. It is also briefly geared to use with the self-study program, CD-ROM *for Integrative Counseling.* For this last product, there is a *Facilitator's Resource Manual Part IV* if you use the CD-ROM in your classes. This *Facilitator's Resource Manual* contains 50 multiple-choice questions based on the CD-ROM *for Integrative Counseling*.

The core textbook presents the basic theories, and the *Student Manual* provides a basis for experiential learning through exercises and many suggested activities. *Case Approach to Counseling and Psychotherapy* has been streamlined to deal exclusively with the case of Ruth. Twenty therapists work with Ruth from their unique theoretical orientations and I describe my approach to counseling Ruth from eleven different theoretical frameworks. In the book, *The Art of Integrative Counseling*, my main aim is to teach students how to design their own counseling orientation, which is based on incorporating various concepts and a range of techniques from diverse theoretical orientations. This book follows the general structure of the CD ROM for *Integrative Counseling,* which is a program designed to assist students in pulling together their own counseling approach.

Let me emphasize that I've prepared this *Instructor's Resource Manual* as a springboard for you to develop your own ideas and approaches to teaching your courses. I am not attempting to prescribe one way of teaching counseling courses; I am merely presenting material that I find of value. Each of you, whether a beginning or advanced/experienced instructor, will have your own ideas that will fit your personal style of teaching and will meet the unique needs of students you teach. There is more material in this *Instructor's Resource Manual* than can possibly be covered fully in any single course.

You may use these materials in a series of courses that span several semesters, or you may want to use some of these materials in your beginning courses and other materials in your advanced courses. My hope is that you'll take from this *Instructor's Resource Manual* whatever you find of value to you, and that you'll modify and expand on (or delete from) this material to suit yourself. In using an experiential approach you can find, I hope, some value in the ideas and content in this *Instructor's Resource Manual,* whether you are teaching a counseling course for the first time or have had many years of experience in teaching such courses.

- All websites listed in ***Theory and Practice of Counseling and Psychotherapy*** as well as the ***Instructor's Resource Manual*** can be accessed through this text's website. You will find the site at: **http://counseling.wadsworth.com/**.

- Professors, you and your students now have access to a new and exciting resource available only through Thomson Learning. You now have the option of ordering this text bundled with a free subscription to ***Infotrac*** for your students. ***Infotrac*** is an on-line database that gives students access to full-length articles from over 900 scholarly and popular periodicals. The database is updated daily and dates back to as much as four years. Students will have access to ***Infotrac*** as well as the ability to print the articles, 24 hours a day from any location that has internet access. ***Infotrac*** is a great tool for conducting research! For a more in-depth discussion of ***Infotrac*** and how to use it, please visit the ***Infotrac*** website found at **http://infotrac.thomsonlearning.com/**. Speak with your local sales representative for more information.

- To better help your students gauge their level of comprehension of the material presented in ***Theory and Practice of Counseling and Psychotherapy***, there are on-line quiz items for each chapter. These quizzes are designed to help students pinpoint areas where they might need further study as well as help them see areas in which they are doing well. Please visit our website and instruct your students to visit our website at **http://counseling.wadsworth.com/** and look under the title for this text to find the quiz items.

- **Thomson Learning *Web Tutor*^{TM}**
  Designed to complement specific Wadsworth texts, this content-rich, Web-based teaching and learning tool helps students succeed by taking the course beyond classroom boundaries to an anywhere, anytime environment. ***Web Tutor*** is rich with study and mastery tools, communication tools, and course content. Professors can use ***Web Tutor*** to provide virtual office hours, post your syllabi, set up threaded discussions, track student progress with the quizzing material, and more.

  For students, ***Web Tutor*** offers real-time access to a full array of study tools, including flashcards (with audio), practice quizzes, online tutorials, and Web links. Professors who have tried ***Web Tutor*** have been especially pleased with the way ***Web Tutor*** allows students – even those in very large classes – to enhance each student's experience with the course content. ***Web Tutor*** also provides rich communication tools to instructors and students, including a course calendar, asynchronous discussion, 'real time' chat, and an integrated e-mail system.

- **Exam View from Wadsworth/Thomson Learning**
  Enhance your range of assessment and tutorial activities – and save yourself time in the process. With ***Exam View*** from Wadsworth, you can easily create and customize tests! ***Exam View*** is the only test generator that offers a "WYSIWYG" feature that allows you to see the test you are creating on the screen exactly as it will print! Also unique is ***Exam View's Quick Test Wizard***, which guides you step-by-step through the process of creating and printing a test in minutes.

I'd be very interested in hearing from you regarding ways that you teach your courses or special materials that you've developed for your courses. Also, I'd like to know how you and your students use the textbook and the ***Student Manual,*** and I welcome any reactions you'd care to share with me. Please communicate with me directly by e-mail at **cordileone@aol.com**, or fax (909) 659-6117.

Gerald Corey

PART I: BASIC ISSUES IN COUNSELING PRACTICE
Chapter 1: Introduction and Overview

Class Preparation/Lecture Tools	Testing Tools/Course Management	Student Mastery/Homework and Tutorials/Beyond the Book
Instructor's Resource Manual: Guidelines for Using Each Chapter, Key Terms for Review, InfoTrac® College Edition Keywords, Case Examples, Study Guides, Objective Test Items with Answer Keys, Transparency Masters **Instructor Book Companion Web Site:** http://helpingprofs.wadsworth.com Includes downloadable Microsoft® PowerPoint® slides. (Contact your local sales representative for the user name and password)	**Instructor's Resource Manual:** Final Examination Questions for *Theory and Practice of Counseling and Psychotherapy, 7e*, Chapter 1; Test Items for *Case Approach to Counseling and Psychotherapy, 5e*; Test Items for *Art of Integrative Counseling*; Comprehension Test for *CD-ROM for Integrative Counseling* **WebTutor™ Toolbox on Web CT and Blackboard:** Preloaded with content and is available free when packaged with the text. Toolbox contains all of the content from the Book Companion Web Site, a chapter on Transactional Analysis, and the sophisticated course management functionality of a WebCT or Blackboard product. **ExamView® Computerized Testing:** Create, deliver, and customize tests and study guides (both print and online) in minutes with this easy-to-use assessment and tutorial system.	**Student Manual:** Pre-Chapter Self-Inventories, Pretest. **Student Book Companion Web Site:** http://helpingprofs.wadsworth.com Includes an Online Quiz, Web links, and InfoTrac College Edition key words. **The Expert Theory Case Analysis Web Site:** http://theories.brookscole.com **WebTutor™ Toolbox on Web CT and Blackboard:** Preloaded with content and is available free when packaged with the text. Toolbox contains all of the content from the Book Companion Web Site, a chapter on Transactional Analysis, and the sophisticated course management functionality of a WebCT or Blackboard product.

Chapter 2. The Counselor: Person And Professional

Class Preparation/Lecture Tools	Testing Tools/Course Management	Student Mastery/Homework and Tutorials/Beyond the Book
Instructor's Resource Manual: Guidelines for Using Each Chapter, Key Terms for Review, InfoTrac College Edition Keywords, Case Examples, Study Guides, Objective Test Items with Answer Keys, Transparency Masters **Instructor Book Companion Web Site:** http://helpingprofs.wadsworth.com Includes downloadable Microsoft PowerPoint slides. (Contact your local sales representative for the user name and password)	**Instructor's Resource Manual:** Final Examination Questions for *Theory and Practice of Counseling and Psychotherapy, 7e*, Chapter 2; Test Items for *Case Approach to Counseling and Psychotherapy, 5e*; Test Items for *Art of Integrative Counseling*; Comprehension Test for *CD-ROM for Integrative Counseling* **WebTutor™ Toolbox on Web CT and Blackboard:** Preloaded with content and is available free when packaged with the text. Toolbox contains all of the content from the Book Companion Web Site, a chapter on Transactional Analysis, and the sophisticated course management functionality of a WebCT or Blackboard product. **ExamView® Computerized Testing:** Create, deliver, and customize tests and study guides (both print and online) in minutes with this easy-to-use assessment and tutorial system.	**Student Manual:** Pre-Chapter Self Inventory; Suggested Activity: *Cultural Diversity in Counseling Practice; Personal Issues in Counseling and Psychotherapy.* Group Exercise: *Personal Strategies for Preventing Burnout.* **Student Book Companion Web Site:** http://helpingprofs.wadsworth.com Includes an Online Quiz, Web links, and InfoTrac College Edition key words. **The Expert Theory Case Analysis Web Site:** http://theories.brookscole.com **WebTutor™ Toolbox on Web CT and Blackboard:** Preloaded with content and is available free when packaged with the text. Toolbox contains all of the content from the Book Companion Web Site, a chapter on Transactional Analysis, and the sophisticated course management functionality of a WebCT or Blackboard product.

Chapter 3. Ethical Issues In Counseling Practice

Class Preparation/Lecture Tools	Testing Tools/Course Management	Student Mastery/Homework and Tutorials/Beyond the Book
Instructor's Resource Manual: Guidelines for Using Each Chapter, Key Terms for Review, InfoTrac Keywords, Case Examples, Study Guides, Objective Test Items with Answer Keys, Transparency Masters **Instructor Book Companion Web Site:** http://helpingprofs.wadsworth.com Includes downloadable Microsoft PowerPoint Slides. (Contact your local sales representative for the user name and password)	**Instructor's Resource Manual:** Final Examination Questions for *Theory and Practice of Counseling and Psychotherapy, 7e*, Chapter 3; Test Items for *Case Approach to Counseling and Psychotherapy, 5e*; Test Items for *Art of Integrative Counseling;* Comprehension Test for **CD-ROM for Integrative Counseling** **WebTutor™ Toolbox on Web CT and Blackboard:** Preloaded with content and is available free when packaged with the text. Toolbox contains all of the content from the Book Companion Web Site, a chapter on Transactional Analysis, and the sophisticated course management functionality of a WebCT or Blackboard product. **ExamView® Computerized Testing: :** Create, deliver, and customize tests and study guides (both print and online) in minutes with this easy-to-use assessment and tutorial system.	**Student Manual**: Pre-Chapter Self-Inventory; Suggested Activities and Exercises **Student Book Companion Web Site:** http://helpingprofs.wadsworth.com Includes an Online Quiz, Web links, and InfoTrac College Edition key words. **The Expert Theory Case Analysis Web Site:** http://theories.brookscole.com **WebTutor™ Toolbox on Web CT and Blackboard:** Preloaded with content and is available free when packaged with the text. Toolbox contains all of the content from the Book Companion Web Site, a chapter on Transactional Analysis, and the sophisticated course management functionality of a WebCT or Blackboard product. **InfoTrac® College Edition:** http://infotrac.thomsonlearing.com *Keywords*: ethical decision making model*; ethical community standard*; standard* practice psych*; Countertransference; transference; Therap* values; values psych*; informed w1 consent; informed consent couns*; informed consent therap*; record* couns*;record* therap*; confidentiality psych*; privileged w1 communication; privacy couns*; privacy psych*; limits w2 confidentiality; duty to warn (17); duty to protect (20); dual relationship* couns*; dual relationship* psych*; multiple relationships

PART II: THEORIES AND TECHNIQUES OF COUNSELING
Chapter 4. Psychoanalytic Therapy

Class Preparation/Lecture Tools	Testing Tools/Course Management	Student Mastery/Homework and Tutorials/Beyond the Book
Instructor's Resource Manual: Guidelines for Using Each Chapter, Key Terms for Review, InfoTrac College Edition Keywords, Case Examples, Study Guides, Objective Test Items with Answer Keys, Transparency Masters **Instructor Book Companion Web Site:** http://helpingprofs.wadsworth.com Includes downloadable Microsoft PowerPoint Slides. (Contact your local sales representative for the user name and password)	**Instructor's Resource Manual:** Final Examination Questions for *Theory and Practice of Counseling and Psychotherapy, 7e*, Chapter 4; Test Items for *Case Approach to Counseling and Psychotherapy, 5e*; Test Items for *Art of Integrative Counseling;* Comprehension Test for **CD-ROM for Integrative Counseling** **WebTutor™ Toolbox on Web CT and Blackboard:** Preloaded with content and is available free when packaged with the text. Toolbox contains all of the content from the Book Companion Web Site, a chapter on Transactional Analysis, and the sophisticated course management functionality of a WebCT or Blackboard product. **ExamView® Computerized Testing:** Create, deliver, and customize tests and study guides (both print and online) in minutes with this easy-to-use assessment and tutorial system.	**Student Manual:** Pre-Chapter Self-Inventory; Key Terms; Questions for Reflection and Discussion; Suggested Activities and Exercises. **Case Approach to Counseling and Psychotherapy, 6e**: Chapter 2-see psychoanalytic oriented therapist, William Blau, work with Ruth. **CD-ROM for Integrative Counseling:** Sessions dealing with resistance, transference and countertransference, and understanding the past. **Student Book Companion Web Site:** http://helpingprofs.wadsworth.com Includes an Online Quiz, Web links, and InfoTrac College Edition key words. **The Expert Theory Case Analysis Web Site:** http://theories.brookscole.com **WebTutor™ Toolbox on Web CT and Blackboard:** Preloaded with content and is available free when packaged with the text. Toolbox contains all of the content from the Book Companion Web Site, a chapter on Transactional Analysis, and the sophisticated course management functionality of a WebCT or Blackboard product. **InfoTrac® College Edition** http://infotrac.thomsonlearing.com Keywords: Erik Erikson; Anna Freud; Sigmund Freud; Otto Kernberg; Heinz Kohut; Margaret Mahler; Donald Winnecott; Psychoanalysis; Psychodynam* ; Ego psychology ; Object relations psych* ;Self psychology ; Freud AND drive; Freud AND id; Freud AND ego; Freud AND superego; Freud AND conscious; Freud AND unconscious; Psychosexual development; Oedipus complex ; Ego-defense W1 mechanisms;Object-relations W1 theory; Transference; Carl Jung; Jung AND psyche; Jung AND ego; Jung AND individuation; Jung AND complex; Jung AND collective unconscious; Jung AND archetype*

Chapter 5: Adlerian Therapy

Class Preparation/Lecture Tools	Testing Tools/Course Management	Student Mastery/Homework and Tutorials/Beyond the Book
Instructor's Resource Manual: Guidelines for Using Each Chapter, Key Terms for Review, Inftrac Keywords, Case Examples, Study Guides, Objective Test Items with Answer Keys, Transparency Masters **Instructor Book Companion Web Site:** http://helpingprofs.wadsworth.com Includes downloadable Microsoft PowerPoint Slides. (Contact your local sales representative for the user name and password)	**Instructor's Resource Manual:** Final Examination Questions for *Theory and Practice of Counseling and Psychotherapy, 7e*, Chapter 5; Test Items for *Case Approach to Counseling and Psychotherapy, 5e*; Test Items for *Art of Integrative Counseling*; Comprehension Test for **CD-ROM for Integrative Counseling** **WebTutor™ Toolbox on Web CT and Blackboard:** Preloaded with content and is available free when packaged with the text. Toolboc contains all of the content from the Book Companion Web Site, a chapter on Transactional Analysis, and the sophisticated course management functionality of a WebCT or Blackboard product. **ExamView® Computerized Testing:** Create, deliver, and customize tests and study guides (both print and online) in minutes with this easy-to-use assessment and tutorial system.	**Student Manual**: <u>Case of Julie</u>: *"It's My Father's Fault That I Can't Trust Men"*; Pre-Chapter Self-Inventory; Key Terms; Questions for Reflection and Discussion; Suggested Activities and Exercises. **Case Approach to Counseling and Psychotherapy, 6e**: See Chapter 3 for how Adlerian therapists Jim Bitter and Bill Nicoll conduct a comprehensive lifestyle assessment of Ruth **CD-ROM for Integrative Counseling:** Final session dealing with evaluation and termination **Student Book Companion Web Site:** http://helpingprofs.wadsworth.com Includes an Online Quiz, Web links, and InfoTrac College Edition key words. **The Expert Theory Case Analysis Web Site:** http://theories.brookscole.com **WebTutor™ Toolbox on Web CT and Blackboard:** Preloaded with content and is available free when packaged with the text. Toolbox contains all of the content from the Book Companion Web Site, a chapter on Transactional Analysis, and the sophisticated course management functionality of a WebCT or Blackboard product. **InfoTrac® College Edition:** http://infotrac.thomsonlearing.com *Keywords:* Alfred Adler; Adler AND social interest; Adler AND superiority; Adler AND inferiority;Inferiority complex; Superiority complex; Phenomenological AND psych*; Family W1 constellation; Birth W1 order

Chapter 6: Existential Therapy

Class Preparation/Lecture Tools	Testing Tools/Course Management	Student Mastery/Homework and Tutorials/Beyond the Book
Instructor's Resource Manual: Guidelines for Using Each Chapter, Key Terms for Review, Inftrac Keywords, Case Examples, Study Guides, Objective Test Items with Answer Keys, Transparency Masters **Instructor Book Companion Web Site:** http://helpingprofs.wadsworth.com Includes downloadable Microsoft PowerPoint Slides. (Contact your local sales representative for the user name and password)	**Instructor's Resource Manual:** Final Examination Questions for *Theory and Practice of Counseling and Psychotherapy, 7e*, Chapter 6; Test Items for *Case Approach to Counseling and Psychotherapy, 5e*; Test Items for *Art of Integrative Counseling;* Comprehension Test for ***CD-ROM for Integrative Counseling*** **WebTutor™ Toolbox on Web CT and Blackboard:** Preloaded with content and is available free when packaged with the text. Toolbox contains all of the content from the Book Companion Web Site, a chapter on Transactional Analysis, and the sophisticated course management functionality of a WebCT or Blackboard product. **ExamView® Computerized Testing:** Create, deliver, and customize tests and study guides (both print and online) in minutes with this easy-to-use assessment and tutorial system.	**Student Manual:** Case of Walt: *"What is there to live for?"* Pre-Chapter Self-Inventory; Key Terms; Questions for Reflection and Discussion; Suggested Activities and Exercises. **Case Approach to Counseling and Psychotherapy, 6e:** SeeChapter 4 for how existential therapist Donald Polkinghorne works with Ruth. **CD-ROM for Integrative Counseling:** See session with an emotive focus and understanding resistance. **Student Book Companion Web Site:** http://helpingprofs.wadsworth.com Includes an Online Quiz, Web links and InfoTrac College Edition key words. **The Expert Theory Case Analysis Web Site:** http://theories.brookscole.com **WebTutor™ Toolbox on Web CT and Blackboard:** Preloaded with content and is available free when packaged with the text. Toolbox contains all of the content from the Book Companion Web Site, a chapter on Transactional Analysis, and the sophisticated course management functionality of a WebCT or Blackboard product. **InfoTrac® College Edition** http://infotrac.thomsonlearing.com *Keywords*: Martin Buber; Viktor Frankl; Rollo May; Jean-Paul Sartre; Irvin Yalom; Existential W1 phenomenology;Existential AND meaning

Chapter 7: Person-Centered Therapy

Class Preparation/Lecture Tools	Testing Tools/Course Management	Student Mastery/Homework and Tutorials/Beyond the Book
Instructor's Resource Manual: Guidelines for Using Each Chapter, Key Terms for Review, Inftrac Keywords, Case Examples, Study Guides, Objective Test Items with Answer Keys, Transparency Masters **Instructor Book Companion Web Site:** http://helpingprofs.wadsworth.com Includes downloadable Microsoft PowerPoint Slides. (Contact your local sales representative for the user name and password)	**Instructor's Resource Manual:** Final Examination Questions for *Theory and Practice of Counseling and Psychotherapy, 7e*, Chapter 7; Test Items for *Case Approach to Counseling and Psychotherapy, 5e*; Test Items for *Art of Integrative Counseling*; Comprehension Test for ***CD-ROM for Integrative Counseling*** **WebTutor™ Toolbox on Web CT and Blackboard:** Preloaded with content and is available free when packaged with the text. Toolbox contains all of the content from the Book Companion Web Site, a chapter on Transactional Analysis, and the sophisticated course management functionality of a WebCT or Blackboard product. **ExamView® Computerized Testing:** Create, deliver, and customize tests and study guides (both print and online) in minutes with this easy-to-use assessment and tutorial system.	**Student Manual:** <u>Case of Don</u>: *Feeling Pressure to Prove Himself;* Pre-Chapter Self-Inventory; Key Terms; Questions for Reflection and Discussion; Suggested Activities and Exercises. **Case Approach to Counseling and Psychotherapy, 6e:** See Chapter 5 demonstration of person-centered therapist David Cain working with Ruth **CD-ROM:** session on the therapeutic relationship **Student Book Companion Web Site:** http://helpingprofs.wadsworth.com Includes an Online Quiz, Web links, and InfoTrac College Edition key words. **The Expert Theory Case Analysis Web Site:** http://theories.brookscole.com **WebTutor™ Toolbox on Web CT and Blackboard:** Preloaded with content and is available free when packaged with the text. Toolbox contains all of the content from the Book Companion Web Site, a chapter on Transactional Analysis, and the sophisticated course management functionality of a WebCT or Blackboard product. **InfoTrac® College Edition** http://infotrac.thomsonlearing.com *Keywords:* Carl Rogers; Client-centered; Person-centered; Humanistic psychology; Nondirective counseling; Self-actualization; Unconditional W1 positive AND regard; Internal W1 locus; Nondirective W1 therapy; Rogers AND self-actualization

Chapter 8: Gestalt Therapy

Class Preparation/Lecture Tools	Testing Tools/Course Management	Student Mastery/Homework and Tutorials/Beyond the Book
Instructor's Resource Manual: Guidelines for Using Each Chapter, Key Terms for Review, InfoTrac College Edition Keywords, Case Examples, Study Guides, Objective Test Items with Answer Keys, Transparency Masters **Instructor Book Companion Web Site:** http://helpingprofs.wadsworth.com Includes downloadable Microsoft PowerPoint Slides. (Contact your local sales representative for the user name and password)	**Instructor's Resource Manual**: Final Examination Questions for *Theory and Practice of Counseling and Psychotherapy, 7e*, Chapter 8; Test Items for *Case Approach to Counseling and Psychotherapy, 5e*; Test Items for *Art of Integrative Counseling;* Comprehension Test for **CD-ROM for Integrative Counseling** **WebTutor™ Toolbox on Web CT and Blackboard:** Preloaded with content and is available free when packaged with the text. Toolbox contains all of the content from the Book Companion Web Site, a chapter on Transactional Analysis, and the sophisticated course management functionality of a WebCT or Blackboard product. **ExamView® Computerized Testing:** Create, deliver, and customize tests and study guides (both print and online) in minutes with this easy-to-use assessment and tutorial system.	**Student Manual**: Case of Christina: *A Student Works With Her Feelings Toward Her Supervisor and Father;* Pre-Chapter Self-Inventory; Key Terms; Questions for Reflection and Discussion; Suggested Activities and Exercises. **Case Approach to Counseling and Psychotherapy, 6e:** Chapter 6 Gestalt therapist Jon Grew works with Ruth. **CD-ROM for Integrative Counseling:** Session on exploring the past **Student Book Companion Web Site:** http://helpingprofs.wadsworth.com Includes an Online Quiz, Web links, and InfoTrac College Edition key words. **The Expert Theory Case Analysis Web Site:** http://theories.brookscole.com **WebTutor™ Toolbox on Web CT and Blackboard:** Preloaded with content and is available free when packaged with the text. Toolbox contains all of the content from the Book Companion Web Site, a chapter on Transactional Analysis, and the sophisticated course management functionality of a WebCT or Blackboard product. **InfoTrac® College Edition** http://infotrac.thomsonlearing.com Keyword: Fritz Perls; Gestalt psychology; Gestalt therapy; Introjection; Awareness AND therap*

Chapter 9: Reality Therapy

Class Preparation/Lecture Tools	Testing Tools/Course Management	Student Mastery/Homework and Tutorials/Beyond the Book
Instructor's Resource Manual: Guidelines for Using Each Chapter, Key Terms for Review, InfoTrac College Edition Keywords, Case Examples, Study Guides, Objective Test Items with Answer Keys, Transparency Masters **Instructor Book Companion Web Site:** http://helpingprofs.wadsworth.com Includes downloadable Microsoft PowerPoint Slides. (Contact your local sales representative for the user name and password)	**Instructor's Resource Manual:** Final Examination Questions for *Theory and Practice of Counseling and Psychotherapy, 7e*, Chapter 9; Test Items for *Case Approach to Counseling and Psychotherapy, 5e*; Test Items for *Art of Integrative Counseling*; Comprehension Test for **CD-ROM for Integrative Counseling** **WebTutor™ Toolbox on Web CT and Blackboard:** Preloaded with content and is available free when packaged with the text. Toolbox contains all of the content from the Book Companion Web Site, a chapter on Transactional Analysis, and the sophisticated course management functionality of a WebCT or Blackboard product. **ExamView® Computerized Testing:** Create, deliver, and customize tests and study guides (both print and online) in minutes with this easy-to-use assessment and tutorial system.	**Student Manual**: <u>Case of Sally</u>: *Hoping to Cure a Social Phobia;* Pre-Chapter Self-Inventory; Key Terms; Questions for Reflection and Discussion; Suggested Activities and Exercises. **Case Approach to Counseling and Psychotherapy, 6e:** See Chapter 7 for Behavior Therapists Arnold Lazarus and Barbara Brownell D'Angelo work with Ruth **CD ROM for Integrative Counseling:** sessions on therapeutic goals and working toward decisions and behavior change **Student Book Companion Web Site:** http://helpingprofs.wadsworth.com Includes an Online Quiz, Web links, and InfoTrac College Edition key words. **The Expert Theory Case Analysis Web Site:** http://theories.brookscole.com **WebTutor™ Toolbox on Web CT and Blackboard:** Preloaded with content and is available free when packaged with the text. Toolbox contains all of the content from the Book Companion Web Site, a chapter on Transactional Analysis, and the sophisticated course management functionality of a WebCT or Blackboard product. **InfoTrac® College Edition** http://infotrac.thomsonlearing.com *Keywords:* Albert Bandura; Ivan Pavlov; Donald Meichenbaum ; B.F. Skinner; E.L. Thorndike; John Watson; Classical conditioning; Operant conditioning; Social Cognitive Theory; Social Learning Theory; Overt behavior; Positive reinforcement; Observational learning; Covert behavior; Systematic desensitization;Exposure W1therapy; Exposure and response prevention; Eye movement desensitization and reprocessing

Chapter 10: Behavior Therapy

Class Preparation/Lecture Tools	Testing Tools/Course Management	Student Mastery/Homework and Tutorials/Beyond the Book
Instructor's Resource Manual: Guidelines for Using Each Chapter, Key Terms for Review, InfoTrac College Edition Keywords, Case Examples, Study Guides, Objective Test Items with Answer Keys, Transparency Masters **Instructor Book Companion Web Site:** http://helpingprofs.wadsworth.com Includes downloadable Microsoft PowerPoint Slides. (Contact your local sales representative for the user name and password)	**Instructor's Resource Manual**: Final Examination Questions for *Theory and Practice of Counseling and Psychotherapy, 7e*, Chapter 10; Test Items for *Case Approach to Counseling and Psychotherapy, 5e*; Test Items for *Art of Integrative Counseling*; Comprehension Test for **CD-ROM for Integrative Counseling** **WebTutor™ Toolbox on Web CT and Blackboard:** Preloaded with content and is available free when packaged with the text. Toolbox contains all of the content from the Book Companion Web Site, a chapter on Transactional Analysis, and the sophisticated course management functionality of a WebCT or Blackboard product. **ExamView® Computerized Testing:** Create, deliver, and customize tests and study guides (both print and online) in minutes with this easy-to-use assessment and tutorial system.	**Student Manual:** Case of Marion: *A Woman Who Lives by "Oughts" and "Shoulds"* Pre-Chapter Self-Inventory; Key Terms; Questions for Reflection and Discussion; Suggested Activities and Exercises. **Case Approach to Counseling and Psychotherapy, 6e:** SeeChapter 8 for two different cognitive-behavior approaches-Albert Ellis' rational emotive behavior and Frank Dattilio's in couples and family therapy **CD -ROM for Integrative Counseling:** the session dealing with a cognitive focus. **Student Book Companion Web Site:** http://helpingprofs.wadsworth.com Includes an Online Quiz, Web links, and InfoTrac College Edition key words. **The Expert Theory Case Analysis Web Site:** http://theories.brookscole.com **WebTutor™ Toolbox on Web CT and Blackboard:** Preloaded with content and is available free when packaged with the text. Toolbox contains all of the content from the Book Companion Web Site, a chapter on Transactional Analysis, and the sophisticated course management functionality of a WebCT or Blackboard product. **InfoTrac® College Edition** http://infotrac.thomsonlearing.com Keywords: Albert Ellis; Rational emotive behavior therapy; Unconditional self-acceptance; Aaron Beck; Cognitive therapy; Cognitive schemas; Automatic thoughts; Cognitive distortions; Catastrophizing; Reattribution; Cognitive W1 restructuring; Beck AND depression

Chapter 11: Cognitive-Behavior Therapy

Class Preparation/Lecture Tools	Testing Tools/Course Management	Student Mastery/Homework and Tutorials/Beyond the Book
Instructor's Resource Manual: Guidelines for Using Each Chapter, Key Terms for Review, InfoTrac College Edition Keywords, Case Examples, Study Guides, Objective Test Items with Answer Keys, Transparency Masters **Instructor Book Companion Web Site:** http://helpingprofs.wadsworth.com Includes downloadable Microsoft PowerPoint Slides. (Contact your local sales representative for the user name and password)	**Instructor's Resource Manual:** Final Examination Questions for *Theory and Practice of Counseling and Psychotherapy, 7e*, Chapter 11; Test Items for *Case Approach to Counseling and Psychotherapy, 5e*; Test Items for *Art of Integrative Counseling;* Comprehension Test for **CD-ROM for Integrative Counseling** **WebTutor™ Toolbox on Web CT and Blackboard:** Preloaded with content and is available free when packaged with the text. Toolbox contains all of the content from the Book Companion Web Site, a chapter on Transactional Analysis, and the sophisticated course management functionality of a WebCT or Blackboard product. **ExamView® Computerized Testing:** Create, deliver, and customize tests and study guides (both print and online) in minutes with this easy-to-use assessment and tutorial system.	**Student Manual**: <u>Case of Manny</u>: *A Loser for Life?* Pre-Chapter Self-Inventory; Key Terms; Questions for Reflection and Discussion; Suggested Activities and Exercises. **Case Approach to Counseling and Psychotherapy, 6e:** See Chapter 9 for examples of two different reality therapists' perspectives-William Glasser and Robert Wubbolding working with Ruth **CD -ROM for Integrative Counseling**: session with a behavioral focus. **Student Book Companion Web Site:** http://helpingprofs.wadsworth.com Includes an Online Quiz, Web links, and InfoTrac College Edition key words. **The Expert Theory Case Analysis Web Site:** http://theories.brookscole.com **WebTutor™ Toolbox on Web CT and Blackboard:** Preloaded with content and is available free when packaged with the text. Toolbox contains all of the content from the Book Companion Web Site, a chapter on Transactional Analysis, and the sophisticated course management functionality of a WebCT or Blackboard product. **InfoTrac® College Edition** http://infotrac.thomsonlearing.com *Keywords:* William Glasser; Reality therapy; Choice theory AND Glasser; Control theory and Glasser; Commitment AND treat*

Chapter 12: Feminist Therapy

Class Preparation/Lecture Tools	Testing Tools/Course Management	Student Mastery/Homework and Tutorials/Beyond the Book
Instructor's Resource Manual: Guidelines for Using Each Chapter, Key Terms for Review, InfoTrac College Edition Keywords, Case Examples, Study Guides, Objective Test Items with Answer Keys, Transparency Masters **Instructor Book Companion Web Site:** http://helpingprofs.wadsworth.com Includes downloadable Microsoft PowerPoint Slides. (Contact your local sales representative for the user name and password)	**Instructor's Resource Manual:** Final Examination Questions for *Theory and Practice of Counseling and Psychotherapy, 7e*, Chapter 12; Test Items for *Case Approach to Counseling and Psychotherapy, 5e*; Test Items for *Art of Integrative Counseling;* Comprehension Test for **CD-ROM for Integrative Counseling** **WebTutor™ Toolbox on Web CT and Blackboard:** Preloaded with content and is available free when packaged with the text. Toolbox contains all of the content from the Book Companion Web Site, a chapter on Transactional Analysis, and the sophisticated course management functionality of a WebCT or Blackboard product. **ExamView® Computerized Testing:** Create, deliver, and customize tests and study guides (both print and online) in minutes with this easy-to-use assessment and tutorial system.	**Student Manual:** Case of Maria: *Torn Between Herself and Her Culture;* Pre-Chapter Self-Inventory; Key Terms; Questions for Reflection and Discussion; Suggested Activities and Exercises. **Case Approach to Counseling and Psychotherapy, 6e:** See Chapter 10 for three feminist therapists-Kathy Evans, Susan Seem, Elizabeth Kincade work with Ruth. **CD-ROM for Integrative Counseling:** First 3 sessions **Student Book Companion Web Site:** http://helpingprofs.wadsworth.com Includes an Online Quiz, Web links, and InfoTrac College Edition key words. **The Expert Theory Case Analysis Web Site:** http://theories.brookscole.com **WebTutor™ Toolbox on Web CT and Blackboard:** Preloaded with content and is available free when packaged with the text. Toolbox contains all of the content from the Book Companion Web Site, a chapter on Transactional Analysis, and the sophisticated course management functionality of a WebCT or Blackboard product. **InfoTrac® College Edition** http://infotrac.thomsonlearing.com *Keywords:* Laura Brown; Carol Gilligan; Jean Baker Miller; Rhoda Unger; Feminist Therapy; Femin* AND psych*; Stone W1 Center; Relational W1 model; Heterosexism; Gender W1 schema*; Feminist W1 consciousness; Assertiveness training; Bibliotherapy

Chapter 13: Postmodern Approaches

Class Preparation/Lecture Tools	Testing Tools/Course Management	Student Mastery/Homework and Tutorials/Beyond the Book
Instructor's Resource Manual: Guidelines for Using Each Chapter, Key Terms for Review, InfoTrac College Edition Keywords, Case Examples, Study Guides, Objective Test Items with Answer Keys, Transparency Masters **Instructor Book Companion Web Site:** http://helpingprofs.wadsworth.com Includes downloadable Microsoft PowerPoint Slides. (Contact your local sales representative for the user name and password)	**Instructor's Resource Manual:** Final Examination Questions for *Theory and Practice of Counseling and Psychotherapy, 7e*, Chapter 13; Test Items for *Case Approach to Counseling and Psychotherapy, 5e*; Test Items for *Art of Integrative Counseling*; Comprehension Test for **CD-ROM for Integrative Counseling** **WebTutor™ Toolbox on Web CT and Blackboard:** Preloaded with content and is available free when packaged with the text. Toolbox contains all of the content from the Book Companion Web Site, a chapter on Transactional Analysis, and the sophisticated course management functionality of a WebCT or Blackboard product. **ExamView® Computerized Testing:** Create, deliver, and customize tests and study guides (both print and online) in minutes with this easy-to-use assessment and tutorial system.	**Student Manual**: Pre-Chapter Self-Inventory; Key Terms; Questions for Reflection and Discussion; Suggested Activities and Exercises. **Case Approach to Counseling and Psychotherapy, 6e:** See Chapter 11 for three postmodern therapists-Jennifer Andrews, David Clark, Gerald Monk work with Ruth. **CD -ROM for Integrative Counseling:** Sessions on an integrative perspective and also the session on working toward decisions and behavior change. **Student Book Companion Web Site:** http://helpingprofs.wadsworth.com Includes an Online Quiz, Web links, and InfoTrac College Edition key words. **The Expert Theory Case Analysis Web Site:** http://theories.brookscole.com **WebTutor™ Toolbox on Web CT and Blackboard:** Preloaded with content and is available free when packaged with the text. Toolbox contains all of the content from the Book Companion Web Site, a chapter on Transactional Analysis, and the sophisticated course management functionality of a WebCT or Blackboard product.

Chapter 14: Family Systems Therapy

Class Preparation/Lecture Tools	Testing Tools/Course Management	Student Mastery/Homework and Tutorials/Beyond the Book
Instructor's Resource Manual: Guidelines for Using Each Chapter, Key Terms for Review, InfoTrac College Edition Keywords, Case Examples, Study Guides, Objective Test Items with Answer Keys, Transparency Masters **Instructor Book Companion Web Site**: http://helpingprofs.wadsworth.com Includes downloadable Microsoft PowerPoint Slides. (Contact your local sales representative for the user name and password)	**Instructor's Resource Manual**: Final Examination Questions for *Theory and Practice of Counseling and Psychotherapy, 7e*, Chapter 14; Test Items for *Case Approach to Counseling and Psychotherapy, 5e*; Test Items for *Art of Integrative Counseling*; Comprehension Test for ***CD-ROM for Integrative Counseling*** **WebTutor™ Toolbox on Web CT and Blackboard:** Preloaded with content and is available free when packaged with the text. Toolbox contains all of the content from the Book Companion Web Site, a chapter on Transactional Analysis, and the sophisticated course management functionality of a WebCT or Blackboard product. **ExamView® Computerized Testing:** Create, deliver, and customize tests and study guides (both print and online) in minutes with this easy-to-use assessment and tutorial system.	**Student Manual:** Pre-Chapter Self-Inventory, Glossary of Key Terms, Questions for Discussion and Evaluation, Suggested Activities and Exercises, Quiz **Case Approach to Counseling and Psychotherapy, 6e:** SeeChapter 12 for family therapist Mary Moline's work with Ruth from a systemic perspective **CD-ROM for Integrative Counseling:** Session on emotive focus **Student Book Companion Web Site:** http://helpingprofs.wadsworth.com Includes an Online Quiz, Web links, and InfoTrac College Edition key words. **The Expert Theory Case Analysis Web Site:** http://theories.brookscole.com **WebTutor™ Toolbox on Web CT and Blackboard:** Preloaded with content and is available free when packaged with the text. Toolbox contains all of the content from the Book Companion Web Site, a chapter on Transactional Analysis, and the sophisticated course management functionality of a WebCT or Blackboard product. **InfoTrac® College Edition** http://infotrac.thomsonlearing.com Keywords: Murray Bowen; Jay Haley; Salvador Minuchin; Virginia Satir; Carl Whitaker; Intergenerational W1 approach; Strategic family therapy; Family therapy; Family systems the*; Genogram*

Part III: INTERGRATION AND APPLICATION
Chapter 15: An Integrative Perspective

Class Preparation/Lecture Tools	Testing Tools/Course Management	Student Mastery/Homework and Tutorials/Beyond the Book
Instructor's Resource Manual: Guidelines for Using Each Chapter, Key Terms for Review, InfoTrac College Edition Keywords, Case Examples, Study Guides, Objective Test Items with Answer Keys, Transparency Masters **Instructor Book Companion Web Site:** http://helpingprofs.wadsworth.com Includes downloadable Microsoft PowerPoint Slides. (Contact your local sales representative for the user name and password)	**Instructor's Resource Manual:** Final Examination Questions for *Theory and Practice of Counseling and Psychotherapy, 7e*, Chapter 15; Test Items for *Case Approach to Counseling and Psychotherapy, 5e*; Test Items for *Art of Integrative Counseling*; Comprehension Test for ***CD-ROM for Integrative Counseling*** **WebTutor™ Toolbox on Web CT and Blackboard:** Preloaded with content and is available free when packaged with the text. Toolbox contains all of the content from the Book Companion Web Site, a chapter on Transactional Analysis, and the sophisticated course management functionality of a WebCT or Blackboard product. **ExamView® Computerized Testing:** Create, deliver, and customize tests and study guides (both print and online) in minutes with this easy-to-use assessment and tutorial system.	**Student Manual**: Applications of theoretical approaches to specific client populations or specific problems; Questions and Issues: Guidelines for developing your personal style of counseling; Suggested Activities and Exercises: Developing Your Philosophy of Counseling; Questions for Reflection and Discussion. **Student Book Companion Web Site:** http://helpingprofs.wadsworth.com Includes an Online Quiz, Web links, and InfoTrac College Edition key words. **The Expert Theory Case Analysis Web Site:** http://theories.brookscole.com **WebTutor™ Toolbox on Web CT and Blackboard:** Preloaded with content and is available free when packaged with the text. Toolbox contains all of the content from the Book Companion Web Site, a chapter on Transactional Analysis, and the sophisticated course management functionality of a WebCT or Blackboard product. **InfoTrac® College Edition** http://infotrac.thomsonlearing.com *Keywords:* Insoo Kim Berg; Arnold Lazarus; John Norcross; James Prochaska; Paul Wachtel; Solution-focused therapy; Brief psychotherapy; Narrative W1 therapy

Chapter 16: Case Illustration: An Integrative Approach in Working With Stan

Class Preparation/Lecture Tools	Testing Tools/Course Management	Student Mastery/Homework and Tutorials/Beyond the Book
Instructor's Resource Manual: Guidelines for Using Each Chapter, Key Terms for Review, InfoTrac College Edition Keywords, Case Examples, Study Guides, Objective Test Items with Answer Keys, Transparency Masters **Instructor Book Companion Web Site:** http://helpingprofs.wadsworth.com Includes downloadable Microsoft PowerPoint Slides. (Contact your local sales representative for the user name and password)	**Instructor's Resource Manual:** Final Examination Questions for *Theory and Practice of Counseling and Psychotherapy, 7e*, Chapter 16; Test Items for *Case Approach to Counseling and Psychotherapy, 5e*; Test Items for *Art of Integrative Counseling*; Comprehension Test for ***CD-ROM for Integrative Counseling*** **WebTutor™ Toolbox on Web CT and Blackboard:** Preloaded with content and is available free when packaged with the text. Toolbox contains all of the content from the Book Companion Web Site, a chapter on Transactional Analysis, and the sophisticated course management functionality of a WebCT or Blackboard product. **ExamView® Computerized Testing:** Create, deliver, and customize tests and study guides (both print and online) in minutes with this easy-to-use assessment and tutorial system.	**Student Manual:** Questions for Reflection and Discussion **Student Book Companion Web Site:** http://helpingprofs.wadsworth.com Includes an Online Quiz, Web links, and InfoTrac College Edition key words. **The Expert Theory Case Analysis Web Site:** http://theories.brookscole.com **WebTutor™ Toolbox on Web CT and Blackboard:** Preloaded with content and is available free when packaged with the text. Toolbox contains all of the content from the Book Companion Web Site, a chapter on Transactional Analysis, and the sophisticated course management functionality of a WebCT or Blackboard product.

I

Some Suggestions for

Teaching the Course

What follows are some approaches that I have used both in the introductory course I regularly teach at California State University at Fullerton (*Theories and Techniques of Counseling*) for undergraduates in the Human Services Program, and for graduate-level courses in advanced counseling theory and practice that I have taught at several universities. I offer these as guidelines as you are preparing your own course, and these suggestions will hopefully generate your own adaptations of teaching techniques. Here are some of the teaching/learning strategies that I continue to experiment with and modify:

1. For the introductory undergraduate-level course, Theories and Techniques of Counseling (3 semester units), I require the following reading:
    A. ***Theory and Practice of Counseling and Psychotherapy*** (abbreviated as ***TPCP***)
    B. ***Student Manual for Theory and Practice of Counseling and Psychotherapy***
    C. ***Case Approach to Counseling and Psychotherapy***

2. In addition to the required reading above, I highly recommend other books, many of which are primary sources. Since the required reading is designed merely to give the students an introduction to the topics, a supplementary reading program is critical for students who want a more in-depth understanding of counseling theory and practice. I recommend, but do not require the book, ***The Art of Integrative Counseling***. Throughout this ***Instructor's Resource Manual*** I will refer you to appropriate selections in the book and to the CD ROM for ***Integrative Counseling***. For suggested readings, I refer students to the annotated readings at the end of each chapter in the core textbook.

3. There is a CD ROM for ***Integrative Counseling*** that demonstrates my own integrative perspective in working with Ruth, the central case in my ***Case Approach to Counseling and Psychotherapy*** text. This educational program is designed as a self-study vehicle and is available at a nominal price if the CD-ROM is bundled with one of the 3 texts listed above. This CD-ROM program can be used as a companion to any of the above texts and the student manual. CD ROM for ***Integrative Counseling*** consists of lecturettes that I present on ways to draw concepts and techniques from the major theories of counseling. I work with Ruth for a total of 13 sessions, demonstrating my own integrative approach. There are short clips of therapy sessions from the initial to termination phase of Ruth's therapy, and a process commentary after each of the 13 counseling sessions.

4. If the class meets for a three-hour segment once a week, I generally use the first half of the time for lecture and/or discussion based on the lecture and readings. The second half stresses applications of the concepts, such as doing the exercises in the ***Student Manual***, discussing the evaluation questions in small groups, role-playing based upon case examples the students bring in (or from the ***Student Manual***), and discussing the case of Ruth from the vantage point of the various therapists who work with her in ***Case Approach to Counseling and Psychotherapy***.

5. I frequently use guest speakers during the course. This adds variety and exposes the students to psychologists with divergent approaches, philosophies, and techniques.

    I have rarely encountered difficulty in securing guest speakers willing to give an hour or two of their time to speak to a class. Community agencies benefit by exposure to the students. Fellow faculty members with a special interest (say a psychologist with a behavioral orientation) have addressed my class, and in return I would speak to one of their classes. This exchange program can work quite well for the advantage of both students and instructors.

6. The nature of the take-home papers is spelled out in more detail later in this ***Instructor's Resource Manual*** in the section that describes my course outline. These papers encourage thought, analysis, and integration of the material. In addition to the directions for these papers given in my course outline, you might want to use the *Questions for Reflection and Discussion* in the ***Student Manual***, and the many questions that I provide in this manual. I often allow students to select specific topics that most appeal to them, or to address questions that will help them delve into their areas of interest in more depth.

7. <u>Peer teaching</u>. Several years ago I began experimenting with the use of former students as peer teachers (or learning assistants or discussion leaders) for part of the class session. It worked out well, for the most part, and students taking the class for the first time appreciated the guidance of former students, who could often identify with their struggles in facing so much new material all at once.

8. **Journal suggestions**. For additional resources for preparing lectures and experiential activities and for gathering data on research in counseling areas, the following journals may be of interest:

- *American Psychologist*
- *APA Monitor*
- *Clinical Psychologist*
- *Community Mental Health Journal*
- *Contemporary Psychology*
- *Journal of Clinical Psychology*
- *Journal of Counseling Psychology*
- *Journal of Humanistic Psychology*
- *Journal of Marriage and Family Therapy*
- *Psychological Abstracts, Psychological Bulletin*
- *Family Therapy Networker*
- *Psychology Today.*

Three journals that I find especially useful are:

- *Journal of Counseling and Development (ACA)*
- *Professional Psychology: Research and Practice (APA)*
- *Psychotherapy Networker*

9. **Suggested books for preparing lectures**. Each instructor will want to develop his or her own emphasis in teaching the theory and practice of counseling. The **TPCP** textbook and the **Student Manual** can provide the students with background material for better understanding of your lectures. As guides for references for the instructor, I refer you to the reference section after each chapter in the textbook and in particular to the annotated *Suggested Readings* at the end of each chapter. These are the books I have found most helpful in preparing my lectures and in gathering the background for writing the textbook.

In addition to the *Suggested Readings*, the following textbooks are commonly used in theory and practice of counseling courses, and you may find them of value in preparing for lectures:

A. Capuzzi, D., & Gross, D. R. (1999). *Counseling and Psychotherapy* (2nd ed.). Upper Saddle River, NJ: Prentice Hall (Merrill).

B. Corey, G. (2005). *Theory and Practice of Counseling and Psychotherapy* (7th ed.). Belmont, CA: Brooks/Cole - Thomson Learning.

C. Corey, G. (2001). *The Art of Integrative Counseling*. Pacific Grove, CA: Brooks/Cole - Wadsworth.

D. Corsini, R., & Wedding, D. (Eds.). (2005*). Current Psychotherapies* (7th ed.). Belmont, CA: Wadsworth.

E. Gilliland, B. E., & James, R. K. (1998). *Theories and Strategies in Counseling and Psychotherapy* (4th ed.). Boston, MA: Allyn & Bacon.

F. Hansen, J. C., Rossberg, R. H., & Cramer, S. H. (1994). *Counseling: Theory and Process* (5th ed.). Boston, MA: Allyn & Bacon.

G. Ivey, A. E., D'Andrea, M., Ivey, M. B., & Simek-Morgan, L. (2002). *Counseling and Psychotherapy: A Multicultural Perspective* (5th ed.). Boston, MA: Allyn Bacon.

H. Kottler, J. A. (2002). *Theories in Counseling and Therapy: An Experiential Approach*. Boston, MA: Allyn Bacon.

I. Patterson, C. H., & Watkins, C. E. (1996). *Theories of Psychotherapy* (5th ed.). NY: Harper/Collins.

J. Parrott, L. (2003). *Counseling and Psychotherapy* (2nd ed.). Pacific Grove, CA: Brooks/Cole.

K.   Prochaska, J. O., & Norcross, J. C. (2003). *Systems of Psychotherapy: A Transtheoretical Analysis* (5th ed.). Pacific Grove, CA: Brooks/Cole.

L.   Seligman, L.(2001). *Systems, Strategies, and Skills of Counseling and Psychotherapy*. Upper Saddle River, NJ: Prentice Hall (Merrill).

M.   Sharf, R. S. (2004). *Theories of Psychotherapy and Counseling: Concepts and Cases* (3rd ed.). Pacific Grove, CA: Brooks/Cole - Wadsworth.

10. **Books, videos, and CD-ROM programs authored and co-authored by Gerald Corey**. The following are books that my colleagues and I have authored or co-authored (and videos/workbooks and CD ROM programs) that might be of interest to you. All textbooks, workbooks and videos, and CD-ROM programs are published by Wadsworth Publishing Company, Belmont, CA 94002.

A.   Corey, G. (2005). *Theory and Practice of Counseling and Psychotherapy*, 7th ed. Presents an overview of eleven contemporary theories of counseling, with an emphasis on the practical applications and the therapeutic process associated with each orientation.

B.   Corey, G. (2005). *Student Manual for Theory and Practice of Counseling and Psychotherapy*, 7th ed. This study guide is designed to accompany the textbook, *Theory and Practice of Counseling and Psychotherapy*, (7th ed., 2005). It provides students with an overview of each chapter, contains a glossary of key terms, questions for discussions and evaluation, suggested activities and exercises, and presents case examples of each of the ten theories.

C.   Corey, G. (2005). *Case Approach to Counseling and Psychotherapy*, 6th ed. Designed to demonstrate how theory can be applied to specific cases. Outline of theories corresponds to your textbook and manual. Readers are challenged to apply their knowledge of theories in working with a single case, Ruth. A proponent of each theory writes about his or her assessment of Ruth and then proceeds to demonstrate a particular therapeutic style in counseling Ruth. I then follow up and show how I would intervene with Ruth by staying within the general framework of each of these theories. In addition, I demonstrate my way of working with Ruth in an integrative fashion.

D.   Corey, G. (2001*)*. *The Art of Integrative Counseling*. This brief supplementary book is an expansion of Chapter 15 in *Theory and Practice of Counseling and Psychotherapy*.

E.   Corey, G., & Haynes, R. (2005). *CD ROM for Integrative Counseling*: This student version of an educational program is designed to bring theory into action as it is applied to the case of Ruth. There are questions and activities that accompanies the 13 counseling sessions that are designed to engage the reader in an interactive learning experience. This interactive self-study program demonstrates my own integrative style in counseling Ruth. Drawing upon the thinking, feeling, and behaving perspectives, I attempt to highlight the value of working with a singular theme from all three modalities of human experience. It is designed to be packaged with any of the three books listed above.

F.   Corey, G. (2004). *Theory and Practice of Group Counseling*, 6th ed. outlines the basic elements of group process, presents an overview of the key concepts and techniques of ten theoretical approaches to group counseling, and shows how to integrate these various approaches.

G.   Corey, G. (2004). *Manual for Theory and Practice of Group Counseling*, 6th ed. Similar to the student manual that accompanies the *TPCP* text.

H.   Corey, M. S., & Corey, G. (2003). *Becoming a Helper*, 4th ed. This book deals with topics of concern to students who are studying in one of the helping professions. Some of the issues explored are examining your motivations and needs, becoming aware of the impact of your values on the counseling process, learning to cope with stress, dealing with burnout, exploring developmental turning points in one's life, and ethical issues.

I.   Corey, G., Corey, M. S., & Callanan, P. (2003). *Issues and Ethics in the Helping Professions*, 6th ed. A combination textbook and student manual that contains self-inventories, open-ended cases and problem situations, exercises, suggested activities, and a variety of ethical, professional, and legal issues facing practitioners.

J. Corey, G., Corey, M. S., & Haynes, R. (2003). *Ethics in Action: CD ROM.* This interactive self-study educational program is aimed at exploring ethical decision-making, the role of values in the counseling process, and managing boundary issues and multiple relationships. This CD ROM program is also designed to be used along with either *Becoming a Helper* or *Issues and Ethics in the Helping Professions.*

K. Corey, G., & Corey, M. S. (2002). *I Never Knew I Had a Choice*, 7th ed. A self-help book for personal growth that deals with such topics as the struggle to achieve autonomy; the roles that work, sex roles, sexuality, love, intimacy, and solitude play in our lives; the meaning of loneliness, death, and loss; and the ways in which we choose values and find meaning in life.

L. * Corey, G., Corey, M. S., & Haynes, R. (2000). *The Evolution of a Group Video: Student Video and Workbook*. This two-hour self-study video/workbook package is geared to demonstrate group process in action and illustrate techniques for all the stages of a group. This video is also designed to be used in conjunction with *Theory and Practice of Group Counseling*, *Groups: Process and Practice*, and *Group Techniques.*

M. Corey, M. S., & Corey, G. (2002). *Groups: Process and Practice*, 6th ed. Outlines the basic issues and concepts of group process throughout the life history of a group. Applies these basic concepts to groups for children, adolescents, adults, and the elderly.

N. Corey, G., Corey, M. S., Callanan, P., & Russell, J. M. (2004). *Group Techniques*, 3rd ed. Describes ideas for creating and implementing techniques for use in groups. Gives a rationale for the use of techniques in all the stages in a group's development.

O. Corey, G., Corey, C., & Corey, H. (1997). *Living and Learning*. Belmont, CA: Wadsworth. This book presents learning as a lifelong journey. By encouraging readers to use the world as their classroom and to "learn from living," this book helps readers to get more out of their college experience and the rest of their lives.

P. Haynes, R., Corey, G., and Moulton, P. (2003). *Clinical Supervision in the Helping Professions: A Practical Guide.* This is a book for those who are interested in learning how to become a supervisor. The book deals with topics such as roles and responsibilities of supervisors; models of supervision; the supervisory relationship; methods of supervision; ethical, legal, and multicultural issues in the supervisory process; managing crisis situations; and evaluation issues.

For a copy of the latest Wadsworth Human Services, Counseling, and Social Work Catalog contact:

Wadsworth Group
10 Davis Dr.
Belmont, CA 94002
(650) 637-7664

11. **Information about professional organizations**. I hope you will encourage your students to consider joining a professional organization early in their career. Below are some of these organizations, all of which offer student memberships at a reduced rate.

AMERICAN COUNSELING ASSOCIATION (ACA)

Student memberships are available to both undergraduate and graduate students enrolled at least half-time or more at the college level.

ACA membership provides many benefits, including a subscription to the *Journal of Counseling and Development* and a monthly newspaper entitled *Counseling Today,* eligibility for professional liability insurance programs, legal defense services, and professional development through workshops and conventions. ACA puts out a resource catalog that provides information on the various aspects of the counseling profession, as well as giving detailed information about membership, journals, books, home-study programs, videotapes, audiotapes, and liability insurance. For further information, contact:

> American Counseling Association
> 5999 Stevenson Avenue
> Alexandria, VA 22304-3300
> Telephone: (703) 823-9800 or (800) 347-6647
> Fax: (703) 823-0252
> Website: *http://www.counseling.org*

AMERICAN PSYCHOLOGICAL ASSOCIATION

The APA has a Student Affiliates category rather than student membership. Journals and subscriptions are extra. Each year in mid-August or late August the APA holds a national convention. For further information contact:

> American Psychological Association
> 750 First Street, NE
> Washington, DC 20002-4242
> Telephone: (202) 336-5500 or (800) 374-2721
> Fax: (202) 336-5568
> Website: *http://www.apa.org*

NATIONAL ASSOCIATION OF SOCIAL WORKERS (NASW)

NASW membership is open to all professional social workers and there is a student membership category. The NASW Press, which produces *Social Work* and the *NASW News* as membership benefits, is a major service in professional development. A number of pamphlets are available through NASW. For information contact:

> National Association of Social Workers
> 750 First Street, NE, Suite 700
> Washington, DC 20002-4241
> Telephone: (202) 408-8600 or (800) 638-8799
> Fax: (202) 336-8311
> Website: *http://www.socialworkers.org*

AMERICAN ASSOCIATION FOR MARRIAGE AND FAMILY THERAPY (AAMFT)

The AAMFT has a student membership category. Members receive the *Journal of Marital and Family Therapy,* which is published four times a year, and a subscription to six issues yearly of *Family Therapy Magazine.* For membership applications and further information, contact:

> American Association for Marriage and Family Therapy
> 112 South Alfred Street
> Alexandria, VA 22314
> Telephone: (703) 838-9808
> Fax: (703) 838-9805
> Web site: *http://www.aamft.org*

NATIONAL ORGANIZATION FOR HUMAN SERVICE EDUCATION (NOHSE)

NOHSE is made up of members from diverse disciplines: mental health, child care, social services, gerontology, recreation, corrections, and developmental disabilities. Membership is open to human service educators, students, fieldwork supervisors, and direct-care professionals. Student membership includes a subscription to the newsletter the *Link,* the yearly journal *Human Services Education,* and a discount price for the yearly conference (held in October). For further information about membership in the National Organization for Human Service Education, contact:

> Chrisanne Christensen
> Sul Ross State University
> Rio Grande College
> Rt. 3, Box 1200
> Eagle Pass, TX 78852
> Telephone: (830) 758-5112
> Fax: (830) 758-5001
> Website: *http://www.nohse.com*

12. **Codes of ethics of professional organizations**. Each of the major mental health professional organizations has its own code of ethics, which can be obtained by contacting the particular organization. All of the following codes of ethics and guidelines for practice are available in the booklet, ***Codes of Ethics for the Helping Professions*** (2nd Edition) (Brooks/Cole and Wadsworth Group, 2004), which is sold at a nominal price when packaged with the textbook, *Theory and Practice of Counseling and Psychotherapy.*

- ACA *Code of Ethics* and Standards of Practice
- ACA Ethical Standards for Internet On-Line Counseling
- Ethical Guidelines for Counseling Supervisors
- Code of Ethics of the American Mental Health Counselors Association
- Ethical Standards for School Counselors
- AAMFT Code of Ethics
- Ethical Principles of Psychologists and Code of Conduct
- Ethics of the International Association of Marriage and Family Counselors
- Code of Ethics of the National Association of Social Workers
- Canadian Counselling Association Code of Ethics
- Code of Professional Ethics for Rehabilitation Counselors
- National Board for Certified Counselors Code of Ethics
- NBCC Standards for the Ethical Practice of Internet Counseling
- Association for Specialists in Group Work Professional Standards for the Training of Group Workers
- Association for Specialists in Group Work Best Practice Guidelines
- Association for Specialists in Group Work Principles for Diversity-Competent Group Workers

13. **On-line resources for your students**:

   A. **On-line quiz items.** In order to help your students gauge their level of comprehension on the material presented in the textbook, there are 120 on-line quiz items. These quizzes are additional items besides the ones contained in each chapter of the ***Student Manual***. The on-line quiz items are designed to help students pinpoint those areas where they might need further study as well as help them see their areas of strength. Please visit our website at: **http://counseling.wadsworth.com/** and look under ***Theory and Practice of Counseling and Psychotherapy*** (7th Edition) to find the quiz items.

   B. *Infotrac* – **On-line resource for journal articles**. Professors have the option of ordering this text bundled with a free subscription to ***Infotrac*** for their students. ***Infotrac*** is an on-line database that gives students access to full-length articles from over 900 scholarly and popular periodicals. The database is updated daily and dates back to as much as four years. Students will have access to ***Infotrac*** as well as the ability to print the articles, 24 hours a day from any location that has internet access. ***Infotrac*** is a great tool for conducting research! For a more in-depth discussion of ***Infotrac*** and how to use it, please visit the ***Infotrac*** website found at: **http://infotrac.thomsonlearning.com/.**

C. **Thomson Learning _Web Tutor_**[TM]. Designed to complement specific Wadsworth texts, this content-rich, Web-based teaching and learning tool helps students succeed by taking the course beyond classroom boundaries to an anywhere, anytime environment. _Web Tutor_ is rich with study and mastery tools, communication tools, and course content. Professors can use _Web Tutor_ to provide virtual office hours, post your syllabi, set up threaded discussions, track student progress with the quizzing material, and more.

For students, _Web Tutor_ offers real-time access to a full array of study tools, including flashcards (with audio), practice quizzes, online tutorials, and Web links. Professors who have tried _Web Tutor_ have been especially pleased with the way _Web Tutor_ allows students – even those in very large classes – to participate in class discussions online. This student-to-student interaction has enormous potential to enhance each student's experience with the course content. _Web Tutor_ also provides rich communication tools to instructors and students, including a course calendar, asynchronous discussion, 'real time' chat, and an integrated e-mail system.

D. _**Exam View**_ **from Wadsworth/Thomson Learning**. Enhance your range of assessment and tutorial activities – and save yourself time in the process. With _**Exam View**_ from Wadsworth, you can easily create and customize tests! _**Exam View**_ is the only test generator that offers a "WYSIWYG" feature that allows you to see the test you are creating on the screen exactly as it will print! Also unique is _**Exam View's Quick Test Wizard**_, which guides you step-by-step through the process of creating and printing a test in minutes.

HUSER 380   Theories and Techniques of Counseling

(3 semester units)
Tuesdays and Thursdays 1:00 to 2:15
Jerry Corey, Ed.D., Professor of Human Services and Counseling
California State University, Fullerton

Required Readings for Huser 380:

1. *Theory and Practice of Counseling and Psychotherapy* (7th ed., 2005)
2. *Student Manual for Theory and Practice of Counseling and Psychotherapy* (7th Edition, 2005)
3. *Case Approach to Counseling and Psychotherapy* (6th Ed, 2005)
4. *CD ROM for Integrative Counseling* (2005)

SCHEDULE FOR READINGS AND ASSIGNMENTS

Week 1   **Introduction and Overview**
Reading assignments: (due Thursday)
  TPCP text, Chapter 1
  Student Manual, Chapter 1
  Case Approach – Introduction to Case of Ruth, Chapter 1
CD ROM for Integrative Counseling
    and
The Counselor as Person and Professional
Reading assignments: (due Tuesday)
  TPCP text, Chapter 2
  Student Manual, Chapter 2
    CD ROM for Integrative Counseling

Week 2   **Ethical Issues in Counseling**
Reading assignment: (due Tuesday)
  TPCP text, Chapter 3
  Student Manual, Chapter 3
Take home **quiz** for Chapters 2 and 3

Week 3   **Psychoanalytic Therapy**
Reading assignments: (due Tuesday)
  TPCP text, Chapter 4
  Student Manual, Chapter 4
  Case Approach, Chapter 2: Case of Ruth
Take home **quiz** for Chapter 4 (due Tuesday)

Week 4   **Adlerian Therapy**
Reading assignments: (due Tuesday)
  TPCP text, Chapter 5
  Student Manual, Chapter 5
  Case Approach, Chapter 3: Case of Ruth
Take home **quiz** for Chapter 5 (due Tuesday)

Week 5   **Test #1** (Tuesday) on Chapters 1 to 5
Existential Therapy
Reading assignments: (due Thursday)
    TPCP text, Chapter 6
    Student Manual, Chapter 6
    Case Approach, Chapter 4: Case of Ruth
Turn in *Student Manual* with all inventories and activities completed (due Thursday)
Chapters 1 to 6
Take home **quiz** for Chapter 6 (due Thursday)

Week 6   **Person-Centered Therapy**
Reading assignments: (due Tuesday)
    TPCP text, Chapter 7
    Student Manual, Chapter 7
    Case Approach, Chapter 5: Case of Ruth
Take home **quiz** for Chapter 7 (due Tuesday)

Week 7   **Gestalt Therapy**
Reading assignments: (due Tuesday)
    TPCP text, Chapter 8
    Student Manual, Chapter 8
    Case Approach, Chapter 6: Case of Ruth
Take home **quiz** for Chapter 8 (due Tuesday)

Week 8   **Behavior Therapy**
Reading assignments: (due Tuesday)
    TPCP text, Chapter 9
    Student Manual, Chapter 9
    Case Approach, Chapter 7: Cases of Ruth
Take home **quiz** for Chapter 9 (due Tuesday)

Week 9   **Test #2** on Chapters 6 to 9 (Tuesday)
Cognitive-Behavior Therapy
Reading assignments: (due Thursday)
    TPCP text, Chapter 10
    Student Manual, Chapter 10
    Case Approach, Chapter 8: Case of Ruth
Take home **quiz** for Chapter 10 (due Thursday)

Week 10   **Reality Therapy**
Reading assignments: (due Tuesday)
    TPCP text, Chapter 11
    Student Manual, Chapter 11
    Case Approach, Chapter 9: Case of Ruth
Take home **quiz** for Chapter 11 (due Tuesday)

Week 11   **PAPER DUE** (Tuesday)
Feminist Therapy
Reading assignments: (due Tuesday)
    TPCP text, Chapter 12
    Student Manual, Chapter 12
    Case Approach, Chapter 10: Case of Ruth
Take home **quiz** for Chapter 12 (due Thursday)

Week 12   **Postmodern Approaches**
Reading assignments: (due Tuesday)
    TPCP text, Chapter 13
    Student Manual, Chapter 13

Case Approach, Chapter 11: Case of Ruth
Take home **quiz** for Chapter 13 (due Tuesday)

Week 13   **Family Systems Therapy**
Reading assignments: (due Tuesday)
TPCP text, Chapter 14
Turn in *Student Manual* (due Tuesday) with all inventories and activities completed
Chapters 7 to 14
Reading assignments: (due Tuesday)
TPCP text, Chapter 14
Student Manual, Chapter 14
Case Approach, Chapter 12: Case of Ruth
Test #3 on Chapters 10 to 14 (Thursday)

Week 14   **Integrative Perspective**
Reading assignments: (due Tuesday)
TPCP text, Chapter 15
Case Approach, Chapter 13 (Bringing the Approaches Together and
Developing Your Own Therapeutic Style)
CD ROM for Integrative Therapy [Turn in all your written responses to the CD ROM program
based on the integrative approach to working with Ruth.]

Week 15   **Case of Stan**
Reading assignments: (due Tuesday)
TPCP text, Chapter 16
Student Manual, Chapter 16
Review of the Course

Week 16   **Final Examination**: (Thursday from 12:00 to 1:50)
Comprehensive Exam consisting of a total of 200 multiple-choice items.
Exam covers a review of all of the theories.

Suggestions of how to study and review for the final exam:

- Review the concise summaries in the student manual for each of the theory chapters.
- Review the comprehension quizzes that are given in the ***Student Manual***, which you have taken each week.
  Re-take these quizzes once more.
- Read carefully the summary and evaluation of each chapter.
- Focus your study on the summary, review and charts given in Chapter 15 – Basic philosophies, key
  concepts, goals of therapy, therapeutic relationship, techniques, applications, contributions, limitations, and
  multicultural implications.
- Pay particular attention to ***Case Approach*** (Chapters 1 & 13) and *Working with Ruth* in Chapters 2 to 12 for
  this exam.

COURSE OBJECTIVES

The purpose of the course is to expose you to a variety of contrasting theoretical models underlying both individual and group practice in counseling. Through lectures, demonstrations, small-group discussions, experiential activities, readings, and writing papers, you are assisted to critically evaluate the practical applications of contemporary counseling perspectives. Specific objectives are:

1. To provide you with information about the therapeutic process and the practical elements of the counseling interaction.

2. To provide you with an experiential laboratory to learn and practice listening and attending skills essential to the counseling process.

3. To expose you to a variety of ethical and professional issues in counseling and to guide you in developing a position on these issues.

4. To develop an interest in reading in the counseling field.

5. To develop self-evaluation skills, writing skills, and critical thinking skills.

6. To encourage your integration of theoretical and experiential learning in order to form your own personal model of the counseling process.

7. To challenge you to look at your own qualities that support and hinder your attempts at being therapeutic for others.

8. To gain an understanding of ways of applying ten theories to specific cases. (The case of Stan in the *TPCP* text; the case of Ruth in the *Case Approach* book; and other cases in the *Student Manual for TPCP*). You will have opportunities to practice working with these cases.

SUGGESTIONS FOR GETTING THE MOST FROM THE COURSE

1. Read the contents in this course outline and study guide. Any questions you have will be clarified during the first week.

2. Decide at the outset if you have the time and are willing to devote the time and effort needed to do a quality job for this important course in your major. As a rough estimate:

   - 45 hours are devoted to attending class meetings
   - 45 hours of class preparation (including reading and studying, as well as preparing for the tests and final examination)
   - 20 hours to write your paper
     110 hours = during the semester, or a minimum of 8 hours weekly. This is only an estimate, as students vary with respect to factors related to how much time and effort any course will require.

3. Don't allow yourself to get behind in your reading! The required readings for the *Theory and Practice of Counseling and Psychotherapy* – and the *Student Manual* – and the supplementary book, *Case Approach to Counseling and Psychotherapy* should be completed each week on time. It is expected that you make use of the *Student Manual* that accompanies the textbook. Come prepared to class to ask questions or raise issues based on the readings. The interactive self-study program, CD ROM for Integrative Counseling, will give you an opportunity to view the theories applied to practice. It is strongly recommended that you view go through this program early in the course, even before we study the theories.

NOTE: All reading assignments are due on the day we discuss an assigned approach covered in the textbook, *Theory and Practice of Counseling and Psychotherapy*, the *Student Manual*, and the *Case Approach* book.

4. It is expected that you make full use of the *Student Manual for Theory and Practice of Counseling and Psychotherapy*. In addition to reading and studying the chapters in the textbook, this manual provides self-inventories for each therapy approach, discussion questions, a concise summary of the basic points of each theory, practical exercises and activities, case studies, and other open-ended situations for you to consider. After you have thoroughly studied the textbook, take the self-tests in the manual and score them to determine your level of mastery of the material. These will be most helpful in reviewing for examinations.

   Weekly take-home quizzes will be turned in consisting of the *Pre-Chapter Self-Inventory* and the *Comprehension Check* for each theory chapter in the *Student Manual*. Be sure to score the quizzes and submit them *on time* each week. If you do, you will receive 10 points (100 possible). You will have a separate answer sheet to record your responses on each pre-chapter self-inventory and comprehension check for each chapter.

5. Come to class with an open frame of mind and be willing to take some risks. This course is designed as a *beginning* survey of counseling theory and practice. Thus, as an introductory course, you are *not* expected to have counseling experience. Don't allow yourself to be intimidated. Hopefully, you will challenge your fears and push yourself to become an *active and involved participant*.

6. Each week, prior to reading the assigned material, carefully look over the study guide that contains focus questions for each week. We will be discussing these topics in class, so do come prepared to raise the questions that you'd most like to discuss. Keep up to date on the reading assignments.

7. Three tests of an objective variety are given as well as a final examination. Look at the suggestions given in this course outline for ways to prepare for these exams, as well as an idea of the content of them.

8. The paper is designed to help you integrate the material. Consult this outline early for the details. This paper must be typewritten, proofread, double-spaced, and is expected to show evidence of clear thought. Plan ahead so that your paper will be turned in *on time* in quality fashion. Late papers will be subject to lowering the overall grade of at least 15%.

9. Of course, you are expected to attend *every* class session, unless there is a valid emergency/reason. *Promptness* is expected and appreciated. *Unexcused absences* do have a bearing on your grade, so if you have a legitimate reason for missing, *do* let me know prior to or immediately upon returning to class. *Active participation* is of the utmost importance in this class. Part of your course grade is determined by *participation* (which includes attendance and promptness, participation in class activities, quality of active participation in class discussions and small groups, and completeness of the exercises and inventories in the *Student Manual*).

10. **Respect confidentiality!** Being actively involved in the class sessions and the small groups entails some level of personal self-disclosure. Because of the nature of the vulnerability, trust, and openness needed to learn about counseling, it is extremely important that confidentiality be maintained. Revealing personal information about others outside of the classroom is a breach of confidentiality. If you wish to share with others outside of the classroom, please reveal only your own reactions and understanding and avoid using names or identifying features of your classmates. It is expected that anyone who participates in a *demonstration* of either an individual session or a group session in this course will have his or her confidentiality respected. Please **do not tape record** any lectures, discussions, or demonstrations. Tape recording parts of class sessions could well pose problems with respect to confidentiality and privacy.

11. **Grading Practices and Policy**. Your grade for this course will be based on the following:

    A. Tests 1, 2, and 3 counts as one-third of your course grade.

    | Test 1 | Chapters 1-5 | (100 points) |
    | Test 2 | Chapters 6-9 | (100 points) |
    | Test 3 | Chapters 10-14 | (100 points) |

    The above three tests are converted into one percentage score.

B. The PAPER will make up one-third of your course grade.

C. The Final Exam (200 points), the *take-home quizzes* (100 points), and *participation* (100 points). Taken collectively these have a possible 400 points. These 400 possible points are converted into one percentage score, which will count for one-third of your grade. *Participation* involves a number of specific factors: attendance and promptness, quality of active participation in class discussions and small groups, participation in activities in class, and completeness of doing the exercises and inventories in the ***Student Manual***.

Each of the three areas above will be recorded as a single percentage score, and then these percentages will be divided by three to arrive at your final GPA for the course.

Grading Scale (percentage) is as follows:

100-98	=	A+	80-78	=	C+
97-94	=	A	77-74	=	C
93-91	=	A-	73-71	=	C-
90-88	=	B+	70-68	=	D+
87-84	=	B	67-64	=	D
83-81	=	B-	63-61	=	D-
			Below 60	=	F

DIRECTIONS FOR YOUR PAPER

This paper – which consists of three topics – will be between 18 to 22 pages in length. Be sure to stay within the page limitations, and also review the guidelines for your papers. Use a title page and put your name only on this title page. Begin each new essay with a new page and identify each essay by number and a title.

1. Show how you would work with the case of Ruth using your own therapeutic strategies. You should emphasize the integration of several theoretical perspectives. Draw upon a variety of concepts and strategies as you demonstrate how you might work with several of Ruth's themes. Consider that you are working with Ruth for a total of six sessions. Show how you would begin and terminate counseling sessions, and what techniques you would employ at various phases in your work with Ruth. Be sure to state your rationale for the interventions you employ. *DO NOT* merely summarize the material in the ***Case Approach*** book Instead, show that you can apply an integration of two or more models in working with Ruth's case. Focus on a few themes or problems in Ruth's life that you are interested in exploring. Say something about how you might evaluate your counseling sessions with Ruth, based upon your own integrative approach. See the ***Case Approach*** book, Chapter 11, for an example of the integrative approach. (Length: Six to seven double-spaced pages).

2. Show how you would work with the case of Stan, using an integrative perspective. Select a few themes from Stan's life that you'd be most likely to focus on, and then demonstrate your style of counseling Stan. As with the case of Ruth, show how you might draw from concepts and techniques from various theoretical approaches if you were to work with Stan for six sessions. However, apply some different concepts and techniques with Stan than you did with Ruth. Give your rationale for your interventions at the various phases in the counseling process. (Length: 4 to 5 double-spaced pages).

3. Write an integrative paper that articulates your personal theoretical orientation to counseling. Your paper should deal with aspects such as:

    • key concepts of your approach
    • view of your role as therapist
    • therapeutic goals
    • relationship issues
    • central techniques and methods

Address specific issues as outlined in the textbook, especially Chapters 13 and 14. This particular essay should be about 8 to 10 pages in length and you should attempt to integrate as many concepts and techniques as you can based upon several of the counseling models.

Suggestions for Writing Papers and Criteria for Grading

DO NOT give a summary of textbook content. Demonstrate that you understand the various models by looking for common denominators among several therapy approaches. Show how you might use key concepts and techniques from the various approaches in working with diverse client groups. You might want to apply your integrative theory to a particular client population and a given setting. See Chapter 14 of the *TPCP* text for ideas. Also, see the guidelines that are given in the *Student's Manual.* Below are specific guidelines:

1. **Quality writing skills.**

   - Write directly and informally, yet write in standard English.
   - I encourage you to use personal examples and to support your points with these examples when appropriate.
   - Make sure your essays reflect university-level writing skills:
     - Use complete sentences
     - develop your paragraphs
     - check your spelling
     - put together a paper that reflects quality
   - You might ask someone to proof read your paper
   - It is essential that you keep strictly within the established page limitations.

2. **Development of a theme.** Look for a central theme or central message in each essay. I suggest that you make an outline, and check to see that each point in your outline pertains to your central message.

   - Create a short title for each essay that conveys your basic idea.
   - State your message clearly and concisely in your opening paragraph.
   - Have a solid and impactful concluding paragraph.
   - The theme should be clear, concise, and specific – rather than global and generalized. Do not write in a general and abstract manner, or else your essays will lose a clear focus.
   - Develop your thoughts fully, concretely, and logically – rather than rambling or being vague and wordy.
   - In terms of form and organization, your paper should flow well, and your points should relate to one another. The reader should not have to struggle to understand your intended meaning.
   - Give reasons for your views – rather than making unsupported statements. When you take a position, provide reasons for your position.
   - Cover a few issues or ideas well and in depth, rather than spreading yourself too thin. For each essay, narrow down your question or topic so that you can manage to develop central paragraphs that expand on your theme.

3. **Use of examples.** In developing your ideas, use clear examples to illustrate your point. Draw upon personal examples, use cases, and apply theoretical concepts to practical settings. Tie your examples into the point you are making – but avoid giving too many details or getting lost in the personal example.

4. **Creativity and depth of thinking.** Write a paper that reflects your own uniqueness and ideas – rather than merely giving a summary of the material in the book.

   - Do not make your papers mere summaries, rather focus on a clear position that you take on a specific question or issue.
   - Approach the material in an original way.
   - Focus on a particular issue or topic that you find personally significant. Since you have a choice in what aspect to focus on, select an aspect of a problem that will allow you to express your beliefs.
   - Show depth in expanding on your thoughts.

5. **Integration and application.** Your papers should emphasize an integration of perspectives and an application of theory/principles to practice.

   - Demonstrate that you know the material or the issues involved through an integration and synthesis of theories, accurate understanding of theoretical concepts, critical evaluation of theories, and ability to apply ideas to practical situations.

- If you are writing a theory essay, focus on those specific aspects of the theory that you'd most like to incorporate into your own style of counseling. Stress the implications for counseling practice. Rather than writing merely about a theoretical issue, show how this issue has meaning in a counseling situation.
- Apply your ideas to specific populations with whom you expect to work – both in counseling and non-counseling situations. You may want to apply your essays to teaching, working with the elderly, working in corrections, working with adolescents, etc. Make these a personal and meaningful experience.
- In writing about ethical issues, be sure to zero in on a specific message. What do you most want to convey?
- In writing about a case, be sure to show that you can apply several approaches or perspectives to this case. Work with the case by attempting to combine a number of perspectives.

II

Guidelines for Using the Chapters in

Theory and Practice of Counseling and Psychotherapy and the *Student Manual*

Case Approach to Counseling and Psychotherapy

and

The Art of Integrative Counseling

In the following sections, I present suggestions for using the special features found in the *Theory and Practice of Counseling and Psychotheray* text, the *Student Manual*, and *The Art of Integrative Counseling* text, such as use of:

- *Guidelines for Using Each Chapter*
- *Key Terms for Review*
- *InfoTrac Keywords*
- *Case Examples*
- *Study Guides*
- *Objective Test Items with Answer Keys*

In addition, essay questions and thought questions for reflection, evaluation, and discussion are offered for each chapter in the *Student Manual*. An answer key follows each of these chapter tests and examinations.

If your students are using the *Student Manual*, have them carefully read *How to Use the Student Manual with the Textbook*, (found in Chapter 1) so that they can get the maximum benefit of the suggestions for fully using the manual.

Guidelines for Using Chapter One

Introduction and Overview

in

Theory and Practice of Counseling and Psychotherapy and the *Student Manual*

Case Approach to Counseling and Psychotherapy

and

The Art of Integrative Counseling

You may have your own preferred organization for the structure of your course. I have made specific suggestions for using the textbook, *Theory and Practice of Counseling and Psychotherapy*, in the preface and the introductory chapter. Also, in the introduction to the *Student Manual for Theory and Practice of Counseling and Psychotherapy*, I make some recommendations that I think will lead to the maximum benefit from the combined package of the textbook and manual.

In addition to these recommendations, I'd like to share some other approaches that I have found useful, as well as share some reactions and suggestions given to me by my students. Perhaps you can incorporate those ideas that seem to fit your teaching style, or you can generate some modifications that are suited to your particular courses.

1. In Chapter 1 of the **Student Manual** is a *Survey of Attitudes and Values Related to Counseling and Psychotherapy: A Self-Inventory and Pretest*. I like to have students take this self-inventory at home during the first week of class. In asking the students to take this questionnaire, I emphasize the following points:

    A. Do not ponder too long on any question. Simply give your response by indicating the answer or answers that seem most appropriate from your viewpoint. More detailed directions are found in the **Student Manual**.

B. During the second session we go over this inventory in class and discuss the items that most stimulated the students. This typically generates excellent discussion and controversy at the beginning of the course. It also gives the student a mental set that the course will involve active participation as opposed to merely sitting passively and listening to lectures. These issues in the inventory touch on most of the key concepts covered in the various chapters of the textbook, so I find that this is an excellent way to introduce the students to an overview of the nature of the course.

C. I ask the students to bring the completed inventory to class and use this as a basis for breaking the class into small discussion groups for about 20 minutes. Their task is to select the top 3 items that they had the most difficulty answering and talk about these items in their small group. This class assignment serves the function of getting them thinking about a variety of issues in counseling practice and it also gives students an opportunity to begin to get acquainted with one another.

2. At the end of the course the students take the same inventory again, and we devote some class time to comparing any changes in their answers. I do this activity in small groups so that everyone has a chance to participate in sharing changes on specific counseling issues. This provides a meaningful way of reviewing the highlights of the course, and it allows students a chance to discover to what degree they have changed any of their attitudes and beliefs concerning the counseling process.

3. I have developed a list of questions that are found in Chapter 15 of the *Student Manual* and I direct the attention of the class to these questions during the first part of the semester (see *Questions and Issues: Guidelines for Developing Your Personal Style of Counseling* and see *Suggested Activities and Exercises: Developing Your Philosophy of Counseling*). I use these questions as reference points during the entire semester, and the hope is that these key questions provide a focus for students to grasp the basic similarities and differences among the theories. Several options are possible:

A. These questions can be considered as potential examination questions for an essay-type final examination or for a take-home final examination. Students might select several of the questions and write about them, or the instructor might decide which questions the students are to address, or a combination of both.

B. There is a possible danger of overwhelming students with too much material too soon, and I readily admit that I tend to do this. To avoid this, these questions could be divided and given at various points in the semester. Another idea is to have each student select one of these questions and briefly present their findings to the class.

C. One approach is to present these questions toward the end of the course, as a guide for review and integration of the various theories. The advantage of this is that students have studied the various counseling theories and these questions could assist them in a meaningful way in their synthesizing and personalizing of the theories.

4. If you are using *Issues and Ethics in the Helping Professions* (Corey, Corey, and Callanan, 2003) as a resource for preparing your lectures, I recommend that you pay particular attention to the pretest in Chapter 1. This is a self-inventory of attitudes and beliefs relating to ethical and professional issues in the practice of counseling. I use this book as a basis for organizing my lectures during the first few weeks of the semester, in conjunction with Chapters 1, 2, and 3 of the *TPCP* textbook. This has stimulated some excellent discussion at the beginning of the course, and it has proven to be a good way to get students thinking and verbally involved from the outset of the course. We typically deal with questions pertaining to the counselor's values, value conflicts, ethics of the therapeutic relationship, problems facing beginning counselors, issues relating to confidentiality, and so forth, during the early sessions.

The *CD ROM for Integrative Counseling* is an interactive self-study program that is based on 13 counseling sessions that I conduct with a client named Ruth. I provide a brief lecturette before each of the 13 sessions, then demonstrate an aspect of integrative counseling as applied to Ruth, and then give a brief commentary of what I saw happening in that particular session with the client. This CD ROM can be packaged with either *Theory and Practice of Counseling and Psychotherapy* or with *Case Approach to Counseling and Psychotherapy* at a major discount.

5. Chapter 1 of *TPCP* provides a framework for the course and an overview of the book, along with specific suggestions for using the textbook and the accompanying *Student Manual*. The table in Chapter 1 of the text

gives a summary of the eleven counseling theories that we focus on in this course. I typically give an overview lecture of the major points of the various theories so that students have a general perspective at the beginning.

6. **Suggestions for preparing your lectures for Chapter 1.** See also *Case Approach to Counseling and Psychotherapy* (Corey, 2005, Chapter 1) for a concise overview of the eleven therapeutic systems with reference to these specific areas:

    *   Basic assumptions
    *   Perspectives on assessment
    *   Therapeutic goals and procedures

    Also, the case of Ruth is introduced in detail in this first chapter. If you present Ruth's case in your class, you will get useful background information in Chapter 1 of *Case Approach*. There is also a section on diagnostic impressions of Ruth that involves various practitioners who give their diagnosis of Ruth based on DSM-IV-TR.

7. **On-line quiz**

    Presented on-line at **http://counseling.wadsworth.com** is a 120-item quiz for your students to determine their level of mastery. This will also be a good way for them to discuss and review some of the key points covered during the semester. An answer key is provided at the end of the test bank.

NOTE: Another alternative use of this 120-item quiz is to use it as part of the final examination in class. This could also be given to students to take home (for no credit or no grade) as a study tool to prepare for the final examination. A copy of the on-line quiz is located in Part VII of this *Instructor's Resource Manual*.

Guidelines for Using Chapter Two

The Counselor: Person and Professional

in

Theory and Practice of Counseling and Psychotherapy and the Student Manual

Case Approach to Counseling and Psychotherapy

and

The Art of Integrative Counseling

1. My own bias is that the issue of the counselor's personhood and behavior should receive primary emphasis in a counseling course. I fear that students are often so eager to learn a range of techniques that they sometimes fail to appreciate that these techniques cannot be divorced from their personhood—their values, philosophy of life, character, and view of their clients.

   During the entire semester, I try to focus on the importance of the counselor's personal characteristics. This chapter is designed to give special attention to the issue of the counselor's personhood and behavior. Many of my students have said that their own growth was the most meaningful aspect of the course. They have said that all the theories they studied were more meaningful when they were encouraged to apply these theories to their own struggles in becoming persons. This is one of my reasons for stressing an experiential approach and for integrating student activities (that deal with them personally) with the didactic material for the course.

2. Chapter 2 in the *TPCP* textbook raises many issues that are open-ended and call upon the student to take a position. The *Student Manual* contains questions that parallel the various topics in the textbook chapter. These questions are the ones I use as a basis for generating class discussion. I think that a discussion format is far more meaningful for this topic than is a lecture approach.

3. In this *Instructor's Resource Manual*, additional questions are raised. These questions can be used for review, for testing, for discussion by guest speakers, for panel discussions, or for research or term-paper topics.

4. In the *Student Manual* is a self-inventory, designed as a review of students' attitudes and beliefs as they relate to the counselor as a person and as a professional . I have students take this at home, and we then discuss in class, or in small groups, those items that seem to be the most popular.

5. Also in the *Student Manual* is a section, *Issues for Personal Application*, which is aimed at helping students identify potential value conflicts they may have with clients. There is also a suggested activity, *Personal Issues in Counseling and Psychotherapy*, which attempts to pinpoint concerns that each student has about counseling.

6. The *Student Manual* (in Chapter 2) contains a section, *Cases Dealing with Value Issues* . The following value issues and case scenarios are described: religious and spiritual concerns, abortion, sexual orientation, end-of-life-decisions, divorce, sexual promiscuity, and relationship issues. Of course, these cases provide good material for discussion either in small groups or in the entire class. It is even better to role-play these situations by having students serve as counselors while the instructor, or a student volunteer, plays out the value conflicts in these cases. This is another good time to show the video, *Ethics in Action* (Institutional Version, by Corey, Corey, & Haynes, 1998), in class. There are four vignettes in this video that deal with issues such as: religion and spirituality, abortion, sexual orientation, and end-of-life decisions. The vignettes in the video are brief role-plays that depict an ethical dilemma and raise questions for discussion. There is another version of *Ethics in Action: CD ROM.* In this second student version of this self-study program there are different role-play vignettes that deal with value conflicts between counselors and clients. Some of these include: divorce, abortion, cultural values, promiscuity, and an extramarital affair. In addition, both of these videos deal with other ethical matters such as the role of multicultural issues in counseling practice, and managing dual relationships and boundary concerns. These role-plays bring up much discussion in most classes – more than we have adequate time for in this beginning course.

7. **Examining Cultural Values and Attitudes.** For Chapter 2, it is well to stress to students the importance of taking an inventory of their beliefs and attitudes toward those who differ from themselves culturally. The beginning of this process can involve students by asking them how their own culture has had a significant impact on their behavior. See the *Student Manual* (Chapter 2) for an inventory that will be helpful in assessing cultural awareness: *Multicultural Counseling Competencies: A Self Examination*. The scoring instructions are given in the *Student Manual*. The section that follows the inventory, *Suggested Activity: Cultural Diversity in Counseling Practice* , asks students to write brief responses based on taking the inventory. If students complete these responses at home, this will greatly contribute to class discussions and provide the fullest use of this exercise. This inventory, and the questions that follow, is a good catalyst for getting students to access their awareness, knowledge, and skills; to understand the worldview of culturally different clients; and to assess their understanding of appropriate intervention strategies and techniques.

    I like to present the importance of examining cultural variables at the outset of the course, especially when we are discussing the counselor as a person. I've found that many students are "culturally encapsulated," and it is critical that they are challenged to assess how well equipped they are to practice counseling with culturally diverse client populations. Four books that I find useful in preparing lecture materials on a multicultural perspective on counseling are:

    *   Pedersen (2000), *A Handbook for Developing Multicultural Awareness*
    *   Atkinson, Morten, and Sue (1998), *Counseling American Minorities: A Cross-Cultural Perspective* (5th ed.)
    *   *Sue, Ivey, and Pedersen (1996), A Theory of Multicultural Counseling and Therapy*
    *   Sue and Sue (2003). *Counseling the Culturally Diverse: Theory and Practice.*

8. **Becoming a multiculturally skilled counselor**. In this chapter I stress what is involved in the process of becoming a multiculturally skilled counselor. I discuss the attitudes, knowledge, and skills that are a basic part of effective counseling in a multicultural society. To accomplish this, I rely on the inventories described above. This is also a good time to introduce experiential activities pertaining to cross-cultural counseling. Pedersen's 2000 book describes his trial model, which makes use of a pro-counselor and an anti-counselor. If you are interested in introducing an experiential dimension to your course, Pedersen's chapter on the trial model will provide you with helpful hints.

9. If you are using *The Art of Integrative Counseling* book to prepare lectures for your course, both Chapters 1 and 2 in that book are relevant to the topics discussed in the first few chapters in *TPCP*. Particularly useful are

the discussions in Chapter 2 regarding the quality of the therapeutic relationship that brings about healing, given on pages 15–16, of Chapter 2. Chapter 1 of *Art of Integrative Counseling* raises issues about ways of obtaining informed consent from the beginning of the therapeutic endeavor (see pages 5–7). The *CD ROM for Integrative Counseling* addresses some specific concerns that are relevant at the initial stage of counseling: ways of listening to client's concerns, educating clients about counseling, and beginning to establish goals for therapy.

Suggested Activities and Exercises

These activities and questions are designed to help students apply their learning to practice. Many of them can profitably be done alone in a personal way or with another person; others can be done in the classroom as discussion activities, either with the whole class or in small groups. Many of these questions are ones that prospective employers ask during job interviews.

1. In small groups in your class, explore the issue of why you are going into a helping profession. This is a basic issue, and one that many students have trouble putting into concrete words. What motivated you to seek this type of work? What do you think you can get for yourself? What do you see yourself as being able to do for others?

2. In class, do the following exercise in pairs. First, discuss areas that each of you might have trouble with in counseling situations because of a conflict of values. For example, one student might anticipate difficulty in working with clients who have fundamentalist religious beliefs. Then, choose one of these situations to role-play, with one student playing the part of a client and the other playing the part of the counselor. The client brings up some problem that involves the troublesome value area. It is important for you and your partner to imagine yourselves in the particular frame of reference being role-played and to experience the part as much as possible.

3. As a variation of the preceding exercise, you can assume the role of a client with whom you have difficulty identifying because of divergent values systems. For instance, if you think you'd have trouble counseling a woman who wanted an abortion, become this client and bring her problem to another student, who plays the part of a counselor. This type of role-reversal exercise can help you understand people whose value systems are different from your own.

4. Invite speakers to class to talk about multicultural factors as they relate to values. Speakers representing special concerns of various ethnic groups can address the topic of certain values unique to their group and can discuss the implications of these values for counseling.

5. In subgroups, explore the issue of how willing you are to be self-disclosing to your clients. Discuss the guidelines you would use to determine the appropriateness of self-disclosure. What are some areas you would feel hesitant about sharing? How valuable do you think it is to share yourself in a personal way with your clients? What are some of your fears or resistances about making yourself known to your clients?

6. In subgroups, discuss some ways that you can stay alive both as a person and as a professional. What are specific remedies for dealing with burnout? What strategies can you use to take care of yourself? After you've explored this issue in small groups, reconvene as a class and make a list of the measures each group came up with to maintain vitality.

7. Think of the type of client you might have the most difficulty working with. Then become this client in a role-playing fantasy with one other student. Your partner attempts to counsel with you. After you've had a chance to be the client, change roles and become the counselor. Your partner then becomes the type of client you just role-played.

8. Chapters 1 and 2 of the *Student Manual* contain some useful self-inventories and self-study and application exercises. The suggested activities and questions in the manual in Chapters 1 and 2 serve as useful guides for writing papers, for class discussion, and for review of key topics that are foundational to counseling practice. Some key questions for class discussion are:

    *   What are the personal characteristics of effective counselors?
    *   How do the counselor's values impact the counseling process?
    *   What are the requirements for becoming a multiculturally skilled counselor?

- What are the major issues and concerns of most beginning counselors?
- How can we stay alive both as persons and as professionals?

As students read this chapter, they can reflect on these questions in a personal way.

Thought Questions for Reflection, Evaluation, and Discussion

1. What does the phrase "the authentic therapist" convey to you? What are the personal characteristics that you deem essential for authenticity?

2. Some theories emphasize that therapist self-disclosure is a vital component of the therapeutic process. List some criteria by which you can differentiate between appropriate and facilitative therapist disclosure and the type of disclosure that is inappropriate.

3. Take a position on the issue: "Therapists should be required to undergo their own personal therapy before they become practitioners." Defend your position.

4. Discuss the degree of importance that you place on the client/therapist relationship as a factor related to successful therapeutic outcomes.

5. What are some of your own personal characteristics that you think might obstruct your ability to effectively work with clients in a counseling relationship?

6. Mention some of your personal strengths, values, beliefs, past experiences, and so on, that you think will work in your favor in establishing a meaningful and therapeutic relationship with clients. Discuss. How might these get in your way?

7. Discuss some of the typical fears that many practitioners experience as they actually begin to work with clients. What are your anxieties? How might you effectively deal with them?

8. If you were looking for a therapist for yourself, what personal and professional qualities would you be seeking. Be specific and explain why you selected these factors.

9. How important do you think it is that each practitioner develops his or her own personal counseling style, opposed to subscribing to any one therapeutic system?

10. Dealing with demanding clients is a problem for many counselors – be they experienced or not. Think of some kinds of demands that you might have trouble with. How might you deal with a client who made unrealistic demands of you?

11. Another problem for many counselors is dealing with uncommitted clients. How might you work with a client who wanted very little?

12. Discuss the possible therapeutic values of developing a sense of humor. When might humor be inappropriate?

13. What is an example of a value you hold that you might be inclined to push with your clients? How would you deal with this?

14. Discuss your own needs for becoming a counselor. How do you think your needs may both help and hinder you and your clients?

ISSUES FOR PERSONAL REFELCTION

Self-Inventory of Major Concerns as a Beginning Counselor

Much of Chapter 2 in the textbook deals with common concerns facing beginning counselors. The following questionnaire is built from the statements I often hear in supervision sessions with counselor interns (and often from experienced professionals in training workshops). Apply each statement to yourself, and determine to what degree this is a concern you face as you think about beginning to counsel others. Use the following scale:

1 = This is rarely a concern of mine.   3 = This matter concerns me quite a bit.
2 = This is a concern I sometimes have.   4 = This issue concerns me greatly.

___ 1. I am concerned that my anxiety will keep me immobilized, and that I will be very passive as a counselor, lest I make mistakes.

___ 2. I fear that I will be so concerned about being appropriate that I will forget to be myself.

___ 3. I might say too much about myself, and in doing so I will burden the client and also take the focus off of him or her and put it on myself.

___ 4. I think that I should be pretty near perfect, and that if I blunder I could really mess up my client.

___ 5. I wonder about how honest I should be with a client.

___ 6. I will feel threatened during moments of silence, thinking that I am expected to do or say something.

___ 7. It will be difficult for me to deal with demanding clients.

___ 8. I will feel helpless with clients who are not committed to working or with involuntary clients.

___ 9. I will probably demand instant results as a way of avoiding getting discouraged.

___ 10. I have an expectation that I should be able to help every client.

___ 11. I worry a lot about whether I am doing the right thing.

___ 12. I worry that I might over-identify with certain clients to the extent that I will take *their* problems on as my own.

___ 13. I think that I might be inclined to give too much advice.

___ 14. I can see myself trying to persuade clients to value what I value.

___ 15. I have trouble in deciding how much responsibility is mine and how much is my client's.

___ 16. I have real doubts about my ability to help someone who is in a crisis.

___ 17. I worry about sounding mechanical and merely following the book.

___ 18. A concern of mine is that I will get burned out.

___ 19. I am concerned about giving everything I have and then not getting any appreciation in return.

___ 20. I wonder if I can do what I believe is important as a counselor and still work within the system.

Suggestions for Using This Inventory

Go back and circle the few items that you find are your *greatest concerns*. It could be useful to bring these concerns up in class and compare your reactions with those of fellow students. Do you have other concerns that were not mentioned above? How can you prepare yourself now so that you will be able to successfully deal with your concerns?

Test Items

Chapters One and Two

Theory and Practice of

Counseling and Psychotherapy

Note: Below are test items for both chapters 1 and 2 of *Theory and Practice of Counseling and Psychotherapy*.

1. It is especially important for counselors who work with culturally diverse client populations to:
   a. be aware of their own cultural heritage.
   b. have a broad base of counseling techniques that can be employed with flexibility.
   c. consider the cultural context of their clients in determining what interventions are appropriate.
   d. examine their own assumptions about cultural values.
   e. all of the above

2. Which one of the following is not considered an experiential and relationship-oriented therapy?
   a. Gestalt therapy
   b. family systems therapy
   c. existential approach
   d. person-centered approach

3. Which one of the following is not associated with the cognitive-behavioral action-oriented therapies?
   a. Gestalt therapy
   b. cognitive therapy
   c. reality therapy
   d. behavior therapy
   e. rational emotive behavior therapy

4. Which approach is rooted in a humanistic philosophy that emphasizes the basic attitudes of the therapist as the core of the therapeutic process?
   a. psychoanalytic therapy
   b. Adlerian therapy
   c. person-centered therapy
   d. cognitive-behavioral therapy
   e. family therapy

5. The concept of the authentic counselor is best described as:
   a. modeling what it means to be a self-actualized person.
   b. being willing to be totally open and self-disclosing.
   c. being a technical expert who is committed to objectivity.
   d. being willing to shed stereotyped roles and being a real person.

6. In the text, all of the following are listed as characteristics of the counselor as a therapeutic person except:
   a. counselors have a sense of humor.
   b. counselors no longer have to cope with personal problems.
   c. counselors feel alive and their choices are life-oriented.
   d. counselors make mistakes and they are willing to admit them.
   e. counselors appreciate the influence of culture.

7. Researchers have identified some traits of the effective counselor. What best captures the spirit of these studies?
   a. Effective counselors are emotionally healthy.
   b. Effective counselors are tolerant of divergent beliefs and lifestyles.
   c. Effective counselors have a deep interest in people.
   d. Effective counselors hold positive beliefs about people and see them as trustworthy and capable.
   e. all of the above

8. In the text, the main reason given for having counseling students receive some form of psychotherapy is to help them to:
   a. work through early childhood trauma.
   b. learn to deal with countertransference.
   c. recognize and resolve their co-dependent tendencies.
   d. become self-actualized individuals.

9. Personal therapy for therapists can be instrumental in assisting them:
   a. to heal their own psychological wounds.
   b. to gain an experiential sense of what it is like to be a client.
   c. to understand their own needs and motives for choosing to become professional helpers.
   d. to work through their own personal conflicts.
   e. all of the above

10. Regarding the role of values in the counseling process, it is most accurate to state that:
    a. counseling can best be considered as teaching and persuading clients to act the right way.
    b. counselors would do well to maintain an indifferent, neutral, and passive role by simply listening to everything the client reports.
    c. counselors should avoid challenging the values of their clients.
    d. counselors avoid imposing their values, but they are likely to expose their values to clients.

11. If you have definite values in certain areas and are intent on directing your client toward your goals, ethical practice states that:
    a. you tell the person he or she holds incorrect values.
    b. you keep your attitudes and beliefs to yourself, and strive to appear accepting and understanding.
    c. you inform potential clients of those values that will certainly influence your intervention with them.
    d. none of the above

12. During an initial session, an adolescent girl tells you that she is pregnant and is considering an abortion. Which of the following would be the most ethical and professional course for you to follow?
    a. Encourage her to get the abortion as soon as possible, without exploring any other option.
    b. Steer her toward having her baby and then consider adoption for her baby.
    c. Suggest a referral for her if your values might interfere with your objectivity.
    d. Help her to clarify the range of her choices in light of her own values.
    e. both (c) and (d)

13. Culturally encapsulated counselors would be most likely to:
    a. depend entirely on their own internalized value assumptions about what is good for people.
    b. have an appreciation for a multicultural perspective in their counseling practice.
    c. recognize the cultural dimensions their clients bring to therapy.
    d. accept clients who have a different set of assumptions about life.

14. An ethnic minority client may be silent during the initial phase of counseling. This silence is probably best interpreted as:
    a. resistance.
    b. a manifestation of uncooperative behavior.
    c. a response to his or her cultural conditioning.
    d. a clear sign that counseling will not work.

15. Which of the following is not considered an essential skill of a culturally effective counselor?
    a. being able to modify techniques to accommodate cultural differences
    b. being able to send and receive both verbal and nonverbal messages accurately
    c. being able to get clients to intensify their feelings by helping them to vividly reexperience early childhood events
    d. assuming the role of consultant and change agent

16. Which of the following is not considered essential knowledge for a culturally effective counselor?
    a. knowing how to analyze transference reactions
    b. understanding the impact of oppression and racist concepts
    c. being aware of culture-specific methods of helping
    d. being aware of institutional barriers that prevent minorities from making full use of counseling services in the community

17. Essential components of effective multicultural counseling practice include all of the following except:
    a. Counselors avoid becoming involved in out-of-office interventions.
    b. Counselors feel comfortable with their clients, values and beliefs.
    c. Counselors are aware of how their own biases could affect ethnic minority clients.
    d. Counselors employ institutional intervention skills on behalf of their clients when necessary or appropriate.

18. In working with culturally diverse clients, it helps to understand and assess:
    a. what these clients expect from counseling.
    b. the degree of acculturation that has taken place.
    c. the attitudes these clients have about seeking professional help for their personal problems.
    d. the messages they received from their culture about asking for professional help.
    e. all of the above

19. Which of the following is *not* listed as a guideline for increasing your effectiveness in working with diverse client populations?
    a. Learn about how your own cultural background has influenced your thinking and behaving.
    b. Realize that practicing from a multicultural perspective will probably make your job very difficult.
    c. Be flexible in apply techniques with clients.
    d. Identify your basic assumptions pertaining to diversity.
    e. Pay attention to the common ground that exists among people of diverse backgrounds.

20. In terms of staying alive as a person and as a professional, a realistic strategy (or strategies) is (are) to:
    a. become aware of the factors that sap your vitality.
    b. deal with those factors that threaten to drain your energy.
    c. look within yourself to determine what choices you are making to keep yourself alive.
    d. assume personal responsibility for finding strategies for remaining vital as a person and as a professional.
    e. all of the above

ANSWER KEY FOR CHAPTERS ONE AND TWO

MULTIPLE-CHOICE TEST QUESTIONS

1. E	8. B	15. C
2. B	9. E	16. A
3. A	10. D	17. A
4. C	11. C	18. E
5. D	12. E	19. B
6. B	13. A	20. E
7. C	14. C	

CASES DEALING WITH VALUE ISSUES

In the **Student Manual**, a *Self-Inventory of Attitudes Relating to Ethical Issues*, provides a way for students to identify what their thoughts are on a range of topics pertaining to ethical practice. This is a good inventory to complete before analyzing the cases. This inventory typically generates excellent discussions in class. The *Cases Involving Ethical Dilemmas* provide useful discussion catalysts. These cases include: sexual attraction, a colleague having an affair with a former student, racism among your colleagues, and confidentiality.

The following are several additional cases dealing with value issues that are not found in the **Student Manual**. You may want to use these cases for role-playing activities in class and for discussion purposes. These cases fit with the discussion in Chapter 2 of **TPCP** on the role of values in the counseling process.

If you are intending on using these cases for role-playing, I find that it is best for someone to assume the client's role, and then several different students can role-play various alternative ways of dealing with each situation. I find that discussion of cases generally proves to be lively if it follows a brief role enactment in class. I generally give instructions such as the following as a way to focus students on the core issues in each case: "Attempt to focus on your own values, and identify any areas where you might tend to impose them on a client. Discuss how you see your values either helping or hindering your intervention in each of these cases."

1. A client who has not questioned her religious beliefs

Brenda, age 22, comes to see you because of problems in living at home with her family. She tells you that she feels dependent both financially and emotionally on her parents and that although she would like to move out and live with a girlfriend, she has many fears of taking this step. She also says that her religion is extremely important to her and that she feels a great deal of guilt over the conflict she has with her parents. After some discussion you find that she has never really questioned her religious values and that it appears that she has completely accepted the beliefs of her parents. Brenda says that if she followed her religion more closely, she would not be having all these difficulties with her folks. She is coming to you because she would "like to feel more like an independent adult who could feel free enough to make my own decisions."

- Where would you begin with Brenda? With her stated goals? With her religious beliefs? With her fear of moving away from home? With her conflicts and guilt associated with her parents? With her dependence/independence struggles?
- Would your religious values influence the direction you were likely to take with Brenda?
- Do you see any connection between her dependence on her parents and her guilt over not following her religion closely enough?

2. A woman struggling over an abortion decision

This case involves Melinda, a 25-year-old Latina who says she wants to have an abortion. She has been married for three years, already has two children, and says: "We had to get married because I was pregnant. We didn't have money then. The second kid was not planned either. But now we really can't afford another child." Her husband is a policeman going to law school at night. She works as a housekeeper and plans to return to school once her husband finishes his studies and it is "her turn." He should graduate in another year, at which time she is scheduled to enroll in classes at the community college. Having another baby at this time would seriously hamper those arrangements in addition to imposing the previously mentioned financial burden. But the client reports:

"I go to call the clinic, and I just can't seem to talk. I hang up the minute they answer. I just can't seem to make the appointment for the abortion, let alone have one. I was never much of a Catholic, and I always thought you should be able to get an abortion if you wanted one. What's wrong with me? And what am I going to do? I don't exactly have a lot of time."

- With the information given here, what do you see as the major value issues that need to be explored?
- How much emphasis would you place on factors such as what is stopping her from making the call? on her ambivalence between wanting to have the abortion and not wanting it?
- If she asked you for your advice, what do you think you would tell her? If you gave her this advice, what might your advice tell you about yourself?
- How would your views on abortion influence the interventions you made with Melinda?

- How would you deal with this situation if you had already established a therapeutic relationship over many months with Melinda?

3. Value issues pertaining to cultural and family background

Michael and Amy appear at your office for crisis counseling. Michael, 22, comes from a somewhat controlling Italian family. Amy, 20, comes from a large and powerful Japanese family that settled in California five generations ago. They want to get married in the fall, but they fear the reactions of their families. After dating casually for six months, they were forced to end their relationship because of objections on both sides. But after not seeing each other for two months, they began to meet in secret and are now determined to marry. Amy has threatened to become pregnant if their decision to get married is not accepted by their families. No one in either of their families is aware of their plans, but they know they must act quickly. They have decided to seek counseling.

- How do you approach this case?
- What kind of information about Amy's and Michael's families would you be interested in, and what would you ask each of them?
- Would you involve both families in the counseling process? Why or why not?
- What value issues are operating in this case, and how would you explore them in counseling?

4. Difficulties of a person adjusting to two cultures

Greta is a young woman who has been in the United States for six months. After living all of her life in Norway, she immigrated as the bride of an American college professor. Ever since arriving in the United States she has suffered from homesickness and is having difficulty adjusting to modern American life. Her husband, who showered her with attention during their courtship, has become distant and preoccupied with schoolwork. When she tries to make friends, she feels she is shunned by the other academic wives. All she really wants now is a divorce and a return ticket to Norway. Greta would like you to be her therapist, but there is a complicating factor. You are a close friend and professional colleague of her husband. When you suggest to her that perhaps she should see another counselor, she begins to cry and tells you that she is not comfortable with many Americans and that it is a relief to be able to talk to you. She begs you not to reject her.

- What reactions do you have toward Greta?
- What would you do or say when she begged you not to reject her?
- Would the fact that you were a close friend and a colleague present ethical problems for you that would make it necessary for you to refer her? What exactly is your responsibility to her?
- Assume that you did not know her husband and that she asked for your help. What values do you have (and what life experiences have you had) that are likely to increase your chances of working with her? What might get in the way of your providing her with this help?

5. A woman who wants her marriage and her affair

Loretta and Bart come to you for marriage counseling. In the first session you see them as a couple. Loretta says that she can't keep going on the way they have been for the past several years. She tells you that she would very much like to work out a new relationship with him. He says that he does not want a divorce and is willing to give counseling his "best shot." Loretta comes to the following session alone because Bart had to work overtime. She tells you that she has been having an affair for two years and hasn't yet mustered up the courage to leave Bart for this other man, who is single and is pressuring her to make a decision. She relates that she feels very discouraged about the possibility of anything changing for the better in her marriage. She would, however, like to come in for some sessions with Bart because she doesn't want to hurt him.

- What would you be inclined to say to Loretta based on what she has told you privately?
- Would you be willing to work with Loretta if her aim was to continue her affair and keep her marriage? Why or why not?
- How would your views on extramarital affairs influence the interventions you made with Loretta and Bart?
- Would you encourage Loretta to divulge what she had told you privately in a later session with Bart? Why or why not?
- Would the element of "the other man" pressuring Loretta to make a decision have a bearing on your intervention in this case?

Guidelines for Using Chapter Three

Ethical Issues in Counseling Practice

In

Theory and Practice of Counseling and Psychotherapy and the *Student Manual Case Approach to Counseling and Psychotherapy*

and

The Art of Integrative Counseling

1. There is a growing trend toward including a study of counselor ethics in courses in the human services, counseling, and intern programs. This chapter contains many open-ended questions and brief case examples designed to make the student aware of ethical issues and problems in the counseling profession. In addition to the frequent examples presented in the textbook, the *Student Manual* contains a series of questions for evaluation and discussion. There are some additional open-ended questions in this *Instructor's Resource Manual* in the test section.

2. Rather than lecture on the topic of ethical issues, I prefer an inquiry approach that urges students to answer for themselves the questions and issues I pose in the textbook and *Student Manual*. Of course, I think it is important that I share my own views and clinical experience with my students, but many of the issues I raise are open-ended and call on the student to make a critical judgment and take a definite stand on the issue. When I teach ethics, I do not provide the students with simple answers. Instead I encourage them to think through an ethical dilemma and come up with an answer that makes sense to them. My emphasis is on ethical reasoning and learning how to grapple with the many dimensions involved in any ethical problem.

3. The *Student Manual* has questions geared to each of the major topics and sections covered in this chapter of the textbook. Have students use these questions as a guide for study, review, and for class discussion of these issues. There is also a self-inventory of ethical issues. The *Student Manual* contains addresses of the major professional organizations in Chapter 3.

4. The *Student Manual* describes several cases involving ethical dilemmas. These all lend themselves to role-playing and discussion. I find that brief cases are a good way to introduce students in this course to the kinds of

ethical dilemmas they are likely to face in practicing counseling. Although most programs have a separate course in ethics, I like to devote a week or two to ethics as a part of the theories course because of my belief that ethics ought to be integrated into the total curriculum. Students will not get an in-depth treatment of ethics in this counseling theory course. However, they can be exposed to ethical dimensions of practice associated with such matters as making a diagnosis at the first session, informed consent, use of techniques, dealing with goals for therapy, and a host of other ethical aspects associated with applying theory to practice.

5. A sample informed consent document is found in the **Student Manual**. If time allows, you might ask your students to write their own informed consent document. As another alternative, students might form small groups and discuss what information they would want to convey to their clients early in the counseling process.

6. I use *Issues and Ethics in the Helping Professions,* 6th ed., 2003, by Corey, Corey, and Callanan as a resource to design lectures for this chapter on ethical issues in counseling. I typically cover in some depth the following topics, which are covered in the above book:

    A. The importance of the counselor's personality and character; some personal characteristics of effective therapists

    B. The issue of personal therapy for therapists

    C. Common concerns facing the counselor; and some ways of struggling and dealing constructively with these personal and professional issues

    D. Values and the therapeutic process: effects of counselor values on client; client/counselor value clashes; imposing versus exposing one's values; practical situations illustrating a variety of value conflicts

    E. Ethics pertaining to therapist responsibility, therapist competence, and confidentiality

    F. Ethics pertaining to the client/therapist relationship

    G. Ethical and professional aspects of dual relationships

    I find that students particularly like the open-ended cases and situations that are presented. The emphasis during the last few weeks is on exploration of issues, sharing of views, and open discussion. I am less concerned that they amass knowledge about ethics; rather at this point my major aim is to introduce the students to a variety of ethical and professional issues that they'll likely face when they are doing their field work or practicing as a paraprofessional on their job. I hope that students learn that developing a sense of professionalism and ethical responsibility is a task that is never finished, that is developmental. I expect that they will remain open to rethinking their positions as they leave school and gain more practical experience.

7. *Ethics in Action: Institutional Video* is a video that is designed to bring to life the ethical issues and dilemmas that counselors often encounter. I use both the *Institutional Version of Ethics in Action (a one-hour video)* and also *Ethics in Action* : CD ROM (available from Brooks-Cole/Wadsworth) as a way to present a host of ethical problems in the short time that we allot to the topic of ethics in the theory course. The video aims to provide opportunity for discussion, self-exploration and problem-solving of a variety of issues and dilemmas. The *Institutional Version* of the video shows a weekend workshop in ethics co-led by Marianne Schneider Corey and Gerald Corey. The workshop includes challenging questions and lively discussion, role-plays where student take on the personalities of a variety of clients and where they demonstrate both helpful and unhelpful interventions. This video is divided into three segments:

    •   *Ethical Decision-Making*
    •   *Values and the Helping Relationship*
    •   *Boundary Issues and Multiple Relationships*

The first segment, *Ethical Decision-Making*, examines the steps necessary in resolving ethical dilemmas and puts this model into practice through role-plays and discussion. The importance of self-awareness, as well as having a multicultural perspective, is also covered as these topics relate to becoming an ethical practitioner. The second segment, *Values and the Helping Relationship*, addresses the fact that every counselor has a value system, which

33

is likely to impact the counseling relationship. Common values influencing the counseling process include those such as abortion, religion, sexual orientation, suicide, and the like. Again, role-plays and discussion bring the issues to life. The final segment, *Boundary Issues and Multiple Relationships*, addresses an ever-growing concern in practice regarding engaging in multiple roles and relationships with clients. Role-plays and discussion focus on topics such as managing boundaries, social relationships, sexual attraction, bartering, and accepting gifts from clients.

The *Institutional Version* one-hour video is designed to be utilized over several class sessions. As the instructor of your course, you may want to use this video in various ways. Ideally, you would stop after each segment and have the class discuss the issues and the role-play and then embark on several role-plays enlisting class members to play the various roles. This can be followed by a discussion which identifies the ethical issues, reviews the relevant codes and laws, and applies the eight-step decision-making model to a specific ethical dilemma, which is briefly described in Chapter 3 of *TPCP* – and also described in the video. The class could then role-play various responses or approaches to the situation.

Suggested Activities and Exercises

The following are some activities that can make the topic of ethical issues in counseling "come alive." While the **Student Manual** contains some activities that can be done alone or in small groups in the classroom, some instructors might want additional exercises. I typically find that students get very involved in discussions of ethical issues, and many of these activities can lead to personal involvement with these topics.

1. In small groups, explore the topic of when and how you might make a referral. If there is time, role-play a referral, with one student playing the client and another the counselor. After a few minutes, the "client" and the other students can give the counselor feedback on how he or she handled the situation. As a variation, one student can play the role of a client who simply does not want to accept a referral. Each person in the group can have a few minutes to work with the client. When everyone has had a chance to work with the client, the client can talk about how he or she felt with each person. This role playing can lead into a discussion about ways of making referrals without alienating a client.

2. In small groups, explore what you think is involved in assisting clients in understanding what counseling is about and how best to make use of the counseling process. What are the elements of informed consent that need to be addressed early in the counseling relationship?

3. In small groups decide what specific rights of clients you deem as most essential. As a group, how would you safeguard those rights? How might you educate your clients with respect to their rights and their responsibilities? (You might draw up a therapeutic contract that you'd want to present to a client.)

4. In a class debate, one side can take the position that absolute confidentiality is necessary to promote full client disclosure. The other side can argue for a limited confidentiality that still promotes effective therapy.

5. In small groups, discuss specific circumstances in which you would break confidentiality, and see whether you can agree on some general guidelines. When your class convenes for a general meeting, the results of all the small groups can be shared and discussed.

6. Consider inviting an attorney who is familiar with the legal aspects pertaining to the client/therapist relationship to address your class. Possible topics for consideration are: What are the legal rights of clients in therapy? What are the most common grounds for malpractice suits?

Thought Questions for Reflection, Evaluation, and Discussion

1. Take a position and defend it: For counseling to make any significant impact on clients, it must deal with the underlying social-environmental-economic factors that are contributing to the psychological problems of the clients.

2. Ethically, it is the counselor's responsibility to terminate a relationship with a client when this relationship is not benefiting the client. What specific guidelines would you use to make this decision? What criteria can you use to judge whether or not your client is benefiting from his or her counseling relationship with you?

3. Assume that your client engages in self-destructive behavior and refuses to change certain of his or her values that you think are a definite danger to his or her life. For example, your adolescent client continues to escape from reality by using hard drugs. How might you deal with this situation?

4. Do you think it is unethical for you as a counselor to meet your psychological needs partly through your work?

5. Assume that you are opposed to involuntary counseling, but you are doing your internship in an agency where all of your clients are sent to you by the judge and very few want counseling. How would you deal with the discrepancy between your philosophical position and the practical realities of your job placement?

6. Assume your client asks you "Is whatever I say in here strictly confidential, and can I be assured that nothing that I talk about with you will go outside of this room?" How would you reply? What specific guidelines could you offer to your client? What kinds of situations might compel you to disclose confidences to others?

7. If you were to encounter an ethical dilemma, what steps would you take in making an ethical decision?

8. If you were in a job interview, how would you respond to the question: "What do you consider to be the most pressing and central ethical issue facing the counselor?"

9. What are some guidelines you might employ to determine when and how to make a referral? Under what conditions might you refer a client or potential client to another counselor?

10. In what ways might you be practicing unethically if you do not address cultural factors in your counseling practice?

11. The therapist has a responsibility primarily (but not exclusively) to the client, but as a therapist you also have a responsibility to the family members of the client, to your own agency or institution, to a referring agency, to society, and to the profession. In cases where there are conflicts of responsibilities, what guidelines could you use to resolve these conflicts? Can you think of any situations where you might be involved in a conflict over deciding where your primary responsibility lies?

12. Some writers have alleged that current theories of counseling are inadequate to describe, explain, predict, and deal with the richness and complexity of a culturally diverse population. As you study the theories in the textbook, keep alert in critiquing each theory from the perspective of its relevance to dealing with diversity.

13. What are some clinical and ethical issues you can see that are associated with diagnostic procedures. What do you think is the appropriate role of diagnosis in counseling?

14. Dual and multiple relationships can be problematic in counseling relationships, yet there can be benefits to certain forms of performing multiple roles. How would you go about determining whether there are more risks or benefits in a particular form of multiple relating?

15. What do you think are some of the most important guidelines for ethical practice?

INFOTRAC KEY WORDS

Multicultural Perspectives and Diversity Issues

The following keywords are listed in such a way as to allow the InfoTrac search engine to locate a wider range of articles o the online library. The keywords should be entered exactly as listed below to include asterisks, "W1," and "AND."
ethic*
multicult*
values couns*
values therap*
values psych*
multicult training couns*
multicultural counseling competencies

Ethics

The following keywords are listed in such a way as to allow the InfoTrac search engine to locate a wider range of articles o the online library. The keywords should be entered exactly as listed below to include asterisks, "W1," and "AND."

ethical decision making model*
ethical community standard*
standard* practice psych*
countertransference
transference
Therap* values
values psych*
informed w1 consent
informed consent couns*
informed consent therap*
record* couns*
record* therap*
confidentiality psych*
privileged w1 communication
privacy couns*
privacy psych*
limits w2 confidentiality
duty to warn
duty to protect
dual relationship* couns*
dual relationship* psych*
multiple relationships

Test Items

Chapter Three

Theory and Practice of

Counseling and Psychotherapy

MULTIPLE-CHOICE TEST ITEMS FOR CHAPTER THREE

ETHICAL ISSUES IN COUNSELING PRACTICE

1. In becoming an ethical practitioner, the clear challenge is to:
   a. learn how to arrive at clear-cut answers for difficult situations.
   b. identify a specific ethical code as the source of answers to ethical dilemmas.
   c. learn how to interpret and apply ethical codes to an ethical dilemma.
   d. avoid making any mistakes in counseling practice.
   e. discover the correct solution for every ethical dilemma that might arise.

2. According to the text, the challenge of providing for informed consent consists of:
   a. telling clients about the nature of confidentiality.
   b. striking a balance between giving clients too much and too little information about the therapeutic process.
   c. convincing clients that counselors know what they are doing.
   d. teaching clients about state laws that pertain to counseling.
   e. getting clients to read the ethical codes of the profession.

3. Most ethical codes state that dual relationships:
   a. should be avoided insofar as possible.
   b. are clearly grounds for revocation of one's professional license.
   c. are helpful in case of counseling one's friends or relatives.
   d. are impossible to avoid.
   e. always result in serious harm to the client.

4. Confidentiality can be considered as:
   a. an absolute that guarantees clients that their disclosures will never be revealed.
   b. central to developing trust in the therapeutic relationship.
   c. both an ethical and a legal issue.
   d. something that is regulated by professional judgment.
   e. all but (a)

5. Confidentiality must be breached and information must be reported by practitioners when:
   a. clients pose a danger to themselves or to others.
   b. child under the age of 16 is the victim of incest, rape, or child abuse.
   c. information is made an issue in a court action.
   d. the therapist determines that the client needs hospitalization.
   e. all of the above

6. Which of the following statements is not true about guidelines for ethical practice in counseling and psychotherapy?
   a. Most professional organizations provide broad guidelines.
   b. Therapists ultimately have to discover their own guidelines for reasonable practice.
   c. Practitioners are free to formulate any ethics they choose.
   d. Ethical issues should be periodically reexamined throughout your professional life.
   e. There are differences of opinion among practitioners about how ethical guidelines apply to certain situations.

7. Under what circumstances should a therapist consult with colleagues or specialists?
   a. when a client complains of physical symptoms
   b. when facing an ethical problem
   c. when working with a client for an extended period of time and losing objectivity
   d. all of the above

8. Clients have a right to be informed about:
   a. their therapist's qualifications.
   b. the general goals of counseling.
   c. the approximate length of the therapeutic process.
   d. all of the above

9. Both feminist therapists and postmodern therapists tend to view diagnosis as it is traditionally done:
   a. as an appropriate part of counseling sessions.
   b. as generally helpful to women clients.
   c. as an essential part of the medical model they follow.
   d. as often oppressive and ignoring of societal contexts.

10. Among the ethical issues related to multicultural counseling are the problems of:
    a. using interventions that were developed in a different cultural context.
    b. counseling culturally different clients by a therapist who has not been taught the necessary skills.
    c. helping clients to accept the values of the dominant culture that they have chosen to live in and be a part of.
    d. all of the above
    e. both (a) and (b)

ANSWER KEY FOR CHAPTER THREE– ETHICAL ISSUES

MULTIPLE CHOICE QUESTIONS

1.	C	6.	C
2.	B	7.	D
3.	A	8.	D
4.	E	9.	D
5.	E	10.	E

Guidelines for Using Chapter Four

Psychoanalytic Therapy

in

Theory and Practice of Counseling and Psychotherapy and the *Student Manual*

Case Approach to Counseling and Psychotherapy

and

The Art of Integrative Counseling

1. I encourage students to take the *Pre-Chapter Self-Inventory* that appears in the first section of each theory chapter in the **Student Manual** before they read that chapter in the **Student Manual** or the **TPCP** textbook.

    I developed each of these inventories by selecting key statements from the given theory under study. I emphasize to my students that their task is to take a position on these statements. What is desired is their evaluation (ranging from strong agreement to strong disagreement) of each statement. Hopefully, this will give the students a reference point to compare their position with that of the key concepts of each theory.

2. During class time we discuss *how* and *why* they answered the various items. We usually focus on the items that students registered strong disagreement with or on those statements that seem to stimulate controversy. The students who have used these inventories have reported that they are most useful in helping them get a focus on the major issues associated with each theory.

3. If you desire, these inventories can be scored by the students. This provides some overall index of the degree of agreement/disagreement with each theory. Class results could be charted, and the results might be of interest to the class.

4. After a given theory has been studied in class and after the students have completed the exercises in the *Student Manual* and read the textbook chapters, I urge them to retake the self-inventory. This gives them a quick basis for comparison to determine if any of their positions have been modified by reading, studying, and discussing the material.

5. In the *Student Manual*, the overview of psychoanalytic therapy provided an encapsulated view of the theory. Admittedly, these summaries are brief, but the purpose is to present an overview of the highlights of each theory. Here is how I recommend that students use the overviews:

    a. These summary overviews should be carefully studied before reading the textbook chapter. I also suggest that the *Questions for Reflection and Discussion* that follow the summary be thought about before reading the textbook chapter.

    b. Then, after the textbook is read and studied, I suggest a review of the overview and questions.

    c. I use these overviews and questions as a general guide to brief lectures that I give for each theory. Other instructors may wish to add their own materials and examples.

6. In this *Instructor's Resource Manual* I have developed questions on psychoanalytic therapy – *Specific Guidelines for the Study of Psychoanalytic Therapy.* Some suggested uses of this material are:

    a. The questions can be duplicated and given to your students as additional questions to guide them in their study of psychoanalysis, and they can provide the material for class discussion.

    b. I have used these questions for small-group discussions. Students work in groups of five, and each group is given (or they select) several questions. After approximately twenty minutes we come together as a complete class, and each group shares with the rest of the class the outcomes of their exploration of the given questions.

    c. Some of these questions lend themselves well to brief classroom debates.

7. There are two case examples, Ruth and Tim, given in the *Student Manual*. After the students have read the theory material in the textbook, I use the cases as ways of relating specific examples to the theory we are studying.

    Sometimes the students form small discussion groups to explore the questions raised after each case. Then we come together as an entire class and discuss how a psychoanalytically oriented therapist might work with Ruth or Tim. Also, we pay attention to the dynamics involved in each case.

    Both the cases of Ruth and Tim lend themselves to role-playing. For example, a student who feels he or she can relate and identify with Tim becomes the "client," and I sometimes demonstrate how an analytic therapist might approach Tim. Students are also given the opportunity to become the "therapist" in these situations.

8. I have developed a book—*Case Approach to Counseling and Psychotherapy* (6th ed., 2005)—that provides opportunities for students to experience counseling vicariously, through reading and discussing in depth the case of Ruth. The newly revised *Case Approach* book is an ideal part of a package including the *TPCP* textbook and *Student Manual*.

    Case Approach provides an opportunity to see how each of the various therapeutic approaches is applied to the same client, Ruth, who is followed throughout the book. A feature of this text is an assessment of Ruth's case by one or more guest consultants in each of the eleven theoretical perspectives. Highly competent practitioners assess and treat Ruth from their particular theoretical orientation; they also provide sample dialogues to illustrate their style of working with Ruth. The book's format includes the guest consultant's commentary, followed by my way of working with Ruth from that particular theoretical perspective. I discuss the theory's basic assumptions, an initial assessment of Ruth, the goals of therapy, and the therapeutic procedures to be used. The therapeutic process is concretely illustrated by client/therapist dialogues, which are augmented by process commentaries explaining the rationale for my interventions. The book contains therapist/client dialogues, and is designed in a consistent format to allow comparisons among the eleven therapies.

For a more complete discussion of counseling Ruth from a psychoanalytic perspective see Chapter 2. In this chapter, Dr. William Blau demonstrates key issues and themes he would focus on with Ruth such as: repression of childhood experiences, using psychoanalytically oriented techniques, and addressing transference and countertransference issues. Also in this chapter students see my version as a psychoanalytically oriented therapist working with Ruth, and they read about what it was like for her in her journal. They learn about transference, resistance, and some analytic techniques. Students are given questions and guidelines for continuing with Ruth. These case discussions of Ruth introduce students to a few of the concepts of this theory, yet the clinical examples of Ruth from a variety of therapy orientations are designed to help students make the transition from the theoretical material in the textbook to actual situations.

9. Also available is the book, *The Art of Integrative Counseling* (Corey, 2001), which is an amplification of the theme of how to design a personal integrative counseling approach. In this book I strive to:

    a. describe the concepts and techniques that I most draw from in my own integrative approach to counseling practice.

    b. demonstrate how concepts and techniques can be borrowed from a variety of theoretical models and applied to the phases of the counseling process from the initial to termination stages; this I do by discussing my work with a single case of Ruth throughout the book, and also by asking readers to imagine they are a client in counseling with me.

    c. suggest ways for readers to think about designing their own integrative approach that will serve as a foundation for what they do in their counseling practice; this I do by both asking readers to assume the role of a therapist at times, and assuming the role of a client at other times.

    In writing about my own personal synthesis to counseling practice, I am in no way suggesting that there is one right way to formulate an integrative perspective. My aim is to provide a framework that will assist students in systematically constructing a counseling approach that works best for them and for the clients whom they will serve. The chapters in this book highlight what I consider to be central elements in an integrative counseling approach – from the beginning to the final session.

10. There is also a new learning package, *CD ROM for Integrative Counseling*, that serves as an ideal companion to both *The Art of Integrative Counseling* book and to *Case Approach to Counseling and Psychotherapy*. In the book, *The Art of Integrative Counseling*, I use examples at the various phases of counseling from Ruth's case as illustrated in the lecturettes and counseling sessions with Ruth. This CD ROM program illustrates my own integrative perspective in counseling Ruth. If you are using *The Art of Integrative Counseling* textbook and also the CD ROM program as a way to prepare for your course, I will be suggesting specific ways to tie these resources into both *TPCP* text and the *Student Manual* in this *Instructor's Resource Manual*. The CD ROM coordinates a number of my texts and this self-study program is structured within the framework of 13 counseling sessions, from the initial to termination phase.

    The format of the video for the 13 sessions consists of: a lecturette on specific dimensions of my integrative approach, a counseling demonstration with Ruth, and a running process commentary of Ruth's and my work together. For example, in Chapter 1, the central focus of my lecturette is on ways that I draw from existential therapy, person-centered therapy, Adlerian therapy, and feminist therapy at the initial stage of my work with clients. Then, in the beginning session, I demonstrate my application of selected concepts and techniques as I would apply them to the initial counseling session with Ruth. After the first counseling session I provide a brief process commentary highlighting salient aspects that I most wanted to address with Ruth. The other 12 sessions utilize the same design for consistency.

    If you are using the *CD ROM for Integrative Counseling*, session #10, *Transference and Countertransference*, is very relevant to the psychoanalytic approach. Session #5, *Understanding and Dealing with Resistance*, also fits well with the psychoanalytic model.

11. *The Suggested Activities and Exercises* in the *Student Manual* have proven to be useful in making the lecture and reading material come to life for the students. With each class session, I devote a portion of the time to lectures and another portion to laboratory activities such as demonstrations, role-playing, client/therapist

simulations, small groups for either discussion or experiential activities, and similar experiential learning experiences.

12. The *Student Manual* contains a glossary of key concepts for psychoanalytic therapy and the other theory chapters, as well. This is an alternative to including a glossary in the text. Also in the *Student Manual* is a quiz (or comprehension check) consisting of objective questions for each theory. You can supplement these quizzes with other items found in this *Instructor's Resource Manual* if you want more comprehensive samples.

13. In the *Summary and Evaluation* sections in the *TPCP* textbook, I attempt to share my own critique of and personal reactions to each theory. I encourage instructors to consider sharing their reactions, both positive and negative to each approach, for I find that my students appreciate knowing my own orientation and bias. It also provides the groundwork for class discussion and the exchange of views between the students and the instructor.

14. For out-of-class assignments, I typically have students type a two-page reaction or position paper. They are asked to avoid writing a summary of psychoanalysis, but they are expected to address themselves to issues such as the main contributions or limitations of the approach, their personal evaluation of the theory, what aspects of the approach they might incorporate into their own counseling style, and so on.

15. A multiple-choice and true-false quiz appears in this *Instructor's Resource Manual* for each of the ten theory chapters. If the instructor chooses to, these quizzes can be given weekly and used as a partial index for determining student grades. Personally, I use them strictly as teaching/learning devices. I photocopy these quizzes and ask my students to take them outside of class, before the lecture on the given theory. I encourage them to retake these quizzes at the end of a review for the final examination.

16. On the Website: **http://counseling.wadsworth.com** are additional questions for each of the chapters in *TPCP* that students may want to access. These questions are different from the ones given in the test-item bank in this *Instructor's Resource Manual*.

KEY TERMS FOR REVIEW AND DEFINITION

Sigmund Freud
libido
life instincts
death instincts
aggressive drive
id
ego
superego
the unconscious
anxiety
ego-defense mechanisms
repression
denial
reaction formation
projection
displacement
rationalization
sublimation
regression
identification
compensation
psychosexual stages
Erik Erikson
psychosocial stages
crisis in development
id psychology
ego psychology

borderline personality disorder
separation/individuation process
transference relationship
working-through
countertransference
free association
interpretation
dream analysis
latent content
manifest contest
dream work
resistance
brief psychodynamic therapy
oral stage
relational psychoanalysis
interpersonal analysts
trust vs. mistrust
anal stage
intrapsychic analysis
Electra complex
contemporary analytic trends
Oedipus complex
male phallic stage
autonomy vs. shame and doubt
Carl Jung
collective unconscious
archetypes

Freud's theory of sexuality
initiative vs. guilt
latency stage
narcissistic character disorder
industry vs. inferiority
genital stage
identity vs. role confusion
intimacy vs. isolation
generativity vs. stagnation
integrity vs. despair
self psychology
object-relations theory
normal infantile autism
symbiosis

animus/anima
persona
shadow
Margaret Mahler
psychological fusion
splitting
notions of grandiosity
insight
cognitive restructuring
unfinished business
maintaining the analytic framework
fixation
identity crisis
intrapsychic conflicts
psychodynamics

INFOTRAC KEYWORDS

The following keywords are listed in such a way as to allow the **InfoTrac** search engine to locate a wider range of articles on the online university library. The keywords should be entered *exactly* as listed below, to include astericks, "W1," "W2," "AND," and other search engine tools.

Psychodynamics
Object-relations W1 theory

Ego-defense W1 mechanisms
Transference

Psychoanalysis
The following keywords are listed in such a way as to allow the **InfoTrac** search engine to locate a wider range of articles o the online library. The keywords should be entered exactly as listed below to include asterisks, "W1," and "AND."

Erik Erikson
Anna Freud
Sigmund Freud
Otto Kernberg
Heinz Kohut
Margaret Mahler
Psychoanalysis
Psychodynamic*
Ego psychology
Object relations psych*
Self psychology
Freud AND drive
Freud AND id
Freud AND ego
Freud AND superego
Freud AND conscious
Freud AND unconscious
Psychosexual development
Oedipus complex
Ego-defense W1 mechanisms
Object-relations W1 theory
Transference
Carl Jung
Jung AND psyche
Jung AND ego
Jung AND archetype*

CASE EXAMPLE

In this *Instructor's Resource Manual*, I generally present one or two brief cases that you might want to use for class discussion. If your students are using the *Student Manual*, they will have the case of Ruth presented for each of the theory chapters, and usually an additional case. In the event that you might want additional cases, you'll find them at the end of each chapter in this manual.

JACK: Afraid that he is "empty inside"

This statement was written by one of my students in an internship program. At the time he wrote it, he was undergoing both individual and group counseling.

"Most of my life I have felt pushed and pulled. My father pushed me into school, sports, and so forth, and over the years my resentment grew for him, as he was always directing and controlling my life and beating me when I challenged his authority. My mother always gave me a warm, unconditional love and tried to pull me under her protective wing, something I have always resisted.

"My parents divorced when I was 16, and without parental control I began a life of permissiveness in my relationships with women and in my use of psychedelic drugs and marijuana.

"On graduating from college, I rejected my father's wishes to pursue a career and returned to school to seek another degree. In some ways it's just a place to be that I like. Most of my life revolves around living for today, a hedonistic style that has no concreteness of goals and aspirations, with a lack of definition of `what a man should be.'

"I float in and out of people's lives. They see an image of me as a despoiler of women, a drug freak, and a cold bastard. My fear is that I am nothing more than that image, that I am empty inside. I want to be able to open up and let people see the warmer, more sensitive sides of me, but I have terrible difficulty doing that. I have a strong need to become close and intimate with others, yet I never let myself become vulnerable because I fear being dependent on them and trapped by their love."

How would you work with Jack?

Assume that Jack comes to you for personal counseling and that all you know about him is what he wrote. Answer the following questions on how you might proceed with Jack within a *psychoanalytic* frame of reference:

1   Do you think that Jack's current unwillingness to become vulnerable to others out of his fear of "being dependent on them and trapped by their love" has much to do with his mother's unconditional love?

2.   Was his mother's "warm, unconditional love" really without conditions? What do you suppose her conditions were for keeping Jack "under her protective wing?" How might this experience be related to his relationships with women now?

3.   Jack describes his father as an authoritarian, controlling, and cruel man who apparently had conventional ideas of what he wanted Jack to become. What are the underlying psychological aspects that you see involved with Jack's rejection of his father's wishes? How might you explain the fact that in many ways he became what his father did not want him to become?

4.   How might you work with Jack's fear that he is nothing more than a "despoiler of women," "a drug freak," and a "cold bastard?"

5.   How might you explain Jack's fear that he is "empty inside"? What are some possible causes of his feelings of emptiness? How would you work on this issue with him?

6.   What else would you want to know about Jack? What specific factors in his case would you focus on, and what would be your treatment plan as you worked with him during the therapy sessions?

STUDY GUIDE FOR CHAPTER FOUR

PSYCHOANALYTIC THERAPY

Note: For each of the chapters in this *Instructor's Resource Manual*, I've developed a study guide that you might want to use as a lecture outline for yourself. These study guides can be reproduced for your students as another resource in addition to the *Student Manual* that they may be using.

In Chapter 4 of the *Student Manual* you will find a *Pre-Chapter Self-Inventory*, which will help you crystallize your attitudes toward psychoanalytic therapy. The overview and the glossary provide you with an excellent guide for review. The quiz gives you a way to check your comprehension once you have studied the textbook and done the exercises in the *Student Manual*.

Case Approach to Counseling and Psychotherapy, Chapter 2, presents a comprehensive view of a psychoanalytically oriented therapist's perspective on Ruth. You will note that each theory chapter begins with an expert's analysis of Ruth and his or her description of a particular therapeutic approach to counseling Ruth. After each expert describes his or her style of assessment and treatment of Ruth within a specific system of therapy, I follow up with my own version of how I would work with Ruth from each of these therapeutic approaches. For making comparisons between approaches clear, each of these theories is applied to Ruth's case and organized along the following dimensions:

- basic assumptions of the theory
- initial assessment of Ruth
- goals of the therapy
- therapeutic procedures
- elements of the therapeutic process
- process commentary
- questions for reflection

With each of the chapters in *Theory and Practice of Counseling and Psychotherapy* I suggest you first look over the entire chapter. The background of the theories is a useful way to evaluate the theory. The *Summary and Evaluation* section, which includes a discussion of the contributions, limitations, and criticisms of the approach, is very important as a way of pulling the chapters together. I suggest that you pay particular attention to the contributions and the limitations of each approach from a multicultural perspective. The implications of working with culturally diverse clients within each of the eleven therapy approaches are discussed in the *Summary and Evaluation* section of each chapter.

Specific Guidelines for Study of Psychoanalytic Therapy

1. What is the Freudian view of human nature? Do you accept the notions that humans are driven by aggressive and sexual instincts, and that humans are determined by irrational and unconscious forces?

2. How is the structure of personality (id, ego, superego) described?

3. In what way is the notion of the unconscious one of Freud's most significant discoveries? What are the implications of this concept for clinical practice?

4. How is anxiety explained from a psychoanalytic view?

5. Know how the ego defenses operate as a way of helping us cope with anxiety. Be able to identify each of the ego-defense mechanisms. How is an understanding of the functioning of ego defenses useful to the counselor?

6. What importance does early development play in Freudian psychoanalysis? In Erikson's psychosocial perspective? To what extent do you think that our first six years of life determines our later personality structure?

7. Concentrate on the comparison of Freud's psychosexual stages with Erikson's psychosocial stages (see textbook, Table 4-1). These differences are important for they represent the evolution of this approach.

8. How does relational psychoanalysis differ from traditional psychoanalysis? Which approach do you prefer, and why?

9. How can an understanding of Erikson's eight stages of life (and the core conflict at each stage) provide you, as a counselor, with a useful framework for making appropriate interventions? How do these stages apply in your own life?

10. Go through the eight stages of psychosocial development outlined by Erikson and look for personal implications of these stages in your own life. What struggles did you face at each stage? How might this relate to your ability to counsel others?

11. What are some of the key features of brief psychodynamic therapy?

12. What are some of Carl Jung's basic concepts? How does his approach differ from Freud's?

13. Be familiar with the contemporary trends in psychoanalytic thinking. What are the key concepts of the object relations theories?

14. Describe the therapeutic process of psychoanalytic therapy, with a focus on: goals, therapist's function/role, client's role, and the relationship variables.

15. What is the working-through process, and how does this process account for the length of psychoanalytic therapy?

16. What is transference and countertransference and how do they operate in the therapeutic relationship? Why is it essential to understand these basic concepts?

17. How is resistance a central issue in analytic therapy? Explain the functions that resistance serves. Discuss some guidelines that you might use in understanding both the resistance of your clients and your reactions to their resistance. What are some ways of therapeutically dealing with resistance as opposed to viewing resistance as a negative force in therapy?

18. Have a clear grasp of the six major therapeutic techniques: maintaining the analytic framework, free association, interpretation, dream analysis, analysis and interpretation of resistance, and analysis and interpretation of transference.

19. What are the main contributions and limitations of the psychoanalytic approach in applications to multicultural counseling?

20. After reading the *Summary and Evaluation*, be able to formulate your own position on what you consider to be the major contributions and limitations of this approach as it applies to the type of counseling that you might do. What do you find most useful about this therapy, and in what ways might you incorporate some aspects of this approach into your own counseling style?

Test Items

Chapter Four

Theory and Practice of

Counseling and Psychotherapy

PSYCHOANALYTIC THERAPY

1. Evidence for postulating the concept of the unconscious includes:
   a. dreams.
   b. post-hypnotic suggestions.
   c. free-association.
   d. all of the above.
   e. direct observation based on experimental research.

2. A person who unconsciously exhibits overly nice behavior to conceal hostile feelings is probably using which ego defense?
   a. displacement
   b. reaction formation
   c. introjection
   d. projection
   e. regression

3. One of the most important Freudian concepts, which consists of pushing unacceptable reality or painful material into the unconscious, is:
   a. repression.
   b. regression.
   c. displacement.
   d. rationalization.
   e. projection.

4. A person who exhibits behavior that clearly shows signs of reverting to less mature stages is likely to be using which ego defense?
   a. fixation
   b. rationalization
   c. regression
   d. introjection
   e. reaction formation

5. Attributing to others the qualities or traits that are unacceptable to our own ego is best described as:
   a. displacement.
   b. introjection.
   c. reaction formation.
   d. projection.
   e. none of the above

6. Resolution of sexual conflicts and sex-role identity is a critical function of the:
   a. oral stage.
   b. anal stage.
   c. phallic stage.
   d. genital stage.

7. Feelings of hostility, destructiveness, anger, rage, and hatred seem most allied with the:
   a. oral stage.
   b. anal stage.
   c. phallic stage.
   d. genital stage.

8. The basic aim of psychoanalytic therapy is:
   a. to treat specific learning disorders.
   b. to change overt behavior.
   c. to correct irrational thinking.
   d. to make the unconscious material conscious.
   e. both (a) and (b)

9. A major characteristic of the psychoanalytic therapist is:
   a. openness and self-disclosure.
   b. a deeply personal and sharing relationship.
   c. a sense of being anonymous.
   d. a focus on specific behavior and an objective appraisal of learned patterns of behavior.
   e. both (a) and (b)

10. The "fundamental rule" for the client in psychoanalysis is:
    a. a necessity to form a contract.
    b. willingness to do "homework assignments."
    c. participating in free association.
    d. writing down dreams.
    e. both (a) and (b)

11. Transference is viewed as:
    a. the core of the psychoanalytic process.
    b. a means to uncover earlier unfinished business from past relationships.
    c. a sign that therapy is not progressing well.
    d. both (a) and (b)

12. The technique whereby the analyst explains the meaning of certain behavior is known as:
    a. transference.
    b. rationalization.
    c. countertransference.
    d. interpretation.
    e. none of the above

13. The concept of resistance can best be described as:
    a. everything that prevents a client from producing unconscious material.
    b. that which needs to be analyzed and interpreted.
    c. an inevitable part of psychoanalytic therapy.
    d. an unwillingness to freely share with the analyst certain thoughts and feelings.
    e. all of the above

14. A person who attempts to deal with anxiety by closing his or her eyes, or by distorting reality is most likely using:
    a. introjection.
    b. sublimation.
    c. denial.
    d. compensation.
    e. undoing.

15. Directing energy toward another object or a person (when anxiety is reduced by focusing on a "safer target") is known as:
    a. sublimation.
    b. repression.
    c. introjection.
    d. displacement.
    e. compensation.

16. Manufacturing "good" reasons to explain away a bruised ego, or to explain away failures or losses, is known as:
    a. rationalization.
    b. projection.
    c. displacement.
    d. introjection.
    e. reaction formation.

17. The abused child, who assumes the abusing parent's way of handling stress and thus continues the cycle of child beating, is an example of:
    a. displacement.
    b. reaction formation.
    c. sublimation.
    d. introjection.

18. The ego defense mechanism that consists of masking perceived weaknesses or developing certain positive traits to make up for limitations is known as:
    a. sublimation.
    b. compensation.
    c. introjection.
    d. reaction formation.
    e. none of the above

19. The process of redirecting sexual energy into creative behaviors or some form of socially acceptable behavior is known as:
    a. displacement.
    b. denial.
    c. compensation.
    d. sublimation.
    e. none of the above

20. The Electra complex and the Oedipus complex are associated with what psychosexual stage of development?
    a. anal stage
    b. genital stage
    c. oral stage
    d. phallic stage
    e. latency stage

21. The concepts of penis envy and castration anxiety are associated with what stage of development?
    a. oral stage
    b. anal stage
    c. phallic stage
    d. latency stage
    e. genital stage

22. A narcissistic orientation is characteristic of what stage of development?
    a. anal
    b. oral
    c. latency
    d. genital
    e. phallic

23. What is the correct sequence of the psychosexual stages?
    a. anal/phallic/latency/genital/oral
    b. oral/anal/phallic/latency/genital
    c. oral/anal/latency/genital/phallic
    d. latency/oral/anal/phallic/genital
    e. latency/anal/oral/phallic/genital

24. In Erikson's view, the major developmental task in adolescence is:
    a.   intimacy vs. isolation.
    b.   integrity vs. despair.
    c.   identity vs. role confusion.
    d.   initiative vs. guilt.
    e.   identity vs. shame and doubt.

25. A person experiencing persistent feelings of inadequacy has probably had difficulty attaining a sense of _____ during the_____ stage.
    a.   intimacy; young adulthood
    b.   identity; adolescent
    c.   integrity; later life
    d.   initiative; preschool age
    e.   industry; school age

26. The important developmental task during the middle age years is:
    a.   to be involved in helping the next generation.
    b.   to look back on one's life with few regrets.
    c.   to adjust to the discrepancy between one's dreams and one's actual accomplishments.
    d.   to feel personally worthwhile.
    e.   both (a) and (c)

27. Self psychology and object-relations theory emphasize:
    a.   the influence of critical factors in early development on later development.
    b.   the origins, transformations and organizational functions of the self.
    c.   the differentiation between self and others.
    d.   all of the above
    e.   (b) and (c) only

28. Which of the following is *not* associated with the relational approach to psychoanalysis?
    a.   The approach is based on an egalitarian model.
    b.   There is an exploration of the subjectivities of both client and therapist.
    c.   There is a process of two subjectivities encountering each other.
    d.   Countertransference provides rich information about the client's dynamics.
    e.   Therapist anonymity is used to foster the transference relationship.

29. Brief psychodynamic therapy (BPT) calls upon the therapist to:
    a. assume a nondirective and even passive role.
    b. deal exclusively with a single presenting problem.
    c. assume an active role in quickly formulating a therapeutic focus that goes beyond the   surface of presenting problems.
    d. avoid treating any underlying issue.

30. The main function of the *ego* is:
    a.   to inhibit id impulses.
    b.   to seek pleasure in life.
    c.   to mediate between the instincts and the surrounding environment.
    d.   to strive for perfection.
    e.   to control the unconscious.

31. All of the following are true about the *superego* except:
    a.   It is the judicial branch of personality.
    b.   It is the internalization of the standards of parents and society.
    c.   It represents the ideal.
    d.   It inhibits id impulses.
    e.   It governs, controls and regulates the personality.

32. Which of the following is true about ego psychology (as compared with id Psychology)?
    a. It emphasizes the striving of the ego for mastery and competence throughout life.
    b. It deals with both early and later developmental stages.
    c. It denies the role of intrapsychic conflicts.
    d. All of the above are true.
    e. both (a) and (b)

33. If a person becomes fixated in the oral stage of development, later personality problems may include:
    a. rejecting others, love.
    b. fear of intimate relationships.
    c. mistrust of others.
    d. all of the above
    e. all but (a)

34. The basic struggle of early childhood involves:
    a. autonomy vs. shame and doubt.
    b. initiative vs. guilt.
    c. identity vs. role confusion.
    d. trust vs. mistrust.
    e. intimacy vs. isolation.

35. The crisis involving initiative vs. guilt occurs during the:
    a. school age.
    b. early childhood stage.
    c. preschool age.
    d. adolescence.
    e. later life.

36. A person who is suffering from feelings of alienation and isolation has probably failed to achieve a sense of _____ during the _____ stage of development.
    a. identity; adolescence
    b. trust; infancy
    c. generativity; middle age
    d. intimacy; young adulthood
    e. integrity; later life

37. A person who is suffering from feelings of despair and hopelessness has not achieved a sense of _____ in the _____ stage.
    a. integrity; later life
    b. generativity; middle age
    c. intimacy; young adulthood
    d. identity; adolescence
    e. initiative; preschool

38. During the separation/individuation process (object-relations theory):
    a. the child moves away from symbiotic forms of relating.
    b. the child stops turning to others for a sense of confirmation.
    c. problems may result in the development of a borderline personality disorder.
    d. the child has a pronounced dependency on the mother.
    e. all of the above

39. All of the following are a part of Jung's view of development except:
    a. individuation.
    b. the shadow.
    c. total behavior.
    d. collective unconscious.
    e. archetypes.

40. Who developed the object-relations view that focuses on separation and individuation?
    a. Perls
    b. Satir
    c. Rogers
    d. Mahler
    e. Erikson

41. Which of the following is not true of the "working-through" process in psychoanalytic therapy?
    a. It involves the exploration of unconscious material and defenses.
    b. It is achieved by free association.
    c. It involves exploring resistances.
    d. It is a very demanding phase of therapy.
    e. It involves the transference relationship.

42. Countertransference occurs when:
    a. the client has positive reactions toward his/her therapist.
    b. the therapist has reactions toward the client that interfere with his or her objectivity.
    c. the therapist has a need to meet his or her own needs by keeping the client infantile.
    d. all of the above are true.
    e. both (b) and (c) are true.

43. During psychoanalytic treatment, clients are typically asked:
    a. to monitor their behavioral changes by keeping a journal that describes what they do at home and at work.
    b. to make major changes in their lifestyle.
    c. not to make radical changes in their lifestyle.
    d. to give up their friendships.
    e. none of the above

44. Countertransference refers to the:
    a. irrational reactions clients have toward their therapists.
    b. irrational reactions therapists have toward their clients.
    c. projections of the client.
    d. client's need to be special in the therapist's eyes.
    e. all except for (a)

45. "Maintaining the analytic framework" refers to:
    a. the whole range of procedural factors in the treatment process.
    b. the analyst's relative anonymity.
    c. minimizes departures from changes in fees..
    d. regularity and consistency of meetings.
    e. all of the above

46. In psychoanalytic therapy (as opposed to classical analysis), which of the following procedures is least likely to be used?
    a. the client lying on the couch
    b. working with transference feelings
    c. relating present struggles with past events
    d. working with dreams
    e. interpretation of resistance

47. In object-relations theory, later relationships build upon:
    a. the child's search for approval from the father.
    b. one's birth order.
    c. one's striving to overcome felt inferiority.
    d. the child's search for a reconnection with the mother.
    e. the quality of relationships with one's siblings.

48. According to object-relations theory, the symbiosis stage is characterized by:
    a. the infant's pronounced dependency on the mother.
    b. the infant's expectation of emotional attunement with the mother.
    c. forming attachments to peers.
    d. Oedipal and Electra struggles
    e. both (a) and (b)

49. Individuals who display exhibitionistic traits, seek attention and admiration from others, and are extremely self-absorbed might have which of the following personality disorders?
    a. narcissistic
    b. manic-depressive
    c. borderline
    d. psychotic

50. A person with a _____ personality disorder is characterized by instability, irritability, self-destructive acts, impulsive anger, and extreme mood shifts. This person is lacking a clear sense of identity, has poor impulse control, and an inability to tolerate anxiety.
    a. narcissistic
    b. manic-depressive
    c. borderline
    d. psychotic

51. Narcissistic disorders seem to be rooted in traumas and developmental disturbances during which phase of development?
    a. symbiosis
    b. normal infantile autism
    c. separation/individuation
    d. a move toward constancy of self and object

52. The goal(s) of Freudian psychoanalytic therapy is (are):
    a. teaching people problem-solving skills.
    b. helping people to change self-defeating cognitions.
    c. making the unconscious conscious.
    d. strengthening the ego so that behavior is based on reality.
    e. both (c) and (d)

53. Analytic therapy is oriented toward:
    a. achieving insight.
    b. identifying and experiencing feelings and memories.
    c. developing an in-depth self-understanding.
    d. reexperiencing and reconstructing childhood experiences.
    e. all of the above

54. As a result of the client/therapist relationship in psychoanalytic therapy:
    a. clients acquire insights into their own unconscious psychodynamics.
    b. clients are better able to understand the association between their past experiences and their current behavior.
    c. awareness is increased on the client's part.
    d. all of the above

55. The techniques of psychoanalytic therapy are aimed at:
    a. fostering insights into the client's behavior.
    b. helping clients to resolve their competitive strivings with their siblings.
    c. teaching people social skills such as assertive behavior.
    d. helping clients see how their thinking leads to certain emotional and behavioral patterns.
    e. all of the above

56. In psychoanalytic therapy, how do clients work with their dreams?
   a. They report their dreams and are encouraged to free-associate to the elements of the dream.
   b. They look for mystical meanings underlying the dream.
   c. They "become" each part of their dream and act out these parts in fantasy.
   d. They look to their dreams as signs of prediction of the future.

57. Which of the following is not typically a standard psychoanalytic technique?
   a. free association
   b. interpretation
   c. exploration of one's position in the family
   d. exploration of patterns of resistance
   e. analysis of transference

ANSWER KEY FOR CHAPTER FOUR – PSYCHOANALYTIC THERAPY
MULTIPLE CHOICE TEST QUESTIONS

1. E	16. A	31. E	46. A
2. B	17. D	32. E	47. D
3. A	18. B	33. D	48. E
4. C	19. D	34. A	49. A
5. D	20. D	35. C	50. C
6. C	21. C	36. D	51. C
7. B	22. B	37. A	52. E
8. D	23. B	38. A	53. E
9. C	24. C	39. C	54. D
10. C	25. E	40. D	55. A
11. D	26. E	41. B	56. A
12. D	27. D	42. E	57. C
13. E	28. E	43. C	
14. C	29. C	44. B	
15. D	30. C	45. E	

TRUE–FALSE TEST ITEMS FOR CHAPTER FOUR

PSYCHOANALYTIC THERAPY

Decide if the following statements are "more true" or "more false" as they apply to psychoanalytic therapy.

1. The ego is the original system of personality.

2. The Freudian view of human nature is deterministic.

3. The id is related to the concept libido.

4. The libido refers to the energy of all the life instincts.

5. Freud postulated the concept of both life instincts and death instincts.

6. According to Freud, consciousness constitutes the largest part of one's psychological functioning.

7. Ego-defense mechanisms, by their very nature, imply psychopathology.

8. Freud postulated the theory of infantile sexuality.

9. The major developmental task of the anal stage is acquiring a sense of trust.

10. During the anal stage, children typically experience a range of negative feelings, including rage, hate, and hostility.

11. According to Freudians, greediness and acquisitiveness may develop as a result of not getting oral needs properly met.

12. The phallic stage typically occurs during the ages of 1 to 3.

13. The latency stage occurs between the ages of 5 to 12.

14. The Oedipal complex and the Electra complex are associated with the genital stage of development.

15. Analytic therapists view the transference relationship as a factor that results from ineffective intervention on the therapist's part.

16. All analytically oriented therapists hold to the anonymous role of the therapist, or the "blank screen" model, as a necessary way to foster transference.

17. Free association is one of the basic tools used to gain access to the unconscious.

18. Analytically oriented therapists typically interpret free associations, dreams, resistances, and transferences.

19. Clients in analytic therapy typically free associate to various symbols in their dreams.

20. Resistance, in the analytic view, results from either a conscious unwillingness on the part of the client to cooperate, or from the ineptness of the therapist in developing a sound therapeutic program.

21. The analysis of transference is a central technique in psychoanalysis.

22. Psychoanalysis provides therapists with a conceptual framework for looking at behavior and understanding the origins and functions of present symptoms.

23. The relational model of psychoanalysis regards transference as being an interactive process between the client and therapist.

24. The relational model of psychoanalysis downplays the role of countertransference.

25. Brief psychodynamic therapies target specific interpersonal problems during the initial session.

26. Brief psychodynamic therapists tend to assume an active role in the therapy process.

ANSWER KEY FOR CHAPTER FOUR – PSYCHOANALYTIC THERAPY

TRUE – FALSE QUESTIONS

1.	F	14.	F
2.	T	15.	F
3.	T	16.	F
4.	T	17.	T
5.	T	18.	T
6.	F	19.	T
7.	F	20.	F
8.	T	21.	T
9.	F	22.	T
10.	T	23.	T
11.	T	24.	F
12.	F	25.	T
13.	T	26.	T

Guidelines for Using Chapter Five

Adlerian Therapy

in

Theory and Practice of Counseling and Psychotherapy and the Student Manual

Case Approach to Counseling and Psychotherapy

and

The Art of Integrative Counseling

1. The **Student Manual** contains a number of devices designed to help students obtain a more concrete grasp of how Adlerian concepts can be translated into practice, especially the following:

    a. *The Lifestyle Assessment:* This contains questions about one's family constellation, early recollections and dreams, and a lifestyle summary. After students complete this assessment form at home, they can form small groups in class to explore their learning. I also include a lifestyle assessment for Stan to provide background on his developmental history, since I refer to Stan's case throughout the **TPCP** text.

    b. *Case example:* Two separate cases, Ruth and Julie, are given in Chapter 5 of the **Student Manual**, with emphasis on the use of Adlerian concepts in counseling.

2. Other ways I encourage students to use the **Student Manual** for this chapter include:

    a. Asking students to take the *Pre-Chapter Self-Inventory*, and to bring into class the specific items that they would most like to discuss.

    b. Encouraging them to carefully study the overview of Adlerian therapy. This section gives a concise summary of: key figures and the major focus of Adlerian therapy; philosophy and basic assumptions; key concepts; therapeutic goals; therapeutic relationship; techniques and procedures; applications; contributions; and limitations.

c. Suggesting that they master the key terms given in the glossary and suggesting that they think carefully about the *Questions for Reflection and Discussion*. These questions and key concepts are a useful way for students to get a focus on each chapter.

3. **Other Resources:** In addition to the cases (generally two) given in each chapter of the ***Student Manual***, you may want to refer to the ***Case Approach to Counseling and Psychotherapy*** (6th ed., 2005) for a detailed treatment of the case of Ruth from an Adlerian perspective. In Chapter 3 Drs. Jim Bitter and Bill Nicoll presents a very detailed and comprehensive lifestyle assessment of Ruth, as well as demonstrating their respective Adlerian styles of working with Ruth at the various stages of therapy. I follow Drs. Bitter and Nicoll's piece with a brief demonstration of my Adlerian slant on working with Ruth cognitively, especially her mistaken beliefs.

4. Session #6 of the ***CD ROM for Integrative Counseling*** presents a demonstration of this kind of work. This video segment reflects Ruth's striving to live up to expectations and measuring up to perfectionistic standards.

5. In my lectures, I've found that students are interested in the background of the theorist. I've highlighted ways that the theorist's life experiences influenced the development of the theory. The life of Alfred Adler is a particularly good example of how his personal background is expressed in the main concepts of his theory. The best book I've found in presenting an interesting sketch of the various personality theorists is Schultz and Schultz, *Theories of Personality* (7th ed.,2001), which I've annotated in the textbook.

6. In preparing your own lectures on Adlerian therapy, the books I most highly recommend are:

    a. *Interventions and Strategies in Counseling and Psychotherapy* (Watts & Carlson, 1999)
    b. *Adlerian Counseling: A Practitioner's Approach* (Sweeney, 1998)
    c. *Techniques in Adlerian Psychology* (Carlson & Slavik, 1997)
    d. *Understanding Life-Style: The Psycho-Clarity Process* (Powers and Griffith, 1987)

    These particular books are annotated in the *Recommended Supplementary Readings* section in Chapter 5 of ***TPCP***.

7. The concepts and techniques that I tend to give primary focus to with the Adlerian approach include the following:

    a. The contrasts between the Adlerian and Freudian view of human nature, with implications for therapeutic practice

    b. The concept of the style of life, including what it is and how it is formed

    c. Social interest, with implications for practice

    d. The client/therapist relationship in the Adlerian approach

    e. The phases of counseling, with emphasis on initial assessment by means of gathering information about the client's life history, family constellation, and early memories

    f. The role of encouragement in therapy

    g. An overview of techniques such as catching oneself, acting "as if," and paradoxical intention

    h. Ways that Adler influences the development of most of the other therapy systems

8. At the end of each chapter is a summary, including my own perspective of the contributions and limitations of each theory. I also talk about ways that I incorporate concepts and techniques into my own approach based upon each of these theories. Adlerian therapy lends itself to providing the framework for an eclectic perspective, since so many Adlerian concepts have found themselves as a part of therapies that have developed since Adler's discoveries.

9. On the *Website* are additional questions for each of the chapters in *TPCP* that students may want to access. These questions are different from the ones given in the test-item bank in this *Instructor's Resource Manual*.

KEY TERMS FOR REVIEW AND DEFINITION

Alfred Adler
phenomenological orientation
subjective reality
individual psychology
teleological explanation of behavior
striving for significance and superiority
basic inferiority
compensation
style of life / lifestyle
fictional finalism
social interest and community feeling
(Gemeinschaftsqefuhl)
mistaken goals
faulty assumptions
motivation modification
family constellation
birth order
early recollections

initial interview
private logic
the encouragement process
dreams
priorities
analysis and assessment
insight
reorientation and reeducation
task setting
basic mistakes
convictions
courage
holism
life tasks
lifestyle assessment
subjective interview
objective interview
"The Question"

INFOTRAC KEYWORDS

Adlerian Therapy

The following keywords are listed in such a way as to allow the *InfoTrac* search engine to locate a wider range of articles on the online university library. The keywords should be entered *exactly* as listed below, to include astericks, "W1," "W2," "AND," and other search engine tools.

Alfred Adler
Adler AND superiority
Inferiority complex
Superiority complex
Phenomenological AND psychol*
Family W1 constellation
Birth W1 order

CASE EXAMPLES

The case of Julie, and the case of working with a couple, Alice and Javier, are presented below. You may want to introduce these two cases in your classes to give students some additional practice in applying Adlerian concepts.

JULIE: "It's my father's fault that I can't trust men"

Some Background Data:

Julie is interested in exploring her relationships with men. She says that she cannot trust me because I am a man and that she cannot trust men because her father was an alcoholic and was therefore untrustworthy. She recalls that he was never around when she needed him and that she would not have felt free to go to him with her problems in any case, because he was loud and gruff. She tells me of the guilt she felt over her father's drinking because of her sense that in some way she was causing him to drink. Julie, who is now 35 and unmarried, is leery of men, convinced that they will somehow let her down if she gives them the chance. She has decided in advance that she will not be a fool again, that she will not let herself need or trust men.

Although Julie seems pretty clear about not wanting to risk trusting men, she realizes that this notion is self-defeating and would like to challenge her views. Though she wants to change the way in which she perceives and feels about men, somehow she seems to have an investment in her belief about their basic untrustworthiness. She is not very willing to look at her part in keeping this assumption about men alive. Rather, she would prefer to pin the blame on her father. It was he who taught her this lesson, and now it is difficult for her to change, or so she reports.

Jerry Corey's Way of Working with Julie from an Adlerian Perspective

Even if it is true that her father did treat her unkindly, my assessment is that it is a "basic mistake" for her to have generalized what she believes to be true of her father to all men. My hope is that our relationship, based on respect and cooperation, will be a catalyst for her in challenging her assumptions about men.

At one point in her therapy, I ask Julie if she knows why she is so angry and upset with men. When she mentions her father, I say: "He's just one man. Do you know why you react in this way to most men – even today?" If it is appropriate to her response, I may suggest: "Could it be that your beliefs against men keep you from having to test your ability to be a true friend?" or, "could it be that you want to give your father a constant reminder that he has wrecked your life? Could you be getting your revenge for an unhappy childhood?" Of course, these interventions would come after we had been working together for a time and trust was established.

As part of the assessment process I am interested in exploring her early memories, especially those pertaining to her father and mother, the guiding lines for male and female relationships. We will also explore what it was like for her as a child in her family, what interpretation she gave to events, and what meaning she gave to herself, others, and the world. Some additional questions that I will pose are:

a. What do you think you get from staying angry at your father and insisting that he is the cause of your fear of men?

b. What do you imagine it would be like for you if you were to act as if men were trustworthy? And what do you suppose really prevents you from doing that?

c. What would happen or what would you be doing differently if you trusted men?

d. If you could forgive your father, what do you imagine that would be like for you? for him? for your dealings with other men?

e. If you keep the same attitudes until you die, how will that be for you?

f. How would you like to be in five years?

g. If you really want to change, what can you do to begin the process? What are you willing to do?

My relationship with Julie is the major vehicle with which to work in the sessions. A male counselor who emphasizes listening, mutual respect, honesty, partnership, and encouragement will give her a chance to examine her mistaken notions and try on new behaviors. A lifestyle assessment will help her see the broad pattern of her life and will reveal the convictions that are leading her to safeguard herself against all male relationships.

Julie needs to take some action if she expects to change her views toward men. Thus, we work together to determine what she can do outside of the sessions. A major part of my work with Julie is directed at confronting her with the ways in which she is refusing to take responsibility for the things in herself that she does not like and at encouraging her to decide on some course of action to begin the process of modifying them. A very important phase of therapy is the reorientation stage, the action-oriented process of putting one's insights to work. As an Adlerian therapist I am concerned that Julie do more than merely understand the dynamics of her behavior. My goal is that she eventually sees a wider range of alternatives. This reorientation phase of her therapy consists of her considering alternative attitudes, beliefs, goals, and behaviors. She is expected to make new decisions. I encourage her to "catch herself" in the process of repeating old patterns. When she meets a man and then immediately assumes that he cannot be trusted, for example, it helps if she is able to observe what she is doing. She can then ask herself if she wants to persist in clinging to old assumptions or if she is willing to let go of them and form impressions without bias.

This phase of counseling is a time for Julie to commit to the specific ways in which she would like to be different. Encouragement during the time that she is trying new behavior and working on new goals is most useful. This encouragement can take the form of having faith in her, of support, of recognizing the changes she makes, and of continuing to be psychologically available for her during our sessions.

Follow-Up: You Continue as Julie's Therapist

1. What are some of your impressions and reactions to my work with Julie? Knowing what you know about these sessions and Julie, what might you most want to follow up with if you could see her for at least a couple of months?

2. How much do you imagine that your approach with Julie would be affected by your life experiences and views? How much would you want to share of yourself with her? In what ways do you think you could use yourself as a person in your work with her?

3. How might you deal with her apparent unwillingness to accept personal responsibility and her blaming of her father for her inability to trust men now?

4. What are some additional Adlerian techniques you might use with Julie?

5. Outline some of the steps in Adlerian counseling that you would expect to take for a series of sessions with Julie, showing why you are adopting that particular course of action.

ALICE AND JAVIER: An interracial couple seeking counseling

Assume that a social worker whom you know conducts groups for couples. In one of these groups a couple indicates to her that they would like to have at least a few counseling sessions with someone different to get another perspective on the problems they are having in their relationship. The counselor knows that your orientation is Adlerian (her's happens to be psychoanalytic). She wants to refer this couple to you, and before you see them, she gives you the following background information.

Some Background Data:

Alice and Javier have been married for 17 years and have three children. This is an interracial marriage. Javier is a Latino, and Alice is a Pacific Islander. Neither his family nor hers was very supportive of marrying a person "not of your own kind." Consequently, Javier and Alice do not see their parents very often. She feels a real gap without this connection with her family; he maintains that if that's the way his family wants it, so be it.

They have been having a great deal of difficulty as a family for several years. The social worker sees Javier as being extremely defensive in his dealings with Alice. He shouts a lot, gets angry, and then slams the door and refuses to talk to her for days at a time. Although he never strikes her, he has threatened to do so, and she is intimidated by his tirades and displays of anger. He has put his fist through the bathroom door, as well as breaking objects in the house.

Alice seems to think that Javier is far too strict with the children, demanding full obedience without question. He admits he is a hard taskmaster, but he says that's the way it was for him in his family. He insists on being the boss in the family. He is constantly yelling at them for making messes as well as for a multitude of offenses in his eyes. He rarely spends time with his two teenage daughters (who see him as a stranger), but he often takes his 10-year-old son on fishing and camping trips. They appear to have a fairly good relationship.

Alice would like to get a job, yet she stops herself from considering it because Javier becomes extremely upset when she even mentions the issue. His response is: "Why can't you be satisfied with what you have? Don't I make enough money for this damn family? It reflects poorly on me if you have to go outside and get work!" Alice has tended to assume the role of keeping peace in the family, almost at any price. This means not doing many of the things she would like to do, lest it lead to an escalation of the conflicts between them. The social worker perceives Alice as quiet, submissive to Javier, very bright and attractive, afraid of the prospects of a divorce, and very disenchanted with her life with him. Alice has finally decided that even if it rocks the boat and causes a storm, she cannot continue living as she has. She has asked Javier to go to counseling with her. He has agreed, reluctantly, mostly to understand her better and "do whatever can be done to help her." His reaction is that he should be able to solve any problems in his family without the help of some professional. Again, he thinks that seeking counseling is somewhat of a slap in his face.

As a couple they rarely have any time together except for Wednesday evenings, when they attend a couples group they recently joined. Alice says she would like to go away to spend at least a weekend alone with Javier, which she cannot ever remember doing. He complains that doing so is too expensive, that it is a problem to get someone to be with the children, and that they could have as much fun by hanging around the house. She feels continually rebuffed when she asks him for time together. He feels typically defensive that he is being asked for more and more, and he thinks he is doing enough in what he refers to as "this damn family."

How Would You Work with This Couple?

Using an Adlerian perspective, show how you might proceed in counseling this couple, assuming that you would see them for four to six sessions. Following are some questions to guide you:

1. If you were to use the lifestyle questionnaire, would you want to administer it to each person, with the spouse in the room at the time? What advantages and disadvantages do you see in this procedure?

2. From the background data given, what guesses do you have about Alice's family background? Javier's family constellation? How might you work with each of their family backgrounds in relation to their current difficulties as a couple?

3. Would the fact that he is a Latino and she is a Pacific Islander be something that you would explore with the couple, especially since their parents were not supportive of their marrying each other? Would you want to discuss the impact of their families of origin on their current family dynamics?

4. How do you see Alice? How do you see Javier? How do you see them as a couple? Do their respective cultural backgrounds provide you with any information about their behavior and their roles in their marriage? Because they are from different ethnic backgrounds, would you be inclined to work with them differently than you would if they shared the same cultural background?

5. Do you think you have enough knowledge about the cultural backgrounds of Javier and Alice to work effectively with them? If you do not have this knowledge, how might you go about acquiring it? What special problems, if any, might you encounter by not sharing the same cultural background?

6. As an Adlerian counselor you will want to make sure that your goals and the goals of Alice and of Javier are in alignment. How might you go about this? What if Javier and Alice have different goals? What kind of contract might you envision developing with them?

7. If you had to speculate at this moment, what are Alice's "basic mistakes"? Javier's? Do you have any ideas of ways in which you might work on such mistaken beliefs with each of them? With them as a couple?

8. What specific Adlerian techniques might you be most inclined to employ in working with this couple? Toward what goals?

STUDY GUIDE FOR CHAPTER FIVE

ADLERIAN THERAPY

The summary, *Overview of Adlerian Therapy*, along with the *Glossary of Key Terms* in the **Student Manual** will be most helpful in your study/review. To learn how the lifestyle assessment actually works, complete the questionnaire in Chapter 5 and look at the lifestyle assessment done on Stan. As usual, the *Pre-Chapter Self-Inventory* and the quiz will be helpful tools for providing you with feedback.

Case Approach to Counseling and Psychotherapy, Chapter 3, gives a concrete example of how the lifestyle assessment proceeds through Ruth's case. You'll see how an Adlerian perspective is used to understand and work with Ruth. These chapters will be an excellent review of basic concepts of each approach.

Specific Guidelines for Study of Adlerian Therapy

1. How are Adler's life experiences expressed in his theory of personality?

2. How is Adler's view of human nature different from Freud's? What importance does Adler give to the role of childhood experiences in terms of adult life?

3. Adler believed that we create ourselves as opposed to being passively scripted by childhood experiences. Do you favor this Adlerian view, or the Freudian view? Explain. Discuss the implications of your view for counseling practice.

4. The following are some key concepts of Adlerian therapy that are helpful for counselors: striving for significance and superiority; style of life; childhood experiences; fictional finalism; social interest; birth order and sibling relationships; subjective perception of reality; purposefulness of behavior, basic mistakes, faulty assumptions.

5. What are the therapeutic goals that guide Adlerians?

6. How do Adlerians view their function and role?

7. If a chronically depressed middle-age man were to experience Adlerian therapy, what is likely to be the main focus of his therapy?

8. Discuss Adler's concept of style of life. Do you agree with him that what is crucial is not our childhood experiences themselves, but our *attitude* toward the early events of our life?

9. What is the Adlerian view of the client/therapist relationship? How does this differ from the classical psychoanalytic view?

10. What is the Adlerian view of the role of dreams in therapy? How does this differ from the psychoanalytic view of dream analysis?

11. Know the four phases of the Adlerian therapeutic process:

    a. How is the proper therapeutic relationship created?

    b. How are the client's dynamics understood and explored via the *family constellation* and *early recollections?* How are *dreams* a part of the lifestyle assessment? What is the use of assessing the client's priorities? How is *encouragement* basic to this process?

    c. What role does *insight* play in therapy? How is interpretation a way to facilitate this process of gaining insight?

    d. What are the main tasks of the action-oriented phase, known as *reorientation?*

12. Discuss the role of encouragement in the process of Adlerian therapy. What are some ways that you might provide encouragement to clients, while at the same time continue to challenge them?

13. How can Adlerian principles be applied to the following: education; marriage counseling; family counseling; group work?

14. In what ways can you apply Adlerian concepts to understanding your own development and the shaping of your personality?

15. Be sure to review carefully the *Questions for Reflection and Discussion* in the **Student Manual**. Which of these questions most stands out for you and why?

16. What do you consider to be the major contribution of this approach? How about its limitations?

17. From the perspective of working with culturally diverse populations, what are the contributions and limitations of Adlerian therapy?

18. What aspects are you most likely to incorporate into your counseling style and why?

19. What are some specific Adlerian concepts and methods that you might apply in your quest for gaining a fuller understanding of yourself?

20. Think of your own experiences in your family. How might Adlerian principles help you gain a clearer grasp of the meaning of these experiences for your life today?

Test Items

Chapter Five

Theory and Practice of

Counseling and Psychotherapy

ADLERIAN THERAPY

1. According to Adler, childhood experiences:
   a. are not relevant to the practice of therapy.
   b. determine the adult personality.
   c. are not as crucial in themselves as is our attitude toward these experiences.
   d. should provide the focus for therapy sessions.
   e. passively shape us.

2. Which is (are) true concerning one's style of life?
   a. All people have a lifestyle, but no two people develop exactly the same style.
   b. The lifestyle is largely set by the age of 6.
   c. One's style of life is a reaction to perceived inferiority.
   d. One's style of life is learned from early interactions in the family.
   e. All of the above

3. Adler believed that human behavior is:
   a. motivated by sexual urges.
   b. motivated by social urges.
   c. purposeful and goal-directed.
   d. all of the above
   e. both (b) and (c)

4. In Adlerian counseling, the client/therapist relationship is characterized by:
   a. cooperation and respect.
   b. equality.
   c. aloofness.
   d. the counselor as "expert," the client as "sick."
   e. both (a) and (b)

5. The purpose of examining a client's family constellation is:
   a. to get a picture of the individual's early social world.
   b. to bring unconscious factors to the surface.
   c. to discover hereditary aspects of the client's behavior.
   d. to determine who else in the family needs help.
   e. both (b) and (c)

6. The term "social interest" refers to:
   a. an individual's attitude in dealing with the social world.
   b. a sense of identification and empathy with others.
   c. striving for a better future for all humans.
   d. all of the above
   e. both (a) and (b)

7. Which of the following is not one of the five basic tasks Adler says we must master?
   a. acceptance
   b. achieving intimacy
   c. intellectual development
   d. work
   e. the spiritual dimension

8. All of the following are stages in Adlerian counseling except:
   a. reorientation.
   b. insight.
   c. establishing a therapeutic relationship.
   d. analysis and assessment.
   e. analysis of resistance.

9. The process of encouragement in Adlerian counseling includes:
   a. helping clients use all their resources.
   b. transforming traits that can be liabilities into assets.
   c. helping clients recognize and accept their positive qualities.
   d. all of the above
   e. all but (b)

10. An Adlerian therapist would ask a client to give their earliest recollections in order to:
    a. discover goals and motivations.
    b. reveal their beliefs and basic mistakes.
    c. give clues as to the development of that individual's lifestyle.
    d. all of the above
    e. both (b) and (c)

11. According to Adlerians, the goal in pointing out a client's top priority is to enable them to recognize:
    a. that it needs to be changed.
    b. the feelings they invoke in others by clinging to it.
    c. the price they pay for clinging to it.
    d. all of the above
    e. both (b) and (c)

12. Adlerians believe that discouragement:
    a. is the basic condition that prevents people from functioning.
    b. is basic to the human condition and is to be accepted as part of being alive.
    c. can be overcome by encouragement.
    d. both (a) and (c)
    e. both (b) and (c)

13. Adlerians view the use of techniques in counseling as:
    a. geared to the phase of therapy and the needs of the client.
    b. more important than paying attention to the subjective experiences of the client.
    c. against their basic philosophy.
    d. both (a) and (b)
    e. all of the above

14. Which of the following techniques is *not* used in Adlerian family counseling?
    a. the initial interview
    b. paradox
    c. analyzing resistances between members of the family
    d. making an appraisal
    e. all are used

15. Adlerian therapy involves a *phenomenological orientation*. This means that the therapist attempts to view the world:
    a. from an objective frame of reference.
    b. from his or her own subjective frame of reference.
    c. from the client's frame of reference.
    d. from the frame of reference of a particular theory.
    e. none of the above

16. Which of the following statements is not true about Alfred Adler?
    a. He created child guidance clinics.
    b. His early childhood was happy.
    c. He worked with Freud for at least eight years.
    d. He had much to say about child-rearing practices.

17. When Adler spoke of individuality, he referred to:
    a. the unique way we rewrite our own life script.
    b. the unique way we deal with the crises of our development.
    c. the unique way we confront our unfinished business.
    d. the unique way we develop our own style of striving for competence.

18. "Fictional finalism" is an Adlerian term that refers to:
    a. the unrealistic ideas that we have about the way life should be.
    b. our strict adherence to certain beliefs that are not based on reality.
    c. an imagined central goal that guides our behavior.
    d. our stubborn resistance to change.

19. In helping clients to examine their mistaken goals and faulty assumptions, an Adlerian therapist does not use:
    a. encouragement.
    b. challenge and confrontation.
    c. tentative interpretations.
    d. interpretation of the transference relationship.
    e. both (b) and (c)

20. Which of the following aspects of family life are assessed when exploring a client's family constellation?
    a. birth order
    b. interactions between siblings and parents
    c. the child's psychological position in the family
    d. all of the above
    e. all but (c)

21. Which of the following is not true about the Adlerian concept of "private logic"?
    a. It comes as a result of the feelings and emotions we experience in our daily lives.
    b. It provides a central psychological unity for US.
    c. It is the philosophy upon which we base our lifestyle.
    d. It often does not conform with the reality of social living.

22. During the phase of analysis and assessment, the Adlerian therapist:
    a. explores the family constellation.
    b. asks for early recollections.
    c. offers tentative interpretations.
    d. all of the above
    e. all but (c)

23. Reorientation, the fourth phase of Adlerian therapy, involves:
    a. putting insights into action.
    b. helping clients see new alternatives.
    c. helping clients come to understand their own part in creating their problems.
    d. both (a) and (b)
    e. both (b) and (c)

24. One way that clients in Adlerian therapy are encouraged to change is:
    a. by changing early decisions.
    b. by understanding the roots of their problems.
    c. by "acting as if" they were already the way they want to be.
    d. both (a) and (b)

25. One contribution of Adlerian therapy is that:
    a. practitioners are given a great deal of freedom in working with their clients.
    b. it offers a well-defined theory of personality.
    c. many of its concepts have been supported by research.
    d. it is a common-sense psychology.
    e. it offers a one-dimensional perspective on personality.

26. Who is primarily credited with popularizing and extending Adler's work by applying Adlerian principles to group work?
    a. Don Dinkmeyer
    b. Erik Erikson
    c. H. L. Ansbacher
    d. Raymond Corsini
    e. Rudolph Dreikurs

27. Which of the following did Adler not stress?
    a. the unity of personality
    b. focus on early childhood experiences as determinants of later personality functioning
    c. behavior is purposeful and goal-oriented
    d. a unique style of life that is an expression of life goals
    e. feelings of inferiority

28. Which child is most likely to demand center stage, tends to have difficulties in life when he or she is no longer the center of attention, and is likely to become dependently tied to the mother?
    a. the oldest child
    b. the second child
    c. the middle child
    d. the youngest child
    e. the only child

29. Which child tends to feel squeezed out and may develop a conviction that life is unfair and a feeling of being cheated?
    a. the oldest child
    b. the second child
    c. the middle child
    d. the youngest child
    e. the only child

30. All of the following are life tasks that Adler taught we must successfully master except for:
    a. building friendships
    b. establishing intimacy
    c. contributing to society
    d. achieving self-actualization

31. The core of the Adlerian therapy experience consists of clients:
    a. working through the transference relationship.
    b. discovering their basic mistakes and then learning how to correct them.
    c. understanding how their relationship with their parents has shaped their personality.
    d. understanding how their birth order has determined the person who they are today.

32. Of the following, on which would an Adlerian therapist place special value?
    a. interpretation of dreams
    b. confronting the ways the client is living dependently since early childhood
    c. modeling of communication and acting in good faith
    d. helping the client to work through the transference neurosis

MULTIPLE CHOICE TEST QUESTIONS

1. C	12. D.	23. D
2. E	13. A	24. C
3. E	14. C	25. A
4. E	15. C	26. E
5. A	16. B	27. B
6. D	17. D	28. E
7. C	18. C	29. C
8. E	19. D	30. D
9. D	20. D	31. B
10. D	21. A	32. C
11. E	22. E	

TRUE–FALSE TEST ITEMS FOR CHAPTER FIVE

ADLERIAN THERAPY

Read each statement and decide if it is "more true" or "more false" as it applies to Adlerian therapy.

1. Alfred Adler believed that what we are born with is not as important as what we choose to do with the abilities and limitations we possess.

2. Striving for superiority is seen as a neurotic manifestation.

3. According to Adler, perfection, not pleasure, is the goal of life.

4. Adler maintained that our style of life was not set until middle age.

5. Adler maintained that individuals attempt to overcome feelings of basic inferiority by developing a lifestyle in which success is possible.

6. We can be fully understood only in light of knowing the purposes and goals toward which we are striving.

7. Adlerians maintain that change is not possible without insight; understanding the causes of one's problems is a prerequisite to behavioral change.

8. In Adlerian counseling, there is a focus on the family constellation and the influence of the family on the individual.

9. Encouragement is a part of the Adlerian counseling process.

10. Adlerians typically do not use techniques of interpretation, for they believe that clients can make their own interpretations without therapist intervention.

11. From the Adlerian perspective, objective reality is more important than how we interpret reality and the meanings we attach to what we experience.

12. Adlerians emphasize reeducating people and reshaping society.

13. For Adlerian counselors, techniques are helpful when adapted to the needs of the client.

14. By having a client discuss his or her earliest recollections, an Adlerian counselor hopes to bring unconscious conflicts to the surface.

15. Adler stressed that our desire to strive for perfection is learned from our parents.

16. One Adlerian concept is that everything we do is influenced by our style of life.

17. "Fictional finalism" is a term that Adlerians use to describe our attitude in dealing with the social world.

18. Clients are viewed by Adlerian therapists as "sick" and in need of a cure.

19. The concept of lifestyle refers to an individual's core beliefs and assumptions through which the person organizes his or her reality and finds meaning in life events.

20. Adlerians maintain that the priorities we choose arise from our personality strengths.

ANSWER KEY FOR CHAPTER FIVE – ADLERIAN THERAPY

TRUE–FALSE TEST QUESTIONS

1.	T	11.	F
2.	F	12.	T
3.	T	13.	T
4.	F	14.	F
5.	T	15.	F
6.	T	16.	T
7.	F	17.	F
8.	T	18.	F
9.	T	19.	T
10.	F	20.	F

Guidelines for Using Chapter Six

Existential Therapy

in

Theory and Practice of Counseling and Psychotherapy and the *Student Manual*

Case Approach to Counseling and Psychotherapy

and

The Art of Integrative Counseling

In my opinion, the existential approach provides rich material for a personal exploration of students who are preparing for becoming counselors or human services professionals.

With this approach I prefer to devote a bulk of the time allotted to explore existential themes and issues that are related to the personal lives of the students. My rationale is that unless future counselors have grappled with personal issues such as the meaning of life, death and dying, anxiety and guilt, freedom and responsibility, and so on, they will not be able to assist their future clients in their exploration of these themes. I believe that it is possible to emphasize an experiential component that encourages the students to critically examine their own values, attitudes, conflicts, and personal lives.

The questions I raise can be material for structured small group experiences that have as their main aim the integration of the cognitive-didactic aspects with the affective-experiential aspects of the course. Students that I teach seem to appreciate the balance between the academic learning of the theory and the application of cognitive structure to their own current interests and concerns. My belief is that a strictly didactic approach will lead to "apparent learning" that will soon be forgotten and not be integrated and that a strictly experiential focus will deprive the students of a conceptual framework to evaluate what they are doing as counselors.

1. I suggest that with each theory you make reference to the case of Stan. In a way, a particular focus can be on the theory under consideration for each week as it applies to Stan. Generally, I make several references to how an existential therapist might work with Stan, what aspects would be attended to, and what conflicts would be stressed. After we have completed the first 15 chapters, I like to devote some time to Stan's case, but more from the perspective of integrating the various approaches and showing the contrasts among the eleven approaches.

2. **Suggestions for demonstrations of therapeutic sessions in the classroom**. As a part of my style of teaching, I typically use demonstrations as a way of making the practical applications of each therapy approach clearer to the students.

    With this approach, I demonstrate how I work using existential concepts. One way of combining the material in this casebook with student concerns is to ask students if they can identify with any of the clients that I've written about. It is not necessary that they role-play, for they can be themselves and work with their own issues, even though these issues may be similar to the cases. It cannot be stressed too much that demonstrating counseling approaches in a class setting is a delicate matter, and that students should be fully aware of the possibilities for getting emotionally involved should they volunteer. While there are risks, there are benefits that I think offset the risks, *if care is taken* on the part of the instructor, *and the students are properly prepared* for this type of personal involvement.

    At this point I'd like to talk further about using demonstrations in class for didactic purposes, as well as some other general comments about how I use a case approach to assist students in seeing the connection between theory and practice.

    It has been my experience that I can "teach" more about a given theory by "showing" how I actually use this theory in working with an individual or a group. At times I ask for a small group of volunteers and I state that I will attempt to show them how I would proceed thinking in existential terms. What I actually do when the group convenes is up to the people who are sitting in the circle with me. I take care to let them know that any of them can say that they'd like to not go any further with an issue at any point. In all honesty, I can say I've never found this a comfortable experience, for while the focus is on demonstrating my approach or a particular therapeutic model, issues often become quite emotionally intense and highly personal.

    My attempt is to create a climate based on trust and respect, and I stress the importance of confidentiality. Also, before the end of a demonstration of a group or individual session I always ask the volunteers how they feel and if there is anything they'd like to say to bring the session to closure. After this, I invite the class to share their personal reactions, and at the same time caution them about talking about the person's "problem" (or worse, attempting to problem-solve or cure the person). The focus is upon how the observers were affected, as well as whatever questions about this demonstration might have arisen.

    In working with an individual who volunteers to be a "client," I typically begin by asking the person what he or she would most hope to get from the next 20 minutes or so. I let the person guide me in how far to go as well as where to go. While I don't see this as a therapy session, I do see this as an opportunity for the volunteer to learn something more about himself or herself, and as a way of clarifying a particular problem or issue that they might want to go further with at another time and place. Frequently volunteers will remark at some later point how participating in the demonstration session actually stimulated them to making an important shift in their thinking or behaving and that the experience was therapeutic for them.

    Counseling demonstrations provide an opportunity for the other students to get some sample of the counseling process in action, as well as learn something about their personal struggles. Again, while I have no clear answers about the use of this approach, all I can do is stress the importance of sensitivity, respect, and taking care not to exploit a volunteer for purposes of teaching a point.

    Every semester I find a number of students who recognize certain conflicts within themselves that they would like to work on therapeutically. In many respects, the counseling course is an opportunity to look at oneself and to consider changes in behavior, as well as being an academic experience. For many, this course provides an impetus for them to seek personal counseling or to get involved in some type of therapeutic group. I make frequent referrals to the university counseling center or to community mental-health centers.

3. In the *Student Manual* are a series of *Questions for Reflection and Discussion*. These questions are designed to help students find ways to apply the major existential propositions to themselves. I use these questions for in-

class seminars and for topics of discussion in small, leaderless groups. The suggested activities that follow can be used in the same way. These activities focus on issues such as "In what ways are we dead but still existing? Do we really want to change? What is the meaning of personal freedom and responsibility?"

4. **Other Resources:** In addition to the cases, Ruth and Walt, given in Chapter 6 of the *Student Manual*, you may want to refer to three other resources: *Case Approach; Art of Integrative Counseling;* and the *CD ROM for Integrative Counseling*. Reviewing the basic dimensions of each therapy will help readers compare and contrast the approaches and is a good way to review the key concepts and techniques.

    Refer to the *Case Approach to Counseling and Psychotherapy* (6th ed., 2005) for a detailed treatment of the case of Ruth from an existential perspective. In Chapter 4 Dr. Donald Polkinghorne presents a comprehensive treatment of dealing with existential themes in Ruth's life such as existential sources of Ruth's symptoms, reconstruction of the self, and manifestations of an authentic existence.

    Refer to the book *The Art of Integrative Counseling* for discussion of existential therapy from a number of vantage points. In Chapter 2 (pp. 15–18) I demonstrate how existential therapy forms the foundation for developing a client/therapist relationship. On pages 18–20 I discuss how existential concepts are related to the collaborative venture of therapy, and on pages 22–25 is a description of drawing upon existential notions in working with Ruth. Chapter 7, *Emotive Focus in Counseling* draws very heavily upon existential therapy. See also Chapter 9, *The Foundation of My Integrative Approach*, (pp. 92–93) for a discussion of how I incorporate existential therapy into my integrative approach.

5. Refer to the *CD ROM for Integrative Counseling*, Session #11: *Exploring the Past*. In the video Ruth and I engage in a role play where Ruth becomes the voice of her church and I take on a new role as Ruth – one in which I have been willing to challenge certain beliefs from church. The video clip illustrates how I deal with existential themes in Ruth's life and how we focus on exploration of values.

    The book, *The Art of Integrative Counseling*, deals with existential themes in Chapters 2 – on the therapeutic relationship, and in Chapter 11 – *Dealing with the Past*.

6. In preparing your own lectures on existential therapy, the books I most highly recommend are:

    a. *Existential Psychotherapy* (Yalom, 1980)
    b. *The Art of the Psychotherapist* (Bugental, 1987)
    c. *Cross-Cultural Counseling: A Casebook* (Vontress, Johnson, & Epp, 1999)

    These particular books are briefly annotated in the *Recommended Supplementary Readings* section in Chapter 6 of *TPCP.* Of course, all of Viktor Frankl's and Rollo May's books are most highly recommended, which are found in the *References and Suggested Readings*.

7. In this *Instructor's Resource Manual*, I am providing some additional materials that deal with applying existential concepts to counseling situations. These practical situations involve existential problems such as the meaning of one's existence, loneliness, anxiety, and so forth. These materials can be duplicated and given to students for additional sources of discussion or laboratory work if you desire. I have used these cases and brief examples in my classes, and they do provide a point of departure for focusing on key issues related to the existential approach.

KEY TERMS FOR REVIEW AND DEFINITION

Frankl	relatedness
Bugental	search for meaning
May	meaninglessness
Kierkegaard	aloneness and isolation
Nietzsche	engagement
Heidegger	"bad faith"
Sartre	"givens of existence"
Buber	commitment
Binswanger	being in the world

Boss   existential anxiety
Logotherapy   death and nonbeing
the will to meaning   restricted existence
the human condition   authenticity
self-awareness   existential guilt
existential vacuum   inauthentic existence
freedom and responsibility   I/Thou relationship
authorship   paradoxes of existence
courage to be   self-determination

INFOTRAC KEYWORDS

The following keywords are listed in such a way as to allow the ***InfoTrac*** search engine to locate a wider range of articles on the online university library. The keywords should be entered *exactly* as listed below, to include astericks, "W1," "W2," "AND," and other search engine tools.

Existential Therapy
Martin Buber
Viktor Frankl
Rollo May
Jean-Paul Sartre
Irvin Yalom
Existential W1 phenomenology
Existential AND meaning
Relatedness AND psychol*

Some Counseling Situations Dealing with Existential Problems

Assume you were counseling people with the following presenting problems. What would you want to say, and what would you hope to do? What would be your strategies, and how would you work with each of these persons? What issues are involved? How have you come to terms with these issues in your own life?

1. I feel like my existence does not matter to anyone. If I were to die today, I fully believe that it wouldn't make a difference to anyone.

2. My fear is that I am empty and vacant inside. I've never really had to look at myself before now, but since my husband left me I am lost. I feel deserted, abandoned, isolated, and I fear that I cannot make it alone. I depended on him to give me a sense of worth, and now that he's gone, I just feel a void.

3. I keep looking outside of me for answers. I try so hard to be whatever anyone else expects me to become. I see myself as a stranger to myself. I really don't know who I am, and what's worse, at this point I don't even know what I would like to become.

4. I find myself terrified when I am alone. I need people around me constantly, and if I'm forced to be alone, then I run from myself by watching television. I'd like to learn how to be alone and feel comfortable about it.

5. Most of the time, I feel a sense of detachment from other people, and I feel cut off from nature too. I am so caught up in traffic, offices, cities, and technology that I feel a sense of isolation. I want to feel at one with somebody – or feel unified with nature.

6. So rarely do I feel close to another person. While I want this closeness, I am frightened of being rejected. Instead of letting anyone get close to me, I build walls that keep them removed. What can I do to lessen my fear of being rejected?

7. When I do allow myself to be vulnerable to others I get scared, then I quickly become defensive. It is as though I see everyone as a potential enemy who is out to hurt me. When I become defensive I have a hard time being anything but closed.

8. I'm not too sure how much I want to change. I have ambivalent feelings concerning how much I want and need others in my life. Often I am aware that I feel hard and uncaring toward others, yet there are times when I would like to be softer and more concerned. I'm struggling with whether or not I care enough to change this.

Counseling Situations and Questions Related to Anxiety

With the following excerpts of counseling problems and the questions for each situation, assume that (1) you are the client posing these conflicts. What are you seeking? What resolution would you like to find? What do you want from and with your counselor? (2) Now assume you are the counselor. What would you say to your client? How would you help your client? What strategies might you take? What are some things you'd want your client to consider?

1. The person has had a lucrative and secure job for years but is now becoming aware that it is sterile, unexciting, and dull. He finally musters the courage to leave this secure job and go into business for himself. He experiences more challenges and excitement, yet he is filled with anxiety of failing. What is the real fear? What are some ways of coping with these fears?

2. A woman decides that she must leave her husband if she is to gain her own dignity. She originally married an "emotional child" but through her therapy decided she wanted a man she could love and give something to as well as receive something from. She encouraged her husband to join a group with her or at least become involved in his own counseling. He flatly and consistently refused. The more she grew, the more open she became, and the more demanding she was, the more he withdrew and became more rigid. She decided to leave her husband and four children, and, while she feels basically good about her choice, she brings new levels of anxiety to the counseling session. "How do I feel about leaving my children? Did I do everything I could have done for him? Was I patient enough? Will I find someone else, or will I live alone? Am I really capable of loving and finding one who will love me? Have I been too selfish?"

3. As a result of attending college classes and receiving some private counseling, a woman finds that she has a right to her own wants and needs. She is discovering that her sole purpose in life is more than simply cooking, cleaning, and always being there for her children. While she is getting in touch with some of her long-denied personal needs, she is also experiencing more anxiety as evidenced by her questions. "Am I being too selfish by going to college two days a week? Don't my kids need me full time? My husband is threatened by my independence, so what do I do with his feelings? I know I need more for myself or I'll dry up, but I'm afraid if I follow my impulses that I'll neglect my duties."

4. A person who has been reared in the strict Baptist tradition begins to question the dogmatic teachings. He eventually decides to separate from the practice of his authoritarian religion that he has followed for over 20 years. He feels a surge of courage in daring to act on his new beliefs, and he likes himself for declaring his independence from beliefs that he no longer accepts as valid. Yet, he experiences much anxiety over this choice. "What if they were really right, and I am wrong? Can I really release myself from my past conditioning? I still have fears that what I was taught might be true after all."

CASE EXAMPLES

The following case examples, Ralph and Pauline, are designed as a catalyst to apply existential concepts in actual counseling. Each case raises issues of the struggle with personal freedom, and students can be encouraged to bring in similar struggles they have encountered in making choices in their own lives.

RALPH: Feeling trapped in his job

Ralph is a 47-year-old father of four children, all of whom are adolescents or older. He says that he is coming to you for counseling in order to find a way to free himself from feeling trapped by meaningless work. He was referred to you by a friend, and he tells you the following at the intake session:

"I feel a need to take some action at this point in my life—I suppose you could say I'm going through a late identity crisis. By now, you'd expect that a guy of my age should know where he's going in life, but all I know is that I feel blah. Just sorta like a zombie!

"I attribute most of my problems to my job. I've worked with this department store chain for more years than I can remember. I'm the manager of a store with quite a few people under me. But now I've come to hate that job! There's nothing to look forward to anymore. It's no challenge. Part of me wants to junk the entire thing, even though I'm not that far away from retirement with a nice pension and many fringe benefits. So the conservative part of me says stay and put up with what you've got! Then another side of me says leave and find something else more challenging. Don't *die* living for a stinking pension plan!

"So I'm really torn whether I should stay or leave. I keep thinking of my kids. I feel I should support them and see them through college – and if I go to another job I'll have to take a big pay cut. I feel guilty about even thinking of letting my kids down when they expect me to see them through. And then my wife tells me I should just accept that what I'm feeling is normal for my age – a midlife crisis, she calls it. She says I should get rid of foolish notions about making a job change at my age. Then there's always the fear that I'll get out there and make that big change and then get fired. What would I do without a job? Who would I be if I couldn't work? I just feel as though there are heavy rocks on my shoulders weighing me down every time I think about being stuck in my job. I sure hope you'll help me get rid of this burden and help me make a decision about what to do with this work situation."

1. Based on his story, what are your impressions of Ralph? Would you like to work with him? Why or why not? Would you share with him any of your initial reactions and thoughts from the intake session? If so, what do you think you would tell him?

2. How might you work with the two sides of Ralph: the part of him that wants to stay in his job and the part that wants to leave?

3. Check what your goals might be in working with Ralph:

_____   to provide him with information about the job market

_____   to give him advice about whether he should remain in his job or look for a new career in life

_____   to encourage him to work with his feelings of "blahness" and guilt over not providing for his children

_____   to help him deal with his fear of changing jobs and then failing

_____   to help him look at what he would be without his work

_____   to challenge him to deal with his feelings toward his wife

4. Depending on which of the above goals you see as being most pressing, how do you think you would work differently with him?

5. Do you have any ideas about how to work with his burden of carrying heavy rocks on his shoulders?

6. What ideas do you have about helping him explore his feeling of being trapped?

PAULINE: A young woman facing death

The existentialist views death as a reality that gives meaning to life. As humans we do not have forever to actualize ourselves. Thus, the realization that we will die jolts us into taking the present seriously and evaluating the direction in which we are traveling. We are confronted with the fact that we have only so much time to do the things we most want to do. Thus, we are motivated to take stock of how meaningful our life is. With this existential perspective in mind, assume that a young woman of 20 comes to the center where you are a counselor.

Some Background Data:

Pauline has recently found out that she has leukemia. Though she is in a period of remission, her doctors tell her that the disease is terminal. Pauline is seeking counseling to help herself deal with this crisis and at least get the maximum out of the remainder of her life. She is filled with rage over her fate; she keeps asking why this had to happen to her. She tells you that at first she could not believe the diagnosis was correct. When she finally got several more professional opinions that confirmed her leukemia, she began to feel more and more anger—toward God, toward her healthy friends, whom she envied, and generally toward the unfairness of her situation. She tells you that she was just starting to live, that she had a direction she was going in professionally. Now everything will have to change. After she tells you this, she is sitting across from you waiting for your response.

Questions for Reflection:

Attempting to stay within the frame of reference of an existential therapist, what direction would you take with her? Think about these questions:

1. What do you imagine your immediate reactions would be if you were faced with counseling this client? What would be some of the things that you would initially say in response to what you know about Pauline?

2. What are your own thoughts and feelings about death? How do you think that your answer will affect your ability to be present for Pauline?

3. What goals would you have in counseling with her?

4. In what ways would you deal with the rage that Pauline says she feels?

5. Pauline tells you that one of the reasons she is coming to see you is her desire to accept her fate. How would you work with her to gain this acceptance? What specific things might you do to help her find ways of living the rest of her life to its fullest?

6. Do you see any possibilities for helping Pauline find meaning in her life in the face of death?

THE CASES OF AL, GLENDA, JIM, AND LUCY

Assume that you are an existential counselor. Read and think about Al, Glenda, Jim, and Lucy in their struggles with freedom. Imagine each of them coming to you for counseling. About them you know only as much as is written below. How would you proceed in your work with each person?

How would you work with Al?

Al decided to become a neuter. His mother was overprotective, overpossessive, and controlled him with guilt. She gave and sacrificed for him. Al became effeminate and did whatever he felt his mother wanted of him. He is overweight, unsexy, passive, nice, and unassertive. As he realizes how his mother lives in him now, he finds that he can decide certain things as indicated by such questions as: "Do I want to continue to be my mother's boy? Am I willing to leave her psychologically, even if it means displeasing her? Do I want self-approval more than her approval? Is it really worth it to try to change? Am I miserable enough? Why should I change, when I am so comfortable in being taken care of by her? If I remain the way I am now, what might I say about myself ten years hence?"

How would you work with Glenda?

Glenda becomes painfully aware that she has perfected the art of manipulating men with her physical appearance. She says the appropriate things, she has an abundance of men in her life, all of her contacts with people are superficial, and she accepts in herself that she has not pursued any depth because she has apparently gotten what she wanted with such little effort. But now she suffers as she comes to grips with her own vacancy and superficiality. The issues of freedom with which she might well wrestle as a result of her dawning awareness could be reflected in questions such as: "Am I tired enough of being plastic that I will risk finding out whether I'm real or not? Since my style has worked so well in the past, will I really change now? What if I pursue depth in a relationship only to find an emptiness? What if I am really empty inside? What if all I am is a pretty exterior? Will I be better off deluding myself that a fine exterior is really better than the experience of nothingness? How do I begin to change? Can I allow myself to hurt, or will I retreat into old ways to repress my pain?"

How would you work with Jim?

Jim is a unique blend of a computer, a robot, and a rock. He is impenetrable. He refuses to make himself vulnerable to any feelings. In the workshop he learned that his father was a model of what he did not want to be. His father was unmovable, indifferent, uncaring, rough, and generally had to exaggerate a sense of pseudo-strength to prove his manliness. Jim accepts the fact that his sample has been limited, and now he wrestles with questions such as: "Will I continue to address myself to being the opposite of my father? Will I invest that much power in him? Will I let myself feel? Can I be a man and decide for myself to be touched and reached by others, or will I build a wall as thick as my father's wall?"

How would you work with Lucy?

Lucy increasingly comes to realize how barren her marriage is. She feels trapped in her assigned roles. She feels unloved by her husband, who she feels takes her for granted. Lucy does very little for herself and gets her total identity from her functions as housewife and mother. Throughout her group-therapy sessions she allows herself to feel fully the pain of her self-denial, of being little more than her sterile roles. With her awareness might come the struggle of her freedom to decide what she might do as she asks herself such questions as: "Should I simply settle for what I have now? Do I dare rock the boat? If I challenge him, will he leave? Maybe things could be worse. Suppose I leave and find that nobody else is out there for me? Will I be threatened if I challenge the deadness of our relationship? How might my life be different if I do challenge it? Do I dare give up being weak and helpless, and, if I do, then whom can I blame?"

STUDY GUIDE FOR CHAPTER SIX

EXISTENTIAL THERAPY

From here on, I'll assume that if you are using the **Student Manual** you will not need specific suggestions. My hope is that you'll find the *Questions for Reflection and Discussion* in Chapter 6 helpful as you apply existential concepts to yourself in a personal way. The best way to really understand this approach is to apply it to your own life and your struggles. Working through the *Suggested Activities and Exercises* is a helpful way to personalize this material. As usual, the *Glossary of Terms* and the *Overview* summary will be very valuable for review. The *Pre-Chapter Self-Inventory* and the quiz are ways for you to get feedback on your comprehension of this approach.

Specific Guidelines for Study of Existential Therapy

1. In what way is existential therapy an approach to therapeutic practice (or a philosophy from which a therapist operates) more than a separate school of therapy or a system of techniques?

2. How might you describe the essence of the existential view of human nature? What are the implications of this view for counseling practice?

3. How is the capacity for self-awareness related to freedom? How is expanding of awareness a goal of this therapy? What are the implications for counseling of this notion?

4. For the existentialist, how are freedom and responsibility related? What implications do freedom and responsibility have for counseling?

5. How are the following notions part of the process of striving for identity?

   - the courage to be
   - the experience of aloneness
   - the experience of relatedness

6. How does the concept of the search for meaning influence what an existential therapist does during sessions?

7. What are Frankl's views of meaninglessness? How can logotherapy help clients deal with this condition by creating new meaning in life?

8. What is the existential view of anxiety? How might you intervene (from an existential perspective) with a client who displays a great deal of anxiety?

9. How does the existentialist view death? How are death and the meaning of life related? What are some counseling implications of the notions of death and nonbeing?

10. Describe the therapeutic process from an existential perspective by addressing basic assumptions, therapy goals, the role of the counselor, the client's experience, and the nature of the client/counselor relationship.

11. Using the basic concepts of the existential approach, show how you would work with the case of Ruth and the case of Stan. How can an existential perspective help you gain a deeper understanding of both Ruth's and Stan's dynamics?

12. From the perspective of counseling culturally diverse client populations, what are some of the contributions and the limitations of the existential approach?

13. How can you apply the existential approach to understanding your own struggles? What specific existential concepts have the most meaning for you?

14. In what ways might you be able to include an existential framework as the background of your counseling practice, even if you draw heavily from other therapy approaches?

15. What key concepts of the existential approach would you be most likely to incorporate into your personal style of counseling?

Test Items

Chapter Six

Theory and Practice of

Counseling and Psychotherapy

EXISTENTIAL THERAPY

1. Which person is not associated with the existential movement?
   a. May
   b. Frankl
   c. Yalom
   d. Skinner
   e. Sartre

2. The basic goal of existential theory is:
   a. to expand self-awareness.
   b. to increase choice potentials.
   c. to help clients accept the responsibility of choosing.
   d. to help the client experience authentic existence.
   e. all of the above

3. Which is not a key concept of existential therapy?
   a. It is based on a personal relationship between client and therapist.
   b. It stresses personal freedom in deciding one's fate.
   c. It places primary value on self-awareness.
   d. It is based on a well-defined set of techniques and procedures.
   e. all of the above

4. The function of the existentially oriented counselor is to:
   a. develop a specific treatment plan that can be objectively appraised.
   b. challenge the client's irrational beliefs.
   c. understand the client's subjective world.
   d. explore the client's past history in detail.
   e. assist the client in working through transference.

5. According to the existential view, anxiety is seen as a:
   a. result of repressed sexuality
   b. part of the human condition.
   c. neurotic symptom that needs to be cured.
   d. result of faulty learning.

6. Existential therapy is best considered as:
   a. an approach to understanding humans.
   b. a school of therapy.
   c. a system of techniques designed to create authentic humans.
   d. a strategy for uncovering dysfunctional behavior.

7. Which might be considered the most crucial quality of a therapist in building an effective therapeutic relationship with a client?
   a. the therapist's knowledge of theory
   b. the therapist's skill in using techniques
   c. the therapist's ability to diagnose accurately
   d. the therapist's authenticity

8. Philosophically, the existentialist would agree that:
   a. the final decisions and choices rest with the client.
   b. people redefine themselves by their choices.
   c. a person can go beyond early conditioning.
   d. making choices can create anxiety.
   e. all of the above

9. The central issue in therapy is:
   a. freedom and responsibility.
   b. resistance.
   c. transference.
   d. examining irrational beliefs.

10. According to the existential viewpoint, death:
    a. makes life absurd.
    b. makes life meaningless and hopeless.
    c. gives significance to living.
    d. should not be discussed or explored in therapy.

11. Which technique is considered essential in existential therapy?
    a. free association
    b. analysis of resistance
    c. analysis of dysfunctional family patterns
    d. role playing
    e. none of the above

12. The existential emphasis is based on:
    a. specific behaviors that can be assessed.
    b. a scientific orientation.
    c. a teaching/learning model that stresses the didactic aspects of therapy.
    d. the philosophical concerns of what it means to be fully human.
    e. an analysis of our position in the family.

13. Expanding awareness is:
    a. a basic goal of existential therapy.
    b. possible only with a few clients.
    c. not given emphasis in existential therapy.
    d. not possible because of our unconscious resistance.

14. Existential therapy is basically:
    a. a behavioral approach to therapy.
    b. a cognitive approach to therapy.
    c. an experiential approach to therapy.
    d. an action-oriented approach to therapy.

15. The philosophical assumptions underlying the existential approach include the notion(s) that:
    a. people are thrust into a meaningless and absurd world and that they are basically alone.
    b. people must create their own meanings through their choices.
    c. freedom is merely an illusion.
    d. human destiny is mainly determined by external forces and social conditioning.
    e. both (a) and (b)

16. The existential approach is:
    a. a reaction against psychoanalysis.
    b. a reaction against behaviorism.
    c. both of the above
    d. neither of the above

17. Viktor Frankl's approach to existential theory is known as:
    a. individual psychology.
    b. logotherapy.
    c. reality therapy.
    d. redecision therapy.
    e. humanistic psychology.

18. Which of the following is not true about Rollo May?
    a. He is most responsible for translating European existentialism into American psychotherapeutic theory and practice.
    b. He focuses on the subjective dimension of therapy.
    c. He is a significant spokesman for the existential approach in the United States.
    d. He believes that we can only escape anxiety by exercising our freedom.
    e. He contends that freedom and responsibility are two sides of the same coin.

19. The existential idea of freedom and responsibility involves the notion that:
    a. our freedom requires us to accept responsibility for directing our own life.
    b. we are free to choose who we will be.
    c. they go hand in hand.
    d. all of the above
    e. all but (b)

20. The notion of authorship states that we are authors of our life in the sense that we create our:
    a. destiny.
    b. life situation.
    c. problems.
    d. all of the above
    e. all but (b)

21. Who was the Danish philosopher that addressed the role of anxiety and uncertainty in life?
    a. Medard Boss
    b. Jean-Paul Sartre
    c. Soren Kierkegaard
    d. Martin Buber
    e. Friedrich Nietzsche

22. Existentialists contend that the experience of relatedness to other human beings:
    a. is just a neurotically dependent attachment.
    b. should be based on our needs and theirs.
    c. can be therapeutic.
    d. is not necessary, since we are basically alone.
    e. all but (c)

23. According to existentialists, all of the following issues are involved in our search for meaning except:
    a. discarding old values.
    b. meaninglessness.
    c. creating our own value system.
    d. exploring unfinished business.
    e. the struggle for significance in life.

24. Who among the following talked about the individuals "will to power" and the "herd morality?"
    a. Soren Kierkegaard
    b. Jean-Paul Sartre
    c. Martin Heidegger
    d. Martin Buber
    e. Friedrich Nietzsche

25. The central theme running through the works of Viktor Frankl is:
    a. that freedom is a myth.
    b. the will to meaning.
    c. self-disclosure as the key to mental health.
    d. the notion of self-actualization.
    e. being thrown into the universe without purpose.

26. According to Yalom, the concern(s) that make(s) up the core of existential psychodynamics is /are:
    a. death.
    b. freedom.
    c. isolation.
    d. meaninglessness.
    e. all of the above

27. A statement that best illustrates "bad faith" is:
    a. Naturally I'm this way, because I grew up in an alcoholic family.
    b. I will not consider others in the choices I make.
    c. I must live by commitments I make.
    d. I am responsible for the choices that I make.
    e. none of the above

28. For Sartre, existential guilt is what we experience when:
    a. we do not live by the Ten Commandments.
    b. we fail to think about the welfare of others.
    c. we allow others to define us or to make our choices for us.
    d. we reflect on all that we might have done and failed to do.
    e. none of the above.

29. Living authentically implies:
    a. following the norms of our social group.
    b. being true to our own evaluation of what constitutes a meaningful existence.
    c. accepting responsibility for the fact that we create our lives by the choices we make.
    d. both (b) and (c)

30. Existential therapy is unlike many other therapies in that:
    a. it does not have a well-defined set of techniques.
    b. it stresses the I/Thou encounter in the therapy process.
    c. it focuses on the use of the therapist's self as the core of therapy.
    d. it allows for incorporation of techniques from many other approaches.
    e. all of the above

31. The concept of "bad faith" refers to:
    a. not keeping up to date with paying one's therapist.
    b. leading an inauthentic existence.
    c. the failure to cooperate with the therapeutic venture.
    d. the experience of aloneness.
    e. the unwillingness to search for meaning in life.

ANSWER KEY FOR CHAPTER SIX – EXISTENTIAL THERAPY

MULTIPLE CHOICE TEST QUESTIONS

1. D	12. D	22. C
2. E	13. A	23. D
3. D	14. C	24. E
4. C	15. E	25. B
5. B	16. C	26. E
6. A	17. B	27. A

7. D	18. D	28. C
8. E	19. D	29. D
9. A	20. D	30. E
10. C	21. C	31. B
11. E		

TRUE–FALSE ITEMS FOR CHAPTER SIX

EXISTENTIAL THERAPY

Decide if each of the following statements is "more true" or "more false" as applied to existential therapy:

1. Rollo May has been instrumental in translating some concepts drawn from existential philosophy and applying them to psychotherapy.

2. Existential therapy can best be considered as a system of highly developed techniques designed to foster authenticity.

3. To its credit, the outcomes of existential therapy have been submitted to rigorous empirical testing, this approach is based on research validation of its techniques.

4. Existential therapy grew out of a reaction to the limitations of both the psychoanalytic and deterministic stance.

5. Existential therapy is rooted in the premise that humans cannot escape from freedom and responsibility.

6. In the existential approach, techniques are primary, while subjective understanding of clients is secondary.

7. Existential therapists show wide latitude in the techniques and procedures that they employ.

8. According to existential thinking, effective therapy does not stop with awareness, for clients are challenged to take action based on their insights.

9. From the existential viewpoint, anxiety is seen as a neurotic manifestation; thus the aim of therapy is to eliminate anxiety so clients can live comfortably.

10. Existential anxiety is seen as a function of our acceptance of our aloneness.

11. The existential therapist sees no basis for counseling and therapy without recognition of the freedom and responsibility each person possesses.

12. Existentialists claim that our experience of aloneness is a result of our making inappropriate choices.

13. According to the existential view, death makes life meaningless.

14. A major criticism of the existential approach is that it lacks a systematic statement of the principles and practices of psychotherapy.

15. This approach puts emphasis on the therapist as a person and the quality of the client/therapist relationship as one of the prime factors in determining the outcomes of therapy.

16. Martin Buber stressed the importance of presence, which allows for the creation of I/Thou relationships in therapy.

17. Existential guilt is being aware of having evaded a commitment, or having chosen not to choose.

18. The existential view is based on a growth mode and conceptualizes health rather than sickness.

19. A strength of the existential approach is that it provides a systematic statement of the pri nciples and practices of psychotherapy.

20. Existential therapy is especially appropriate for clients who are struggling with developmental crises.

ANSWER KEY FOR CHAPTER SIX – EXISTENTIAL THERAPY

TRUE–FALSE TEST QUESTIONS

1.	T	11.	T
2.	F	12.	F
3.	F	13.	F
4.	T	14.	T
5.	T	15.	T
6.	F	16.	T
7.	T	17.	T
8.	T	18.	T
9.	F	19.	F
10.	T	20.	T

Guidelines for Using Chapter Seven

Person-Centered Therapy

in

Theory and Practice of Counseling and Psychotherapy and the *Student Manual*

Case Approach to Counseling and Psychotherapy

and

The Art of Integrative Counseling

1. In the **Student Manual** there are some issues for *Practical Application* that deal with the goals of the person-centered approach, along with a series of problem situations that call for practical applications. Two brief cases, Ruth and Don, are designed to give students practice in staying within the person-centered framework. These problem situations and cases are useful exercises for helping students develop their skills in *actively listening* to client messages and practice reflecting to the client what was heard. Since the person-centered approach emphasizes listening, hearing, and reflecting, I think that these exercises, to sharpen the students skills in these areas, are timely and appropriate. I generally have the class form dyads. One person becomes the "speaker" and the other the facilitator, who attempts to accurately clarify the subtle messages that are received. Then the roles are reversed. After the exercise, we use class time to share what the experience was like from both sides.

2. I routinely devote some class time to role-playing Stan's case. Several students can try their hands at becoming a person-centered therapist as they work with Stan. This gives me an opportunity to show some areas of contrast between the person-centered therapist's approach and the psychoanalytically oriented therapist's approach. It also provides an opportunity to show the relationship between the existential therapist and the person-centered therapist. I attempt to make comparisons among the various therapy models during the semester. Stan's case provides a concrete vehicle for discussing the similarities and differences among the various therapies and a way of encouraging students to continually relate each theory to preceding theories. In the following chapters, some of

the contrasts I focus on are person-centered therapy versus rational emotive behavior therapy, reality therapy versus psychoanalytic therapy, and existential therapy versus behavior therapy.

3. **Other Resources:** In addition to the cases, Ruth and Don, examined in Chapter 7 of the *Student Manual*, you may want to refer to three other resources: *Case Approach; Art of Integrative Counseling;* and the *CD ROM for Integrative Counseling.* Reviewing the basic dimensions of each therapy will help readers compare/contrast the approaches and is a good way to review the key concepts and techniques.

   Refer to the *Case Approach to Counseling and Psychotherapy* (6th ed., 2005) for a detailed treatment of the case of Ruth from an existential perspective. In Chapter 5 Dr. David Cain describes his view of assessment and treatment of Ruth from a person-centered therapist's perspective. He shows how he intervenes at the various phases of Ruth's therapy.

4. Refer to the *CD ROM for Integrative Counseling* for a concrete illustration of how I view the therapeutic relationship as the foundation of therapy practice. The first three sessions of the video, (Session #1 *Beginning of Counseling*; Session #2 *The Therapeutic Relationship*; Session #3 *Establishing Therapeutic Goals*), consists of a demonstration of some of the principles pertaining to the person-centered approach

5. In preparing your own lectures on the person-centered approach, the books I most highly recommend are:

   a. *On Becoming a Person* (Rogers,1961)
   b. *A Way of Being* (Rogers, 1980)
   c. *The Psychology of Carl Rogers* (Farber, Brink, & Raskin, 1996)
   d. *Facilitating Emotional Change: The Moment-by-Moment Process* (Greenberg, Rice, & Elliott, 1996)
   e. *Humanistic Psychotherapies: Handbook of Research and Practice* (Cain & Seeman, 2002).

   These particular books are briefly annotated in the *Recommended Supplementary Readings* section in Chapter 7 of *TPCP*.

KEY TERMS FOR REVIEW AND DEFINITION

Carl Rogers	acceptance
nondirective counseling	accurate empathic understanding
client-centered therapy	nondirective psychotherapy
person-centered approach	reflective psychotherapy
existentialism and humanism	experiential psychotherapy
self-actualization	holistic psychotherapy
openness to experience	clarification
self-trust	reflection
internal locus of evaluation	congruence
growth promoting climate	core therapeutic conditions
incongruence	actualizing tendency
genuineness	humanistic psychology
unconditional positive regard	here-and-now experience

INFOTRAC KEYWORDS

The following keywords are listed in such a way as to allow the *InfoTrac* search engine to locate a wider range of articles on the online university library. The keywords should be entered *exactly* as listed below, to include asterisks, "W1," "W2," "AND," and other search engine tools.

Congruence AND therap*	Client-centered
Congruence AND psychol*	Unconditional W1 positive AND regard
Internal locus	Nondirective W1 therapy

Person-Centered Therapy
Carl Rogers

Client-centered
Person-centered
Humanistic psychology
Congruence AND psychol*
Self-actualization
Unconditional W1 positive AND regard
Internal locus
Rogers AND self-actualization

CASE EXAMPLES

HELGA: A depressed client with suicidal impulses

Helga has spent time in mental institutions because of deep depression, marked feelings of worthlessness, and several attempts to kill herself. She was born and reared in Germany and came to live in New Jersey in her late teens. She relates that she has never felt at home since she left Germany but that there is now nothing there for her to return to. She frequently mentions how lonely and isolated she feels. There are no friends in her life, no intimate relationships, and she feels a deep sense of rejection. Although she has been out of the last institution for over a year, she is an outpatient and has come to the day-treatment center on a regular basis. Assume that you are a new counselor and are seeing her for the first time. Think about how you might deal with her in the first five minutes of your initial session. At this first session Helga relates:

"I just dread getting up every morning. Everything seems like such a chore. I'm afraid that anything I do will turn to failure. I see no real sense in going on. I have constant thoughts of ending my life. I'm surely no use to anyone around me. I couldn't hold a husband or any job, and then I lost my kids. I just feel so worthless and rotten and full of guilt and hate for myself. No matter what I do or try, I just can't see any light at the end of that long, dark, cold, scary tunnel. I look forward to death, because then I won't have to suffer anymore."

1. What are your personal reactions to what Helga is saying? How does it affect you? What are you feeling as you listen to her?

2. What do you mainly hear Helga saying?

3. Given the way Helga presents herself, do you see much hope? Do you believe that there is a positive, trustworthy, and actualizing tendency within her?

4. In what ways might you use yourself as a person to create a relationship with Helga so that she might work through her depression? Do you think that your relationship with her by itself is sufficient, or would you see a need for interpretation, direction, and active techniques?

5. Would you be able to accept any direction or decision that Helga chose for herself, including suicide? What are the ethical and legal ramifications of accepting her choice to end her life? How would you deal with her suicidal ideation and threats?

6. To what extent would you want to explore her German background with her, especially since she does not feel at home in either culture?

7. Have you had enough life experiences similar to Helga's to enable you to empathize with her and enter her experiential world? How would you respond to her if she said: "You can't understand how uprooted I feel. I don't belong anywhere. But I just don't think you can know what this is like for me."

DORIS: Leaving her husband and child

Doris comes to a community counseling center at the recommendation of a friend, who expresses concern that Doris intends to leave her child. The friend thinks she is confused and needs professional help.

Some Background Data:

Doris was born and reared in Arkansas. Her father is a reformed alcoholic who drank heavily when the client was a child. Both parents are religious, and the father is described as a strict fundamentalist. Doris has a younger brother who is now an enlisted man in the army and is described as the family favorite. She says her parents were stricter with her than with their son and emphasized the importance of marriage as well as the woman's dependent and inferior role in that relationship.

Doris dropped out of high school in the tenth grade. She worked as a manicurist in Arkansas until marrying and moving to Kentucky three years ago. She then worked as a waitress. Her husband says that they have had no fights or arguments during their three-year marriage, and the client agrees. Six months ago Doris gave birth to a baby boy. There were no medical complications, and she maintains that she adjusted well to the baby, but she reports just not being able to feel much of anything except tired. Two months ago she and her husband moved to Houston so that he could join an amateur band. She began working as a cashier at a drugstore. In the course of her work she began to have a series of brief sexual affairs with fellow workers as well as customers. At the same time, although her husband is happy with the band, he has not been able to find a steady job. He has asked her to try to find a second job or to take overtime hours at the drug store.

Doris is considering leaving her husband and her child, although she is uncertain how she would continue to support herself financially. She is also concerned with what would happen to her son, because her husband has no means of support. She insists that she does not want to take the child with her.

Questions for Reflection:

1. What is your attitude about Doris wanting to leave her husband and her child? What are your values on this matter, and how would they influence the way you would work with her?

2. Assume that Doris asked you for your advice regarding her plan to leave her husband and child. What would you say? To what degree do you think Doris can function without advice?

3. If you accepted Doris as a client, in what ways do you think you could be of most help to her?

4. Are there feelings about herself and her husband that Doris is currently unwilling to accept? How would a person-centered approach help with acceptance of feelings and with denied parts of the self?

5. What are some of the advantages of working with Doris within a person-centered framework?

Suggestion:

Now that you have attempted to stay within the person-centered framework in working with both Helga and Doris, form small groups in class. One person can volunteer to "become" the client (Doris or Helga) while another volunteer shows how he or she would approach this client within the spirit of the person-centered approach. I recommend that you do this type of role playing in small groups for most of the cases presented in this manual. If you experience the roles of *both* client and counselor, you will be in a good position to discuss meaningfully what you like and don't like about each of the theoretical approaches. And you may learn a good bit about yourself by assuming the identity of the clients presented here.

1. See the *Student Manual* for a list of key terms and definitions for this chapter.

2. Briefly describe the historical development of the person-centered approach.

3. Differentiate between existentialism and humanism.

4. Summarize the basic characteristics of the person-centered approach.

5. What is Rogers's view of human nature, and what are the implications for the practice of counseling?

6. How is the personal life of Carl Rogers reflected in his theory?

7. What are the therapeutic goals of this approach? How do the counselor's role and function fit with these goals?

8. What importance is placed on the client/counselor relationship? Describe the six therapeutic conditions necessary and sufficient for personality change to occur. Evaluate this view.

9. Discuss the concept of therapist congruence as a critical variable in the therapy process.

10. Discuss the concept of empathy as the therapist's ability to subjectively understand the client's world. What are some barriers that might limit a therapist's capacity to be empathic?

11. Critically evaluate this approach, mentioning the main contributions and limitations. With what kinds of populations do you think this approach has the most applicability?

12. What are some contributions and limitations of concepts of the person-centered approach as applied to multicultural counseling? In what ways might you modify the techniques you might use depending on the client's cultural background?

13. What aspects of the person-centered orientation might you integrate into your own perspective? Discuss the concepts that you would want to include as a basic part of your own personal counseling style.

14. In what ways might you use a person-centered base yet at the same time draw upon other therapy approaches for specific techniques? Explain the importance of developing a solid relationship with a client before you attempt to actively intervene in a client's life with too many techniques.

15. Review the section in the *Student Manual* that contains a *Quiz for Comprehension Check*. Also, check *on-line* for additional quiz items besides those given below.

Test Items

Chapter Seven

Theory and Practice of

Counseling and Psychotherapy

MULTIPLE-CHOICE TEST ITEMS FOR CHAPTER SEVEN

PERSON-CENTERED THERAPY

1. The person-centered view of human nature:
   a. contends that people are basically competitive.
   b. holds that humans are driven by irrational forces.
   c. is rooted in a faith in the person's capacity to direct his or her own life.
   d. assumes that, while humans have the potential for growth, there is a tendency toward remaining stagnant.
   e. both (a) and (b)

2. Person-centered therapy is best described as:
   a. a completed and fixed "school" of counseling.
   b. a dogmatic set of therapeutic principles.
   c. a systematic set of behavioral techniques.
   d. a set of tentative principles describing how the therapy process develops.
   e. none of the above

3. The founder of person-centered therapy is:
   a. Rollo May.
   b. Frederick Perls.
   c. Abe Maslow.
   d. B. F. Skinner.
   e. none of the above

4. Which of the following is not a characteristic of the person-centered approach?
   a. Emphasis is on the subjective (phenomenal) world of the client.
   b. Emphasis is on learning in therapy derived from ongoing research.
   c. Emphasis is on the attitudes and beliefs of the therapist.
   d. Emphasis is given to a contract for therapy.
   e. Emphasis is on the personal relationship between the client and the therapist.

5. Person-centered therapy is a form of:
   a. psychoanalysis.
   b. humanistic therapy.
   c. behavioral therapy.
   d. cognitive-oriented therapy.
   e. both (c) and (d)

6. Which of the following is considered important in person-centered therapy?
   a. accurate diagnosis
   b. accurate therapist interpretation
   c. analysis of the transference relationship
   d. all of the above
   e. none of the above

7. What is the central variable related to progress in person-centered therapy?
   a. defining concrete and measurable goals
   b. the therapist's technical skills
   c. the relationship between the client and therapist
   d. the client's ability to think logically and employ the scientific method to solving problems

8. "Therapist congruence" is a term that refers to the therapist's:
   a. genuineness.
   b. empathy for clients.
   c. positive regard.
   d. respect for clients.

9. In person-centered therapy, transference is:
   a. seen as a necessary, but not sufficient, condition of therapy.
   b. viewed as a core part of the therapeutic process.
   c. regarded as a neurotic distortion.
   d. a result of ineptness on the therapist's part.
   e. not an essential or significant factor in the therapy process.

10. Which statement(s) is (are) true of the person-centered approach?
    a. Therapists should give advice when clients need it.
    b. The techniques a therapist uses are less important than his or her attitudes.
    c. Therapists should function largely as teachers
    d. Therapy is primarily the therapist's responsibility.
    e. both (c) and (d)

11. Which of the following is *not* a key concept of the person-centered approach?
    a. The focus is on experiencing the immediate moment.
    b. The person has the capacity to resolve his or her own problems in a climate of safety.
    c. The client is primarily responsible for the direction of therapy.
    d. The focus is on exploration of a client's past.

12. The person-centered therapist is best described as a:
    a. facilitator.
    b. teacher.
    c. human engineer.
    d. friend.

13. The concept of "unconditional positive regard" implies:
    a. the therapist's acceptance of the client's right to all his or her feelings.
    b. acceptance of all behavior on the client's part.
    c. the therapist's acceptance of the client without stipulations.
    d. both (a) and (c)

14. "Accurate empathic understanding" refers to the therapist's ability to:
    a. accurately diagnose the client's central problem.
    b. objectively understand the dynamics of a client.
    c. like and care for the client.
    d. sense the inner world of the client's subjective experience.

15. Which technique(s) is (are) most often used in the person-centered approach?
    a. questioning and probing
    b. analysis of resistance
    c. free association
    d. active listening and reflection

16. The person-centered approach uses which technique?
    a. diagnosis
    b. probing and questioning
    c. interpretation
    d. none of the above

17. Which statement is most true of person-centered therapy?
    a. Therapists should be judgmental at times.
    b. Therapists should direct the session when clients are silent.
    c. The skill a therapist possesses is more important than his or her attitudes toward a client.
    d. The techniques a therapist uses are less important than are his or her attitudes.
    e. both (a) and (b)

18. Which of the following is a contribution of the person-centered viewpoint?
    a. It calls attention to the need to account for a person's inner experience.
    b. It has relied on research to validate the concepts and practices of the approach.
    c. It provides the therapist with a variety of therapeutic techniques.
    d. It focuses upon an objective view of behavior.
    e. both (a) and (b)

19. What is a limitation of person-centered therapy?
    a. The approach does not make use of research to study the process or outcomes of therapy.
    b. The therapist has more power to manipulate and control the client than is true of most other therapies.
    c. People in crisis situations often need more directive intervention strategies.
    d. The client is not given enough responsibility to direct the course of his or her own therapy.
    e. It is a long-term approach to therapy.

20. One point of disagreement between existential and humanistic thought involves:
    a. a respect for the client's subjective experience.
    b. a trust in the capacity of the client to make positive choices.
    c. an emphasis on freedom.
    d. the idea of an innate self-actualizing drive.
    e. both (a) and (b)

21. Which of the following is *not* true about Carl Rogers?
    a. He was raised with strict religious standards in his home.
    b. He developed cognitive therapy.
    c. At one point in his life, he was preparing to enter the ministry.
    d. He made a contribution toward achieving world peace.
    e. He was a pioneer in humanistic approaches to counseling.

22. Which of the following is the correct order in terms of the historical development of Rogers's approach to counseling?
    a. client-centered/person-centered/nondirective
    b. client-centered/nondirective/person-centered
    c. nondirective/client-centered/person-centered
    d. nondirective/person-centered/client-centered
    e. person-centered/client-centered/nondirective

23. According to Rogerian therapy, an "internal source of evaluation" is defined as:
    a. internalizing the validation one receives from others.
    b. looking more to oneself for the answers to the problems of existence.
    c. going on one's instincts when judging the behavior of others.
    d. a neurotic tendency to be self-critical.
    e. a success identity.

24. Which of the following personal characteristics of the therapist is most important, according to Rogers?
    a. unconditional positive regard
    b. acceptance
    c. genuineness
    d. accurate empathic understanding
    e. accurate active listening

25. Which of the following is not true about the most recent trends in person-centered therapy?
    a. It could be referred to as holistic therapy.
    b. Acceptance and clarification are the main techniques used.
    c. It emphasizes an increased involvement of the therapist as a person.
    d. It allows the therapist greater freedom to be active in the therapeutic relationship.
    e. The therapist is encouraged to bring his or her values to the therapeutic relationship.

26. Rogers's current position on confronting the client is that:
    a. confrontation is to be avoided at all costs.
    b. confrontation causes clients to stop growing.
    c. confrontation reflects that the therapist has a need to be in control.
    d. caring confrontations can be beneficial.
    e. all but (d)

27. Carl Rogers drew heavily from existential concepts, especially as they apply to:
    a. the transference relationship.
    b. countertransference, or unfinished business of the counselor.
    c. the client/therapist relationship.
    d. guilt and anxiety.
    e. death and nonbeing.

28. A consistent theme that underlies most of Rogers's writings is:
    a. the need to find meaning in life through love, work, or suffering.
    b. the need for a religion to find meaning in life.
    c. the importance of expressing feelings that stem from childhood issues.
    d. a faith in the capacity of individuals to develop in a constructive manner if a climate of trust is established.
    e. the need for clients to relive past traumatic situations in the here-and-now.

29. Person-centered therapy is best conceived as:
    a. a dogma.
    b. a fixed and completed approach to therapy.
    c. a set of techniques to build trust in clients.
    d. all of the above
    e. none of the above

30. The person-centered therapist's most important function is:
    a, to begin therapy with a comprehensive lifestyle assessment.
    b. challenge clients to examine how their past influences them in the present.
    c. to be skillful in techniques of confrontation so that clients will give up their defenses.
    d. to be willing to be real in the relationship with a client.
    e. both (a) and (b)

31. From Rogers's perspective the client/therapist relationship is characterized by:
    a. a sense of equality.
    b. a reliving of the transference relationship.
    c. the therapist functioning as the expert.
    d. a clearly defined contract that specifies what clients will talk about in the sessions.
    e. none of the above

32. The person-centered approach has been applied to:
    a. personal-growth groups.
    b. training of workers in the Peace Corps and VISTA.
    c. family therapy.
    d. foreign relations.
    e. all of the above

33. One of the limitations of the person-centered approach is that:
    a. its basic tenets have not been subjected to research.
    b. it does hot have a grounding in personality theory.
    c. therapists can strip away a client's defenses by its confrontive methods,
    d. there can be a tendency to give too much support and not enough challenge.
    e. both (a) and (b)

34. One of the strengths of the person-centered approach is that:
    a. it offers a wide range of cognitive techniques to change behavior.
    b. it teaches clients ways to explore the meaning of dreams.
    c. it emphasizes reliving one's early childhood memories.
    d. therapists have the latitude to develop their own counseling style.
    e. clients are given a concrete plan to follow.

35. As a result of experiencing person-centered therapy, it is hypothesized that the client will move toward:
    a. self-trust.
    b. an internal source of evaluation.
    c. being more open to experience.
    d. a willingness to continue growing.
    e. all of the above

36. In the 1960s and 1970s Rogers did a great deal to spearhead the development of:
    a. organizational management seminars.
    b. private colleges aimed at training person-centered therapists.
    c. personal-growth groups and encounter groups.
    d. the National Training Laboratories and T-groups.
    e. registration and certification of person-centered counselors.

37. According to Rogers, the three core conditions that create a growth-promoting climate are:
    a. congruence, conditional acceptance, faith in a client.
    b. congruence, unconditional positive regard, empathic understanding.
    c. total love and caring, therapist transparency, and empathy.
    d. realness, objectively viewing the client's world, full acceptance.
    e. commitment, compassion, and confrontation.

38. Concerning research on psychotherapy, it can be said that Rogers:
    a. stated his concepts as testable hypotheses and submitted them to research.
    b. literally opened the field for psychotherapy research.
    c. inspired others to conduct extensive research on counseling process and outcome.
    d. all of the above
    e. none of the above

39. Person-centered research has been conducted predominantly on:
    a. the effectiveness of various techniques in promoting change.
    b. the hypothesized necessary and sufficient conditions of therapeutic personality change.
    c. comparing the outcomes of person-centered therapy with other approaches to therapy.
    d. follow-up studies of individual counseling.
    e. the application of the approach to specific behavioral problems.

40. Accurate empathy helps clients to:
    a. pay attention and value their experience.
    b. see earlier experiences in new ways.
    c. modify their perceptions of themselves, others, and the world.
    d. increase their confidence in making choices and in pursuing a course of action.
    e. all of the above

41. One of the limitations of the person-centered approach for counseling ethnic-minorities clients is:
    a. not enough emphasis is given to understanding the world of a client who is different from the counselor.
    b. the tendency on these clients' part to expect a more structured approach.
    c. the fact that this approach is grounded on the therapist's expertise.
    d. that it is easy to translate the core conditions into actual practice in certain cultures.
    e. none of the above.

MULTIPLE-CHOICE TEST QUESTIONS

1. C	15. D	29. E
2. D	16. D	30. D
3. E	17. D	31. A
4. D	18. E	32. E
5. B	19. C	33. D
6. E	20. D	34. D
7. C	21. B	35. E
8. A	22. C	36. C
9. E	23. B	37. B
10. B	24. C	38. D
11. D	25. B	39. B
12. A	26. D	40. E
13. D	27. C	41. B
14. D	28. D	

TRUE–FALSE TEST ITEMS FOR CHAPTER SEVEN

PERSON-CENTERED THERAPY

Decide if each of the following statements is "more true" or "more false" from the person-centered perspective.

1. Rogers's original emphasis was on reflection of feelings expressed by the client.

2. Rogers's approach is based on the assumption that humans can be trusted, that clients can find their own way without directive interpretation from therapists, and that clients have a growth urge.

3. The person-centered approach is based on a set of specific therapeutic techniques designed to promote behavior change.

4. According to Rogers, personality change will occur only when clients develop insight into the origin of their personality problems.

5. Free association and dream analysis are a typical part of the person-centered therapist's procedures.

6. Concepts developed by Rogers have been applied to schools, business, international relations, community development, and marriage and family life.

7. Congruence is a basic personality characteristic of effective therapists.

8. Therapists are best advised to withhold positive regard for clients until clients behave in such ways as to be deserving of this regard.

9. The concept of unconditional positive regard implies that therapists develop an accepting and approving attitude toward any actions taken by their clients.

10. Therapists who have little respect for their clients can anticipate that their therapeutic attempts will produce little fruit.

11. Accurate empathic understanding implies an objective understanding of a client and some form of diagnosis.

12. Diagnosis of clients is seen as the beginning point in person-centered therapy.

13. The person-centered approach evolved from a nondirective therapy to an experiential therapy.

14. The person-centered model has become a fixed theory.

15. A major contribution of this approach is Rogers's willingness to state his formulations as testable hypotheses and submit them to research.

16. Person-centered therapy places primary responsibility for the direction of therapy upon the therapist, though the therapist is directing his or her knowledge toward client goals.

17. This approach emphasizes the personal relationship between the client and therapist, stating that the therapist's attitudes are more important than specialized knowledge and skills.

18. An assumption of person-centered therapy is that the counselor's presence is far more powerful than techniques he or she uses to bring about change.

19. Rogers encourages counselors to use caring confrontations with their clients.

20. The core conditions are centered more in attitudes and values of the therapist rather than being reflected in skills.

ANSWER KEY FOR CHAPTER SEVEN – PERSON-CENTERED THERAPY

TRUE–FALSE QUESTIONS

1.	T	11.	F
2.	T	12.	F
3.	F	13.	T
4.	F	14.	F
5.	F	15.	T
6.	T	16.	F
7.	T	17.	T
8.	F	18.	T
9.	F	19.	T
10.	T	20.	T

Guidelines for Using Chapter Eight

Gestalt Therapy

in

Theory and Practice of Counseling and Psychotherapy

and the *Student Manual*

Case Approach to Counseling and Psychotherapy

and

The Art of Integrative Counseling

1. In my opinion, the Gestalt approach lends itself well to experiential exercises and activities. The **Student Manual** contains many activities that can be done both during and outside class.

2. I often begin my presentation on Gestalt therapy by having the student experience some of the Gestalt techniques and exercises. Then, after the demonstrations and small-group experiential activity, I stress the key concepts of this approach. I think it is important to talk about the rationale underlying the various Gestalt techniques, so that students are not left with the impression that Gestalt therapy is merely a bag of tricks to be learned.

3. This approach, like the existential approach, seems well suited to applying the concepts to the students' own self-exploration and personal growth. During class sessions, specific concepts I tend to focus on as they relate to the students' personal struggles are:

   - their "unfinished business"
   - ways of avoiding experiencing the "here-and-now"

- their own "catastrophic expectations"
- experiences when they felt "stuck" – the impasse

4. The Gestalt approach focuses on body language and on the client's nonverbal language. I often design exercises in class to help students become increasingly aware of their overt speaking habits, their gestures, their posture, and their tone of voice. In addition to this, I typically work with what our language patterns tell us, with a focus on using "it" for "I"; "you talk"; questions; and words that deny power.

5. If you feel comfortable enough with Gestalt, you might demonstrate how a Gestaltist might work by asking for volunteers. When I work with a volunteer in class I frequently stop and check with the student what he or she is experiencing. I stop the demonstration before we get involved in intensive exploration that might be inappropriate in the classroom setting. Also, I usually share with the volunteer and the class what I am experiencing as I am working with the person. This modeling of "what it is like for the therapist" is a crucial part of the teaching component.

6. The Gestalt approach lends itself to working with dreams. I generally demonstrate a Gestalt approach to dream work, either by working with the dream of a student, who volunteers for such work, or by giving an example of a dream and showing how I might proceed with this client's dream in a Gestalt fashion. An example of how I worked with one of my dreams is included in this chapter. I encourage students to keep a journal of their dreams, and to experiment with "Gestalting" their own dreams, by becoming each part in their dream and looking for the meaning in their dreams. We also talk about the differences between the psychoanalytic and the Gestalt approach to working with dreams.

7. **Exercise on Doing Gestalt Dream Work.** I find Gestalt therapy to be one of the most creative approaches to understanding and exploring dreams. Of course, I would want to very cautiously interpret dreams of students in classes, but I still want to give some opportunity for applying the principles of dream work that are described in the text to the students' personal lives. Below is an illustration of a dream I had many years ago that I have used as a demonstration of applying Gestalt ideas. The dream is always reported in the present tense, as can be seen in my account that follows.

The Dream. I am talking with the principal of Whittier High School (a school where I used to teach). He is telling me that he is annoyed with me because I expected a private office and a three-day teaching schedule. I reply: "I didn't *demand* a private office, I merely requested one. I wonder why you seem so irritated?" He keeps telling me that he is put off by my demanding tone of voice and that he sees me as being unreasonable. I tell him that I also want to do more than teach standard courses; I would like to offer therapy groups for adolescents in the school. He immediately seems closed to the idea and tells me that it cannot be done. I continue to argue with him, and I say: "I don't enjoy arguing with you, but I won't be a 'yes man' either. After all, I've written a lot of books, and I think that ought to count for something." Then a car hits his car (the one we are riding in together), and I want to pursue our conversation. He says, "Now is not a good time for me to talk." I reply: "Well, let me see if I hear what you are saying. You really seem to object to my tone and manner." He is obviously preoccupied with his smashed fender and the other driver, who is taking off after hitting his car. At the same time, I am insisting on finishing this discussion!

Become the Dream. The Gestalt approach to exploring the messages of the dream is to "become" each of the various parts of the dream. Let me illustrate:
- *Be the principal*: "I wish you'd get off my back. You're continually asking for special treatment, and after all I have a lot of other teachers. I have to treat everyone the same."
- *Be Jerry Corey*: "Look, if I don't at least tell you what I'd like, then you'll never know, and I'll never get it. I can contribute in some special ways, and I'd like the chance to do this."
- *Be the principal's gray hair* (he had gray hair in the dream): "I'm older and wiser than you are. It's not your place to argue with me. Listen to me, and don't come at me with special requests."
- *Be Jerry Corey's books* (I was trying to tell him of my writing): "Notice me as important, damn it! I am special! I'm read and appreciated by many students in many places. Don't shove me aside!"
- *Be the smashed fender, and talk to the principal:* "I'm hurt and need immediate attention. The woman who hit me is speeding away. I'll push in against the tire and cut the tire, and then you can't move."
- *Be the principal talking to the bent fender:* "This is an important matter. I need to catch the woman who hit my car. Look at what she did to you, and she's just running off without telling me."

- *Be Jerry Corey, and talk to the fender:* "Gee, it's a shame that you're all bent that way and that she's speeding away. Maybe I can see her license plate. Nope, it's too faint. Oh well, what's the big deal, you're only a fender—one of many."

Commentary. This can go on for some time, with dialogue between various parts of the dream. It's important that I avoid intellectualizing about the dream or merely reporting *about* the dream in the past tense. As much as possible, it is useful to really relive my dream, fully "get into" each role, and let uncensored reactions flow. It helps me to change voices and inflections as I become each part of my dream. Once this process is done, it is useful for me to ask: "What is the main feeling I get from my dream? What is my dream telling me?" One of the messages I get from my dream is that I won't settle for being ignored or brushed away. I want the freedom to work in my own way, yet I have some fear that an "authority figure" will tell me what to do and won't take me seriously. I feel that I have to fight at times to keep my identity and not get lost in the shuffle.

Recording and Working with Your Dreams

Attempt for a period to recall (or, even better, write down) your dreams. Practice reliving your dreams via here-and-now Gestalt procedures. Try to let yourself go, censoring as little as possible. Make your dreams come alive! Don't worry about being appropriate or correct. Just create a script with the material provided in your dream, and let interactions happen with these parts of your dream. It would be ideal for you to report your dreams in the present tense into a tape recorder and to actually "Gestalt" these dreams on tape. Make comments and observations *after* you have done this. You may become aware of certain patterns and clear messages. It could be an interesting class exercise to at least share in small groups what this process is like for you, even if you do not interpret one another's dreams.

8. **Other Resources:** In addition to the cases of Ruth and Christina given in Chapter 8 of the *Student Manual*, you may want to refer to three other resources: *Case Approach; The Art of Integrative Counseling* book; and the *CD ROM for Integrative Counseling.*

   Refer to the *Case Approach to Counseling and Psychotherapy* (6th ed., 2005) for a detailed treatment of the case of Ruth from the perspective of a Gestalt therapist. In Chapter 6 both Dr. Jon Frew describes his views of assessment and key themes he would focus on in working with Ruth.

   Refer to the book *The Art of Integrative Counseling* for discussions of Gestalt therapy from a number of vantage points. In Chapter 5 (pp. 48–53) I demonstrate Gestalt approaches in working with resistance. On pages 55–56 I show how I draw on Gestalt therapy in dealing with resistance with Ruth. Chapter 7, *Emotive Focus in Counseling*, draws very heavily upon Gestalt concepts and methods, especially in the section *Becoming the Client: Experiencing Emotionally Focused Therapy*, (pp. 70–73). I also demonstrate working with Ruth in Gestalt ways on pages 75–77. See also Chapter 9, *The Foundation of My Integrative Approach*, pp. 92–95, for a discussion of how I incorporate Gestalt therapy into my integrative approach. Chapters 7 and 9 of this text tie in very nicely to the corresponding sessions in the video.

   In the *CD ROM for Integrative Counseling* (see Session #7 *Emotive Focus*) I demonstrate how I create experiments to heighten Ruth's awareness. In this video segment I employ a Gestalt experiment whereby Ruth talks to me as John, in which she becomes quite emotional. In the book, *The Art of Integrative Counseling*, there is considerable discussion of Gestalt experiments in Chapters 7, 9, and 11.

9. The following are books that I consider "musts" in preparing my lectures:
   - *Gestalt Therapy Verbatim* (Perls, 1969)
   - *Gestalt Therapy Integrated* (Polster & Polster, 1973)

   Other useful books for getting ideas for lectures include:
   - *Creative Process in Gestalt Therapy* (Zinker, 1978)
   - *Awareness, Dialogue and Process: Essays on Gestalt Therapy* (Yontef, 1993)
   - *The Healing Relationship in Gestalt Therapy: A Dialogic/Self Psychology Approach* (Hycner & Jacobs, 1995).
   - *From the Radical Center: The Heart of Gestalt Therapy* (E. Polster & Polster, 1999).

KEY TERMS FOR REVIEW AND DEFINITION

Fritz Perls
awareness
the "now ethos"
"why" questions
unfinished business
layers of neurosis
contact
resistances to contact
introjection
projection
retroflection
Field theory
blocks to energy
catastrophic expectations
impasse or "stuck point"
projection screen
confluence
deflection
"You" talk
questions
language that denies power
"shoulds" and "oughts"
I/Thou relationship
Exercises

the dialogue experiment
making the rounds
playing the projection
reversal technique
the rehearsal experiment
staying with the feeling
dream work
empty chair technique
integration of polarities
body language
energy
exaggeration exercise
holism
Laura Posner Perls
here-and-now experiencing
figure-formation process
ground or background
organismic self-regulation
internal dialogue exercise
boundary disturbance
"top dog"
"underdog"
confrontation
experiments

INFOTRAC KEYWORDS

The following keywords are listed in such a way as to allow the *InfoTrac* search engine to locate a wider range of articles on the online university library. The keywords should be entered *exactly* as listed below, to include astericks, "W1," "W2," "AND," and other search engine tools.

Gestalt AND therapy
Confrontation AND psychol*
Projection AND psychol*
Gestalt psychology

Awareness AND psych*
Awareness AND therap*
Gestalt Therapy
Introjection

CASE EXAMPLES

KAREN: Anxiety over choosing for herself

Assume the perspective of a Gestalt therapist, and show how you would proceed with Karen, a 27-year-old Asian American who is struggling with value conflicts pertaining to her religion, culture, and sex-role expectations. Here is what she has related to you during the first session.

Throughout her life Karen has identified herself as a "good Catholic" who has not questioned much of her upbringing. She has never really seen herself as an independent woman; in many ways she feels like a child, one who is strongly seeking approval and directions from those whom she consider authorities. Karen tells you that in her culture she was taught to respect and honor her parents, teachers, priests, and other elders. Whenever she tries to assert her own will, if it differs from the expectations of any authority figure, she experiences guilt and self-doubt. She went to Catholic schools, including college, and she has followed the morals and teachings of her church very closely. She has not been married, nor has she even had a long-term relationship with a man. Karen has not had sexual intercourse, not because she has not wanted to but because she is afraid that she could not live with herself and her guilt. She feels very restricted by the codes she lives by, and in many ways she sees them as rigid and unrealistic. Yet she is frightened of breaking away from what she was taught, even though she is seriously questioning much of its validity and is aware that *her* views on morality are growing more and more divergent from those that she at one time accepted. Basically, Karen asks: "What if I am wrong? Who am I to decide what is moral and immoral? I've always been taught that morals are clear-cut and do not allow for individual conveniences. I find it difficult to accept many of the teachings of my church, but I'm not able to really leave behind those notions that I don't accept. What if there is a hell, and I'll be damned forever if I follow my own path? What if I discover that I 'go wild' and thus lose any measure of self-respect? Will I be able to live with my guilt if I don't follow the morality I've been taught?"

Karen is also struggling with the impact of cultural restraints on her view of what it means to be a woman. Generally, she sees herself as being dependent, unassertive, fearful of those in authority, emotionally reserved, socially inhibited, and unable to make decisions about her life. Although she thinks that she would like to be more assertive and would like to feel freer to be herself around people, she is highly self-conscious and "hears voices in her head" that tell her how she should and should not be. She wishes she could be different in some important respects, but she wonders if she is strong enough to swim against what she has learned from her culture, her parents, and her church.

Assume that Karen is coming for a series of counseling sessions in a community clinic. You know the above information about her, and what she wants from you is help in sorting out what she really believes about living a moral life versus what she has been told is the moral way to be. She says that she would like to learn how to trust herself and, in essence, have the courage to know her convictions and live by them. At the same time, she feels unable to act on her values, for fear that she will be wrong. How would you proceed with her?

1. What do you see as Karen's basic conflict? How would you summarize the nature of her struggle?

2. Do you think that in some ways she might be looking to you as another authority figure to tell her that it is all right for her to reject some of the moral codes she was taught and to follow her own? How might you test out this possibility? How could you help her without becoming another source of either approval or disapproval for her?

3. This case raises a number of key issues for you to consider, a few of which are:

   a. Can you respect her cultural values and at the same time help her make the changes she wants, even if they go against some of her traditions?

   b. Perhaps the values of her culture specify that women should be somewhat reserved, unassertive, emotionally restrained, and deferential to authority. Would you attempt to help her adjust to these cultural norms, or would you encourage her to live by a new set of standards?

   c. Would you be able to avoid imposing your own views or values on Karen? In what direction would you encourage her to move, if any?

   d. What are your views pertaining to sex-role and gender issues that are apparent in this case? How would your values here affect the interventions you make with Karen?

4. Below are some Gestalt techniques that you might consider using with Karen. Check those that you think you would use:

_____ Ask her to carry on a dialogue between different parts or sides of a conflict.

_____ Invite her to have a dialogue between the Asian side of her and the American side of her.

_____ Suggest that she write an uncensored letter (that she does not mail) to one of her parents. in which she tells them the ways in which she would like to be different than she is expected to be.

_____ Invite her to create a dialogue between an assertive woman and an unassertive woman.

_____ Ask her to rehearse out loud whatever she is thinking.

_____ Ask her to "become" a significant authority and then lecture to "Karen" in an empty chair.

_____ Ask her to carry on a fantasy dialogue with her boyfriend and say to him everything that she has not yet told him.

_____ Ask her to imagine herself being as wild as possible, along with the worst things that could happen if she were to lose all control.

5. List some other Gestalt-oriented techniques that you might use in your session with Karen:

6. Karen says that she feels very restricted by her morals and sees them as rigid and unrealistic. At the same time, she is frightened of breaking away from what she was taught. Thinking in a Gestalt framework, how might you proceed with helping her sort through her values and clarify them for herself?

7. What are your values as they pertain to the issues that Karen has brought up, and how do you think they will affect the way in which you counsel her? Explain.

LINDA: In crisis over her pregnancy

Assume that you are a counselor in a community mental-health clinic, that you have a Gestalt orientation, and that the counselor at the local high school tells you about Linda, a 15-year-old client he has seen several times. He feels that she needs further counseling, but he is limited by a school policy that does not permit personal counseling of any duration. He would like for you to see her for at least three months, as she is facing some difficult decisions. Here is what you learn about her from the counselor.

Some Background Data:

Linda comes from a close-knit family, and in general she feels that she can seek her parents out when she has problems. But now she says that she just *cannot* turn to them in this time of crisis. Even though she and her boyfriend had been engaging in sexual intercourse for a year without using birth-control measures, she was convinced that she would not get pregnant. When she did learn that she was pregnant, she expected that her 16-year-old boyfriend would agree to get married. He did not agree, and he even questioned whether he was the father. She felt deeply hurt and angry over this. On the advice of a girlfriend, she considered an abortion for a time. But she decided against it because she felt she could not deal with the guilt of terminating a life within her. The possibility of putting her child up for adoption was suggested to her. But she felt this to be totally unacceptable, because she was sure she could not live knowing that she had created a life and then "abandoned" the child. She considered having her baby and becoming a single parent. Yet when the counselor pointed out all the realities involved in this choice, she could see that this option would not work – unless she told her parents and lived with them, which she was *sure* she could not do. Her pregnancy is moving toward the advanced stages, and her panic is mounting.

Questions for Reflection:

Linda agrees to work with you for several months, and you will be using Gestalt procedures with her.

1. What do you imagine would be your initial reactions and responses to the counselor's account? What might your first words be to Linda after you were introduced to her? What do you think you would *most* want to say to her?

2. What are *your values* as they relate to the above matters, and what role do you see your values playing in the approach you will take with Linda? Might you be inclined to share your values, so that she knows where you stand? Might you be inclined to push your values and thus steer counseling in a particular direction?

3. At some point you might work with Linda's feelings of anger and hurt toward her boyfriend. What Gestalt techniques can you think of to help her explore these feelings? What techniques could you use to work with her feelings of guilt over not having lived up to her parents' high expectations? What other Gestalt approaches might you use (with what expected outcomes) to explore with Linda her other feelings associated with being pregnant?

4. As you proceed with Linda, what importance will you place on her nonverbal communication? Can you think of examples of how Linda's body messages might contradict her words?

5. What are the limitations, if any, of staying within a Gestalt framework in this case? Do you feel that you could say and do what you would like within this theory?

6. What are some advantages of using a Gestalt perspective in this case?

STUDY GUIDE FOR CHAPTER EIGHT

GESTALT THERAPY

1. In what way is Gestalt therapy a form of existential therapy? How is the approach experiential? What is the primary focus of this approach?

2. Summarize the view of human nature underlying Gestalt, and explain its implications for counseling.

3. Define the following important terms in Gestalt and provide examples of each: awareness, confluence, confrontation, deflection, dichotomy, experiments, introjection, modes of defense, projection, retroflection, unfinished business. (See *Student Manual.*)

4. How is "the now" a basic concept in Gestalt? How is the past dealt with in this approach? How about the future?

5. How does unfinished business from the past manifest itself in current behavior? What is the most frequent source of unfinished business?

6. What is the impasse, and how is it worked with in this approach? How is the impasse related to avoidance?

7. What is the Gestalt view of energy and blocks to energy? How is this frequently manifested in the body, and how can you combine Gestalt and body oriented methods?

8. What are the important therapeutic goals of Gestalt theory? How does the therapist's role/function relate to accomplishing these goals? In discussing the therapist's function, bring in issues such as: paying attention to the client's body language, noting client's language patterns, role of interpretation, frustrating the client, and creating experiments.

9. What are the client's responsibilities in therapy? How is the relationship between client and counselor viewed in Gestalt?

10. Discuss the importance of preparing clients for Gestalt techniques. How might you modify Gestalt techniques in working with a culturally diverse population?

11. What role does confrontation play in Gestalt therapy? What are some guidelines for effective confrontation?

12. Know the rationale underlying the techniques of Gestalt therapy. What is the main purpose of most of the experiments created in the Gestalt process? Be able to briefly describe these techniques, such as the dialogue experiment, reversal technique, rehearsal technique, working with dreams, etc.

13. What is the essence of the Gestalt approach to dream work? How would a Gestalt therapist help a client to understand the meaning of his or her own dreams?

14. Mention some applications of Gestalt approaches. How can it be used in individual counseling? group counseling? With what kind of clients (or problems) is Gestalt most effective? least effective?

15. What is your critique of Gestalt therapy? Mention what you see as its major contribution and its major limitation. In working with culturally diverse clients, what guidelines might you employ in the use of Gestalt techniques? What are some contributions and limitations of Gestalt therapy with culturally diverse populations? What aspects of this approach would you be inclined to incorporate into your own style of counseling?

Test Items

Chapter Eight

Theory and Practice of

Counseling and Psychotherapy

GESTALT THERAPY

1. The founder of Gestalt therapy is:
    a. Carl Rogers.
    b. Carl Whitaker.
    c. Albert Ellis.
    d. William Glasser.
    e. none of the above

2. Gestalt therapy is a form of:
    a. Freudian psychoanalytic therapy.
    b. neo-Freudian analytic therapy.
    c. behavior therapy.
    d. existential therapy.

3. Which is not true of Gestalt therapy?
    a. The focus is on the *what* and *how* of behavior.
    b. The focus is on the here-and-now.
    c. The focus is on integrating fragmented parts of the personality.
    d. The focus is on unfinished business from the past.
    e. The focus is on the *why* of behavior.

4. Which of the following is not a key concept of Gestalt therapy?
    a. acceptance of personal responsibility
    b. intellectual understanding of one's problems
    c. awareness
    d. unfinished business
    e. dealing with the impasse

5. According to the Gestalt view:
    a. awareness is by and of itself therapeutic.
    b. awareness is a necessary, but not sufficient, condition for change.
    c. awareness without specific behavioral change is useless.
    d. awareness consists of understanding the causes of one's problems.

6. The basic goal of Gestalt therapy is to assist the client to:
    a. move from environmental support to self-support.
    b. uncover his or her cognitive distortions.
    c. uncover unconscious motivations.
    d. work through the transference relationship with the therapist.
    e. challenge his or her philosophy of life.

7. The *impasse* is the point in therapy at which clients:
    a. avoid experiencing threatening feelings.
    b. experience a sense of "being stuck."
    c. imagine something terrible will happen.
    d. all of the above
    e. none of the above

8. The Gestalt therapist:
    a. freely makes interpretations for the client.
    b. pays attention to the client's nonverbal language.
    c. is mainly nondirective.
    d. helps the client understand why he or she is behaving in self-defeating ways.
    e. all of the above

9. Gestalt therapy can best be characterized as:
   a. an insight therapy.
   b. an experiential therapy.
   c. an action-oriented therapy.
   d. all of the above
   e. none of the above

10. When a person experiences an internal conflict (namely a conflict between top dog and underdog), which of the following techniques would be most appropriate?
   a. making the rounds
   b. reversal technique
   c. dialogue technique
   d. the rehearsal experiment
   e. the exaggeration experiment

11. Gestalt-therapy techniques are designed to help the client:
   a. expand awareness of the here-and-now.
   b. intensify feelings and experiencing.
   c. make a value judgment of his or her behavior.
   d. free himself or herself of specific behavioral symptoms.
   e. both (a) and (b)

12. A Gestalt technique that is most useful when a person attempts to deny an aspect of his or her personality (such as tenderness) is:
   a. making the rounds.
   b. reversal technique.
   c. the rehearsal experiment.
   d. playing the projection.

13. The Gestalt approach to dreams:
   a. rests with the therapist's skill in interpreting the meanings of the dreams to the client.
   b. consists of teaching the client the universal meanings of symbols in dreams.
   c. asks the client to become all parts of his or her own dream.
   d. has the client interpret and discover the meaning of the dream for himself or herself.
   e. both (c) and (d)

14. Gestalt therapy encourages clients to:
   a. experience feelings intensely.
   b. stay in the here-and-now.
   c. work through the impasse.
   d. pay attention to their own nonverbal messages.
   e. all of the above

15. The basic goal of Gestalt therapy is:
   a. attaining awareness, and with it greater choice.
   b. to understand why we feel as we do.
   c. to uncover repressed material.
   d. all of the above
   e. none of the above

16. A limitation of Gestalt therapy is that:
   a. it does not specify techniques.
   b. it is not grounded in solid theory.
   c. it discounts cognitive factors in therapy.
   d. it dwells too much on the past.
   e. both (b) and (c)

17. A contribution of this therapeutic approach is that:
    a. it enables intense experiencing to occur quickly.
    b. it can be a relatively brief therapy.
    c. it stresses doing and experiencing, as opposed to talking about problems.
    d. all of the above
    e. none of the above

18. According to Gestalt theory, people use avoidance in order to:
    a. keep themselves from facing unfinished business.
    b. keep from feeling uncomfortable emotions.
    c. keep from having to change.
    d. all the above
    e. both (a) and (b)

19. Perls's concept of the five layers of neurosis includes all of the following except:
    a. the phony layer.
    b. the borderline layer.
    c. the impasse layer.
    d. the implosive layer.
    e. the phobic layer.

20. According to Gestalt theory, all of the following are true about contact except:
    a. contact is necessary for change and growth to occur.
    b. one does not lose one's sense of individuality as a result of good contact.
    c. withdrawal after a good contact experience indicates neurosis.
    d. contact is made by seeing, hearing, smelling, touching, and moving.
    e. we often tend to resist contact with others.

21. In Gestalt therapy, the relationship between client and counselor is seen as:
    a. a joint venture.
    b. an existential encounter.
    c. an I/Thou interaction.
    d. both (a) and (b)
    e. all of the above

22. Which of the following is not true about Gestalt techniques?
    a. "Exercises" are ready-made techniques.
    b. "Experiments" grow out of the interaction between therapist and client.
    c. Clients need to be prepared for their involvement in Gestalt techniques.
    d. Experiments are always carried out during the therapy session, rather than outside it.
    e. Techniques are for the purpose of increasing the client's awareness.

23. Which of the following is not true about Fritz Perls?
    a. He developed Gestalt therapy.
    b. During his childhood, he was a model student.
    c. He was trained in psychoanalysis.
    d. He gave workshops and seminars at the Esalen Institute.
    e. He aroused various reactions in the people he met.

24. Gestalt therapists say that clients resist contact by means of:
    a. retroflection.
    b. projection.
    c. introjection.
    d. all of the above
    e. both (a) and (c)

25. Which of the following aspects of a client's use of language would a Gestalt therapist not focus on?
    a. "it" talk
    b. "you" talk
    c. questions
    d. language that denies power
    e. semantics

26. Which of the following is not true about the Gestalt view of the role of confrontation in therapy?
    a. It is not possible to be both confrontive and gentle with clients.
    b. It is important to confront clients with the ways they are avoiding being fully alive.
    c. Confrontation does not have to be aimed at negative traits.
    d. Confrontation should be a genuine expression of caring.

27. Which of the following Gestalt techniques involves asking one person in a group to speak to each of the other group members?
    a. playing the projection
    b. reversal technique
    c. making the rounds
    d. the exaggeration technique

28. The process of distraction, or fleeting awareness, that makes it difficult to maintain sustained contact is the definition of:
    a. introjection.
    b. projection.
    c. retroflection.
    d. confluence.
    e. deflection.

29. The process of turning back to ourselves what we would like to do to someone else is the definition of:
    a. introjection.
    b. projection.
    c. retroflection.
    d. confluence.

30. The tendency to uncritically accept others' beliefs without assimilating or internalizing them is the definition of:
    a. introjection.
    b. projection.
    c. retroflection.
    d. confluence.

31. The process of the blurring of awareness of differentiation between the self and the environment is the definition of:
    a. introjection.
    b. projection.
    c. retroflection.
    d. confluence.

32. What is a limitation (or limitations) of Gestalt therapy as it is applied to working with culturally diverse populations?
    a. Clients who have been culturally conditioned to be emotionally reserved might not see value in experiential techniques.
    b. Clients may be "put off" by a focus on catharsis.
    c. Clients may believe that to show one's vulnerability is to be weak.
    d. all of the above

ANSWER KEY FOR CHAPTER EIGHT – GESTALT THERAPY

MULTIPLE-CHOICE TEST QUESTIONS

1. E	12. B.	23. B
2. D	13. E	24. D
3. E	14. E	25. E
4. B	15. A	26. A
5. A	16. E	27. C
6. A	17. D	28. E
7. D	18. D	29. C
8. B	19. B	30. A
9. B	20. C	31. D
10. C	21. E	32. D
11. E	22. D	

TRUE–FALSE TEST ITEMS FOR CHAPTER EIGHT

GESTALT THERAPY

Decide if each of the following statements is "more true" or "more false" from the perspective of Gestalt therapy.

1. Gestalt theory is best considered as a form of psychoanalytic therapy.

2. The Gestalt therapist typically uses diagnosis and interpretation as a basic part of the therapeutic process.

3. One of the functions of the Gestalt therapist is to pay attention to the client's body language.

4. A Gestalt therapist pays attention to ways the client uses language.

5. Therapy is based upon the successful resolution of the transference relationship.

6. Both contact and withdrawal are necessary and important to healthy functioning.

7. Gestalt therapy makes use of a wide variety of techniques that are designed to increase the client's awareness of his or her present experiencing.

8. According to Perls, awareness of and by itself is not sufficient to lead to change; clients must also put their experiences into some type of cognitive framework if change is to happen.

9. The Gestalt approach to dream work consists of the therapist interpreting the meaning of the symbols in the dream.

10. Gestalt therapy relies mainly on psychoanalytic techniques.

11. Gestalt therapy is designed for individual counseling, and it typically does not work well in groups.

12. One of the contributions of Gestalt therapy is the vast empirical research that has been done to validate the specific techniques used.

13. The goal of Gestalt therapy is to solve basic problems, to resolve one's polarities, and to help the individual to adjust to his or her environment.

14. Gestaltists typically ask *why* questions in the attempt to get clients to think about the source of their problems.

15. Gestalt therapy focuses on the cognitive aspects of therapy.

16. Gestalt techniques can be considered as experiments.

17. Part of success in using Gestalt techniques is contingent upon preparing clients for these techniques.

18. Most of the Gestalt techniques are designed to intensify one's experiencing.

19. Gestalt therapies view a client's avoidance behavior as related to unfinished business.

20. When we experience our "explosive" layer, we let go of phony roles and pretenses and we release a tremendous amount of energy that we have been holding in by pretending to be who we are not.

21. Retroflection involves doing to others what we would like them to do to us.

22. In Gestalt therapy, a client's resistance is welcomed and used to deepen their therapeutic work.

23. Gestalt experiments are ready-made techniques that are often used to evoke the expression of certain emotions.

24. A current trend in Gestalt therapy is toward greater emphasis on the client/therapist relationship rather than on techniques divorced from the context of this encounter.

25. Gestalt therapists focus more on *why* clients are doing than *what* they are doing.

26. Since Gestalt therapy focuses on the here-and-now, the past is not explored or given emphasis in this approach.

27. In Gestalt therapy, resistance refers to defenses we develop that prevent us from experiencing the present in a full and real way.

28. Preparing clients for Gestalt exercises destroys both their spontaneity and effectiveness.

29. Although Perls used a highly confrontational approach in dealing with client avoidance and resistance, the confrontational model is not representative of contemporary Gestalt therapy.

ANSWER KEY FOR CHAPTER EIGHT – GESTALT THERAPY

TRUE–FALSE QUESTIONS

1.	F	15.	F
2.	F	16.	T
3.	T	17.	T
4.	T	18.	T
5.	F	19.	T
6.	T	20.	T
7.	T	21.	F
8.	F	22.	T
9.	F	23.	F
10.	F	24.	T
11.	F	25.	F
12.	F	26.	F
13.	F	27.	T
14.	F	28.	F
		29.	T

Guidelines for Using Chapter Nine

Behavior Therapy

in

Theory and Practice of Counseling and Psychotherapy and the *Student Manual*

Case Approach to Counseling and Psychotherapy

and

The Art of Integrative Counseling

1. In the ***Student Manual***, I have an outline for designing a self-management program. For students who want to actually apply behavioral principles to changing some of their behavior, I have encouraged them to get involved in a self-directed change program. This might relate to weight control, teaching oneself relaxation methods in coping with stress, or learning how to stick to an exercise program. A reference that I often suggest for those who want to learn more about a self-directed program for change is: Watson and Tharp (2002) *Self-Directed Behavior: Self-Modification for Personal Adjustment*.

2. The questions in the ***Student Manual*** can be used for class discussion and lecture material. They are also appropriate for panel presentations, debates, take-home position papers, and essay-exam questions.

3. The *Questions for Reflections and Discussion* and the *Issues for Personal Application* in the ***Student Manual*** are designed to give students practice in translating general therapeutic goals into concrete goals. I ask my students to complete these exercises before they come to class for the lecture/lab session on behavior therapy. During our experiential or laboratory session of that class, various students are asked to state the specific goals they wrote. Sometimes I do this as an entire-class activity, and other times I have them share their responses in smaller subgroups.

   As part of this exercise, the students are also asked to practice learning how to develop their own personal goals in specific terms. In their ***Manual*** the students are asked to design a self-management program and to list

119

specific behavioral changes they might want for themselves. In the *Practical Application* section of the **Student Manual** students are asked to translate broad goals into specific goals and to list concrete goals. From here there are several possibilities:

a. Students can be asked to discuss what it is like for them to define specific and concrete goals, as opposed to broad and elusive goals.

b. Students can be asked how they would go about acquiring the behavioral changes they desire.

c. After doing the above, students can participate in role-playing exercises using a behavior-therapy approach. One student can volunteer to be the "client," and either a student or the instructor can become the "therapist" and demonstrate how to work with this client by using specific behavioral techniques.

4. There are some *Suggested Activities and Exercises* for behavior therapy in the **Student Manual**.

a. One exercise is designed to show students how they can apply behavioral techniques by self-control methods. Consider giving a lecture on the topic of self-relaxation procedures, as well as conduct a classroom demonstration. Students can then practice these techniques outside of class, and in a week or two can report back on their progress in learning relaxation procedures.

b. To illustrate assertion training, you can use the same suggestions as given in (a) above. For useful readings for your lectures I suggest Alberti and Emmons (2001a), *Your Perfect Right: A Guide to Assertive Behavior*; and Alberti and Emmons (2001b), *Your Perfect Right: A Manual for Assertiveness Trainers.*

During a lab session I will first give lecture material on the key concepts associated with assertive training in interpersonal relationships. I ask for volunteers from the class, and specific social situations are explored. Role-playing, modeling, coaching, behavior rehearsal, feedback, experimenting, and practice are all a vital part of this demonstration.

5. As is the case with each of these theory chapters, I briefly describe a behavior therapist's way of working with Stan in the textbook. Students can gain practice by counseling Stan from a behavioral perspective. Either the instructor or a student can play the role of Stan, while one or more students can work with him behaviorally.

6. In the *Summary and Evaluation* section in the textbook, I list some commonly raised major objections to behavior therapy. You may want to raise these criticisms before the students read the chapter and have them evaluate and explore their preconceived notions toward this approach. As another suggestion, you may ask the students to discuss their reactions to my replies to each of these criticisms.

7. **Other Resources:** In addition to the cases (Ruth and Sally) given in Chapter 9 of the **Student Manual**, you may want to refer to three other resources: **Case Approach; Art of Integrative Counseling** book; and the **CD ROM for Integrative Counseling.**

Refer to the **Case Approach to Counseling and Psychotherapy** (6th ed., 2005) for a detailed treatment of the case of Ruth from the perspective of behavior therapists. In Chapter 8 Dr. Arnold Lazarus describes his multimodal assessment of Ruth, shows how he selects techniques based on the assessment, and describes a conjoint session with Ruth and her husband. Additionally, Dr. Barbara D'Angelo describes a systematic application of behavioral concepts applied to Ruth. I follow up with my own style of drawing on behavior therapy concepts in counseling Ruth.

Refer to the book **The Art of Integrative Counseling** book, Chapter 8 (*Behavioral Focus in Counseling*) for a discussion of how to apply behavioral concepts and techniques in counseling practice. On page 80 I identify some of the benefits and limitations of a behavioral focus. On pages 81–82 I describe how the seven modalities of human functioning can be a crucial aspect of assessment. See pages 85–86 for specific suggestions for creating an action plan based on a behavioral contract. I describe a behavioral focus with Ruth on pages 86–88, which coordinates with the video.

In the **CD ROM for Integrative Counseling** you will note ways that I attempt to assist Ruth in specifying concrete behaviors that she will target for change (see Session #8, *Behavioral Focus*). I do this in considerable more detail in **The Art of Integrative Counseling** book in Chapter 8.

8. Books in behavior therapy that I draw on for preparing lectures include:

- *Contemporary Behavior Therapy* (Spiegler & Guevremont, 2003)
- *Interviewing and Change Strategies for Helpers: Fundamental Skills and Cognitive Behavioral Interventions* (Cormier & Nurius, 2003)
- *Behavior Modification: Principles and Procedures* (Miltenberger, 2004)
- *Behavior Modification in Applied Settings* (Kazdin, 2001)
- *Brief But Comprehensive Psychotherapy: The Multimodal Way* (Lazarus, 1997a)
- *Self-Directed Behavior: Self-Modification for Personal Adjustment* (Watson and Tharp, 2002)

KEY TERMS FOR REVIEW AND DEFINITION

B. F. Skinner
behavior modification
behavior theory
classical conditioning
operant conditioning
cognitive trend/processes
self-management
self-directed behavior
self-monitoring
behavioral diary
self-reinforcement
self-contracting
self-training therapy
mediational concepts
scientific method
goal setting
summary statement
contingency contracting
phobic behavior
relaxation training
autogenic training
social reinforcement
behavior rehearsal
modeling
feedback
flooding
stress inoculation
reinforcement
negative reinforcement
positive reinforcement
behavioral assessment
social skills training
self-efficacy
applied behavioral analysis
punishment
positive punishment

systematic desensitization
biofeedback
meditation procedures
hypnosis
reinforcers
target behaviors
reinforcement techniques
homework
observational learning
imitation
multimodal therapy
technical eclecticism
cognitive behavioral coping skills
the BASIC I. D.
ethical accountability
Joseph Wolpe
Arnold Lazarus
Hans Eysenck
Albert Bandura
E. Jacobson
homework assignments
social learning
exposure therapy
assertion training
in vivo desensitization
eye movement desensitzation and
    reprocessing, (EMDR)
technical eclecticism
Donald Meichenbaum
Albert Ellis
visualization techniques
Francine Shapiro
generalization of learning
extinction
functional assessment
negative punishment

The following keywords are listed in such a way as to allow the ***InfoTrac*** search engine to locate a wider range of articles on the online university library. The keywords should be entered *exactly* as listed below, to include astericks, "W1," "W2," "AND," and other search engine tools.

EMDR	Social-learning W1 theory
Behavior W1 modification	Cognitive W1 processes
Exposure W1 therapy	Reinforcer
Classical W1 conditioning	Operant W1 conditioning

Behavior Therapy

Albert Bandura
Donald Meichenbaum
Ivan Pavlov
B.F. Skinner
E.L. Thorndike
Classical conditioning
Operant conditioning
Social Cognitive Theory
Social Learning Theory
Overt behavior
Positive reinforcement
Observational learning
Covert behavior
Cognitive W1 process*
Systematic desensitization
Exposure W1 therapy
Exposure and response prevention
Eye movement desensitization and reprocessing

CASE EXAMPLES

EDDIE: An attention-getting child

A third-grade teacher seeks your professional help with an 8-year-old boy in her class. She tells you that Eddie's behavior is highly disruptive because he is continually acting out his problems in a hostile or aggressive manner. He punches other children for no apparent reason, tears up others' work, rarely follows instructions, continually talks at times that are disruptive, and draws attention to himself through negative behavior. He seems to take delight in seeing other children get angry.

The teacher tells you that she is at a loss to know how to deal with Eddie's behavior. She considered asking that he be removed from her classroom, but she hesitated because she believes that he has many pressing conflicts and is a deeply troubled child. She asks you to see him for a session and give her some guidance in dealing with his behavior.

You see Eddie for an individual session, during which you discover that his father is both verbally and physically abusive. Without provocation his father calls him names and beats him up. One time, Eddie was beaten so badly that he had severe cuts and bruises, and his father threatened him with a "real beating" if he did not agree to say that he had had a bicycle accident. You also discover that Eddie comes from a single-parent family. His father has had custody since his parents divorced when he was in preschool. Eddie tells you that he would feel really lost if he didn't have his father. He thinks that maybe he has done many wrong things to deserve the treatment he gets.

Working within a behavioral framework, show how you would proceed in this session with Eddie so that you might be in a better position to make recommendations to his teacher and might offer him some direct help yourself.

1. What goals would you have in mind during this session? How would you attempt to meet them? What questions would you ask of Eddie? How might you approach the issue of his disruptive behavior in class? What might you want to tell him? What would you tell his teacher?

2. What speculations can you offer about the reasons for Eddie's disruptive behavior? Where might he have learned his aggressive behaviors?

3. How do you expect that you would handle the issue of Eddie's beatings by his father? How would you deal with Eddie on this matter? Might you approach his father? If so, what would you say, and what would you hope to accomplish? Might you consult the authorities? What are your legal obligations in this case?

4. During your session what behaviors would you most want to observe? What would you do with your observations as far as Eddie is concerned? How much would you share with him of what you know from his teacher and of what you actually observe?

5. Would the fact that Eddie comes from a single-parent home influence your interventions? How would you deal with him when he told you that he would be lost without his father?

6. If you were to continue working with Eddie as his counselor, what *specific behavioral procedures* might you employ, and toward what end?

KATHRINA: Learning to cope with anxiety

Kathrina, a Native American in her early 20s, comes to the clinic where you are a behaviorally oriented therapist. Assume that this is your initial meeting with her and that you know nothing else about her. Also assume that she would very much like to become involved in short-term behavioral counseling, mainly to deal with chronic anxiety that is getting in the way of her personal and professional life.

Some Background Data:

During the initial interview Kathrina tells you:

"I've just *got* to learn how to cope with stress. I feel as if there's a dark cloud over my head – a constant feeling of apprehension. I'm so worked up during the day that when I try to go to sleep, I just toss and turn most of the night, ruminating over everything that happened to me that day. I keep telling myself that I've got to get to sleep or I won't be worth a damn the next day. I just lie there and can't seem to stop thinking of what I did or will do the next day. When I do get up the next morning, I'm a basket case. I sell real estate, and lately I'm getting more anxious about my future. I'm fearful of contacting people because I might say the wrong thing and blow the potential sale, and I'm afraid they'll notice my anxiety. I just don't seem to be able to relax at any time. And what's even worse is that I feel less able to cope with stress now than I used to. Stress is getting the best of me, and I'm afraid that unless I can learn to recognize and deal with the situations I'm in, my anxiety will do me in."

Kathrina also tells you that she is experiencing many problems in leaving home and feeling that she can make it on her own. She says that she is not following the family "program" and lets you know that her parents are disappointed with some of the ways in which she is living. She does not want to cut herself off from her family, yet she has trouble in being everything her parents expect of her.

Assume that you and Kathrina agree to several counseling sessions to help her deal with her anxieties. Specifically, she wants guidance in learning coping skills that she can use on her own. Show how you would view her as a behaviorally oriented counselor and how you might proceed for several sessions.

Questions for Reflection:

1. How do you view Kathrina's anxiety? How will your answer to this question have a direct bearing on the manner in which you work with her in your sessions?

2. What cultural themes would you pay attention to, if any? To what extent would you focus on her alienation from her family? Would you be inclined to focus more on her anxiety? her stress? her concerns over not living up to the expectations of her family?

3. What might you want to know from Kathrina about the ways in which her cultural experiences have affected her? If you are from a different background, would you expect any difficulties in understanding and working with her?

4. What specific behavioral procedures might you employ during your sessions? What suggestions would you make to Kathrina for work she can do by herself outside of the sessions?

5. What ways can you think of to teach her how to cope with stress? What self-help or self-management techniques could you suggest?

6. How might you deal with Kathrina's insomnia? How might you design a program for her that would help her relax and sleep at night?

STUDY GUIDE FOR CHAPTER NINE

BEHAVIOR THERAPY

1. Summarize the four trends in behavior therapy (classical conditioning, operant conditioning, social learning, and the cognitive trend).

2. In what way can behavioristic methods be used to attain humanistic goals? What is the basis for an integration of the behavioral and humanistic perspectives?

3. In what ways does behavior therapy differ from the experiential approaches to counseling?

4. List the basic characteristics and agreed-on assumptions that apply to the behavioral approach. What are the key characteristics of behavior therapy that distinguish it from other therapy approaches

5. Key terms for behavior therapy are defined in the **Student Manual** in Chapter 9. See the *Glossary of Key Terms* in the manual.

6. How is the behavior therapist likely to work with a client in identifying and specifying therapeutic goals? In behavior therapy, the client determines *what* behavior will be changed, while the therapist determines *how* behavior will be changed. What is your reaction to this view of goal setting in therapy?

7. Discuss the role of the client/therapist relationship from the behavior therapist's point of view.

8. Briefly describe some of the main principles involved in applied behavioral analysis --- mention some of the main operant conditioning techniques.

9. Differentiate between positive reinforcement and negative reinforcement.

10. Discuss some advantages and disadvantages to the use of punishment as a way to control behavior. What are some ethical considerations in using punishment and other aversive events as a way to change problematic behavior.

11. How does relaxation training work? What are some relaxation procedures that you might apply to yourself? What is the value of these techniques? What are some of its main uses and applications?

12. What are the basic principles involved in systematic desensitization, and what are its main therapeutic applications? Describe how you would set up a systematic-desensitization procedure for a client who wanted to overcome his or her fear of flying in airplanes.

13. *In vivo* desensitization and flooding are two forms of exposure therapies. Briefly describe each of these exposure

therapies.

14. Put yourself in the place of a client and think of a particular problem you might have, such as some form of fear or avoidance. As a client, how do you think you would relate to *in vivo* desensitization or flooding?

15. Eye movement desensitization reprocessing is a new form of behavior therapy. Briefly describe this approach by listing the highlights of the various phases of this form of treatment. What kinds of problems lend themselves to this type of treatment?

16. What are some basic assumptions underlying assertion training? What are its main uses and applications? What are the common clinical strategies that therapists typically employ as part of assertion training?

17. Give a few examples of self-management programs. What are the characteristics of an effective self-management program? What are the specific steps involved in setting up such a program? What are the features of a good self-contract? How might you apply a self-management program to some behavior that you would like to change in your life?

18. In what way is multimodal therapy an open system that encourages technical eclecticism? What are some ways that you might integrate this approach into your own counseling style?

19. What are some implications to consider in counseling culturally diverse clients within the framework of multimodal therapy?

20. What are some specific contributions of behavior therapy? What are some selected problem areas for which this approach is particularly effective?

21. Discuss how ethical accountability is a strength of behavior therapy. What are some ethical guidelines for using behavioral methods?

22. Mention some limitations of behavior therapy. Identify (and respond to) some common criticisms leveled against this approach.

23. From the perspective of multicultural counseling, what are some contributions and limitations of the behavioral approach?

24. What aspects of behavior therapy would you be inclined to incorporate into your own counseling style?

25. How would you apply behavioral procedures to the cases of Stan and Ruth in the *TPCP* book? To the cases of Eddie and Katrina in this *Instructor's Resource Manual*?

Test Items

Chapter Nine
Behavior Therapy

Theory and Practice of

Counseling and Psychotherapy

BEHAVIOR THERAPY

1. Behavior therapy is grounded in:
   a. the psychodynamic aspects of a person.
   b. the principles of learning.
   c. a philosophical view of the human condition.
   d. the events of the first five years of life.

2. Behavior therapy assumes that:
   a. behavior is the result of unconscious forces.
   b. behavior is the result of free choices.
   c. behavior is determined by psychic energy.
   d. behavior is learned.
   e. both (a) and (c)

3. Behavior therapy is characterized by:
   a. a focus on overt specific behavior.
   b. a formulation of precise treatment goals.
   c. the design of an appropriate treatment plan.
   d. the objective assessment of the results of therapy.
   e. all of the above

4. Behavior therapy is based on:
   a. applying the experimental method to the therapeutic process.
   b. a systematic set of concepts.
   c. a well-developed theory of personality.
   d. the principle of self-actualization.
   e. both (b) and (c)

5. In behavior therapy, it is generally agreed that:
   a. the therapist should decide treatment goals.
   b. the client should decide the treatment goals.
   c. goals of therapy are the same for all clients.
   d. goals are not necessary.

6. The main goal of behavior therapy is:
   a. providing for self-actualization.
   b. expanding self-understanding and insight.
   c. assisting clients in making value judgments concerning their behavior.
   d. eliminating unadaptive learning and providing for more effective learning.

7. Which is not true of behavior therapy?
   a. Insight is necessary for behavior change to occur.
   b. Therapy should focus on behavior change and not attitude change.
   c. Therapy is not complete unless actions follow verbalizations.
   d. A good working relationship between client and therapist is necessary for behavior change to occur.

8. What is the function of the behavior therapist?
   a. to provide modeling for the client
   b. to apply his or her skills in developing a treatment plan
   c. to assess specific behavior problems
   d. to provide reinforcement for clients
   e. all of the above

9. According to most behavior therapists, a good working relationship between the client and therapist is:
    a. a necessary and sufficient condition for behavior change to occur.
    b. a necessary, but not sufficient, condition for behavior change to occur.
    c. neither a necessary nor a sufficient condition for behavior change to occur.
    d. none of the above

10. Which of the following is not true regarding behavior therapy?
    a. The client must be an active participant.
    b. The client is merely passive while the therapist uses techniques.
    c. Therapy cannot be imposed on unwilling clients.
    d. Both therapist and client need to work together for common goals.

11. Which of the following is not a key concept of behavior therapy?
    a. Behavior is learned through reinforcement.
    b. Present behavior is stressed over past behavior.
    c. Emphasis is on cognitive factors.
    d. Emphasis is on action and experimenting with new behaviors.
    e. Emphasis is on the role of insight in treatment.

12. Which technique is aimed at teaching the client to emit a response that is inconsistent with anxiety?
    a. assertive training
    b. operant conditioning
    c. systematic desensitization
    d. social reinforcement
    e. stress inoculation

13. Behavior therapy techniques:
    a. must be suited to the client's problems.
    b. are assessed to determine their value.
    c. are geared toward behavior change.
    d. all of the above
    e. none of the above

14. Behavior therapy is suited for:
    a. individual therapy.
    b. group therapy.
    c. institutions and clinics.
    d. classroom learning situations.
    e. all of the above

15. What is (are) the contribution(s) of behavior therapy?
    a. It gives a psychodynamic explanation of behavior disorders.
    b. It intensifies the client's feelings and subjective experiencing.
    c. It makes explicit the role of the therapist as a reinforcer.
    d. The client is clearly informed of specific procedures used.
    e. both (c) and (d)

16. Which statement contains the most truth?
    a. Behavioristic and humanistic approaches cannot be reconciled.
    b. Current behavior therapy is grounded on a deterministic view of persons.
    c. Behavioristic methods can be used to attain humanistic ends.
    d. Contemporary behavior therapy focuses on how people are determined by their social and cultural environments.
    e. Contemporary behavior therapy is increasingly concerned with behavioral control.

17. Which of the following is not a basic characteristic of behavior therapy?
    a. Treatment goals are specific and concrete.
    b. Target problems in therapy are specifically defined.
    c. There is reliance on basic research concerning use of specific techniques.
    d. There is an emphasis on client expression of feelings.
    e. Emphasis is given to observing overt behaviors.

18. Who has done most of the work in the area of modeling?
    a. Joseph Wolpe
    b. Hans Eysenck
    c. E. Jacobson
    d. Arnold Lazarus
    e. Albert Bandura

19. B. F. Skinner is associated with which of the following trends in the behavioral approach?
    a. classical conditioning
    b. operant conditioning
    c. the cognitive trend
    d. all of the above
    e. both (a) and (c)

20. Which of the following is not true about how behavior therapists function in the therapeutic setting?
    a. They use techniques such as summarizing, reflection, clarification, and open-ended questioning.
    b. They focus on specifics.
    c. They systematically attempt to get information about all aspects of the problem.
    d. They serve as a model for the client.
    e. All of the above are true.

21. Which of the following is not a characteristic of an effective self-management program?
    a. A single strategy is usually more useful than a combination of strategies because it eliminates confusion.
    b. Consistent use of self-management strategies is essential.
    c. Realistic goals must be set and ongoingly evaluated.
    d. The use of self-reinforcement is important.
    e. Environmental support is important in maintaining changes.

22. What is not a part of the steps in a self-directed change program?
    a. exploration of one's family constellation
    b. selection of specific goals
    c. self-monitoring
    d. self-reinforcement procedures
    e. working out a plan for change

23. Which of the following is not one of the seven major areas of personality functioning described by the acronym "BASIC ID"?
    a. behavior
    b. cognition
    c. interpersonal relationships
    d. aspirations
    e. sensation

24. Which of the following is true about "technical eclecticism" in multimodal therapy?
    a. It is discouraged.
    b. It is encouraged.
    c. The client is fit into a predetermined treatment.
    d. It is considered confusing to the client.
    e. both (a) and (d)

25. In terms of ethical accountability, behavior therapy:
    a. does not address this issue.
    b. provides a basis for responsible practice.
    c. offers a greater chance of abusing interventions than do other approaches.
    d. makes use of techniques that have questionable validity.
    e. both (c) and (d)

26. Which of the following is credited with initially developing the progressive relaxation procedure?
    a. Bandura
    b. Mahoney
    c. Wolpe
    d. Jacobson
    e. Alberti

27. Which of the following distinguishes the cognitive trend in behavior therapy from the trends of classical and operant conditioning?
    a. a focus on experimental analysis
    b. a focus on evaluating therapeutic procedures
    c. the reference to mediational concepts in understanding behavior
    d. all of the above
    e. both (a) and (b)

28. Multimodal therapy is a therapeutic approach that is grounded on:
    a. cognitive behavior therapy.
    b. social learning theory.
    c. applied behavior analysis
    d. operant conditioning
    e. both (c) and (d)

29. According to Bandura, which of the following are characteristic of effective models (whether they be live, symbolic or multiple)?
    a. similar to the observer with regard to age, sex, race and attitudes
    b. possessing a degree of prestige and status
    c. exhibiting warmth
    d. all of the above
    e. both (a) and (c)

30. Which of the following clinical strategies is not necessarily employed during assertion training?
    a. feedback
    b. modeling
    c. social reinforcement
    d. homework assignments
    e. self-monitoring via keeping a behavioral diary

31. Which of the following would not be considered a feature of a good self-contract?
    a. It emphasizes the positive.
    b. It is a verbal agreement between client and therapist.
    c. It is clear and specific.
    d. It involves the participation of another person.
    e. It includes a balance of appropriate rewards and sanctions.

32. A limitation of behavior therapy is:
    a. the overemphasis on feeling and the neglect of cognition.
    b. the overemphasis upon insight.
    c. the lack of empirical research validating its techniques.
    d. the need for long-term treatment to effect change.
    e. none of the above

33. Behavior therapy emerged as a major force in psychotherapy and experienced a significant growth spurt during the:
    a. 1950s.
    b. 1960s.
    c. 1970s.
    d. 1980s.
    e. 1990s.

34. Behavior therapy developed new concepts and methods that went beyond traditional learning theories and searched for new horizons during the:
    a. 1950s.
    b. 1960s.
    c. 1970s.
    d. 1980s.
    e. none of the above

35. Wolpe's systematic desensitization is based on the principles of:
    a. classical conditioning.
    b. operant conditioning.
    c. cognitive therapy.
    d. both (a) and (b)
    e. all of the above

36. The situation in which behaviors are emitted from an active organism is known as:
    a. classical conditioning.
    b. operant conditioning.
    c. either (a) or (b)
    d. neither (a) nor (b)

37. Skinner's view of controlling behavior is based on the principles of:
    a. classical conditioning.
    b. operant conditioning.
    c. cognitive therapy.
    d. none of the above

38. _____ involves the removal of unpleasant stimuli from a situation once a certain behavior has occurred.
    a. Negative reinforcement
    b. Positive reinforcement
    c. Punishment
    d. Systematic desensitization
    e. none of the above

39. Cognitive-behavioral therapy is:
    a. considered a passing fad.
    b. not really accepted by most practicing behavior therapists.
    c. now established as a part of mainstream behavior therapy.
    d. declining in popularity.

40. The person who is considered a key pioneer of clinical behavior therapy because of his broadening of its conceptual bases and development of multimodal therapy is:
    a. Albert Bandura.
    b. Joseph Wolpe.
    c. Robert Alberti.
    d. Arnold Lazarus.
    e. Alan Kazdin.

41. All of the following are characteristics of behavioral approaches except:
    a. Behavior therapy relies on the principles and procedures of the scientific method.
    b. Behavior therapy specifies treatment goals in concrete and objective terms.
    c. Behavior therapy focuses on the client's current problems and the factors influencing them.
    d. Behavior therapy employs the same procedures to every client with a particular dysfunctional behavior.

42. In conducting a behavioral assessment, the client's functioning is taken into account in which area(s)?
    a. affective dimensions
    b. cognitive dimensions
    c. behavioral dimensions
    d. interpersonal dimensions
    e. all of the above

43. Goals serve the function in behavioral counseling of:
    a. providing a meaningful direction for counseling.
    b. providing a basis for selecting specific counseling strategies.
    c. providing a framework for evaluating counseling outcomes.
    d. making it possible to compare progress before and after therapy.
    e. all of the above

44. Behavior therapists tend to:
    a. be active and directive.
    b. function as consultants.
    c. function as problem solvers.
    d. all of the above

45. All of the following are steps in the use of systematic desensitization except for:
    a. hypnosis.
    b. relaxation training.
    c. the development of an anxiety hierarchy.
    d. systematic desensitization proper.

46. Most of the assertion-training methods are based on principles of:
    a. classical conditioning.
    b. operant conditioning.
    c. the cognitive-behavioral therapies.
    d. a stimulus-response psychology.

47. Effective assertion-training programs:
    a. teach people skills and techniques for dealing with difficult situations.
    b. challenge one's beliefs that accompany lack of assertiveness.
    c. involve changing the environment so that clients will be able to function more assertively.
    d. both (a) and (b)

48. Self-management strategies include:
    a. self-monitoring.
    b. self-award.
    c. self-contracting.
    d. stimulus control.
    e. all of the above

49. If your client wanted to change a behavior, for instance, learning to control smoking, drinking, or eating, which behavioral technique would be most appropriate to employ?
    a. systematic desensitization
    b. self-management
    c. assertion training
    d. punishment

50. A temporary strategy that is used until people can implement new behaviors in everyday life is known as:
    a. self-monitoring.
    b. self-reinforcement.
    c. self-contracting.
    d. self-assessment.

51. From a multimodal therapy perspective, enduring change is seen as a function of:
    a. gaining emotional and intellectual insight into one's problems.
    b. a client's ability to experience catharsis.
    c. the level of self-actualization of the therapist.
    d. combined techniques, strategies, and modalities.

52. Lazarus argues in favor of:
    a. technical eclecticism.
    b. theoretical eclecticism.
    c. both (a) and (b)
    d. practicing exclusively within the framework of behavior therapy so as to avoid confusing the client.

53. Who is the developer of multimodal therapy?
    a. Albert Bandura
    b. Robert Goulding
    c. Joseph Wolpe
    d. Arnold Lazarus
    e. Rollo May

54. Which is not true as it applies to multimodal therapy?
    a. Therapeutic flexibility and versatility are valued highly.
    b. Therapists adjust their procedures to effectively achieve the client's goals in therapy.
    c. Great care is taken to fit the client to a predetermined type of treatment.
    d. The approach encourages technical eclecticism.
    e. The therapist makes a comprehensive assessment of the client's level of functioning at the outset of therapy.

55. Which of the following is not based on the principles of operant conditioning?
    a. positive and negative reinforcement
    b. punishment
    c. extinction
    d. cognitive behavior therapy

56. The following is (are) example(s) of exposure therapy:
    a. traditional systematic desensitization
    b. flooding
    b. *in vivo* desensitization
    d. all of the above
    d. (a) and (c) above

57. *In vivo* flooding consists of:
    a. brief and graduated series of exposures to feared events.
    b. intense and prolonged exposure to the actual anxiety-producing stimuli.
    c. phases commonly used in behavior therapy.
    c. none of the above

58. EMDR is used to help clients:
    a. restructure their cognitions or to reprocess information.
    b. resuscitate an individual who has experienced a heart attack.
    c. reexperience repressed material.
    d. none of the above

59. Dialectical behavior therapy
    a. has no empirical support for its validity.
    b. is a promising blend of behavioral and psychoanalytic techniques.
    c. is a long-term therapy for treating depression.
    d. is a form of operant conditioning.
    e. is a form of classical conditioning.

60. Which is *not* true of dialectical behavior therapy (DBT)?
    a. The approach was formulated for treating borderline personality disorders.
    b. DBT emphasizes the importance of the client/therapist relationship.
    c. DBT incorporates mindfulness training and Zen practices.
    d. DBT is a blend of Adlerian concepts and behavioral techniques.
    e. DBT relies on empirical data to support its effectiveness.

ANSWER KEY FOR CHAPTER NINE – BEHAVIOR THERAPY

MULTIPLE-CHOICE TEST QUESTIONS

1. B	21. A	41. D
2. D	22. D	42. E
3. E	23. D	43. E
4. A	24. B	44. D
5. B	25. B	45. A
6. D	26. D	46. C
7. A	27. C	47. D
8. E	28. B	48. E
9. B	29. D	49. B
10. B	30. E	50. B
11. E	31. B	51. D
12. C	32. E	52. A
13. D	33. C	53. D
14. E	34. D	54. C
15. E	35. A	55. D
16. C	36. B	56. D
17. D	37. B	57. B
18. E	38. A	58. A
19. B	39. C	59. B
20. E	40. D	60. D

TRUE–FALSE TEST ITEMS FOR CHAPTER NINE

BEHAVIOR THERAPY

Decide if the following statements are "more true" or "more false" from the perspective of the behavior therapy approach.

1. Albert Bandura is credited with originally developing the progressive relaxation procedure.

2. Systematic desensitization typically includes the use of relaxation procedures.

3. Research studies show that systematic desensitization has been effective in eliminating fears related to animals.

4. Modeling is a form of systematic desensitization.

5. Reviews of research indicate that a model who is similar to the observer with respect to age, sex, race, and attitudes is more likely to be imitated than a model who is unlike the observer.

6. Modeling methods have been used in treating people with snake phobias and in teaching new behaviors to socially disturbed children.

7. A trend in contemporary behavior therapy is the increased emphasis on the role of thinking and "self-talk" as a factor in behavior.

8. Systematic desensitization is associated with the principles of operant conditioning.

9. A behavior therapist makes use of the technique of open-ended questioning for the purpose of obtaining important information related to the client's problem.

10. Research has shown that behavior therapists are more self-disclosing than psychoanalytic therapists.

11. In behavior therapy, changes are all or nothing.

12. Multimodal therapy encourages its practitioners to fit their procedures to the needs of the client by borrowing techniques from many other approaches.

13. Behavior therapy has been shown to be effective in the prevention and treatment of cardiovascular disease.

14. There is no place for the role of thinking process and attitudes in contemporary behavior therapy.

15. Behavior therapy has undergone important changes and has expanded considerably.

16. Dialectical behvior therapy integrates behavioral techniques with psychoanalytic concepts and mindfulness training of Eastern psychological and spiritual practices.

17. Dialectical behavior therapy stresses the importance of the therapeutic relationship.

18. Multimodal therapy does not fit well with the goals and aspirations of managed care.

19. The basic therapeutic conditions stressed by person-centered therapists can be integrated into a behavioral framework.

20. Evidence-based procedures are a part of both behavior therapy and cognitive behavior therapy.

ANSWER KEY FOR CHAPTER NINE – BEHAVIOR THERAPY

TRUE-FALSE TEST QUESTIONS

1.	F	11.	F
2.	T	12.	T
3.	T	13.	T
4.	F	14.	F
5.	T	15.	T
6.	T	16.	T
7.	T	17.	T
8.	F	18.	F
9.	T	19.	T
10.	T	20.	T

Guidelines for Using Chapter TEN

Cognitive-Behavior Therapy

in

Theory and Practice of Counseling and Psychotherapy and the *Student Manual*

Case Approach to Counseling and Psychotherapy

and

The Art of Integrative Counseling

1. The *Issues and Questions for Personal Application* in the **Student Manual** are meant to help students apply this theory to their personal lives. In my lectures I use many of these questions as catalysts for discussion, and I typically raise some of these questions and then address myself to them by bringing in examples of clients I have worked with both individually and in groups. The following are areas I try to supplement by describing some of my clinical experience:

    *   common "irrational beliefs" of clients
    *   the tendency of clients to reindoctrinate themselves with inappropriate standards that they have accepted without challenge
    *   how cognition influences feelings and behavior
    *   ways in which some clients have learned to challenge certain self-defeating attitudes

2. The *Rational Emotive Behavior Therapy Self-Help Form* in the **Student Manual** can be most helpful if students will take the time for even one week to apply the A-B-C model to situations they encounter during the week. At the end of the week, in small groups in the classroom, students can discuss patterns they detected in their own thoughts about particular events. They can pinpoint some of their faulty thinking and identify constructive self-statements and healthy cognitions. Assigning this self-help form as homework, and following it up with

discussion in small groups, is one way of helping students apply what they are learning about REBT to themselves.

3. The "homework assignment" method is one way of assisting clients to implement in daily life new behaviors that they acquire during the therapy session. The sections entitled *Issues and Questions for Personal Application*, and the *Practical Applications*, in the **Student Manual** contain exercises that should provide the student with practice in thinking about possible "homework assignments."

   I ask my students to do these exercises at home, and we discuss the results in class. As a variation, you might consider having students give themselves specific "homework assignments" relating to some behavior they would like to change. For example, if one of your students says that he rarely participates in class for fear of looking stupid or giving the wrong answer, that student might be encouraged to actively participate in each of his classes for one week. He can bring the results of the assignment to class and discuss how this method worked for him. I attempt each week to give the class some type of out-of-class exercise that they can practice on during the week. This usually corresponds to some exercise or technique that we are studying at the time. I find that this intensifies student interest and makes the concepts we are studying more meaningful and concrete.

4. In my lectures on REBT I give considerable emphasis to the various cognitive, emotive, and behavioral methods that are described in the textbook. Both students and I value brief demonstrations of these various techniques in class, so I often ask for volunteers and provide a brief demonstration of various techniques such as disputing faulty beliefs, suggesting cognitive homework, cognitive role playing, rational-emotive imagery, and so forth. As an alternative, in small groups students can practice a particular technique such as cognitive disputing by alternating between the role of counselor and client.

5. The work of Aaron Beck is noteworthy in the development of cognitive therapy. In my lectures on cognitive therapy I pay particular attention to some of the commonalities and differences between REBT and cognitive therapy – most of which are discussed in the **TPCP** text. Topics I emphasize in both lecture and demonstrations of counseling sessions are:

   • the concept of automatic thoughts
   • common cognitive distortions (such as selective abstraction, overgeneralization, polarized thinking)
   • collaborative empiricism
   • the therapeutic alliance in cognitive therapy
   • homework in cognitive therapy

   What I find works well is to ask students to share examples of automatic thoughts or faulty cognitions, and then I proceed to ask for volunteers to demonstrate how I might work with their thoughts as a cognitive therapist. I often suggest homework assignments in these demonstrations as a way to illustrate how to encourage students to actually think about their thinking after participating in a counseling demonstration as a client. For this modality, I ask all the students in class to "become clients," even if they do so silently and write down examples of problematic thoughts and ways they can practice challenging these thoughts outside of class.

6. As a way to engage students in learning how to cope with stress more effectively, I give at least a very brief lecture on the key points of Meichenbaum's approach to stress management. The textbook describes some of the main steps Meichenbaum uses in stress-management training. This can be amplified with even one demonstration with a student who is willing to serve as a "client" who wants to reduce stress in a particular area. When I demonstrate I strive to apply some of Meichenbaum's key concepts so that students get a sense of how they can apply what they are reading in the text.

7. Constructivism is a trend in cognitive behavior therapy, and especially a trend in Meichenbaum's approach. Time only allows very brief coverage of the key themes of constructivism, but we do return to a more detailed discussion of social constructionism in Chapter 13 that deals with the postmodern approaches.

8. As I attempt to do with each theory we discuss, I include a brief critique of the strengths and weaknesses of cognitive behavioral approaches in a multicultural context. I generally like to ask students what they think are the contributions (and some limitations as well) of CBT in working with diverse client populations. It is useful to ask students: "If you were a client with a cognitive behavioral therapist, what do you imagine this would be like for you? What are you most likely to find helpful from this approach? What aspect, if any, of this approach might present problems for you as a client?"

9. I typically refer to Stan's case as we study each therapeutic system. Consult Chapter 10 of the textbook for specific questions and guidelines for reviewing Stan within a cognitive-behavioral framework. Again, for comparison and contrast, I usually refer to the major points of likeness and difference among REBT and cognitive therapy.

10. Using some of the other cognitive therapies, demonstrate ways of working with themes in Stan's life. Examples include:

    • How might A. T. Beck explain Stan's depression and his suicidal impulses? Using Beck's cognitive methods, how might you therapeutically work with Stan's depression?

    • How would Meichenbaum analyze and conceptualize Stan's cognitive structures and his self-statements? Using Meichenbaum's three-phase change process, how might you help Stan develop a new way of thinking and acquire a new set of skills? If you wanted to teach Stan coping skills, how might you do this by using Meichenbaum's stress inoculation methods?

11. **Other Resources:** In addition to the cases, Ruth and Marion, given in Chapter 10 of the *Student Manual*, you may want to refer to three other resources: *Case Approach; The Art of Integrative Counseling*; and the *CD ROM for Integrative Counseling.*

    Refer to the *Case Approach to Counseling and Psychotherapy* (6th ed., 2005) for a detailed treatment of the case of Ruth from the perspective of cognitive behavior therapists. In Chapter 9 Dr. Albert Ellis describes a range of cognitive, emotive, and behavioral techniques he employs with Ruth. Following Ellis, Dr. Frank Dattilio applies cognitive behavioral concepts and techniques in couples and family therapy with Ruth. I follow up with my own style of drawing on cognitive behavior therapy concepts in counseling Ruth.

    Refer to *The Art of Integrative Counseling* book, Chapter 6, *Cognitive Focus in Counseling*, for a discussion of how I utilize concepts and techniques from cognitive behavioral approaches in my integrative perspective. Some of these topics are highlighted: *The Benefits and Limitations of a Cognitive Focus* (pp. 59–61), *Becoming the Client: Experiencing Cognitive Behavioral Techniques* (pp. 61–63). There is also a section that describes my integrative approach in counseling Ruth by exploring her cognitive structures and exploring her cognitive distortions (pp. 63–68). See the following cognitive distortions as applied to Ruth on pages 67–68: arbitrary inferences, overgeneralization, personalization, labeling and mislabeling, and polarized thinking. This section of the text on cognitive focus in working with Ruth coordinates well with the video (Sessions #6 and #8).

    If you are using the *CD ROM for Integrative Counseling*, refer to the three sessions where I demonstrate my way of working with Ruth from a cognitive and behavioral focus (Sessions #6 and #8). See also Session #9, *Integrative Focus*, which illustrates the interactive nature of working with Ruth on thinking, feeling, and doing levels. For *The Art of Integrative Counseling* book , Chapters 6 and 8 deal with an elaboration on techniques I draw from the cognitive-behavioral approaches.

12. Books in rational emotive behavior therapy that I draw on for preparing lectures include:

    • *Feeling Better, Getting Better, Staying Better* (Ellis, 2001a)
    • *Overcoming Destructive Beliefs, Feelings, and Behaviors* (Ellis, 2001b)
    • *Rational Emotive Behavior Therapy: A Therapist's Guide* (Ellis & MacLaren, 1998)
    • *How to Make Yourself Happy and Remarkably Less Disturbable* (Ellis, 1999)

For preparing lectures and background reading for the cognitive therapies, the following are very useful resources:

    • *Cognitive Therapy: Basics and beyond* (Beck, 1995)
    • *Cognitive Therapy of Depression* (Beck et al., 1979)
    • *Mind Over Mood: Change How You Feel by Changing the Way You Think* (Greenberger & Padesky, 1995)
    • *Clinician's Guide to Mind Over Mood* (Padesky & Greenberger, 1995)

KEY TERMS FOR REVIEW AND DEFINITION

Albert Ellis
irrational beliefs
cognitions
unconditional "shoulds"
absolutistic "musts"
musturbatory philosophies
self-talking
self-evaluating
simple preferences
emotional disturbance
autosuggestion
self-repetition
blame
anxiety
A-B-C theory
philosophical reevaluation
social interest
full acceptance or tolerance
therapeutic collaboration
collaborative empiricism
disputing irrational beliefs
changing one's language
rational-emotive imagery
role playing
shame-attacking exercises
cognitive behavioral therapies
cognitive therapy
rational emotive behavior therapy
Aaron Beck
alternative interpretations
Beck Depression Inventory

internal dialogue
coping-skills program
stress inoculation
cognitive coping
self-observation
faulty assumptions
automatic thinking
self-sustaining
schema restructuring
cognitive distortions/errors
schema
"family schemata"
arbitrary inferences
relapse prevention
cognitive triad
selective abstraction
Socratic questioning
cognitive homework
constructivist narrative perspective (CNP)
distortion of reality
overgeneralization
magnification and minimization
personalization
labeling and mislabeling
polarized thinking
self-deprecation
Donald Meichenbaum
cognitive behavior modification
constructivism
self-instructional therapy
cognitive restructuring

INFOTRAC KEYWORDS

The following keywords are listed in such a way as to allow the **InfoTrac** search engine to locate a wider range of articles on the online university library. The keywords should be entered *exactly* as listed below, to include astericks, "W1," "W2," "AND," and other search engine tools.

Cognitive W1 behavioral
Cognitive W1 restructuring
Rational-emotive

Cognitive W1 therapy
Cognitive W1 structure
Beck AND depression

Cognitive Behavior Therapy

Albert Ellis
Rational emotive behavior therapy
Rational W1 emotive
Aaron Beck
Cognitive therapy
Automatic thoughts
Cognitive distortions
Catastrophizing
Reattribution
Cognitive W1 restructuring
Beck AND depression

CASE EXAMPLES

CAROL: "I'm to blame for all the problems in my family"

As the oldest of three children, Carol (who is 29) berates herself for her family's tension and dissension. Her father is depressed most of the time (which Carol feels responsible for); her mother feels overburdened and ineffectual (Carol feels she contributes to this); and both her sisters are doing poorly in school and having other personal problems (Carol also assumes responsibility for this). Somehow she is convinced that if she were different and did what she *should do*, most of these problems would greatly diminish. Assume, as you listen to her, that you hear her saying some of the following things:

- "My father looks to me to be the strong one in the family. I *must* be strong if I'm to gain his approval, which I feel I *must* have."

- "Since my mother is overworked, I *should* take on more of the responsibility for taking care of my younger sisters. I *ought* to be able to talk with them and help them with their problems."

- "My sisters both expect me to do their chores for them, to help them at school, and to live up to the image they have of me. I *ought* to meet their ideals, and it would be absolutely horrible of me to fail in this regard. Then if they grow up with problems, I'll have only myself to blame for the rest of my life."

1. Rank the following in order of importance, from the perspective of rational emotive behavior therapy:

   _____ providing Carol with support and understanding

   _____ creating a warm and personal relationship with her

   _____ telling her that she should not think the way she does

   _____ confronting her with her irrational assumptions

   _____ asking her to question the origin of her beliefs

   _____ asking her what she most wants to change

   _____ teaching her how to identify her own faulty thinking and how to dispute it

   _____ providing her with reassurance

   Are there some of the above things that you would *not* do? If so, what are they? Are there some things that you would stress that are not mentioned above? If so, what are they?

2. One of the things a rational emotive behavior therapist would do is teach Carol that her thinking and her evaluation of events are causing her problems (feelings of inadequacy, anxiety, and insecurity). What do you hear her saying to herself that is irrational?

3. As a rational emotive behavior therapist you would want to help her undermine her self-destructive thinking, once she had identified disturbance-creating beliefs. Check the therapeutic techniques that you might be inclined to use:

   _____ active teaching methods

   _____ readings

   _____ relaxation exercises

   _____ fantasy exercises in which she relives past experiences

   _____ specific homework assignments

_____ therapist interpretation

_____ free-association exercises

_____ a journal of events, thoughts, feelings, and outcomes

_____ behavioral rehearsal

_____ writing her autobiography

_____ writing a "letter" to her sisters and parents

_____ methods of disputing irrational beliefs

List some other procedures you would be inclined to use:

4. Discuss in greater length which of the above techniques you would expect to rely on the most. What might you expect to occur through the use of these procedures? What outcomes would you hope for?

5. Assume that Carol holds steadfastly to her beliefs and tries to convince you that they are _not_ irrational? For example, she tells you: "I just _know_ that if I were more adequate as a daughter, my father wouldn't be depressed.

6. "It's because I've let him down so that he feels useless as a father." How would you respond?

7. If Carol seems to hang on to the idea that she _must_ have the approval of her father in order to feel adequate as a person, what direction might you take?

8. What value do you see in asking Carol to do a written _REBT Self-Help Form_?

9. Apply the technique of rational-emotive imagery in Carol's case. How would you help her imagine herself thinking, feeling, and behaving in the way she would ideally like to?

10. What differences, if any, might there be between using Beck's cognitive therapy and using Ellis's REBT?

HAL AND PETE: A gay couple seeks counseling

Hal and Pete have been living together for several years. Much as heterosexual couples do, they experience conflicts in their relationship. Lately, the situation has taken a turn for the worse, and Hal wants to either resolve certain problems or break up the relationship. Pete is very anxious about being deserted, and he agrees to come for counseling as a couple. Neither of them is troubled with the fact that they are in a gay relationship, and from their perspective this is not the problem. They want you to know at the outset that they are not seeking counseling to "cure" them of their homosexuality. Rather, they seem to be having major problems that they are unable to work out by themselves and that lead them to wonder if they want to continue living together.

Pete feels unappreciated, and he does not feel that Hal cares for him in "the way I would like." He initially tells you the following:

"I try so hard to do what I think Hal expects. It's really important that I please him, because I'm afraid that if I don't, he'll get fed up and simply leave. And if he left, I imagine all sorts of terrible things happening. First of all, I feel the constant threat of being left. I need someone to rely on – someone who will listen to me, who I know cares for me and accepts me the way I am, who wants to be with me, and who will approve of what I do. I feel I _must_ have this in the person I live with. If I don't, this just proves that the other person doesn't love me. I need to be loved. My parents didn't love me, they never gave me the approval I needed to have, and I think that this alone is more than enough for me to bear. I feel that life often plays dirty tricks on me. For a long time I felt that I could _really_ trust Hal and that he'd stay with me and approve of me and care about me, regardless of who I was. Now, after I trust him, he decides to tell me that I'm too demanding and that he's not able to handle all my demands. I don't think I'm demanding – I just want to be loved and accepted by some other significant person. If I can't find this in at least one person, then I can't see much value in living."

142

Hal responds with the following initial statement, in which he describes how it is for him to be in this relationship: "Frankly, I'm so tired of always feeling that I *must prove myself* and my constant love for Pete. No matter what I do or say, I typically end up feeling that I'm not enough and that regardless of what I do, it just won't measure up. I'm tired of hearing that I don't care. I'm sick of being made to feel that I'm insensitive, I hate being made to feel inadequate, and I don't want to constantly feel that I have to weigh everything I say for fear that I'll offend Pete and make him upset. I just can't stand having people be upset at me – it makes me feel lousy and guilty – as if I should somehow be more than I am, that I ought to be better than I am. If I can't get over being made to feel inadequate around Pete, I want out!"

Questions for Reflection:

Assume that Hal and Pete agree to attend six sessions as a couple. By the end of that time they would like to have decided whether they want to stay together. If they do decide to continue living together, they would be open to considering further counseling to continue working on their separate problems and finding ways of improving their relationship.

1. From the perspective of rational emotive behavior therapy, some of the following could be identified as *Pete's irrational beliefs*. Show how you would demonstrate to him that they are self-defeating attitudes that are the direct cause of his misery:

    *   I *must* please Hal, and if I don't he'll leave, and the consequences will be horrible!
    *   I *must* have someone to rely on, or else I can't make it on my own!
    *   I *must* have someone to show me caring, love, and approval, and if I don't get this, life is hardly worth living!
    *   If I don't get what I want from life, then life is damn unfair!

2. Again as an REBT counselor, how might you work with *Hal's irrational beliefs*? How would you teach him to dispute them? How would you show him that these beliefs are at the root of his problems?

    *   I *must* prove myself, I *must* be able to meet another's expectations of me – and if I don't, I'll feel inadequate, guilty, rotten, and deficient as a person!
    *   If I don't meet Pete's needs, I'm *made* to feel inadequate.

3. Show how both Hal's and Pete's beliefs and assumptions are related to the problems they are having in their relationship. In what ways do you imagine that working on their irrational beliefs will affect their relationship?

4. If you were to work with Hal and Pete from Beck's cognitive therapy perspective, how might this approach be different from REBT?

STUDY GUIDE FOR CHAPTER TEN

COGNITIVE-BEHAVIOR THERAPY

1. In what way is REBT the parent of today's cognitive-behavioral therapies? Discuss the relationship between REBT and other cognitive-behavioral approaches.

2. Mention the basic hypothesis of REBT. How is REBT therapy seen as an educational process?

3. What are the philosophical assumptions of REBT pertaining to human nature? To what degree do you agree or disagree with the REBT view of human nature? What implications do you see for therapeutic practice?

4. From the REBT perspective, why and how do people develop emotional disturbances? How is blame the core of most emotional problems?

5. List some of the main irrational ideas that people often internalize. Think about a few of your own irrational beliefs. What REBT strategies could you apply to the exploration of your own belief system?

6. Know the key terms in this chapter (defined in the *Student Manual*).

7. Provide an example from your own life experience that illustrates the A-B-C theory of personality. Mention specific steps that explain how philosophical restructuring changes our dysfunctional personality.

8. What are the general goals that cognitive-behavior therapists focus on with their clients? To achieve these goals, what are the specific tasks of the therapist? What are some main ideas that cognitive-behavior therapists teach their clients?

9. For therapy to be effective, what must the client do? What are the expectations of clients in rational emotive behavior therapy and cognitive therapy?

10. What are Albert Ellis's views on the role of the client/therapist relationship? Compare and contrast this perspective with Carl Rogers's thoughts. What are your thoughts about Ellis's view on the nature of the therapeutic relationship? Do you agree or disagree with Ellis's notion that the therapist's personal warmth and liking for a client is not a necessary condition for clients to improve?

11. Describe at least one cognitive method, one emotive technique, and one behavioral technique used in the practice of REBT.

12. Discuss some applications of the principles and procedures of REBT to individual therapy, group therapy, brief therapy and crisis intervention, and marital therapy.

13. What are some of the major concepts and principles of A. T. Beck's cognitive therapy? Provide an example showing how cognitive therapy could be applied. How is this form of therapy used in the treatment of depression?

14. Discuss some of the main differences between REBT and Beck's cognitive therapy.

15. Describe each of the following common distortions that lead to faulty assumptions: arbitrary inference, selective abstraction, overgeneralization, magnification and exaggeration, personalization, and polarized thinking.

16. Discuss the concepts of therapeutic collaboration and collaborative empiricism as they apply to the practice of cognitive therapy.

17. How does cognitive restructuring play a central role in Donald Meichenbaum's cognitive behavior modification? According to Meichenbaum, how does behavior change? Discuss these three phases of the change process: self-observation, starting a new internal dialogue, and learning new skills.

18. Describe the rationale for coping-skills programs and list the five steps of such programs. What are some applications of a coping-skills program?

19. Describe these three phases involved in Meichenbaum's stress inoculation training program: the conceptualization phase, the skills-acquisition phase, and the application and follow-through phase. Describe the primary focus and key tasks associated with each phase of the stress inoculation training program.

20. Summarize the characteristics of Meichenbaum's constructivist approach to cognitive behavior therapy.

21. What are some of the main contributions of the cognitive-behavioral approaches? Some of the main limitations and criticisms? What are some contributions and limitations of the cognitive-behavioral approaches in working with culturally diverse populations?

22. What are some ways that you might apply the principles and techniques of the cognitive-behavioral approaches to your personal life? Which approach do you think would be most useful to you if you were a client in therapy: Ellis's REBT? Beck's cognitive therapy? Meichenbaum's cognitive behavior modification? Think about some specific areas of your life that you may want to change and then identify some cognitive and behavioral strategies that you would be willing to employ as a means of bringing about these changes.

23. Discuss some specific concepts and techniques of the cognitive behavior therapies that you would want to incorporate into your own style of counseling.

24. In what ways can you integrate some cognitive and behavioral methods with some of the experiential approaches (existential therapy, person-centered therapy, and Gestalt therapy)?

25. Show how you might apply a cognitive perspective in working with the cases of Hal and Pete, and Carol at the beginning of this chapter.

Test Items

Chapter Ten

Cognitive Behavior Therapy

Theory and Practice of

Counseling and Psychotherapy

COGNITIVE-BEHAVIOR THERAPY

1. The founder of rational emotive behavior therapy is:
   a. William Glasser.
   b. Frederick Perls.
   c. Albert Ellis.
   d. Joseph Wolpe.
   e. none of the above

2. Rational emotive behavior therapy belongs to which category of therapy?
   a. existential-humanistic
   b. client-centered
   c. psychoanalytic
   d. Gestalt
   e. cognitive-behavior/action oriented

3. The cognitive-behavioral approach to therapy stresses:
   a. support, understanding, warmth, and empathy.
   b. awareness, unfinished business, impasse, and experiencing.
   c. thinking, judging, analyzing, and doing.
   d. subjectivity, existential anxiety, self-actualization, and being.
   e. transference, dream analysis, uncovering unconscious, and early experience.

4. REBT is based on the philosophical assumption that human beings are:
   a. innately striving for self-actualization.
   b. determined by strong unconscious sexual and aggressive forces.
   c. potentially able to think rationally but have a tendency toward irrational thinking.
   d. basically trying to develop a lifestyle to overcome feelings of basic inferiority.
   e. determined strictly by environmental conditioning.

5. REBT views emotional disturbances as the result of:
   a. inadequate mothering during infancy.
   b. failure to fulfill our existential needs.
   c. excessive feelings.
   d. irrational thinking and behaving.

6. According to REBT, what is the core of most emotional disturbance?
   a. blame
   b. resentment
   c. rage
   d. unfinished business
   e. depression

7. REBT contends that people:
   a. have a need to be loved and accepted by everyone.
   b. need to be accepted by most people.
   c. will become emotionally sick if they are rejected.
   d. do not need to be accepted and loved.
   e. both (b) and (c)

8. According to REBT, we develop emotional disturbances because of:
   a. a traumatic event.
   b. our belief about certain events.
   c. the abandonment by those we depend on for support.
   d. the withdrawal of love and acceptance.

9. REBT employs what kind of method to help people resolve their emotional, behavioral problems?
    a. the phenomenological method
    b. the empirical method
    c. the Gestalt method
    d. the philosophical method

10. The main therapeutic goal of REBT is:
    a. to teach clients how to recognize which ego state they are in.
    b. to make the unconscious conscious.
    c. to assist the client in becoming aware of his or her "being-in-the-world."
    d. to challenge the client in making both a value judgment and moral decision about the quality of his or her behavior.
    e. none of the above

11. The main function of the rational emotive behavior therapist is to:
    a. become an "existential partner" with the client.
    b. create a climate of safety and freedom from threat.
    c. challenge clients to reevaluate their ideas and philosophy of life.
    d. encourage the client to experience fully the here-and-now.
    e. help the client relive past emotional traumas.

12. REBT can best be considered as:
    a. an educative process.
    b. a didactic process.
    c. a process challenging ideas and thinking.
    d. a teaching/learning process.
    e. all of the above

13. Ellis contends that human beings are:
    a. self-talking.
    b. self-evaluating.
    c. self-sustaining.
    d. all of the above
    e. none of the above

14. The role of the client in rational emotive behavior therapy is like that of a:
    a. co-therapist.
    b. passive observer.
    c. student or learner.
    d. partner.

15. Which method is often employed in REBT?
    a. the "homework assignment" method
    b. the contract method
    c. the logical-analysis method
    d. behavioral and action methods
    e. all of the above

16. Who has developed a cognitive theory of behavior change?
    a. D. Meichenbaum
    b. Albert Bandura
    c. B. F. Skinner
    d. Joseph Wolpe
    e. all of the above

17. Cognitive restructuring plays an important role in whose approach to therapy?
    a.   Albert Ellis
    b.   D. Meichenbaum
    c.   A. T. Beck
    d.   all of the above

18. A feature of REBT that distinguishes it from other cognitive-behavioral therapies is:
    a.   its use of the A-B-C theory in analyzing the client.
    b.   its use of behavioral techniques.
    c.   its applicability to group work.
    d.   its systematic exposition of irrational beliefs that result in emotional and behavioral disturbance.
    e.   both (a) and (d)

19. Beck's cognitive therapy involves:
    a.   helping clients recognize and discard self defeating thinking.
    b.   looking at a client's "internal dialogue."
    c.   correcting erroneous beliefs.
    d.   all of the above
    e.   all but (b)

20. According to Meichenbaum, behavioral change:
    a.   occurs as a result of a three-phase change process.
    b.   occurs strictly as a result of starting a new internal dialogue.
    c.   will come about if clients are simply taught more effective coping skills.
    d.   begins with self-observation.
    e.   both (a) and (d)

21. Which of the following is the correct order of the three phases of Meichenbaum's stress-inoculation program?
    a.   conceptual-application-rehearsal
    b.   application-conceptual-rehearsal
    c.   application-rehearsal-conceptual
    d.   rehearsal-conceptual-application
    e.   conceptual-rehearsal-application

22. According to Ellis, we develop emotional and behavioral difficulties because:
    a.   we think of simple preferences as dire needs.
    b.   we live by the values our parents gave us.
    c.   we refuse to deal with unfinished business.
    d.   we have learned maladaptive behaviors.
    e.   we do not possess any self-actualizing tendencies.

23. An REBT therapist would contend that anxiety stems from:
    a.   unresolved issues of the past.
    b.   inadequate ego-defense mechanisms.
    c.   the internal repetition of irrational sentences.
    d.   a normal human condition that should be accepted.
    e.   none of the above

24. In REBT, what method is taught to clients to help them challenge irrational beliefs?
    a.   autogenic method
    b.   disputational method
    c.   self-management method
    d.   phenomenological method
    e.   multimodal method

25. Which of the following is true about the relationship between a client and a rational emotive behavior therapist?
    a. Therapists make value judgments in helping their clients gain insight.
    b. It is characterized by full acceptance and tolerance.
    c. Personal warmth is considered to be very important.
    d. The therapist assumes a nondirective stance.
    e. Transference is encouraged to develop.

26. Which of the following REBT techniques helps a client gradually learn to deal with anxiety and challenge basic irrational thinking?
    a. changing one's language
    b. cognitive homework
    c. dream analysis
    d. skill training
    e. assertiveness training

27. According to REBT, it is important to change the way one uses language because:
    a. imprecise language is one of the causes of distorted thinking processes.
    b. language shapes thinking and behavior.
    c. language shapes feelings.
    d. all of the above
    e. both (a) and (b)

28. The REBT technique that involves having clients imagine themselves in situations where they feel inappropriate feelings is called:
    a. cognitive homework.
    b. disputing irrational beliefs.
    c. role playing.
    d. shame-attacking exercises.
    e. rational-emotive imagery.

29. Which of the following is *not* true about role playing in REBT?
    a. It is a way of surfacing unfinished business.
    b. It involves emotional components.
    c. It involves behavioral components.
    d. It helps pinpoint irrational beliefs.
    e. It allows the client to work through underlying irrational beliefs.

30. Which REBT technique involves having the client do the very thing they avoid because of "what people might think?"
    a. role playing
    b. desensitization
    c. cognitive homework
    d. shame-attacking exercises
    e. changing one's language

31. All of the following are true as they apply to self-instructional therapy, except that:
    a. it was developed by Meichenbaum.
    b. it is a form of cognitive restructuring.
    c. it focuses directly on changing a client's behavior in social situations.
    d. it is also known as cognitive behavior modification.

32. Which of the following is not part of the five-step treatment procedure used in a coping-skills program?
    a. exposing clients to anxiety-provoking situations by means of role playing and imagery
    b. evaluating the anxiety level of the client by using both physiological and psychological tests
    c. teaching clients to become aware of the anxiety-provoking cognitions they experience in stressful situations
    d. having the clients examine their thoughts through reevaluating their self-statements
    e. noting the level of anxiety following reevaluation

33. All of the following are cognitive methods of REBT except for:
    a. shame-attacking exercises.
    b. disputing irrational beliefs.
    c. changing one's language.
    d. completing homework assignments.

34. Which of the following is not true of Beck's cognitive therapy?
    a. It is an insight therapy.
    b. It is a short-term or time-limited structured approach.
    c. It is an active and focused form of therapy.
    d. It asserts that irrational beliefs lead to emotional problems.
    e. It is based on the assumption that the way people feel and behave is determined by the way they structure their experience.

35. One of the main ways that Beck's cognitive therapy differs from Ellis's REBT is that in Beck's approach, more so than in Ellis's approach:
    a. reality testing is highly organized.
    b. thinking is considered to influence feeling and action.
    c. the quality of the therapeutic relationship is basic to the therapy process.
    d. clients are asked to look for evidence to support their conclusions.

36. In Meichenbaum's cognitive behavior modification, what is given primary importance?
    a. using a Socratic dialogue to get clients thinking
    b. collaborative empiricism
    c. automatic thoughts
    d. inner speech
    e. a multimodal approach to changing one's thinking and behaving

37. Stress inoculation training consists of:
    a. behavioral rehearsals.
    b. self-monitoring.
    c. cognitive restructuring.
    d. problem solving.
    e. all of the above

38. Cognitive therapy is based on the assumption that:
    a. our feelings determine our thoughts.
    b. our feelings determine our actions.
    c. cognitions are the major determinants of how we feel and act.
    d. the best way to change thinking is to reexperience past emotional traumas in the here and now.
    e. insight is essential for any type of change to occur.

39. In cognitive therapy, therapy techniques are designed to:
    a. assist clients in substituting rational beliefs for irrational beliefs.
    b. help clients experience their feelings more intensely.
    c. assist individuals in making alternative interpretations of events in their daily living.
    d. enable clients to deal with their existential loneliness.
    e. teach clients how to think only positive thoughts.

40. The type of cognitive error that involves thinking and interpreting in all-or-nothing terms, or in categorizing experiences in either/or extremes, is known as:
    a. magnification and exaggeration.
    b. polarized thinking.
    c. arbitrary inference.
    d. overgeneralization.
    e. none of the above

41. Beck's cognitive therapy differs from Ellis's REBT in that Beck's approach emphasizes:
    a. more of a Socratic dialogue.
    b. helping clients to discover their misconceptions by themselves.
    c. working with the client in collaborative ways.
    d. more structure in the therapy process.
    e. all of the above

42. Beck's cognitive therapy has been most widely applied to the treatment of:
    a. stress symptoms.
    b. anxiety reactions.
    c. phobias.
    d. depression.
    e. cardiovascular disorders.

43. In Meichenbaum's self-instructional therapy, focus is on:
    a. detecting and debating irrational thoughts.
    b. learning the power of reexperiencing childhood events.
    c. learning the A-B-C theory of emotional disturbances.
    d. carrying out shame-attacking exercises in daily life.
    e. none of the above

44. The cognitive distortion of making conclusions without supporting and relevant evidence is:
    a. labeling and mislabeling.
    b. overgeneralization.
    c. arbitrary inferences.
    d. selective abstraction.
    e. personalization.

45. The cognitive distortion that consists of forming conclusions based on an isolated detail of an event is:
    a. labeling and mislabeling.
    b. overgeneralization.
    c. arbitrary inferences.
    d. selective abstraction.
    e. personalization.

46. The process of holding extreme beliefs on the basis of a single incident and applying them inappropriately to dissimilar events or settings is known as:
    a. labeling and mislabeling.
    b. overgeneralization.
    c. arbitrary inferences.
    d. selective abstraction.

47. The tendency for individuals to relate external events to themselves, even when there is no basis for making this connection, is known as:
    a. labeling and mislabeling.
    b. overgeneralization.
    c. arbitrary inferences.
    d. selective abstraction.
    e. personalization.

48. The cognitive distortion that involves portraying one's identity on the basis of imperfections and mistakes made in the past and allowing them to define one's true identity is:
    a. labeling and mislabeling.
    b. overgeneralization.
    c. arbitrary inferences
    d. selective abstraction.
    e. personalization.

49. To a large degree, cognitive therapy is:
    a. an experiential model.
    b. a psychoeducational model.
    c. a psychodynamic model.
    d. based on principles borrowed from Gestalt therapy.

50. The concept of automatic thoughts plays a central role in whose theory?
    a. Ellis
    b. Beck
    c. Meichenbaum
    d. Lazarus
    e. none of the above

51. Of the following cognitive techniques, which one would Beck be least likely to employ?
    a. exploring cognitive distortions
    b. helping clients to replace negative imagery with more positive and successful coping scenes
    c. confronting the musturbatory thinking of a client
    d. encouraging clients to participate in cognitive rehearsal
    e. teaching clients ways of testing hypotheses

52. According to Meichenbaum, the first step in the change process involves:
    a. learning the A-B-C model of disputing irrational thinking.
    b. learning a new dialogue.
    c. observing one's behavior and thinking patterns.
    d. learning coping skills.
    e. discovering insight into the cause of one's problem.

53. The constructionist perspective in cognitive therapy holds that:
    a. clients must accept objective reality if they hope to change.
    b. there is really no difference between objective and subjective reality.
    c. one's problems are merely a product of one's imagination.
    d. there are multiple realities and a therapist's task is to help clients appreciate how they construct their realities and how they author their own stories.
    e. we all construct irrational beliefs and must change those if we hope to find happiness.

54. Which of the following is *not* a characteristic of Meichenbaum's constructivist approach to cognitive behavior therapy?
    a. It is more structured and more directive than standard cognitive therpy.
    b. It give more emphasis to the past.
    c. It tends to target deeper core beliefs.
    d. It explores the behavioral impact and emotional toll a client pays for clinging to certain metaphors.

ANSWER KEY FOR CHAPTER TEN – COGNITIVE-BEHAVIOR THERAPY

MULTIPLE-CHOICE TEST QUESTIONS

1.	C	14.	C	27.	D	40.	B
2.	E	15.	E	28.	E	41.	E
3.	C	16.	A	29.	A	42.	D
4.	C	17.	D	30.	D	43.	E
5.	D	18.	D	31.	C	44.	C
6.	A	19.	D	32.	B	45.	D

7. D	20. E	33. A	46. B
8. B	21. E	34. D	47. E
9. B	22. A	35. C	48. A
10. E	23. C	36. D	49. B
11. C	24. B	37. E	50. B
12. E	25. B	38. C	51. C
13. D	26. B	39. C	52. C
			53. D
			54. A

COGNITIVE-BEHAVIOR THERAPY

Decide if the following statements are "more true" or "more false" as applied to rational emotive behavior therapy.

1. Ellis contends that research has shown that REBT is effective in helping all types of clients.

2. Ellis claims that his methods are applicable to individual therapy but that his approach does not work well in group therapy.

3. REBT can be considered a form of behavior therapy.

4. REBT makes use of cognitive and behavioral techniques, but it does not use any emotive techniques.

5. Ellis maintains that REBT is an eclectic form of therapy.

6. Ellis maintains that in order for clients to change their behavior, they must be willing to actively carry out assignments in everyday life.

7. According to Ellis, events themselves do not cause emotional disturbances; rather it is our evaluation of these events that causes the problem.

8. REBT hypothesizes that we keep ourselves emotionally disturbed by the process of self-indoctrination.

9. Ellis shares Rogers's view of the client/therapist relationship as a condition for change to occur within clients.

10. REBT contends that humans need the love and acceptance of significant others in order to feel worthwhile.

11. Part of Ellis's motivation for developing REBT was to deal with his own problems.

12. The cognitive-behavioral therapies are largely based on the idea that the reorganization of clients' self-statements is a key to changing their behavior.

13. There is no concept in REBT that in any way agrees with Rogers's idea of unconditional positive regard.

14. Rational-emotive imagery involves teaching relaxation techniques.

15. REBT can be effectively employed in crisis intervention.

16. According to REBT, what is rational corresponds to a description of subjective reality.

17. Beck's therapeutic approach focuses on specific symptoms of depressed clients and the reasons they give for these symptoms.

18. Meichenbaum believes that our self-statements affect us much as statements made by another person do.

19. Stress inoculation is a coping-skills approach designed to change a person's self-statements.

20. From a cognitive perspective, depression is largely due to one's attitudes and beliefs.

ANSWER KEY FOR CHAPTER TEN – COGNITIVE BEHAVIOR-THERAPY

TRUE-FALSE TEST QUESTIONS

1.	F	11.	T
2.	F	12.	T
3.	T	13.	F
4.	F	14.	F
5.	T	15.	T
6.	T	16.	F
7.	T	17.	T
8.	T	18.	T
9.	F	19.	T
10.	F	20.	T

Guidelines for Using Chapter Eleven

Reality Therapy

in

Theory and Practice of Counseling and Psychotherapy and the *Student Manual*

Case Approach to Counseling and Psychotherapy

and

The Art of Integrative Counseling

1. In my lectures on choice theory and reality therapy, I emphasize issues such as: the relationship of reality therapy to behavior therapy, the focus on the present, the controversial idea that mental illness is a myth, the contrasts between psychoanalytic therapy and reality therapy, Glasser's views on the rejection of transference, and the de-emphasis on the client's past. In my lectures on contemporary reality therapy I emphasize such aspects as ways that we choose our misery; how we can explain our behavior; how we are responsible for what we think, feel, and do; and ways that we can increase personal control. These topics, which are covered by Glasser (1998, 2000), lend themselves to lively class discussion.

2. Other key concepts that I focus on in my classes to contrast reality therapy with psychoanalysis include:

   - the existential-phenomenological orientation
   - the nature of choice theory
   - the rejection of the medical model
   - the emphasis on responsibility
   - the de-emphasis on the role of dreams
   - de-emphasis on exploration of the past and focus on the present
   - de-emphasis on transference

Reality therapy provides an interesting contrast to several of the approaches studied earlier, especially psychoanalytic and Gestalt therapies. I tend to focus on ways of applying the basic principles of reality therapy to a variety of problems. In many ways, reality therapy shares common ground with both behavior therapy and cognitive behavior therapy. Reality therapy is primarily concerned with what a client is doing and thinking, and in this respect, it can be considered as a form of cognitive behavior therapy.

3. Case examples, practical situations, and specific problem situations are found in this *Insructor's Resource Manual,* the *Case Approach* book, *Student Manual,* and *The Art of Integrative Counseling* books. These cases can serve as anchors for applying the key concepts of reality therapy. Critical issues include:

    - Is a person's past ever responsible for his or her present life condition? Are individuals victims of their past or of their environment?
    - How might you help a person challenge his or her values?
    - In what ways might you reach a person who engages in antisocial behavior?
    - What might you do if your client threatened suicide? Is this a choice that you would consider acceptable? What if your client made a value judgment of his or her life and decided that he or she no longer wanted to live?

4. I find that applying the procedures of reality therapy to Stan is an effective way of illustrating reality therapy in action. Again, the instructor might "become" Stan and ask one or more students to "become" reality therapists. For comparison, one student might counsel Stan from a person-centered or a Gestalt perspective, and then another student could continue with a reality therapy perspective.

5. **Other Resources:** In addition to the cases Ruth and Manny given in Chapter 11 of the *Student Manual,* you may want to refer to three other resources: *Case Approach; The Art of Integrative Counseling*; and the *CD ROM for Integrative Counseling.*

    Refer to the *Case Approach to Counseling and Psychotherapy* (6th ed., 2005) for a detailed treatment of the case of Ruth from the perspective of reality therapists. In Chapter 9 both Dr. William Glasser and Dr. Robert Wubbolding describe different styles of applying the principles of choice theory to the practice of reality therapy with Ruth. I follow up with my own style of drawing on reality therapy concepts in counseling Ruth.

    Refer to Chapter 8 of *The Art of Integrative Counseling* for a discussion of reality therapy. See the section *Becoming the Client: Behaviorally Oriented Therapy* (pp. 82–85) for a description of how to formulate action plans with clients. As an exercise, I often ask students to devise their own action plan as a way to change one of their behaviors. The WDEP model of reality therapy is especially helpful in bringing about change. Specific suggestions are given on pages 85–86 for developing a behavioral contract, which is often a part of reality therapy. See also pp. 97–98 in Chapter 9 for a discussion of how I incorporate reality therapy into my integrative approach.

    In the *CD ROM for Integrative Counseling*, Session #8 *Behavioral Focus*, you will note ways that I attempt to assist Ruth in specifying concrete behaviors that she will target for change. I do this in considerable more detail in *The Art of Integrative Counseling* book in Chapter 8.

6. Books in reality therapy that I draw on for preparing lectures include:
    - *Choice Theory: A New Psychology of Personal Freedom* (Glasser, 1998)
    - *Counseling with Choice Theory: The New Reality Therapy* (Glasser, 2000)
    - *Reality Therapy for the 21st Century* (Wubbolding, 2000)

KEY TERMS FOR REVIEW AND DEFINITION

William Glasser	punishment
choice theory	reasonable consequences
skillful questioning	total behavior
mental illness	involvement
personal responsibility	responsibility
autonomy	counseling environment
the cycle of counseling	WDEP
present behavior	self-evaluation
past successes	basic human needs

value judgments   quality world or "picture album"
action plan   "paining" behavior
commitment   perceived world
"no excuses"

INFOTRAC KEYWORDS

The following keywords are listed in such a way as to allow the *InfoTrac* search engine to locate a wider range of articles on the online university library. The keywords should be entered *exactly* as listed below, to include astericks, "W1," "W2," "AND," and other search engine tools.

Autonomy AND psych*   Commitment AND psych*
Self-evaluation AND psych*

Reality Therapy

William Glasser
Reality therapy
Choice theory AND Glasser
Control theory and Glasser
Commitment AND treat*
Commitment AND psychol*
Commitment AND therap*
Commitment treatment therapy
Self evaluation AND psychol*
Autonomy AND psychol*

CASE EXAMPLES

CANDY: An adolescent in rebellion

Fourteen-year-old Candy, her father, and her mother are sitting with you in your office for an initial counseling session. Her father begins:

"I'm just at the end of my rope with my daughter! I'm sick and tired of what I see her doing to disrupt our family life. I'm constantly wondering what she'll pull next in her long line of antics. She's gone to the Colorado River with some guys who are older than she is, in outright defiance of my order not to go. She's done any number of things she knows I disapprove of, and the result is that she's suspended from school for three weeks or until she gets some counseling. This was the last straw that broke my back. Her getting kicked out of school was just too much. It moved me to call you, so we can get to the bottom of Candy's problem and get her straightened out. God only knows she needs some straightening out. She's into drugs and dating older men, and I strongly suspect that she's been messing around. Candy knows what my values are, and she knows that what she's doing is wrong. I just don't know how to convince her that if she doesn't change, she'll come to a bad end."

Candy's mother is rather quiet and does not list complaints against Candy. She generally agrees that Candy does seem defiant and says she does not know how to handle her. She says she becomes very upset at seeing her husband get angry and worried over the situation, and she hopes that counseling will help Candy see some of what they see.

As for Candy she initially says very little other than "I guess I've got a problem." She appears very withdrawn, sullen, and not too eager to open up in this situation with her parents. She is in your office mainly because she was brought by her parents.

Show how you would proceed to use the cycle of counseling as a reality therapist if Candy were your client for three sessions.

1. What are your initial reactions, thoughts, and feelings about this situation? How willing would you be to work with Candy as your primary client if she had come in simply because her father said that she needed counseling?

2. Assume that in an individual session with Candy she does open up with you, and you find out that her father's presentation of the problems is correct. In fact, matters are worse than he imagined. Candy tells you that she had an abortion recently after a short affair with a married man in his early 30s. She also tells you that she has been experimenting with various drugs. How might you proceed in working with her if you found yourself being very concerned over where her behavior might lead her? What might you want to say to her?

3. Your central task as a reality therapist is to guide Candy toward making an honest assessment of her current behavior and to help her evaluate the results of her behavior. Show how you will attempt to do this. How will you respond if she resists looking at her own behavior, insisting that her problems stem from her demanding and moralistic father, who is driving her to rebellion?

4. What are *your values* regarding drug usage, sexual experimentation, abortion, accepting parental values, Might you attempt to influence her subtly to change her behavior in the way you think she should? Or do you think that you could accept her choices, *providing* that she made an evaluation of her behavior and decided that she did not really want to change?

5. Assume that you have a session with Candy, her father, and her mother after seeing Candy for three individual sessions. The purpose of this session is to talk about where to go from here and to make recommendations. What would you be inclined to tell the parents? What would you *not* tell the parents? What specific recommendations might you make?

6. The focus has been on Candy. Might you direct the focus to either or both of the parents? Might you want them to look at their actions and attitudes and to see their role in Candy's problem? If so, how might you go about doing this in a way that would not be likely to increase their defensiveness?

JANET: Struggling with substance abuse

The client, a troubled woman of 33, is in your office at a community mental-health center because it is a requirement of her parole. She reports that she has always had difficulties handling her family and her personal life. She says that she had a relatively stable marriage until she found out her "old man was running around with other women." Although she filed for a divorce from him, she never appeared in court, so she is uncertain about her marital status. She reports that after the separation he "disappeared" until quite recently, when he "reappeared out of nowhere" and took their son, now 10, to live with him. She also has two girls, ages 8 and 10, who still live with her. The clients says that once her husband left, she was forced to resort to stealing to support the family and her drug habit.

Janet has been addicted to cocaine for four years. During this period she has had behavioral problems with her two daughters, as well as the son. Eventually she moved in with her current boyfriend, and the behavioral problems with the children escalated. She reports that she is on parole for a theft charge and is afraid that she will have to go back to prison for parole violation because of her drug use.

Janet lets her parole officer know that she has seen you and that she wants to get some help "to get her life together." A few days later her parole officer calls and says that her urine test is "dirty," showing traces of several drugs. The parole officer asks about your treatment plan for therapy and requests that you write your opinion on whether the client should be back in prison.

STUDY GUIDE FOR CHAPTER ELEVEN

REALITY THERAPY

1. What are the characteristics that define reality therapy? Be able to explain these key concepts of reality therapy: basic psychological needs, choice theory, rejection of the medical model, responsibility, role of the past, and role of transference.

2. What is the view of human nature in current reality therapy?

3. What is the overall goal of reality therapy? What is the focus of this approach? What are the main tasks of the reality therapist? What are clients expected to do in therapy?

4. Describe the elements involved in the cycle of counseling. Discuss the two major components of the cycle of counseling: the counseling environment, and specific procedures that lead to behavior change.

5. Discuss each of the following dimensions of the counseling environment:
   - personal involvement with the client
   - counselor attitudes and behaviors that promote change

6. Discuss each of the following procedures in the practice of reality therapy that lead to change: exploring wants, needs, and perceptions, focus on current behavior, getting clients to evaluate their behavior, planning and commitment.

7. Take the cases of Candy and Janet in this *Instructors Resource Manual* and show how you would apply the concepts and procedures of reality therapy to their cases. Review the cases presented in *Case Approach* and in the *Student Manual* to see how other therapists utilize reality therapy in their practice.

8. What role do diagnostic techniques play in reality therapy?

9. What part does commitment play in reality therapy?

10. What are Glasser's views on mental illness and mental health?

11. What is the purpose of developing an action plan? How might a client and counselor develop such a plan?

12. Why does a reality therapist consider it essential that clients make an evaluation or value judgment of their current behavior?

13. Mention some of the main applications of reality therapy.

14. Mention what you consider to be the main contributions and the main limitations of the approach from a multicultural perspective.

15. Think of some areas of your life that you want to change. How might the principles and procedures of reality therapy be useful to you in bringing about these changes?

16. How might you integrate some of the concepts and procedures of reality therapy with some of the other therapeutic approaches you have studied?

17. What is your personal evaluation of reality therapy? Discuss what you consider the main contributions and limitations of reality therapy.

18. What are some aspects of reality therapy that you would most want to incorporate into your personal style of counseling?

Chapter Eleven

Theory and Practice of

Counseling and Psychotherapy

MULTIPLE-CHOICE TEST ITEMS FOR CHAPTER ELEVEN

REALITY THERAPY

1. The founder of reality therapy is:
   a. Albert Ellis.
   b. Albert Bandura.
   c. Joseph Wolpe.
   d. none of the above

2. Reality therapy is best categorized as:
   a. a brand of psychoanalytic therapy.
   b. a form of nondirective therapy.
   c. a derivative of Gestalt therapy.
   d. a derivative of Adlerian therapy.
   e. a form of cognitive behavior therapy.

3. Reality therapy has gained popularity with:
   a. school counselors and administrators.
   b. school teachers, both elementary and secondary.
   c. rehabilitation workers.
   d. all of the above
   e. none of the above

4. Reality therapy is *best* described as:
   a. an intensive and long-term therapy.
   b. a rational therapy.
   c. an insight therapy.
   d. a short-term therapy that stresses doing.
   e. an experiential therapy stressing feelings and attitudes.

5. According to choice theory:
   a. insight is necessary before behavior change can occur.
   b. insight is not necessary for producing behavior change.
   c. insight will come only with changed attitudes.
   d. insight can be given to the client by the teachings of the therapist.
   e. insight is achieved by the technique of free association.

6. Which is not a key concept of reality therapy?
   a. Focus is on the present not the past.
   b. Emphasis is given to unconscious motivation.
   c. Emphasis is on client self-evaluation.
   d. Commitment is part of the therapy process.
   e. Stress is on assisting clients in developing satisfactory relationships

7. Which of the following is not true of reality therapy?
   a. Punishment is eliminated.
   b. Clients must make commitments.
   c. Therapists do not accept excuses or blaming.
   d. Therapy is a didactic process.
   e. Working through the transference relationship is essential for therapy to occur.

8. Regarding the goals of reality therapy:
   a. it is the therapist's responsibility to decide specific goals for clients.
   b. clients are helped to get connected or reconnected with the people they have chosen to put in their quality world and are taught choice theory.
   c. the goals of therapy should be universal to all clients.
   e. society must determine the proper goals for all clients.

9. The function of the reality therapist is:
   a. to assist clients in dealing with the present.
   b. to encourage clients to make a value judgment concerning the quality of their behavior.
   c. to confront clients about specific irrational thoughts and ideas and to teach them to think rationally.
   d. to reindoctrinate clients with the acceptable standards for living.
   e. none of the above

10. Concerning the role and place of evaluation in therapy:
   a. it is the therapist's function to evaluate the appropriateness of the client's behavior.
   b. it is the client's place to make his or her own evaluation concerning his or her behavior.
   c. evaluation should not be a part of therapy.
   d. therapist evaluation should be given only when clients ask their therapists for such feedback.

11. Which statement is not true of reality therapy?
   a. The therapist establishes involvement with the client.
   b. It focuses on attitude change as a prerequisite for behavior change.
   c. Planning is essential.
   d. Commitment is essential.
   e. The focus is on the client's strengths.

12. Which method(s) is (are) often used in reality therapy?
   a. behavior-oriented methods
   b. the contract method
   c. use of role playing
   d. confronting clients
   e. all of the above

13. Which of the following would not be used by a reality therapist?
   a. the use of drugs and medication
   b. the use of hypnosis
   c. the analysis of dreams
   d. the search for causes of current problems
   e. none of the above would be used

14. Which of the following procedures would a reality therapist be least likely to employ?
   a. skillful questioning
   b. encouraging clients to look at what they are doing
   c. making action plans
   d. engaging in homework to change behaviors
   e. reliving an early childhood event

15. Which of the following is not a function of the reality therapist?
   a. focusing on areas in the client's life that need improvement so that they can achieve a "success identity"
   b. setting limits in the therapeutic setting
   c. getting clients to be specific about how they will make desired changes
   d. confronting clients by not accepting their excuses
   e. helping clients reformulate their plans, if necessary

16. All of the following are true about *planning* and *commitment* in reality therapy, except:
   a. Clients make a commitment to carry out their plans.
   b. There is a connection between a person's identity and their level of commitment.
   c. A great deal of time is spent on this step of reality therapy.
   d. Commitment puts the responsibility for changing on the client.
   e. Therapists only ask for commitments that are reasonable.

17. Reality therapy is based on which of the following orientations to understanding human behavior?
    a. radical behavioristic
    b. psychoanalytic
    c. existential-phenomenological
    d. deterministic
    e. person-centered theory0

18. According to reality therapy, which of the following is not true as it relates to mental illness and mental health?
    a. Psychosis can be directly related to distorted thinking patterns.
    b. Mental health is equated with responsibility in fulfilling one's needs.
    c. Mental illness is what happens when people cannot control the world to satisfy their needs.
    d. Mental illness is not a reaction to external events.
    e. We choose neurotic or psychotic behavior.

19. Reality therapists are likely to deal with all of the following except for:
    a. what a client is currently doing.
    b. what clients are thinking and feeling, when this relates to what they are doing.
    c. a client's relationships with significant others.
    d. assisting clients in developing an action plan geared for change.
    e. asking clients to recall, report, and share dreams.

20. A reality therapist will primarily focus on:
    a. past behavior.
    b. present behavior.
    c. feelings.
    d. thoughts.
    e. the client's personal history.

21. When reality therapists explore a client's past, they tend to focus on:
    a. relationships within the family.
    b. early traumatic events.
    c. problems in school performance.
    d. past successes.
    e. developmental problems.

22. In reality therapy, the purpose of developing an action plan is:
    a. to encourage clients to stretch beyond their limits.
    b. to teach clients to "think big."
    c. to arrange for successful experience.
    d. to arrive at the ultimate solution to a client's problem.
    e. both (a) and (b)

23. In reality therapy, when a client fails to carry out their plans, the therapist will:
    a. use a behavioral form of punishment.
    b. "put the client down" to arouse their anger and motivate them to change.
    c. accept their excuses.
    d. make a value judgment about the client's behavior.
    e. challenge the client to accept the reasonable consequence of their behavior.

24. Which of the following is (are) a contribution of reality therapy?
    a. It helps clients deal emotionally with unfinished business from their past.
    b. It provides insight into the causes of one's problems.
    c. It provides a structure for both clients and therapist to evaluate the degree and the nature of changes.
    d. Most of its concepts have been subjected to empirical testing.
    e. both (a) and (b)

25. Reality therapy rests on the central idea that:
    a. thinking largely determines how we feel and behave.
    b. we choose our behavior and are responsible for what we do, think, and feel.
    c. environmental factors largely control what we are doing.
    d. the way to change dysfunctional behavior is to reexperience a situation in which we originally became psychologically stuck.

26. Glasser would agree with all of the following conclusions except:
    a. We are most likely to change if we are threatened by punishment.
    b. We do not have to be the victim of our past.
    c. We have more control over our lives than we believe.
    d. We strive to change the world outside ourselves to match our internal pictures of what we want.
    e. We often seek therapy when we do not have the relationships we want.

27. The core of reality therapy consists of:
    a. teaching clients how to acquire rational beliefs instead of irrational beliefs.
    b. helping clients to understand their unconscious dynamics.
    c. giving clients opportunities to express unresolved feelings.
    d. teaching clients to take effective control of their own lives.
    e. identifying their cognitive distortions by means of a Socratic dialogue.

28. Glasser identifies four psychological needs, which are the forces that drive us. Which of the following is *not* one of the needs that he focuses on?
    a. self-actualization
    b. belonging
    c. power
    d. freedom
    e. fun

29. All of the following are procedures that are commonly used in reality therapy except:
    a. exploring wants, needs, and perceptions.
    b. exploring early recollections.
    c. focusing on current behavior.
    d. planning and commitment.
    e. skillful questioning.

30. Which of the following procedures would a reality therapist be least likely to employ?
    a. self-help procedures
    b. the use of humor
    c. homework assignments
    d. asking a client to emotionally reexperience a childhood experience
    e. asking questions to get a better sense of the client's inner world

31. Which of the following statements is true as it applies to control theory?
    a. Behavior is the result of external forces.
    b. We are controlled by the events that occur in our lives.
    c. We can control the behavior of others by learning to actively listen to them.
    d. We are motivated completely by internal forces, and our behavior is our best attempt to get what we want.
    e. We can more easily control our feelings than our actions.

32. According to Glasser, all of the following are basic psychological needs except:
    a. competition.
    b. belonging.
    c. power.
    d. freedom.
    e. fun.

33. Sometimes it seems as if people actually choose to be miserable (depressed). Glasser explains the dynamics of *depressing* as based on:
    a. keeping anger under control.
    b. getting others to help us.
    c. excusing our unwillingness to do something more effective.
    d. all of the above
    e. none of the above

34. All of the following are procedures in reality therapy that are said to lead to change except for:
    a. exploring wants, needs, and perceptions.
    b. focusing on current behavior.
    c. the therapist evaluating the client's behavior.
    d. the client evaluating his or her own behavior.
    e. the client committing to a plan of action.

35. According to Glasser, many of the problems of clients are caused by:
    a. unfinished business with parents.
    b. sibling rivalry.
    c. early childhood trauma.
    d. their inability to connect or to have a satisfying relationship with at least one of the significant people in their lives.
    e. the failure to receive praise and approval from the members of their family.

36. All of the following are key characteristics of contemporary reality therapy except for which one?
    a. There is a focus on talking about symptoms that bring a client into therapy.
    b. Emphasis is on choice and responsibility.
    c. There is a rejection of the notion of transference.
    d. Therapy is kept in the present.
    e. Clients are helped to get connected or reconnected with the people they have chosen to put in their quality world.

ANSWER KEY FOR CHAPTER ELEVEN – REALITY THERAPY

MULTIPLE-CHOICE TEST QUESTIONS

1. D	13. E	25. B
2. E	14. E	26. A
3. D	15. A	27. D
4. D	16. C	28. A
5. B	17. C	29. B
6. B	18. A	30. D
7. E	19. E	31. D
8. B	20. B	32. A
9. A	21. D	33. D
10. B	22. C	34. C
11. B	23. E	35. D
12. E	24. C	36. A

TRUE–FALSE TEST ITEMS FOR CHAPTER ELEVEN

REALITY THERAPY

Decide if the following statements are "more true" or "more false" from the reality therapy perspective.

1. Choice theory is the theoretical foundation for the practice of reality therapy.

2. Reality therapy is based on the assumption that it is the therapist's job to make an evaluation of the client's present behavior.

3. Reality therapy cautions against the therapist mentoring the client.

4. Contemporary reality therapy is based on the assumption that people are moved by inner forces; that is, that behavior is not caused by environmental factors.

5. Choice theory emphasizes that what happens outside us in the real world is of little significance unless it relates to what is inside us in our personal world.

6. One of the procedures of reality therapy is to work through unfinished business from the past.

7. Reality therapists see therapeutic value in working with a client's dreams.

8. Glasser's more recent writings give more emphasis to a noncritical, nonjudgmental, and accepting attitude on the therapist's part.

9. Reality therapists ask clients to take a hard look at whether their current actions are working for them.

10. Reality therapy sees transference as a way for the therapist to avoid getting personally involved in the clients' lives.

11. The core of reality therapy is developing a plan for change as a way of translating talk into action.

12. The first step in the process of reality therapy consists of a comprehensive assessment leading to a specific diagnosis.

13. Commitment puts the responsibility directly on clients for changing.

14. Reality therapists refuse to accept excuses.

15. Reality therapists use punishment as a way to help clients follow through with their plans and commitments.

16. Reality therapy tends to be a long-term approach.

17. Reality therapy is a popular approach in correctional work.

18. Therapeutic contracts are frequently used in reality therapy.

19. Reality therapy is basically active, directive, practical, didactic, cognitive, and behavioral.

20. Choice theory is based on the assumption that people are in charge of their own destiny.

21. Reality therapists maintain that clients will not change unless they assume a self-critical attitude.

22. Clients are expected to focus on their feelings and attitudes, and then their behavior will change.

23. Glasser recommends that therapists look back for the causes of a client's present failures.

24. A main function of the reality therapist is to encourage clients to assess their behavior to determine how well it is working for them.

25. Reality therapy is often used in treating drug and alcohol abusers.

26. It is the job of the reality therapist to convey the idea that no matter how bad things are there is hope.

ANSWER KEY FOR CHAPTER ELEVEN – REALITY THERAPY

TRUE–FALSE TEST QUESTIONS

1.	T	14.	T
2.	F	15.	F
3.	F	16.	F
4.	T	17.	T
5.	T	18.	T
6.	F	19.	T
7.	F	20.	T
8.	T	21.	F
9.	T	22.	F
10.	T	23.	F
11.	T	24.	T
12.	F	25.	T
13.	T	26.	T

Guidelines for Using Chapter Twelve

Feminist Therapy

in

Theory and Practice of Counseling and Psychotherapy and the *Student Manual*

Case Approach to Counseling and Psychotherapy

and

The Art of Integrative Counseling

1. The pre-chapter self-inventory in the **Student Manual** is a good device for assisting students in assessing the degree to which they agree with the basic principles of feminist therapy. You could ask students to identify the differences between feminist therapy and the prior theoretical approaches they have studied.

2. You might consider asking a guest speaker who identifies herself as a feminist therapist to talk to your class about how her theory influences her work with both women and men. For example, the director of the Women's Center at California State University, Fullerton often presents a special lecture to my classes on gender issues in counseling practice.

3. In your lectures, you might want to briefly show some of the unique aspects of the various forms of feminist philosophy: liberal feminism, cultural feminism, radical feminism, social feminism, postmodern feminism, women of color feminism, lesbian feminism, and global/international feminism.

4. A topic of interest for a lecture is a comparison between the psychoanalytic perspective on personality development (addressed in Chapter 4) and the feminist perspective on personality development. What are some of the key differences? Are there possible ways to combine some core aspects from both theoretical orientations and apply them to a more comprehensive understanding of personality development?

5. As a classroom activity, you might develop some exercises aimed at helping your students identify and challenge traditional roles for both women and men. Ask your students to identify a few personality characteristics they see in themselves that have been strongly influenced by socialization. Are there certain gender roles that your students have grown up with that they are now seriously questioning? You might refer to the chapter on gender roles for women and men in *I Never Knew I Had a Choice* (Corey & Corey, 2002) for ideas on creating exercises that can be applied to small group discussions.

6. The goal of feminist therapy is transformation both in the individual client and in society as a whole. As a part of your lecture, you might want to stress how this perspective differs from the primary goals of the other therapeutic approaches covered thus far in ***TPCP***. There are implications of this goal for the therapist's role and function that you might want to elaborate upon in your lecture.

7. A small group activity for this chapter consists of asking students to explore ways that feminist therapy emphasizes some unique concepts, especially when these concepts are compared with key concepts of the traditional counseling approaches.

8. A useful focus for a lecture on this chapter is to describe some of the main techniques and strategies that are uniquely associated with feminist therapy such as: gender-role analysis, gender-role intervention, power analysis and power intervention, and social action. Of course, there are other techniques shared with other theories such as assertiveness training, reframing and relabeling, and bibliotherapy.

9. The case of Stan will be of special interest in this chapter, since feminist therapy is being applied to conceptualizing many of Stan's problems. You might ask students to note particular aspects of this therapist's work with Stan such as: establishing an egalitarian relationship at the initial session; conducting a gender-role analysis; reviewing with Stan messages he incorporated regarding being a man; challenging societal expectations; assigning homework and use of bibliotherapy; ways of dealing with Stan's mother and father in therapy; and combining several approaches with feminist therapy.

10. In the ***Student Manual,*** for each of the chapters, the case of Ruth has been highlighted. This would be a good time to concentrate on Ruth's case from a comparative perspective. How would a feminist therapist deal with Ruth in a somewhat different manner than the other therapeutic models thus far considered? Below are some questions that would be useful as catalysts for discussion on this topic:

    a. What are some of the ways that you might integrate concepts and techniques from the other therapy orientations you've studied with feminist therapy? Are there any theories that you think would not fit with a feminist perspective? If so, which ones, and why?

    b. What are some of the major contributions of the feminist perspective in working with Ruth? What themes from this approach would you most want to incorporate in counseling Ruth?

    c. Feminist therapists believe in the value of educating clients about the therapy process and stress the importance of an egalitarian relationship. What other counseling approaches share these values? What are your thoughts about demystifying therapy and establishing collaborative (and equal) relationships with a client such as Ruth?

    d. Feminist therapy takes a dim view of traditional diagnosis and assessment. What other therapies share this view? At this point, what are your thoughts about the use of the DSM-IV-TR as a basis for making an assessment and arriving at a diagnosis?

    e. Feminist assessment and diagnosis requires a cooperative and phenomenological approach. If you accept the feminist perspective on assessment and diagnosis, what problems might you expect to encounter in an agency that required you to come up with a diagnosis during an intake session? What would you say to Ruth if she were enrolled in a managed care program that permitted a maximum of six therapy sessions, and then only if a suitable diagnosis is submitted to the health provider?

    f. Feminist therapy focuses on gender-role and power analysis. What ways might you employ these interventions in your work with Ruth? To what degree have you thought about ways that your gender-role socialization have influenced your views of what it means to be a woman or a man? How might you views influence your work with a client like Ruth?

g. How might your values pertaining to equality in relationships either work for or against you if Ruth tells you that see is seeking adjustment more than change in her life?

h. As you read about the basic tenets of feminism, to what extent do you think a feminist therapist might impose her values on a client? Do you think that it is appropriate for a therapist to teach clients ways of challenging the status quo and a patriarchial system? What modifications, if any, might you make in applying feminist therapy to clients who embraced cultural values that kept women in a subservient role?

i. If Ruth were your client, how specifically might you encourage her to take social and political action?

11. Refer to *Case Approach to Counseling and Psychotherapy* for examples of several feminist therapists who demonstrate their own perspectives on counseling Ruth. The basic assumptions, goals of therapy, and therapy strategies of feminist therapy have been detailed in the section written by Drs. Kathy Evans, Susan Seem, and Elizabeth Kincade in their discussion of Ruth. Dr. Pam Remer, a feminist therapist, demonstrates principles and techniques in dealing with Ruth as a sexual assault survivor. In my description of counseling Ruth from a feminist perspective, I deal with how I would enlist her as a collaborator. In working with Ruth from a feminist perspective my intention is to be clear about the core principles and premises that are underlying my counseling practice.

12. Refer to *The Art of Integrative Counseling* text for several discussions of how I draw from feminist therapy principles and techniques. See especially Chapter 2, *The Therapeutic Relationship*, for a discussion of how feminist therapy ideas are most useful as a foundation for developing a working therapeutic relationship (pp. 15–22). Chapters 1 to 5 contain references to how feminist therapy can be applied to the topics under discussion. Chapter 9, *An Integrative Focus*, details ways that feminist and family systems approaches can be incorporated into an integrative counseling model (pp. 99–100).

13. The *CD ROM for Integrative Counseling* will be especially useful to illustrate some principles and procedures of feminist therapy. If you are using this video as a part of the course, this would be a good time to ask students to look for feminist issues in the counseling with Ruth. The video and workbook will be especially useful as a demonstrations of interventions I make with Ruth that illustrate some principles and procedures of feminist therapy. (See especially Sessions #1 to #5, and #11). *The Art of Integrative Counseling* book (especially Chapters 1 to 5 and 11) reflect some basic principles drawn from feminist therapy as they are applied to an integrative perspective.

14. In preparing your lectures on feminist therapy, there are many references cited throughout the chapter. A few books that I have found useful are:

- *Feminist Perspectives in Therapy: An Empowering Diverse Women* (Worell & Remer, 2003)
- *Shaping the Future of Feminist Psychology: Education, Research, and Practice* (Worell & Johnson, 1997)
- *Feminist Theories and Feminist Psychotherapies* (Enns, 1997, 2003)
- *The Healing Connection: How Women Form Relationships in Therapy and Life* (Miller & Stiver, 1997)
- *Women's Growth in Diversity: More Writings from the Stone Center* (Jordon, 1997)
- *Subversive Dialogues: Theory in Feminist Therapy* (Brown, 1994)

KEY TERMS FOR REVIEW AND DEFINITION

Androcentricism	gender-fair counseling
egalitarian relationship	gender-based phenomena
ethnocentricism	feminist consciousness
gendercentricism	status quo
gender-fair theory	assertiveness training
gender-role analysis	white privilege
gender-role intervention	white male privilege
gender schema theory	feminist consciousness
heterosexism	gender equity
life-span perspective	social action
personal is political	patriarchy

power analysis   institutionalized sexism
power intervention   social transformation
reframing   self-in-relation model of development
relabeling   liberal feminism
self-in-relation theory
relational-cultural theory   cultural feminists
interactionist theories   radical feminists
gender-role expectations   socialist feminists
gender-role socialization   engendered lives
consciousness-raising techniques gender stereotypes
postmodern feminists   women of color feminists
lesbian feminists   global/international feminists

INFOTRAC KEYWORDS

The following keywords are listed in such a way as to allow the **InfoTrac** search engine to locate a wider range of articles on the online university library. The keywords should be entered *exactly* as listed below, to include astericks, "W1," "W2," "AND," and other search engine tools.

Heterosexism   Femin* AND psych*
Gender W1 schema   Interdependence AND femin*
Feminist W1 consciousness   Interdependence AND psych*

Feminist Therapy

Laura Brown
Carol Gilligan
Jean Baker Miller
Feminist Therapy
Femin* AND psychol*
Stone W1 Center
Relational W1 model
Heterosexism
Gender W1 schema*
Feminist W1 consciousness
Assertiveness training
Bibliotherapy

STUDY GUIDE FOR CHAPTER TWELVE

FEMINIST THERAPY

1. Feminist therapy is built on the premise that it is essential to consider the social and cultural context that contributes to a person's problems in order to understand that person. This implies that therapy should be aimed not only for individual change, but for social change. If you accept this principle, how would this affect your way of working with clients? How does this approach differ from the prior theories that you have studied?

2. What is the view of human nature from a feminist perspective? What are the basic characteristics of a gender-biased theory? What are the basic constructs of a gender-fair therapy?

3. What is the primary goal of feminist therapy? What is the focus of this approach?

4. In what ways do feminist therapists carry out functions that are similar to traditional therapy? What are some unique roles and functions that distinguish feminist therapists?

5. How can feminist principles and methods be incorporated in other therapeutic orientations?

6. Feminist therapists do not restrict their practices to women clients; they also work with men, couples, families, and children. What are some ways you think that feminist therapy concepts can be applied to counseling men?

7. There is debate over the issue of men being able to do feminist therapy. Do you believe that men can practice feminist therapy? Do you think it is essential that women clients seek female therapists?

8. In feminist therapy, the therapeutic relationship is based on empowerment and egalitarianism. If you were to practice from this perspective, how could you work to equalize the power differential in the therapy relationship? What interventions would you make to increase the empowerment of clients?

9. What are some of the ways that you could demystify the therapeutic process at the initial session? What kinds of information would you most want to give to your clients? What would you do to promote a collaborative partnership?

10. What are some feminist therapy interventions that you are most likely to employ in working with both women and men? What techniques from other therapy schools would you be inclined to use along with feminist strategies?

11. Social action is a main feminist intervention. Can you think of some examples of social action strategies that you might suggest for certain clients?

12. Feminist therapists do not use diagnostic labels, or they use them reluctantly. They are critical of traditional assessment and diagnosis because of the belief that these procedures are often based on sexist assumptions. What are your thoughts concerning the feminist critique of assessment and diagnosis?

13. A part of the feminist critique is assessment and diagnosis is that these procedures are often influenced by subtle forms of sexism, racism, ethnocentricism, heterosexism, ageism, or classism. What are your views pertaining to this feminist critique?

14. The role of feminist therapists cannot be separated from certain personal characteristics. They are committed to monitoring their own biases and distortions, they are willing to share themselves during the therapy hour, they model proactive behaviors, and they are committed to their own consciousness-raising process. To what degree do you see these characteristics in yourself?

15. Feminist therapists are committed to understanding oppression in all its forms --- sexism, racism, heterosexim --- and the impact of oppression and discrimination on psychological well-being. To what extent do you think that this broad agenda is an appropriate role for counselors to assume? Would you want to prepare yourself as a counselor to be able to deal with oppression in any form it may take with your clients?

16. Some feminist therapist writers maintain that although individuals are not to blame for their personal problems that are largely caused by dysfunctional social environments, they are responsible for working toward change. What are your thoughts on this position? If you accept this contention, what implications might this have for the way in which you practice therapy?

17. Feminist therapists tend to used self-disclosure to equalize the client/therapist relationship, to normalize women's collective experiences, to empower the client, and to establish informed consent. What guidelines might you use to determine the therapeutic value of your self-disclosures to clients? What are some reasons that you would share your experiences with your clients?

18. It is clear that feminist therapists have certain agendas such as social change, addressing political factors contributing to oppression, and striving for gender equity. To what degree do you think that having an agenda for a client poses potential problems involving imposition of a therapist's values or pushing clients in a certain direction?

19. What are some criticisms or shortcomings of the feminist approach?

20. What do you consider to be some of the major contributions of the feminist approach to the counseling profession?

Test Items

Chapter Twelve

Theory and Practice of Counseling and Psychotherapy

MULTIPLE CHOICE TEST ITEMS FOR CHAPTER TWELVE

FEMINIST THERAPY

1. From the perspective of feminist therapy, the socialization of women inevitably affects their:
   a. identity development.
   b. self-concept.
   c. goals and aspirations.
   d. emotional well-being.
   e. all of the above

2. The four feminist philosophies of liberal, cultural, radical, and socialist have in common:
   a. the same view of the sources of oppression of women.
   b. the same methods of bringing about societal change.
   c. the same goal of activism.
   d. a basic agreement that the therapist is the expert.
   e. a basic agreement on the value of diagnosis in counseling.

3. Feminist therapists, regardless of their philosophical orientation, believe all of the following except that:
   a. gender is at the core of therapeutic practice.
   b. human development and interaction are similar across races, cultures, and nations.
   c. understanding a client's problems requires adopting a sociocultural perspective.
   d. the client-therapist relationship should be an egalitarian one.
   e. empowerment of the individual and societal changes are core goals of therapy.

4. All of the following are characteristic of gender-biased theories except for the concept or practice of:
   a. gendercentricism.
   b. heterosexism.
   c. intrapsychic orientation.
   d. interactionist orientation.
   e. determinism.

5. Which of the feminist principles views the therapist as simply another source of information, rather than as the expert in the therapy process?
   a. the person is political.
   b. the counseling relationship is egalitarian.
   c. women's experiences are honored.
   d. definitions of distress and mental illness are reformulated.
   e. an integrated analysis of oppression.

6. Which of the following feminist principles recognizes the importance of working against oppression on the basis of race, class, culture, religious beliefs, sexual orientation, age, and disability?
   a. the person is political.
   b. the counseling relationship is egalitarian.
   c. women's experiences are honored.
   d. definitions of distress and mental illness are reformulated.
   e. an integrated analysis of oppression.

7. Which of the following feminist principles implies that what has been typically viewed as individual clients' personal problems are really socially and politically caused?
   a. the person is political.
   b. the counseling relationship is egalitarian.
   c. women's experiences are honored.
   d. definitions of distress and mental illness are reformulated.
   e. an integrated analysis of oppression.

8. All of the following are goals of feminist therapy except for:
   a. striving for gender equality.
   b. confronting forms of institutional oppression.
   c. resolving intrapsychic conflicts from early childhood.
   d. helping clients embrace their personal power.
   e. freeing clients of gender role socialization.

9. Although feminist therapy shares many of the premises of person-centered therapy, feminist therapy does not agree with the notion that:
   a. the therapeutic relationship is, in an of itself, sufficient to produce change.
   b. therapy is based on unconditional positive regard and acceptance.
   c. the therapeutic relationship should be a non-hierarchical one.
   d. therapy aims to empower clients to live according to their own values and to rely on an internal locus of control.
   e. therapists should be genuine rather than hiding behind an expert role.

10. Which of the following themes would clients in feminist therapy be least likely to explore?
    a. messages received in growing up
    b. critically evaluating social dictates and expectations
    c. power and control
    d. transference reactions toward their therapist
    e. external forces influencing behavior

11. Which of the following techniques would a feminist therapist be least likely to employ?
    a. interpretation of the transference relationship
    b. therapeutic contracts
    c. assertiveness training
    d. gender-role analysis
    e. power analysis and intervention

12. Of the following, which intervention would a feminist therapist probably consider most essential?
    a. challenging irrational beliefs
    b. making use of the empty-chair technique
    c. conducting a lifestyle analysis
    d. social action
    e. interpretation of resistance

13. All of the following are reasons many feminist therapists do not use diagnostic labels, or use them reluctantly, except for which one?
    a. Diagnostic labels reinforce gender role stereotypes.
    b. Diagnostic labels reflect the inappropriate application of power in the therapeutic relationship.
    c. Diagnostic labels focus on the social factors that cause dysfunctional behavior.
    e. Diagnostic labels encourage adjustment to the norms of the status quo.

14. An alternative to traditional diagnosis and assessment that is preferred by feminist therapists is:
    a. power analysis.
    b. gender role analysis.
    c. lifestyle analysis.
    d. analysis of transference and resistance.

15. Which of the following interventions involves a shift from "blaming the victim" to consideration of social factors in the environment that contribute to a client's problem?
    a. paradoxical intention
    b. reframing
    c. relabeling
    d. cognitive homework

16. All of the following strategies are unique to feminist therapy except for:
    a. cognitive restructuring.
    b. encouraging clients to take social action.
    c. being an advocate in challenging conventional attitudes about roles for women.
    d. power analysis and intervention.
    e. gender-role analysis and intervention.

17. Cognitive behavioral therapies and feminist therapy have a number of features in common. Of the following, which is not one an assumption shared by both approaches?
    a. viewing the therapeutic relationship as collaborative
    b. taking the position that the therapeutic relationship alone is necessary and sufficient to bring about change
    c. helping clients to take charge of their own lives
    d. commitment to demystifying therapy
    e. providing information to clients about how the therapy process works

18. A defining theme in the practice of feminist therapy is:
    a. the inclusion of the client in the assessment process.
    b. the inclusion of the client in the treatment process.
    c. the therapist conducting a lifestyle analysis early during the therapy process.
    d. expecting clients to be willing to engage in long-term therapy.
    e. both (a) and (b)

19. A feminist therapy is likely to become an advocate for change in the social structure by arguing for:
    a. the right to self-determination.
    b. the freedom to pursue a career outside the home.
    c. the right to an education.
    d. equality in power in relationships.
    e. all of the above.

20. Of the following, which is one of the major contributions that feminists have made to the field of counseling?
    a. a focus on dealing with family dynamics
    b. a focus on exploring the unconscious factors contributing to current problems
    c. paving the way for gender-sensitive practice
    d. placing the therapeutic relationship at the core of the therapy process
    e. assisting clients to increase awareness of here and now experiencing

21. Which of the following is not associated with the "third wave" of feminism?
    a. postmodern feminists
    b. cognitive behavioral feminists
    c. women of color feminists
    d. lesbian feminists
    e. global/international feminists

22. The constructs of feminist theory, in contrast to traditional theories, include all of the following except for which characteristic?
    a. intrapsychic orientation
    b. gender-fair
    c. flexible/multicultural
    d. life-span oriented
    e. interactionist

23. The relational-cultural theory emphasizes the vital role:
    a. that relationships and connectedness with others play in the lives of women.
    b. of a spiritual or religious perspective in providing women with strength.
    c. in understanding how early childhood is a crucial factor in a woman's personality development.
    d. that siblings play in the shaping of personality.
    e. all of the above

24. The feminist perspectives on the development of personality:
   a. encompass the diversity and complexity of women's lives.
   b. attend to the ways in which diversity influences self-structures.
   c. recognize the inextricable connection between internal and external worlds.
   d. acknowledge the political and social oppression of women.
   e. all of the above

25. Which of the following principles of feminist psychology provides a major vehicle for integrating diversity into feminist therapy?
   a. The personal is political.
   b. Personal and social identities are interdependent.
   c. The counseling relationship is egalitarian.
   d. Women's perspectives are valued.
   e. all of the above

ANSWER KEY FOR CHAPTER TWELVE – FEMINIST THERAPY

MULTIPLE-CHOICE TEST QUESTIONS

1.	E	11.	A
2.	C	12.	D
3.	B	13.	C
4.	D	14.	B
5.	B	15.	B
6.	E	16.	A
7.	A	17.	B
8.	C	18.	E
9.	A	19.	E
10.	D	20.	C
		21.	B
		22.	A
		23.	A
		24.	E
		25.	B

TRUE–FALSE TEST ITEMS FOR CHAPTER TWELVE
FEMINIST THERAPY

Decide if the following statements are "more true" or "more false" from the feminist therapy perspective.

1. Feminist therapy is not static, but is continually evolving.

2. Feminist therapists do not tend to engage in self-disclosure because of their concern over unduly influencing the client.

3. By considering contextual variable, *symptoms* are reframed as survival strategies.

4. The female therapist may share some of her own struggles with sex role oppression with her client.

5. Feminist therapists restrict their practices to women clients.

6. Feminist therapist avoid sharing their values to clients in order to reduce the chance of value imposition.

7. Feminist therapists work to demystify the counseling relationship.

8. Bibliotherapy is frequently used in feminist therapy.

9. Feminist therapy incorporates techniques from many of the various traditional approaches.

10. Traditional theories of counseling place the cause of problems with external circumstances and environmental factors.

11. It is possible to incorporate the principle of feminist therapy with a multicultural perspective.

12. A feminist therapist generally does not expect the client to assume responsibility for making internal or external changes.

13. According to feminist therapists, an intrapsychic orientation tends to result in blaming the victim.

14. Gender-free theories explain differences in the behavior of women and men on the basis of true natures, rather than on learning.

15. An andocentric theory uses female-oriented constructs to draw conclusions about human nature.

16. Heterosexism views a heterosexual orientation as normative and desirable, and devalues same-sex life styles.

17. Gendercentric theories propose two separate paths of development for women and men.

18. Feminist therapists emphasize that societal gender role expectations profoundly influence a person's identity from birth and become deeply engrained in adult personality.

19. According to the relational-cultural model, a woman's sense of self depends largely on how she connects with others.

20. In feminist therapy, adjustment rather than transcendence is a primary goal of therapy.

21. Today's feminists believe that gender can be considered separately from other identity areas such as race, ethnicity, class, and sexual orientation.

22. The contemporary version of feminist therapy and the multicultural approach to counseling practice have a great deal in common.

23. At the present time there is a unified feminist theory.

24. Feminist therapy is not static, but is continually evolving and maturing.

25. While most feminist therapists believe that gender is always an important factor, they realize that ethnicity, sexual orientation, and class may be more important factors in certain situations for many women.

ANSWER KEY FOR CHAPTER TWELVE – FEMINIST THERAPY

TRUE–FALSE TEST QUESTIONS

1.	T	11.	T
2.	F	12.	F
3.	T	13.	T
4.	T	14.	F
5.	F	15.	F
6.	F	16.	T
7.	T	17.	T
8.	T	18.	T
9.	T	19.	T
10.	F	20.	F
		21.	F
		22.	T
		23.	F
		24.	T
		25.	T

Guidelines for Using Chapter Thirteen

Postmodern Approaches

in

Theory and Practice of Counseling and Psychotherapy and the *Student Manual*

Case Approach to Counseling and Psychotherapy

and

The Art of Integrative Counseling

1. In my lectures on the postmodern approaches to therapy, my attempt is to illustrate how these approaches differ from many of the theories that the students have already studied in the text. The pre-chapter self-inventory in the *Student Manual* is a good device for assisting students in assessing the degree to which they agree with the basic principles of the various postmodern therapies. You could ask students to identify the differences between the postmodern perspectives and the prior theoretical approaches they have studied.

2. Case examples, practical situations, and specific problem situations are found in the *Case Approach* book and *Student Manual.* These cases can serve as anchors for applying the key concepts of social constructionism, solution-focused brief therapy, and narrative therapy. Some key issues that lend themselves to lecture and discussion are:

   - Is there any such thing as objective reality and objective truth, or is all reality a subjective matter?
   - Is the task of therapy to construct solutions and restory one's life?
   - If you agree with the premise that the client is an expert on his or her own life, what implications does this have for how you are likely to practice therapy?
   - If therapy is a collaborative partnership, how would you teach clients ways to become active partners in the therapy process?

3. **Other Resources:** In addition to the case of Ruth given in Chapter 13 of the *Student Manual*, you may want to refer to three other resources: *Case Approach; The Art of Integrative Counseling*; and the *CD ROM for Integrative Counseling.*

    Refer to the *Case Approach to Counseling and Psychotherapy* (6th ed., 2005) for a detailed treatment of the case of Ruth from the perspectives of three different postmodern therapists. In Chapter 11, Dr. Jennifer Andrews describes the way she would assess and treat Ruth from a social constructionist's perspective. This is followed by Dr. David Clark's demonstration of his application of solution-focused therapy with Ruth. Then Dr. Gerald Monk discusses many of the basic concepts of narrative therapy and applies these concepts and narrative techniques to counseling Ruth. I follow up with my own thoughts on aspects of the postmodern therapies that would influence my work with Ruth.

    Refer to the book *The Art of Integrative Counseling* for a discussion of existential therapy from a number of vantage points. In Chapter 2 (pp. 15–18) I demonstrate how I draw from the postmodern approaches as a foundation for developing a client/therapist relationship. On pages 18–20 I discuss how concepts from both solution-focused therapy and narrative therapy are related to the collaborative venture of therapy. On pages 22-25 my work with Ruth clearly reflects ideas taken from narrative therapy (focusing on the relationship, listening to Ruth's story, and helping Ruth externalize her problem. In Chapter 11 on pages 121-123 I am particularly borrowing from solution-focused therapy in demonstrating how future aspirations influence the present. The use of the miracle question is found on page 122.

    In the *CD ROM for Integrative Counseling*, the first three sessions illustrate some principles in action that reflect basic ideas of solution-focused therapy and narrative therapy. From the very beginning of my work with Ruth, I am operating on the assumption that she is the expert on her own life and that I am not the person who will provide her with answers to her problems.

4. In preparing your own lectures on the postmodern therapies, the books I most highly recommend are:

    a. *Becoming Solution-Focused in Brief Therapy* (Walter and Peller, 1992)
    b. *Recreating Brief Therapy: Preferences and Possibilities* (Walter and Peller, 2000).
    c. *Handbook of Solution-Focused Brief Therapy (*Miller, Hubble, and Duncan, 1996)
    d. *Collaborative, Competency-Based Counseling and Therapy* (Bertolino and O'Hanlon, 2002)
    e. *Narrative Therapy: The Social Construction of Preferred Realities* (Freedman and Combs, 1996)
    f. *Narrative Counseling in Schools* (Winslade and Monk, 1999)
    g. *Narrative Therapy in Practice: The Archaeology of Hope* (Monk, Winslade, Crocket, and Epston, 1997)

These particular books are briefly annotated in the *Recommended Supplementary Readings* section in Chapter 13 of *TPCP.*

KEY TERMS FOR REVIEW AND DEFINITION

social constructionism	postmodern approaches
solution-focused brief therapy	narrative therapy
alternative story	coauthoring a new story
deconstruction	dominant story
exception questions	externalizing conversations
formula first session task	mapping-the-influence questions
miracle question	not-knowing position
pre-therapy change	problem-saturated story
re-authoring	scaling questions
totalizing descriptions	unique outcome
documenting the evidence	storied lives
reflecting team	news of difference
problem talk	change talk
narrative letters	sparkling moments
client as expert	

INFOTRAC **KEY WORDS**
Postmodern Approaches

The following keywords are listed in such a way as to allow the InfoTrac search engine to locate a wider range of articles o the online library. The keywords should be entered exactly as listed below to include asterisks, "W1," and "AND."

Insoo Kim Berg
Steve de Shazer
Michael White
David Epston
Solution-focused therapy
Brief psychotherapy
Narrative W1 therapy

CASE EXAMPLE

THE CASE OF RUTH: VIEWING HER FROM A NARRATIVE THERAPY PERSPECTIVE

In the book, *Case Approach to Counseling and Psychotherapy* (Corey, 2005: Chapter 11) there are three different contributors who present three postmodern approaches to counseling with Ruth: Dr. Jennifer Andrews (social constructionist), Dr. David Clark (solution-focused brief therapy), and Dr. Gerald Monk (narrative therapy). Because of their detailed descriptions of their respective perspectives and illustrations of their counseling with Ruth, I refer you to that source for excellent examples that bring to life these three postmodern therapies. Since Ruth is featured in both the *Case Approach* and *Art of Integrative Counseling* books, and also in the *CD ROM for Integrative Counseling,* here I make only brief mention of a few aspects of working with Ruth from the narrative perspective and give a general sense of how I would conceptualize Ruth's therapy.

From the perspective of narrative therapy, I base my work on the assumption that Ruth's life story influences what she notices and remembers, and in this sense her story influences how she will face the future. Although I am somewhat interested in Ruth's past, we certainly do not spend a great deal of our time talking about her past problems. Instead, therapy time is devoted to what Ruth is currently doing and on her strivings for her future.

I further assume that many of Ruth's problems have been produced by the contradictory cultural messages she has received from society about what kind of person, woman, mother, and partner she should be in the world. Part of our work together will be to look for personal resources Ruth has that will enable her to create a new story for herself. As a narrative therapist, my efforts are devoted to helping Ruth rewrite the story of her life. Our collaborative partnership is likely to result in her reviewing certain events from her past and rewriting her future. I am very concerned about focusing Ruth on her strengths and not so interested in having her merely talk about her problems. I believe that a problem-focused approach to therapy is likely to cement unhelpful modes of behavior.

Many of the various theories that have already been covered in this textbook emphasize the importance of a working relationship and a collaborative spirit in therapy (Adlerian therapy, person-centered therapy, existential therapy, Gestalt therapy, the cognitive behavioral approaches, and feminist therapy). Working within the framework of narrative therapy, I am influenced by the notion that our collaboration will be aimed at freeing Ruth from the influence of oppressive elements in her social environment and empowering her to become an active agent who is directing her own life.

Narrative therapy can help Ruth feel motivated, understood, and accepted. A method of supporting Ruth with the challenges she faces is to get her to think of her problems as external to the core of her selfhood. A key concept that influences therapeutic practice is that the problem does not reside in the person. From our initial therapy session, I strive to assist Ruth in separating her total identity from her problems by raising questions that lead her in the direction of externalizing her problem. I view Ruth's problems as something separate from her, even though her problems are influencing her thoughts, feelings, and behaviors. Ruth presents many problems that are of concern to her, yet we cannot deal with all of them at once.

One of Ruth's central problems is the anxiety that she often experiences. When I ask her what one problem most concerns her right now, she replies, "Anxiety. I feel anxiety so often and I often have panic attacks." Ruth feels anxious about making choices in her life and accepting the responsibility for her decisions. She has wrestled with trusting her ability to make good choices. The fear of the unknown also is a source of anxiety for Ruth.

My intention is to help Ruth come to view her problem of anxiety as being separate from who she is as a person. I ask Ruth how her anxiety occurs and ask her to give examples of situations where she experiences anxiety. I am interested in charting the influence of the problem of anxiety. I also ask questions that externalize the problem, such as the following: "What is the mission of this anxiety, and how does it recruit you into this mission?" "How does the anxiety get you, and what are you doing to let it become so powerful?" "How has anxiety dominated and disrupted your life?"

In this narrative approach, I follow up on these externalizing questions with further questions aimed at finding exceptions: "Can you remember any times when anxiety could have taken control of your life but didn't? What was it like for you? How did you do it?" "How is this different from what you would have done before?" "What does it say about you that you were able to do that?" "How do you imagine your life would be different if you didn't have bouts of anxiety?" "Can you think of ways you can begin to take even small steps toward divorcing yourself from anxiety?" "How have you successfully coped with panic attacks in the past?"

When we identify times when Ruth's life was not disrupted by anxiety, we have a basis for considering how life would be different if anxiety were not in control. As our therapy proceeds, I expect that Ruth will gradually come to see that she has more control over her problem of anxiety than she believed. As she is able to distance herself from defining herself in terms of problematic themes (such as anxiety), she will be less burdened by her problem-saturated story and will discover the resources within herself to construct the kind of life she wants. Applying narrative therapy with Ruth is distinct to the extent that this approach encourages her to create a richer life story by exploring new cultural meanings that are desirable to her. In this sense, therapy is a new beginning.

Questions for Reflection:

1. Looking at Ruth's strengths is not unique to the postmodern approaches, for other theories also emphasis the resources of the client. Building on a client's strengths is part of Adlerian therapy, the humanistic therapies, cognitive behavioral therapies, feminist therapy, and reality therapy. What basic concepts would you draw upon from the various theories in assisting Ruth identify internal resources?

2. What are some of the advantages to the approach of externalizing the problem from the client? How might you attempt to do this with Ruth? Any disadvantages to this approach?

3. To what degree might you want to incorporate using "solution talk" as opposed to "problem talk?" How would you deal with Ruth if she insisted that she came to see you so she could talk about her problems?

4. Asking clients to think of exceptions to their problems often gets them to think about a time when a particular problem did not have such intense proportions. What are some of the advantages you can see in asking Ruth to talk about a time when she did not have a given problem? How might you build on times of exceptions?

5. In what ways are some of the basic ideas of narrative therapy compatible with a multicultural perspective on counseling practice? What applications do you see for using narrative therapy with culturally diverse client populations?

6. How comfortable would you be in counseling Ruth from a narrative perspective? What challenges might you face in working within the framework of this approach?

STUDY GUIDE FOR CHAPTER THIRTEEN

POSTMODERN APPROACHES

1. The social constructionist perspective emphasizes a collaborative approach with clients rather than directing them. What are some basic differences of this perspective from many of the traditional approaches thus far covered in this text?

2. The postmodern therapies are based on the assumption that the therapist takes a not-knowing position. This means that, clients are viewed as the experts on their own lives, not the therapist. If the therapist is not an expert, why would a client pay a therapist for help?

3. In cases where the therapist assumes a "not-knowing" position, clients become the experts who are informing and sharing with the therapist the significant narratives of their lives. To what extent might you be inclined to adopt this not-knowing stance, and why?

4. In what ways do you see the postmodern approaches as having some different assumptions about clients and about counseling than most of the previous therapy approaches you have studied? What are some different key concepts?

5. Narrative therapy stresses externalizing questions by asking "Was there ever a time in your life when you did not have this problem, and, if so, how was that for you?" This approach tries to help clients see that a presenting problem is separate from their identity as persons. What are your thoughts about this process?

6. Solution-oriented therapists use the following three kinds of questions: the miracle question, the exception question, and the scaling question. Define each of these methods of questioning. How might you react, as a client, to each of these forms of questions?

7. What is the value of asking clients to talk about the exceptions to their problems and to adopt a positive focus on what they are doing that is working in their lives? If a therapy practice is built on the notion of helping clients recognize their strengths and resources, what implications does this have for both the client and the therapist?

8. Solution-focused therapists often ask clients the miracle question. What potential value is there in asking clients to imagine their problems will vanish one night when they were asleep? How does the miracle question enable clients to ways of creating solutions? Are there any problems with using the miracle question technique?

9. Solution-focused brief therapy eschews the past in favor of both the present and the future. What implications does this time perspective have for the practice of therapy? How is this perspective the same or different from reality therapy on this point?

10. Solution-focused brief therapists strive to get their clients away from talking about their problems, and instead, talking about solutions. How does solution-oriented therapy differ from problem-oriented therapy? If clients are accustomed to talking about problems, what are some ways to get them to begin thinking about solutions? How might you help a client who is fused to a problem-saturated story begin to co-construct another story?

11. Solution-focused brief therapy is grounded on the optimistic assumption that people are healthy and competent with the ability to construct solutions that can enhance their lives. If you accept this assumption as being valid, how is this likely to impact the manner in which you relate to clients?

12. Solution-focused brief therapists do not look for pathology and avoid reducing clients to a diagnostic label. Instead, they look for what clients are doing that is working and encourage them to continue in that direction. What do you think of this perspective?

13. Many solution-focused therapists take a 5 to 10 minute break toward the end of each session to compose a summary message, provide clients with feedback, and assign a task to be completed by the following session. Would you be likely to use this procedure with your clients? Why or why not?

14. Both narrative therapists and solution-focused therapists are very concerned with establishing truly collaborative relationships with their clients. Clients are co-creators of solutions and are co-authors in the process of re-authoring

their life stories. What are some specific steps a therapist can take early in the course of therapy to establish this collaborative partnership? What if the client does not want to be a partner, but instead expects the therapist to be the expert?

15. In narrative therapy, the emphasis is on being able to listen to the problem-saturated story of the client without getting stuck. What are the possible advantages of the narrative approach of separating the person from the problem?

16. In practicing narrative therapy, there is no recipe, no set agenda, and no formula for practice. Instead, the attitudes of the therapist are at least as important as the therapist's techniques. What are some therapist attitudes that are most important in encouraging clients to share their stories and discover ways to create alternative stories?

17. Narrative practitioners believe that new stories take hold only when there is an audience to appreciate and support such stories. The therapist looks for ways to document the evidence and to assist clients in finding significant people in their lives that will support their changes. What are your thoughts about these procedures?

18. The narrative therapist often writes a letter to clients as a way to assist them in consolidating what they have gained and to record highlights of a session. This kind of letter often highlights the struggle clients have had with a problem and draws distinctions between the problem-saturated story and the developing new and preferred story. What values might there be in therapist letters to clients? Would you be inclined to make use of narrative letters to your clients? Why or why not?

19. What are some specific ways that the postmodern approaches can be applied to working with culturally diverse client populations? What are some concepts of the postmodern therapies that particularly lend themselves to examining a client's cultural context?

20. What are some contributions and strengths of both the solution-focused and narrative approaches to the practice of therapy? What are some specific aspects of both of these approaches that you might incorporate into your counseling approach?

Test Items

Chapter Thirteen

Theory and Practice of

Counseling and Psychotherapy

POSTMODERN APPROACHES

1. Which of the following is true of narrative therapy and solution-focused therapy?
    a.   The client is an expert on his or her own life.
    b.   The therapeutic relationship should be hierarchical.
    c.   The therapist is the expert on a client's life.
    d.   Clients should adjust to social and cultural norms.
    e.   For change to occur, clients must first acquire insight into the cause of their problems.

2. Of the following, a major goal of narrative therapy is to
    a.   shift from problem-talk to solution-talk.
    b.   assist clients in designing creative solutions to their problems.
    c.   invite clients to describe their experience in new and fresh language, and in doing this opening up new vistas of what is possible.
    d.   uncover a client's self-defeating cognitions.
    e.   enable clients to gain clarity about the ways their family of origin still impacts them today.

3. All of the following are ways narrative therapy differs from traditional therapy except for
    a.   viewing problems in a sociopolitical and cultural context.
    b.   assisting clients in developing an alternative life story.
    c.   accepting the premise that diagnosis is a basic prerequisite for effective treatment.
    d.   creating a therapeutic relationship that is collaborative.
    e.   recognition that clients know what is best for their life and are experts in their own life.

4. Which of the following interventions is least likely to be used by a narrative therapist?
    a.   externalizing conversations
    b.   mapping the influence of a problem
    c.   power analysis and intervention
    d.   the search for unique outcomes
    e.   documenting the evidence

5. All of the following are techniques used in solution-focused therapy except for
    a.   using the reflecting team
    b.   scaling questions
    c.   the miracle question
    d.   formula first session task
    e.   exception questions

6. A major strength of both solution-focused and narrative therapies is the
    a.   empirical evidence that has been conducted on both approaches.
    b.   attention given to how one's early history sheds light on understanding current problems.
    c.   history taking procedures used during the intake interview.
    d.   use of questioning.
    e.   none of the above

7. Two of the major founders of solution-focused brief therapy are
    a.   Michael White and David Epston.
    b.   Insoo Kim Berg and Steve deShazer.
    c.   Harlene Anderson and Harold Goolishian.
    d.   Tom Andersen and Bill O'Hanlon.
    e.   John Walter and Jane Peller

8. Two of the major founders of narrative therapy are
    a.   John Walter and Jane Peller
    b.   Insoo Kim Berg and Steve deShazer.
    c.   Harlene Anderson and Harold Goolishian.
    d.   Tom Andersen and Bill O'Hanlon.
    e.   Michael White and David Epston.

9. The therapeutic process in solution-focused brief therapy involves all of the following except for the notion
    a. of creating collaborative therapeutic relationships.
    b. of asking clients about those times when their problems were not present or when the problems were less severe.
    c. that clients are the experts on their own lives.
    d. that solutions evolve out of therapeutic conversations and dialogues.
    e. that therapists are experts in assessment and diagnosis.

10. Which of the following is *false* as it applies to the practice of solution-focused brief therapy?
    a. Individuals who come to therapy have the ability to effectively cope with their problems.
    b. There are advantages to a positive focus on solutions and on the future.
    c. Clients want to change, have the capacity to change, and are doing their best to make change happen.
    d. Using techniques in therapy is a way of discounting a client's capacity to find his or her own way.

11. In solution-focused therapy, which of the following kind of relationship is characterized by the client and therapist jointly identifying a problem and a solution to work toward?
    a. customer-type relationship
    b. the complainant
    c. a visitor
    d. a compliant client

12. Pre-therapy change is a solution-focused therapy technique that
    a. is arrived at by asking clients about exceptions to their problems.
    b. asks clients to address changes that have taken place from the time they made an appointment to the first therapy session.
    c. is based on a series of tests that the client takes prior to beginning therapy to get baseline data.
    d. involves comparing the use of both pre-test and post-test data from instruments that report client satisfaction of therapy.

13. Which of these solution-focused therapy techniques involves asking clients to describe life without the problem?
    a. pre-therapy change
    b. the miracle question
    c. exception questions
    d. scaling
    e. formula first session task

14. In narrative therapy, the process of finding evidence to bolster a new view of the person as competent enough to have stood up to or defeated the dominance or oppression of the problem refers to
    a. the initial assessment
    b. exploring problem-saturated stories
    c. objectifying the problem
    d. search for unique outcome

15. Which of the following statements about creating alternative stories is *not* true?
    a. Constructing new stories goes hand in hand with deconstructing problem-saturated narratives.
    b. The narrative therapist analyzes and interprets the meaning of a client's story.
    c. The therapist works with clients collaboratively by helping them construct more coherent and comprehensive stories that they live by.
    d. The development of alternative stories is an enactment of ultimate hope.
    e. The narrative therapist listens for openings to new stories.

16. From a social constructionist perspective, change begins with:
    a. deconstructing the power of cultural narratives.
    b. understanding the roots of a problem.
    c. the therapist's skill in using confrontational techniques.
    d. understanding and accepting objective reality.

17. Of the following, what is an interest that social constructionists tend to share?
    a. helping clients better understand objective reality
    b. using paradoxical techniques
    c. using a genogram to teach families about conflicts
    d. generating new meaning in the lives of individuals

18. The techniques of externalization and developing unique events are associated primarily with:
    a. solution-oriented therapy.
    b. the linguistic approach.
    c. the narrative approach.
    d. the reflecting team.

19. Narrative therapists attempt to
    a. engage people in deconstructing problem-saturated stories.
    b. discover preferred directions and new possibilities.
    c. create new stories.
    d. all of the above
    e. none of the above

20. Narrative therapists pay attention to "sparkling events." These are
    a. moments when the client feels exhilarated.
    b. events that contradict problem-saturated narratives.
    c. times when significant other give the client unconditional love.
    d. events characterized by a striving to overcome barriers.
    e. none of the above

ANSWER KEY FOR CHAPTER THIRTEEN – POSTMODERN APPROACHES

MULTIPLE-CHOICE TEST QUESTIONS

1.	A	11.	A
2.	C	12.	B
3.	C	13.	B
4.	C	14.	D
5.	A	15.	B
6.	D	16.	A
7.	B	17.	D
8.	E	18.	C
9.	E	19.	D
10.	D	20.	B

POSTMODERN APPROACHES

1. Narrative therapists believe that new stories take hold only when there is an audience to appreciate and support such stories.

2. One of the functions of a narrative therapist is to ask questions of the client, and based on answers, generate further questions.

3. The effective application of narrative therapy is primarily a function of a therapist being polished in the use of techniques.

4. Narrative practitioners encourage clients to avoid being reduced by totalizing descriptions of their identity.

5. Narrative therapists pay more attention to a client's present and future than they do to the past.

6. In solution-focused therapy, gathering extensive information about a problem is a necessary step in helping clients to find a solution to the problem.

7. Solution-focused therapists assist clients in paying attention to the exceptions to their problem patterns.

8. Solution-focused therapists use questions that presuppose change, posit multiple answers, and remain goal-directed and future-oriented.

9. In narrative therapy, the role of the client is to create, explore, and co-author his or her evolving story.

10. Because solution-focused therapy is designed to be brief, it is essential that therapists teach clients specific strategies for understanding what caused their problems so that they can resolve these problems.

11. Solution-oriented therapy differs from both strategic and traditional models by eschewing the past in favor of focusing on the future.

12. Assessment and therapy technique are more important than empathy to a social constructionist.

13. In postmodern thinking, language and the use of language in stories create meaning.

14. The linguistic approach stresses the expert role of the therapist in suggesting solutions to a family's problems.

15. The narrative approach is part of the social construction model.

16. According to feminist therapists, gender equality permeates most narratives about normal human development.

17. Solution-focused therapists often use scaling questions.

18. Social constructionists differ from many early family therapists in believing that it is neither the person nor the family that is the problem.

19. The narrative approach utilizes the technique of externalizing one's problems.

20. In social constructionism, the therapist assumes the role of expert, rather than adopting a collaborative or consultative stance.

ANSWER KEY FOR CHAPTER THIRTEEN – POSTMODERN APPROACHES

TRUE–FALSE TEST QUESTIONS

1.	T	11.	T
2.	T	12.	F
3.	F	13.	T
4.	T	14.	F
5.	T	15.	T
6.	F	16.	F
7.	T	17.	T
8.	T	18.	T
9.	T	19.	T
10.	F	20.	F

Guidelines for Using Chapter Fourteen

Family Systems Therapy

in

Theory and Practice of Counseling and Psychotherapy and the *Student Manual*

Case Approach to Counseling and Psychotherapy

and

The Art of Integrative Counseling

1. The *Pre-Chapter Self-Inventory* in the **Student Manual** is a good device for helping students assess the degree to which they are inclined toward systemic thinking. You might ask students to identify the differences between an individual orientation and a systemic orientation in working with clients.

2. I warn students about the complexity of considering the family systems approach. Unlike the other chapters in the text, this chapter is made up of several historical approaches to family therapy. It is good to emphasize that this chapter is merely an introductory survey of the basic elements in the theory and practice of family therapy. In the text, there are numerous references to other reading sources for those who want to explore a particular approach to family therapy.

3. The chart in Chapter 14 of the textbook are designed to give students a capsule summary of the basic elements of the major historical approaches to systemic thinking. Table 14–1 compares six theoretical viewpoints in family therapy. This is a good way to summarize specific dimensions of each approach, including therapy goals, role and function of the therapist, how change occurs, and techniques employed.

4. In the **Student Manual** (see Chapter 14) there are a number of suggested activities and exercises. Some of these are:

   • *How Your Past Influences Your Present*

- *Understanding Your Family Structure*
- *A Balance of Being Separate and of Belonging in a Family*
- *Understanding the Rules of Your Family*
- *Significant Developments in Your Family*

These exercises provide good material for journal writing, which can be followed up with in-class experiential activities. Some of the questions may tap painful memories of students and may even open up highly personal issues. I recommend that instructors provide specific guidelines for in-class activities so that students do not open up personal material that might be better dealt with in personal therapy. In my classes, I encourage students to reflect on their personal experiences in their family of origin as a way to make the material more meaningful. However, I am aware of the fine line between personal discussions that are appropriate for the classroom and exploring certain dimensions of topics that are more appropriately reserved for therapy. For example, I do not probe, nor do I encourage students to share family secrets. If students do bring up issues such as incest or family violence, I attempt to help them see how such experiences are likely to affect them in the future as therapists. However, I do not encourage them to disclose details in the context of class discussions. If students recognize that they have specific unresolved personal problems relating to their family, they can be supported in finding appropriate resources to enable them to deal with these concerns. Teacher guidance is clearly important in introducing experiential activities in the **Student Manual**, and it is well to state this to students at the outset.

5. Stan will be of special interest in this chapter, since an integrative approach to family therapy is being applied to conceptualizing Stan's case. Ask students to note the ways family therapy differs in emphasis from the other models studied.

6. In the **Student Manual** for this chapter Ruth's case appears again. This would be a good time to concentrate on Ruth's case from a comparative perspective. How would a family systems therapist deal with Ruth in a somewhat different manner than the first other ten models considered in the **TPCP** text? Below are some questions that would be useful as catalysts for discussion on this topic:

   a. What are some of the ways that you might integrate concepts and techniques from the other therapy orientations you've studied with family therapy? Are there any theories that you think would not fit with a family systems perspective? If so, which ones, and why?

   b. What are some of the major contributions of the family systems perspective in working with Ruth? What themes from this approach would you most want to incorporate in counseling Ruth?

   c. Family therapy focuses on Ruth as a member of a family unit and the assumption is that each person in the system influences one another and the system as a whole. If you were to counsel Ruth from a systemic perspective, would you be inclined to work with her entire family? Why or why not?

7. Refer to **Case Approach to Counseling and Psychotherapy** (see Chapter 12) for a family therapist who demonstrates concepts and strategies in working with Ruth's family. The basic assumptions, goals of therapy, and therapy strategies of family systems therapy have been spelled out in detail by Dr. Mary Moline who uses an integrative model in counseling Ruth in a family context.

8. The **CD ROM for Integrative Counseling**, along with **The Art of Integrative Counseling** text, has minimal direct reference to working with Ruth from a family systems approach. At times when it was relevant, I incorporated family systems concepts. An example is working with Ruth from an integrative perspective, how Ruth's past influences her today, and exploring Ruth's early decisions and encouraging her to make new decisions.

9. In preparing your lectures on family systems therapy, there are many references cited throughout Chapter 14. Check the end of the chapter under the *Recommended Suggested Readings* for a lengthy list of resources you will find useful for class preparation. Below are some of the resources that are highly recommended for background reading in preparing lectures.

- *Ethnicity and Family Therapy (*McGoldrick, Pearce, & Giordano, 1996)
- *Family Therapy Basics* (Worden, 2003)
- *Family therapy: Concepts and Methods* (Nichols and Schwartz, 2001)
- *Family Therapy: Ensuring Treatment Efficacy* (Carlson, Sperry, and Lewis, 1997)

- *Family Therapy: History, Theory, and Practice* (Gladding, 2002)
- *Family Therapy: An Overview* (Goldenberg and Goldenberg, 2004)
- *Family Therapy: A Systemic Integration* (Becvar and Becvar, 2003)
- *Metaframeworks: Transcending the Models of Family Therapy* (Breunlin, Schwartz, and MacKune-Karrer, 1997)
- *Theories and Strategies of Family Therapy* (Carlson and Kjos, 2002)

KEY TERMS FOR REVIEW AND DEFINITION

accommodating	family systems theory
boundary	functional family
coaching	fusion
closed family system	genogram
developmental lens	gender lens
detriangulation	identified patient
differentiation of self	joining
disengagement	metaframeworks
dysfunctional family	mistaken goals
emotional cutoff	multicultural lens
emotional divorce	multigenerational transmission process
enactment	multilensed family systems approach
enmeshment	multilensed process of family therapy
nuclear family emotional system	organization lens
experiential therapy	open family system
paradoxical directive	patriarchy
family atmosphere	personal priorities
family constellation	process lens
family dysfunction	
family life chronology	reframing
family life cycle	restraining
family myths	sequencing
family of origin	strategic therapy
family projection process	structural therapy
family rules	triangle
family sculpting	triangulation
family structure	teleological lens

INFOTRAC KEYWORDS

Family W1 dysfunction	Disengagement AND family
Family W1 constellation	Multigenerational
Family W1 origin	Family W1 system

Family Systems Therapy

Murray Bowen
Jay Haley
Salvador Minuchin
Virginia Satir
Carl Whitaker
Intergenerational W1 approach
Strategic family therapy
Family therapy

Family systems the*	Family systems theory	Family systems therapy
Family W2 system*	Family W2 dysfunction	Family W2 origin
Genogram*		

CASE EXAMPLE

THE KLINES: Family with a son in trouble

Assume that a person in the agency where you work has done an intake interview and that you are given the following information:

The Kline family consists of Gail and George, their two daughters, Jessie, 10, and Jaimi, 12, and their son Gary, 16. George called for the intake interview. He said that his son was in trouble for stealing and dealing drugs. Gary is on probation, and the court ordered him to undergo therapy. It was suggested that the entire family be involved in some kind of family therapy.

George is following the suggestion of the court and involving the entire family in counseling sessions. However, he does not have much hope that therapy will be of great help. According to him, the one who is responsible for the family's problems is his wife, who, he says, is an alcoholic. George, a businessman who does a great deal of traveling, is convinced that he is doing all he can to hold the family together. He comments that he is a good provider and that he does not understand why Gail insists on drinking. He feels that Gary has gotten everything that he ever wanted, and he maintains that the young people of today are "just spoiled rotten." The father says that his eldest daughter, Jaimi, is the best one of the bunch, and he has no complaints about her. He sees her as being more responsible than his wife as well as being more attentive to him. He views his younger daughter, Jessie, as pampered and spoiled by her mother, and he has little hope for her.

George is willing to give family counseling a try and says he hopes that the therapist can straighten them all out. He says that he, Gail, and Jessie are all willing to come in for a family session. Jaimi does not want to attend, however, because she says she has no problems and sees no purpose in therapy for herself. Gary is very reluctant to appear, even for one session, because he feels sure that the others in the family will see him as the source of their problems. To satisfy the conditions of his probation, Gary would rather choose "the lesser of two evils" and see a therapist privately.

The counselor who did the intake interview saw only the father for an initial session. He suggests that you see the entire family for at least one session and then decide how to proceed.

Questions for Reflections:

1. What are your initial reactions after reading the intake interview? What are the themes that interest you the most in this case? Why?

2. How would you proceed as a family therapist in an initial session if you saw the entire family? What issues would you want to discuss with this family at the first meeting?

3. George does not seem very open to looking at his role in contributing to the problems within his family. If you were to see him as your client, how would you go about establishing a relationship with him?

4. If you believed in the value of seeing the family as a unit for one or more sessions, how might you go about getting the entire family to come in? Assume that all agreed to attend one session. What would be your focus, and what would you most want to achieve in this family session?

5. What are the key dynamics of the family as a system? What does the family atmosphere seem like?

6. Do you see any aspects of yourself in this case? Can you identify with any of the family members? How do you think this similarity or dissimilarity would help or hinder you in working with this family?

7. Show how you would work with this family, and discuss any problems that you might expect to encounter. Say how you would deal with these problems.

FAMILY SYSTEMS THERAPY

1. In your own words, define and describe the essence of the family systems perspective.

2. What are the similarities and differences of individual theories with family system approaches?

3. Explain the following key concepts of Bowen's multigenerational approach to family therapy.

   - differentiation of self
   - triangulation

4. Outline in a sentence the basic therapy goals of each of these approaches to family therapy:

   - Adlerian family therapy
   - multigenerational family therapy
   - human validation process model
   - experiential/symbolic family therapy
   - structural family therapy
   - strategic family therapy

5. Identify in about a sentence the major roles and functions of the therapist according to each of these approaches to family therapy:

   - Adlerian family therapy
   - multigenerational family therapy
   - human validation process model
   - experiential/symbolic family therapy
   - structural family therapy
   - strategic family therapy

6. Describe in about a sentence the way that the process of change occurs in each of these approaches to family therapy:

   - Adlerian family therapy
   - multigenerational family therapy
   - human validation process model
   - experiential/symbolic family therapy
   - structural family therapy
   - strategic family therapy

7. List some of the major techniques and intervention strategies used by each of the following family systems models:

   - Adlerian family therapy
   - multigenerational family therapy
   - human validation process model
   - experiential/symbolic family therapy
   - structural family therapy
   - strategic family therapy

8. Discuss the cultural values associated with the family therapy concept of differentiating oneself from the family. What modifications might you need to make in applying a family therapy approach that emphasizes the primacy of differentiation of self? How might the concept of triangulation need to be modified to fit certain cultural contexts? Many family therapists view triangles as being problematic in a family. Can you think of cultural situations where triangles may be appropriate?

9. What are the values of genograms in working with a family? How might you use a genogram in working with members of a family?

10. Some approaches to family therapy focus on developing collaborative relationships with members of a family, while other therapeutic approaches stress the role of therapist as expert and consultant who helps a family change its structure. Which approach do you favor and why?

11. If you were working with an individual client and thought it was appropriate to include the family, how would you go about getting the family involved?

12. What would you do if an individual client resisted your efforts to involve other family members in his or her therapy?

13. Do you think it is possible to think and practice systematically, even if you are doing individual counseling with a client? What are some ways you might focus on a systemic perspective in working with an individual?

14. Satir differentiates functional (emotionally honest) from dysfunctional communication in a family. In your view, what are some key differences between healthy and unhealthy patterns of communication?

15. According to Whitaker, the goal of family therapy is to promote the feeling dimension, including spontaneity, creativity, the ability to play, and the willingness to be "crazy." What do you think of this goal?

16. Identify the key themes that characterize Adlerian family therapy. What do you consider some of the main contributions of the Adlerian perspective as applied to family therapy? How might you incorporate Adlerian concepts into other family therapy approaches?

17. Some approaches to family therapy focus on the here-and-now interactions within the therapy session, some models focus on the past, and some focus on the future. Can you think of ways to work with all of these time frames and, if so, how? In working with families, what time frame might you be drawn to most and why?

18. Minuchin's structural family therapy deals with boundaries, especially with concepts such as enmeshment and disengagement. What are some potential boundary problems in your own life that might affect your working with a family with boundary disturbances? From a cultural perspective, how might the concept of enmeshment make sense? Are enmeshed relationships necessarily problematic? Or might they represent a value of a particular family?

19. After reading the chapter on family therapy, what kind of specialized training and education do you think would be necessary for you to practice with families in an effective and ethical manner?

20. In strategic family therapy, considerable emphasis is given to power, control, and hierarchies in families. Therapy tends to be brief, process-focused rather than content-oriented, and solution-focused. What are your reactions to the focus of strategic therapy? What aspects of this approach do you find most valuable? How might this approach work for you?

21. Strategic therapists make use of directives. How comfortable do you feel using directives in working with clients? What are some advantages of using directives? Can you think of any drawbacks?

22. From what you learned about feminist therapy in Chapter 12, how might feminists criticize some approaches to family therapy? What specific concepts in family therapy do you think would be objectionable from a feminist therapist's perspective? For example, what is the feminist's view of the notion of patriarchy?

23. How might you address a theme such as patriarchy if you were working with a family whose culture places the father in the key role of making decisions for the entire family? Do you see it as your job to challenge certain cultural values if you think that such values lead to oppression of women?

24. Briefly describe each of the following eight lenses (metaframeworks) in family systems therapy.
    • The individual's internal family system
    • The teleological lens
    • Sequencing and tracking patterns of interaction

- The organization lens
- The developmental lens
- The multicultural lens
- The gender lens
- The process lens

25. The eight lenses described in the chapter can be considered as a blueprint for family therapy. The multilensed approach also allows for an enlarged integration of ideas from multiple models of family therapy. What are some of the possible advantages of a multilensed process of family therapy?

26. If you were to develop your own integrated approach to family therapy, which models would you tend to draw from? Which aspects would you make central to your theory of family therapy? Identify the key concepts that you find most valuable from the various theories. Also identify the basic techniques from the different approaches that you are most interested in studying.

27. Read and review the case of Stan in Chapter 14 of the *TPCP* textbook. What kinds of questions does the therapist's work with Stan's genogram raise for you? How would you interpret Stan's drinking problem from a systemic perspective based on the genogram of Stan's family?

28. If you were assigned to Stan's case, what would be a few areas you'd most like to explore with him from a systemic perspective?

29. What are some of the main contributions that you see in working with clients from a family systems perspective?

30. Mention some of the limitations you see in the family systems perspective. What limitations are there, if any, in working with families from culturally diverse backgrounds?

Test Items

Chapter Fourteen

Theory and Practice of

Counseling and Psychotherapy

FAMILY SYSTEMS THERAPY

1. Who was the first person of the modern era to do family therapy?
   a. Adler
   b. Minuchin
   c. Bowen
   d. Satir
   e. Haley

2. Who is the family therapist who made most use of innovative interventions such as metaphor, reframing, rules for interaction, parts party, family reconstructions, family sculpting, communication stances, family life-fact chronologies, and family maps?
   a. Bowen
   b. Minuchin
   c. Satir
   d. Whitaker
   e. Haley

3. Which of the following statements about strategic family therapy is *not* true?
   a. Therapy is brief, process-focused, and solution-oriented.
   b. Change results when the family follows the therapist's directions and change transactions.
   c. The focus is on solving problems in the present.
   d. The therapist designs strategies for change.
   e. Presenting problems are viewed as being symptomatic of a dysfunction within the system.

4. Alfred Adler was the first to notice that the development of children within family constellations was heavily influenced by:
   a. the power structure within the family.
   b. cultural context in which a family resides.
   c. balance of leadership between parents.
   d. jealousy and rivalry among the children.
   e. birth order.

5. Differentiation of self is the cornerstone of which theory?
   a. Bowenian family therapy
   b. Adlerian family therapy
   c. social constructionism
   d. strategic family therapy

6. Who was the person who refined Adler's concepts into a typology of mistaken goals and an organized approach to family therapy?
   a. Virginia Satir
   b. Jay Haley
   c. Cloe Madanes
   d. Carl Whitaker
   e. Rudolf Dreikurs

7. The concept of triangulation is most associated with
   a. Virginia Satir.
   b. Murray Bowen.
   c. Salvador Minuchin.
   d. Carl Whitaker.
   e. Rudolf Dreikurs

8. What type of boundaries results in disengagement?
   a. clear boundaries
   b. diffuse boundaries
   c. rigid boundaries
   d. flexible boundaries
   e. shrinking boundaries

9. What is the technique in family therapy that casts a new light on a problem and provides a different interpretation for a problematic situation?
   a. reorganization
   b. family mapping
   c. restructuring
   d. reframing
   e. joining

10. A major contribution of Bowen's theory is the notion of
    a. birth order as a determinant of personality.
    b. differentiation of the self.
    c. family rules and communication patterns.
    d. spontaneity, creativity, and play as therapeutic factors in family therapy.

11. Directives and paradoxical procedures are most likely to be used in which approach to family therapy?
    a. Bowenian family therapy
    b. human validation process model
    c. social constructionism
    d. strategic therapy
    e. experiential/symbolic family therapy

12. Which is(are) a key role (or roles) of most family therapists?
    a. teacher
    b. model
    c. coach
    d. consultant
    e. all of the above

13. Which of the following techniques is a strategic family therapist least likely to use?
    a. asking about attempted solutions to a problem
    b. directives
    c. family sculpting
    d. reframing
    e. paradoxical interventions

14. A tool for collecting and organizing key turning points in a three-generational extended family is a
    a. lifestyle assessment.
    b. family sketch.
    c. genogram.
    d. projective test.
    e. none of the above

15. Which of the following roles and functions would be most atypical for a structural family therapist?
    a. joining the family in a position of leadership
    b. giving voice to the therapist's own impulses and fantasies
    c. mapping the underlying structure of a family
    d. intervening in ways designed to transform an ineffective structure of a family
    e. being a stage director

16. Which of the following is least associated with Satir's human validation process model?
    a. family rules
    b. functional versus dysfunctional communication patterns
    c. family roles and triads
    d. storied lives and narratives
    e. defensive stances in coping with stress

17. Triangles in family relationships can best be explained by which factor?
    a. reducing anxiety and emotional tension in relationships
    b. a method of disengagement
    c. a method of becoming enmeshed
    d. an attempt to develop intimacy

18. Which approach to family therapy contends that problems manifested in one's current family will not significantly change until relationship patterns in one's family of origin are understood and directly challenged?
    a. Bowenian family therapy
    b. human validation process model
    c. structural family therapy
    d. strategic family therapy

19. The techniques of joining, accommodating, unbalancing, tracking, and boundary making would be most likely to be part of which approach to family therapy?
    a. Bowenian family therapy
    b. Adlerian family therapy
    c. structural family therapy
    d. strategic family therapy
    e. experiential/symbolic family therapy

20. A major contribution of Whitaker's approach to family therapy is
    a. birth order as a determinant of personality.
    b. differentiation of the self.
    c. genogram work.
    d. spontaneity, creativity, and play as therapeutic factors in family therapy.
    e. none of the above

21. Which of the following is *not* a key general movement of the multilensed approach to family systems therapy?
    a. forming a relationship
    b. conducting an assessment
    c. hypothesizing and sharing meaning
    d. facilitating change
    e. conducting empirical research to evaluate therapy outcomes

22. Which of the following lenses addresses these questions: What goals do you have for yourself and for other people in the family? What purposes do you seem to have for how the behave?
    a. internal family systems
    b. the teleological lens
    c. sequences
    d. the organization lens
    e. the developmental lens

23. What lens raises questions such as: How does a typical day go? Are there processes and patterns that characterize current or past transitions for the family? What routines support your daily living?
    a. internal family systems
    b. the teleological lens
    c. sequences
    d. the organization lens
    e. the developmental lens

24. Which approach operates on the assumption that a family can best be understood when it is analyzed from at least a three-generational perspective?
    a. Bowenian family therapy
    b. human validation process model
    c. social constructionism
    d. strategic family therapy
    e. experiential/symbolic family therapy

25. Which approach operates on the assumption that unresolved emotional fusion to one's family must be addressed if one hopes to achieve a mature and unique personality?
    a. Bowenian family therapy
    b. Adlerian family therapy
    c. social constructionism
    d. strategic family therapy
    e. solution-oriented therapy

26. A couple directs the focus of their energy toward a problematic son as a way to avoid facing or dealing with their own conflicts. This is an example of:
    a. enmeshment.
    b. normal love.
    c. displacement.
    d. triangulation.
    e. diffusion.

27. In working with a triangulated relationship, Bowen would be inclined to place primary emphasis on:
    a. joining the family.
    b. engaging in personal self-disclosure to build trust.
    c. maintaining a stance of neutrality.
    d. siding with one member involved in the triangle.
    e. identifying behavioral goals to guide the therapy.

28. Structural family therapy includes all of the following goals except for bringing about structural change by:
    a. modifying the family's transactional rules.
    b. developing more appropriate boundaries.
    c. creating an effective hierarchical structure.
    d. reducing symptoms of dysfunction.
    e. the therapist taking a not-knowing stance with a family.

29. What lens deals with questions such as: Are the parents effective leaders of the family? How do the children respond to parental leadership? Is the process of leadership balanced or imbalanced? Does it lead to harmony or conflict?
    a. internal family systems
    b. the teleological lens
    c. sequences
    d. the organization lens
    e. the developmental lens

30. What lens most addresses these questions: Where is the family in the family life cycle, and how are they handling transitions? What relational processes have been established over time and how have the changed through transitional periods?
    a. internal family systems
    b. the teleological lens
    c. sequences
    d. the developmental lens
    e. the multicultural lens

31. What best defines the focus of family therapy?
    a. Most of the family therapies tend to be brief.
    b. Family therapy tends to be solution-focused.
    c. The focus is on here-and-now interactions in the family system.
    d. Family therapy is generally action-oriented.
    e. all of the above

32. Which approach would be most interested in the appropriateness of hierarchical structure in the family?
    a. Bowenian family therapy
    b. human validation process model
    c. structural family therapy
    d. social constructionism

33. Which lens of family therapy is most likely to be concerned with the question, "How does the family's level of economics, education, ethnicity, religion, race, regional background, gender, and age affect the family's processes?"
    a. internal family systems
    b. the teleological lens
    c. sequences
    d. the multicultural lens
    e. the developmental lens

34. Family atmosphere, family constellation, and mistaken goals are key concepts of:
    a. Adlerian family therapy.
    b. structural family therapy.
    c. experiential family therapy.
    d. none of the above

35. A family systems perspective is grounded on the assumption(s) that a client's problematic behavior may:
    a. serve a function or purpose for the family.
    b. be a function of the family's inability to function productively.
    c. be a symptom of dysfunctional patterns handed down across generations.
    d. all of the above
    e. none of the above

36. According to Dreikurs, four goals of children's misbehavior include:
    a. attention getting, power struggle, revenge, and assumed disability.
    b. attention getting, control, affection, and nurturing.
    c. nurturing, education, security, and attention getting.
    d. none of the above

37. Adlerian family therapy strives to _____ as its goal.
    a. establish a hierarchy of power
    b. establish and support parents as effective leaders of the family
    c. replace automatic, often nonconscious, negative interactions with a conscious understanding of family process
    d. all of the above
    e. none of the above

38. Problem descriptions and goal identification, typical day, and the child interview and goal disclosure are techniques used in:
    a. multigenerational family therapy.
    b. strategic family therapy.
    c. social constrictionist therapy.
    d. Adlerian family therapy.
    e. none of the above

205

39. Which of the following is not one of the eight lenses of family systems therapy?
   a. the gender lens
   b. the multicultural lens
   c. the cognitive behavioral lens
   d. the process lens
   e. the developmental lens

40. The therapy goals of promoting growth, self-esteem, connection, and helping family members achieve congruent communication and interaction is most associated with which theory of family therapy?
   a. Bowen's multigenerational family therapy
   b. Satir's human validation process model
   c. Whitaker's experiential/symbolic family therapy
   d. Minuchin's structural family therapy
   e. Haley's strategic family therapy

ANSWER KEY FOR CHAPTER FOURTEEN – FAMILY SYSTEMS THERAPY

MULTIPLE-CHOICE TEST QUESTIONS

1. A	11. D	21. E	31. E
2. C	12. E	22. C	32. C
3. E	13. C	23. C	33. D
4. E	14. C	24. A	34. A
5. A	15. B	25. A	35. D
6. E	16. D	26. D	36. A
7. B	17. A	27. C	37. B
8. C	18. A	28. E	38. D
9. D	19. C	29. D	39. C
10. B	20. D	30. D	40. B

TRUE–FALSE TEST ITEMS FOR CHAPTER FOURTEEN

FAMILY SYSTEMS THERAPY

Decide if the following statements are "more true" or "more false" as applied to the perspective of family systems therapy.

1. Bowen's multigenerational approach stresses techniques more than it does theory.

2. Family systems represents a paradigm shift that is sometimes called "the fourth force."

3. Experiential family therapy relies on the expert use of directives aimed at changing dysfunctional patterns.

4. The focus of Bowen's multigenerational approach is on dealing with family of origin issues and detriangulating relationships.

5. The cornerstone of Bowen's theory is differentiation of self.

6. Carl Whitaker's style focuses on his own spontaneous reactions and craziness as a way to tap material that a family keeps secret.

7. Whitaker's experiential/symbolic approach is based on a well-developed theory of how a family changes.

8. Satir's human validation model focuses on functional versus dysfunctional communication in families.

9. Because Bowen's multigenerational approach looks at families from a three-generational perspective, the therapist is mainly interested in past happenings and does not pay much attention to present issues.

10. Minuchin's structural therapy is based on the notion that an individual's symptoms are best understood from the vantage point of interactional patterns within a family, and that structural changes must occur in a family before an individual's symptoms can be resolved.

11. Structural family therapy deals with boundaries.

12. The goal of structural family therapy is to break down any hierarchical structure and replace it with equal relationships among all family members.

13. Structural family therapists limit their interventions to families alone.

14. Minuchin's approach to therapy is geared more toward insight, rather than being a therapy of action.

15. Strategic family therapy has its foundation in communications theory.

16. Strategic family therapists do not generally deal with the presenting problem; rather, they focus on the underlying symptom of a dysfunctional system.

17. The focus of strategic family therapy is on growth and resolving historical conflicts in a family rather than on dealing with present problems of a family.

18. Strategic family therapy stresses some of the same basic concepts as the structural approach to family therapy.

19. The role of the strategic therapist involves being in charge of the session.

20. Strategic therapists do not rely on therapy techniques to bring about change but instead give more stress to the therapist's relationship with a family.

21. A multilensed approach to family therapy is best supported by a collaborative relationship.

22. Conducting an assessment is one of the phases of the multilensed approaches.

23. Understanding family process is almost always facilitated by "how" questions.

24. In terms of assessment, it is useful to inquire about family perspectives on issues inherent in each of the lenses.

25. The multilensed process of family therapy is similar to the "blueprints for therapy" as proposed by a metaframeworks model.

26. The teleological lens in concerned with the study of how intuition and telepathy inform family therapy.

27. Reframing is the art of putting what is known in a new, more useful perspective.

28. From a family systems perspective, an individual's dysfunctional behavior grows out of the interactional unit of the family as well as the larger community and societal systems.

29. There is a trend in the field of family therapy toward adopting a single theory approach rather than striving to develop integrative models of practice.

30. Bowenian therapists function in ways to bring about change through action-oriented directives and paradoxical interventions.

31. Bowenian therapists place more emphasis on techniques than they do on understanding the dynamics of a family system.

32. According to Haley, who the therapist is as a person is far more important than specific intervention techniques.

33. In Whitaker's experiential therapy, there is a greater focus on exploring past experiences than on here-and-now interaction between the family and the therapist.

34. In experiential therapy, techniques are secondary to the relationship that the therapist is able to establish with the family.

35. Joining, accommodation, and boundary making are techniques likely to be used by structural family therapists.

36. Strategic therapists emphasize the value of therapist interpretation, exploring unresolved issues from the past, and insight.

37. A multicultural lens challenges dominant culture and introduces diversity and complexity into our understanding of the human condition.

38. The gender lens makes use of lifestyle assessments during the intake interview.

39. Because an individual is connected to a living system, change in one part of that system will result in change in the other parts.

40. The main focus of family therapy is on past interactions and past conflicts as the best way to understand the dynamics of the family system.

ANSWER KEY FOR CHAPTER FOURTEEN – FAMILY SYSTEMS THERAPY

TRUE–FALSE TEST QUESTIONS

1. F	14. F	27. T
2. T	15. T	28. T
3. F	16. F	29. F
4. T	17. F	30. F
5. T	18. T	31. F
6. T	19. T	32. F
7. F	20. F	33. F
8. T	21. T	34. T
9. F	22. T	35. T
10. T	23. T	36. F
11. T	24. T	37. T
12. F	25. T	38. F
13. F	26. F	39. T
		40. F

Guidelines for Using Chapter Fifteen

An Integrative Perspective

in

Theory and Practice of Counseling and Psychotherapy and the *Student Manual*

Case Approach to Counseling and Psychotherapy

and

The Art of Integrative Counseling

1. Please refer to Chapter 15 of the ***TPCP*** textbook for the objectives of this chapter. I have written this chapter to raise basic issues that are common to all the contemporary therapies.

2. In a lecture on the topic of *Review of Basic Issues: An Integrative Perspective,* I recommend emphasizing the following areas as they apply to all the models:

    *   the philosophical assumptions
    *   the key concepts
    *   the issue of therapeutic goals
    *   the issue of the role and function of the therapist
    *   the experience of the client in the therapy process
    *   the issue of the client/therapist relationship
    *   issues related to the practice of multicultural counseling

    I stress comparison and contrast among the theories. The student is asked to look for common underlying themes and for areas of divergence as well.

3. In the ***Student Manual*** (see Chapter 15) I developed a series of brief situations that can be found in the section entitled *Applications of Theoretical Approaches to Specific Client Populations or Specific Problems.* In this

section I ask students to determine which approach (or approaches) they'd use in each problem situation; their reasons for their selection, and what techniques they'd likely employ for this particular client. The basic purpose of these exercises is to stimulate their thinking in applying the theories they've studied to a specific case. This is followed by a review of common integrative counseling techniques used with Ruth; students are to determine which kinds of techniques they might or might not use. There are some questions that pertain to issues in using techniques which can be used for small-group discussions.

4. In the **Student Manual** (see Chapter 15) there is a section on working with Ruth from an integrative perspective. There is a brief discussion of each of the 13 counseling sessions with Ruth, which are the subject matter of the **CD ROM for Integrative Counseling** and also for the book, **The Art of Integrative Counseling**. There are also a few key questions in the student manual geared to assist students in thinking about their way of working with Ruth for each session.

5. In **The Art of Integrative Counseling** book (Chapter 9: *An Integrative Perspective*) there is a discussion of ways of drawing from various theories in utilizing specific techniques from an integrative perspective. I describe the theories that I use for the foundation of my integrative model. Also, see Session #9 in the **CD ROM for Integrative Counseling** that deals with an integrative perspective for my comments on ways of thinking about counseling integration. In the last few minutes of the CD ROM program (in Session #13) I make some concluding comments that consists of suggestions to students regarding how to develop an integrative style of counseling.

6. See Chapter 13 in the **Case Approach to Counseling and Psychotherapy**, *Bringing the Approaches Together*. What is the basis for an integrative perspective? How can a client such as Ruth work in therapy within an integrated model – exploring cognitions, expressing and working through feelings, and experimenting with new behaviors? What are some elements of the various theories you would most likely draw from in your integrative work with Ruth? Some specific questions you might pose to your students pertaining to an integrative approach in working with Ruth are listed below:

    •   How might you help Ruth design homework that would allow her to practice challenging her belief system, identifying and expressing her emotions, and changing dysfunctional behaviors (and learning and practicing new and more effective ways of acting)?

    •   If you were a client in counseling, what kind of collaboration would you want to have with your counseling in designing meaningful homework assignments? Can you think of ways to increase the chances that you would carry out these homework assignments in your daily life?

    •   If you were Ruth's therapist, how would you make an assessment of the outcomes of your work with her?

    •   From what you have seen in the CD ROM program and read about Ruth, which therapy approaches might you be most inclined to draw from in your work with Ruth? If Ruth were your client, how effective do you think you would be with her?

7. As a guideline for students in their review of these therapies and as a resource for helping them begin to understand the areas of convergence and divergence among the systems, I have developed *Questions and Issues: Guidelines for Developing your Personal Style of Counseling* in Chapter 15 of the **Student Manual**.

    Students have found these questions useful for integrating and reviewing the course. My additional hope is that these questions help students critically examine the theories, so they will have some *rationale* for selecting or rejecting certain therapeutic concepts.

8. In the **Student Manual** is a detailed outline for a paper on *Developing Your Philosophy of Counseling*. Specific suggestions on using this assignment are given. You might consider having your students write their philosophy during the initial class session, or at least a few paragraphs or a brief outline. These could be collected and then returned to them at the end of the semester after they have written a more complete paper. If they attempt this assignment at the beginning of the course, then as they read and explore these various therapies, they are more likely to critically evaluate them in the background of their own values and attitudes. I routinely devote at least one class session to an exploration of their philosophy of counseling after they have written their papers.

9. **Resources for Lectures.** *Theory and Practice of Counseling and Psychotherapy* (Chapter 15: *An Integrative Perspective*) contains a discussion of issues related to the therapeutic process and a set of summary and review charts of the eleven models covered in the book, which will be a useful guide in thinking about an integrative approach. There are also two chapters dealing with an integrative approach in my two books: (1) See Chapter 13 (*Bringing the Approaches Together*) in *Case Approach to Counseling and Psychotherapy*; and (2) See Chapter 9 (*An Integrative Perspective*) in the *Art of Integrative Counseling*. These resources provide examples of integration in action as applied to Ruth's case.

STUDY GUIDE FOR CHAPTER FIFTEEN

AN INTEGRATIVE PERSPECTIVE

Note: This chapter is designed to help you pull your knowledge together and see a basis for integration of the various theories. The following *Summary and Review* charts (see Tables 15-1 through 15-10) in Chapter 15 of the *TPCP* textbook will be most useful in comparing and contrasting the approaches and will serve as a review for the final exam: Basic philosophies, key concepts, goals of therapy, the therapeutic relationship, techniques of therapy, applications, contributions and limitations of the approaches, and contributions and limitations for multicultural counseling.

In Chapter 15 of the *Student Manual* are exercises on applications of theoretical approaches to specific client populations or specific problems. There are also some guidelines for studying counseling theories in working with Ruth from an integrative perspective. Additionally, there are questions and issues to consider as guidelines for developing your own counseling perspective.

The following questions can be presented as essay questions for your students, as discussion questions for small groups, or as review questions for the final exam:

1. How does theory affect practice?

2. Discuss the meaning of the integrated perspective. What are some of the advantages and disadvantages of drawing from more than one school?

3. What do you consider to be the most important therapeutic goals? Which theoretical orientations would most guide you in formulating your goals?

4. How would you describe your function and role as a helper or a counselor? What do you see as your major responsibility as a helping agent? What would you expect of your clients? How do you view the relationship between you and your clients? Again, what theoretical perspectives do you draw from as a helper?

5. What are your basic assumptions about human nature? Which approach to therapy, of the ten you have studied, comes the closest to your beliefs about human nature?

6. When you consider the philosophical assumptions underlying the approach you chose in the question above, what are its implications for therapeutic practice? In what ways do our basic assumptions determine the procedures we use in working with our clients?

7. What are some general goals that you value as you counsel others? Why are these goals important to you? How might your own goals influence your client? How do your goals influence the interventions you make?

8. What reactions do you have to this statement made in the text? "As a counselor, *you* are your very best technique. There is no substitute for developing techniques that are an expression of your personality and that fit for you."

9. Most counselors must deal with the issue of structuring in such areas as time limits, action limits, role limits, and process limits. The following questions can be useful as guidelines for examining your own views on the degree of control you deem important both during the sessions and outside the therapy hour.

    a. What effect does the counselor's behavior have on the client in the session?

b.   What matters of control should be clarified at the outset – length of session? frequency of meetings? duration of sessions? general goals? contracts and assignments? division of responsibility? limitations? confidentiality?

c.   Should counselors outline or suggest certain themes or topics for the client to pursue in the sessions?

d.   To what degree should counselors attempt to control the client's behavior outside the session? Should they ask the clients to keep journals, record dreams, think about certain topics, and so on?

e.   Should they encourage clients to go further and put into practice what they have been exploring? Should "homework assignments" be given? Should contracts be developed? Who should develop these – the counselor, the client, or both? What is the value of assignments and contracts?

f.   Who should decide when the client is ready to terminate – the client, the counselor, or both?

10.   Now that you have studied eleven therapy models, what kinds of criteria could you develop to create your own integrative approach to counseling? What basis do you have for including or excluding certain major concepts of the various approaches? Describe your rationale for your personalized theory of counseling.

Test Items

Chapter Fifteen

Theory and Practice of

Counseling and Psychotherapy

AN INTEGRATIVE PERSPECTIVE

A. *Basic Philosophies*

1. According to psychoanalytic therapy, human beings are:
    a.   motivated by social interest.
    b.   determined by psychic energy and early experiences.
    c.   inclined toward becoming fully functioning.
    d.   free to choose who they will become.

2. Which of the following approaches contends that the nature of the human condition includes self-awareness, freedom of choice, responsibility, and anxiety as basic elements?
    a.   Gestalt therapy
    b.   person-centered therapy
    c.   existential therapy
    d.   Adlerian therapy
    e.   reality therapy

3. Which of the following approaches to therapy focuses on the unique style of life we create at an early age?
    a.   family systems therapy
    b.   reality therapy
    c.   rational emotive behavior therapy
    d.   psychoanalytic therapy
    e.   Adlerian therapy

4. Which of the following approaches is based on the premise that there are multiple realities and multiple truths?
    a.   behavior therapy
    b.   postmodern approaches
    c.   rational emotive behavior therapy
    d.   Gestalt therapy
    e.   reality therapy

5. Which of the following orientations avoids exploring problems, and instead, focuses on creating solutions in the present and the future?
    a.   Freud's psychoanalytic approach
    b.   family therapy
    c.   person-centered therapy
    d.   solution-focused therapy
    e.   Gestalt therapy

6. Which statement most closely reflects the philosophy of feminist therapy?
    a.   Feminist therapy depicts an accurate assessment of the psychosexual stages of development.
    b.   Androcentricism, gendercentricism, and ethnocentricism are important bias-free concepts of feminist therapy.
    c.   Constructs of feminist therapy include being gender-fair, flexible, interactionist, and life-span oriented.
    d.   both (b) and (c) are correct

B. *Key Concepts*

7. Adlerian therapy emphasizes the individual's:
    a.   positive capacities to live in society cooperatively.
    b.   quality world.
    c.   irrational, crooked thinking.
    e.   polarities.

8. Which of the following approaches would contend that normal personality development depends on the successful resolution of specific stages of development?
   a. narrative therapy
   b. family systems therapy
   c. psychoanalytic therapy
   d. solution-focused therapy

9. A key concept of Gestalt therapy is:
   a. externalizing conversations.
   b. unfinished business.
   c. belief systems.
   d. family of origin issues.
   e. importance of the past.

10. Which of the following therapies emphasizes that a person's belief system is the cause of emotional problems?
    a. solution-focused brief therapy
    b. existential therapy
    c. Gestalt therapy
    d. behavior therapy
    e. rational emotive behavior therapy

11. Person-centered therapy puts faith in the client's:
    a. ability to uncover repressed experiences.
    b. ability to integrate their polarities.
    c. capacity for recognizing how birth order affects their choices.
    d. capacity for self-direction.
    e. ability to change their belief system.

12. Which of the following approaches most emphasizes principles of learning?
    a. Gestalt therapy
    b. behavior therapy
    c. narrative therapy
    d. family systems therapy
    e. solution-focused brief therapy

13. Which is not a key concept of feminist therapy?
    a. the personal is political
    b. the counseling relationship is egalitarian
    c. commitment to confronting oppression
    d. women's problems are viewed from an intrapsychic perspective
    e. the personal and social and interrelated

C. Goals of Therapy

14. Personal change and social transformation are goals of:
    a. Adlerian therapy.
    b. solution-focused therapy.
    c. person-centered therapy
    d. feminist therapy.
    e. none of the above

15. Which of the following approaches to therapy most attempts to provide a safe climate (based on unconditional positive regard) that is conducive to a client's self-exploration?
    a. psychoanalytic therapy
    b. Gestalt therapy
    c. reality therapy
    d. family therapy
    e. person-centered therapy

16. One of the goals of rational emotive behavior therapy is to:
    a. assist clients in acquiring a more tolerant and rational view of life.
    b. make the unconscious conscious.
    c. provide opportunities for reliving early traumas.
    d. assist clients in gaining awareness of moment-to-moment experiencing.
    e. help clients become aware of their family constellation.

17. Which of the following approaches places emphasis on challenging clients to recognize that they are responsible for events that they formerly thought were happening *to* them?
    a. psychoanalytic therapy
    b. existential therapy
    c. behavior therapy
    d. Adlerian therapy
    e. solution-focused therapy

18. One of the major goals of reality therapy involves:
    a. reconstructing the basic personality.
    b. identifying factors that block freedom.
    c. encouraging clients to be willing to be a process.
    d. challenging clients to evaluate what they are doing.
    e. learning to express feelings.

19. Which of the following approaches to therapy focuses on the scientific method?
    a. person-centered therapy
    b. Gestalt therapy
    c. behavior therapy
    d. reality therapy
    e. existential therapy

D. *The Therapeutic Relationship*

20. Empowerment and egalitarianism are the basis of the _____ therapeutic relationship.
    a. existential
    b. feminist
    c. Gestalt
    d. psychoanalytic

21. According to traditional psychoanalytic therapy, the therapist:
    a. must establish an authentic encounter with the client.
    b. should display genuineness and warmth.
    c. remains anonymous.
    d. is a teacher.
    e. refuses to give up on the client.

22. In which of the following approaches does the therapist show concern for the client by a process of involvement throughout the course of therapy?
    a. reality therapy
    b. Gestalt therapy
    c. family systems therapy
    d. psychoanalytic therapy
    e. solution-focused therapy

23. In which therapy approach is the client viewed as the expert on his or her own life, while the therapist is seen as an expert questioner who assists clients in freeing themselves of their problem-saturated stories and create new life-affirming stories?
    a. existential therapy
    b. narrative therapy
    c. rational emotive behavior therapy
    d. person-centered therapy
    e. psychoanalytic therapy

24. Which of the following approaches encourages therapists to accurately grasp the client's "being in the world"?
    a. psychoanalytic therapy
    b. Adlerian therapy
    c. behavior therapy
    d. rational emotive behavior therapy
    e. existential therapy

25. An Adlerian therapist would:
    a. maintain an aloof stance.
    b. establish a cooperative relationship based on equality.
    c. take the role of expert.
    d. take the role of a friendly parent.
    e. avoid sharing personal reactions.

26. In which of the following approaches to therapy does the therapist become active and directive, functioning as a trainer for the client?
    a. existential therapy
    b. person-centered therapy
    c. behavior therapy
    d. Gestalt therapy
    e. psychoanalytic therapy

E. *Therapy Techniques*

27. A key technique of Adlerian therapy is:
    a. free association
    b. dialogue with polarities.
    c. family sculpting.
    d. changing one's language.
    e. the assessment of one's family constellation.

28. Which of the following approaches to therapy stresses understanding first and technique second?
    a. Gestalt therapy
    b. existential therapy
    c. rational emotive behavior therapy
    d. family systems therapy
    e. behavior therapy

29. One of the techniques used by behavior therapists in dealing with a client's anxiety is:
    a. the miracle question.
    b. encouragement.
    c. externalizing the problem.
    d. systematic desensitization.
    e. shame-attacking exercises.

30. Which of the following approaches to therapy stresses the attitude of the therapist over the use of techniques?
    a. person-centered therapy
    b. psychoanalytic therapy
    c. cognitive-behavior therapy
    d. behavior therapy
    e. family systems therapy

31. The technique of reliving and reexperiencing unfinished business is associated with:
    a. Gestalt therapy.
    b. person-centered therapy.
    c. existential therapy.
    d. reality therapy.
    e. solution-focused therapy

32. In feminist therapy, the following technique(s) is/are used to help clients recognize the impact of gender-role socialization:
    a. free association
    b. genograms
    c. scaling questions
    d. consciousness-raising
    e. all of the above

33. In psychoanalytic therapy, a technique of great importance is:
    a. "The Question."
    b. re-authoring one's life story.
    c. value judgments.
    d. interpretation.
    e. solution talk as opposed to problem talk.

F. *Applications*

34. Narrative therapy can be applied to:
    a. eating disorders.
    b. depression.
    c relationship concerns.
    d. all of the above

35. Which of the following therapies is most recommended for the treatment of phobic disorders?
    a. behavior therapy
    b. narrative therapy
    c. existential therapy
    d. rational emotive behavior therapy
    e. solution-focused brief therapy

36. Which of the following approaches to therapy is based on the A-B-C theory of personality?
    a. reality therapy
    b. rational emotive behavior therapy
    c. psychoanalytic therapy
    d. solution-focused brief therapy
    e. none of the above

37. Which of the following approaches is *least* likely to be applied to short-term crisis intervention?
    a. existential therapy
    b. person-centered therapy
    c. reality therapy
    d. psychoanalytic therapy
    e. cognitive-behavior therapy

38. Existential therapy can be especially helpful for:
    a. individuals with phobic disorders.
    b. children with behavior disorders.
    c. patients in a mental hospital.
    d. couples needing sex therapy.
    e. individuals facing a transition in life.

39. Which of the following approaches to therapy is best suited for helping people to create an alternative life story?
    a. narrative therapy
    b. psychoanalytic therapy
    c. person-centered therapy
    d. Adlerian therapy
    e. behavior therapy

G. *Contributions*

40. One contribution of psychoanalytic therapy has been its:
    a. subjective approach.
    b. reliance on research for validation.
    c. detailed and comprehensive description of personality structure and functioning.
    d. emphasis on an I/Thou relationship.

41. Which of the following approaches is credited with an emphasis on assessment and evaluation?
    a. behavior therapy
    b. existential therapy
    c. psychoanalytic therapy
    d. reality therapy
    e. Gestalt therapy

42. Which of the following approaches challenges social and cultural injustices that lead to oppression of certain groups?
    a. family systems therapy
    b. psychoanalytic therapy
    c. person-centered therapy
    d. narrative therapy
    e. reality therapy

43. Which of the following approaches consists of simple and clear concepts that are easily grasped in many helping professions?
    a. psychoanalytic therapy
    b. reality therapy
    c. narrative therapy
    d. Gestalt therapy
    e. family systems therapy

44. One contribution of Adlerian therapy has been an emphasis on:
    a. unconscious motivations.
    b. empirical validation.
    c. unleashing buried feelings.
    d. precision.
    e. social and psychological factors.

45. Which of the following approaches to therapy is noted for using numerous cognitive, emotive, and behavioral techniques?
    a. person-centered therapy
    b. Gestalt therapy
    c. rational emotive behavior therapy
    d. narrative therapy
    e. existential therapy

46. The negative impact of discrimination and oppression for both men and women has surfaced as a result of:
    a. rational emotive behavior therapy.
    b. person-centered therapy.
    c. family systems therapy.
    d. feminist therapy.

H. *Limitations*

47. Some are critical of the "not-knowing" stance of the therapist and the negative stance on formal diagnosis in which of these therapies?
    a. behavior therapy
    b. solution-focused therapy
    c. narrative therapy
    d. both (b) and (c)
    e. Adlerian therapy

48. A limitation of reality therapy is that it:
    a. consists of simple concepts that are easily grasped.
    b. discounts the therapeutic value of dreams.
    c. does not appeal to resistant clients.
    d. has limited applicability.
    e. goes along with the medical model of therapy.

49. A limitation of person-centered therapy is:
    a. the possible danger of the therapist remaining passive and inactive.
    b. the emphasis on complex ideas and concepts.
    c. the lack of research to support the theory.
    d. neglect of the value of the therapeutic relationship.
    e. the overemphasis on unconscious factors.

50. A limitation of existential therapy is its:
    a. emphasis on the therapist as an expert.
    b. adherence to the medical model.
    c. limited applicability to nonverbal clients.
    d. use of simplistic concepts.
    e. neglect of feelings.

51. A limitation of Gestalt therapy is that it:
    a. does not allow for full expression of feelings.
    b. discounts the therapeutic value of dreams.
    c. completely ignores the past.
    d. offers few techniques.
    e. may neglect cognitive factors.

52. A limitation of behavior therapy is that it:
    a. does not provide a basis for accountable practice.
    b. does not identify specific problems.
    c. does not make room for cognitive factors.
    d. fails to explicitly define the role of the therapist.
    e. none of the above

1. B	14. D	27. E	40. C
2. C	15. E	28. B	41. A
3. E	16. A	29. D	42. D
4. B	17. B	30. A	43. B
5. D	18. D	31. A	44. E
6. C	19. C	32. D	45. C
7. A	20. B	33. D	46. D
8. C	21. C	34. D	47. D
9. B	22. A	35. A	48. B
10. E	23. B	36. B	49. A
11. D	24. E	37. D	50. C
12. B	25. B	38. E	51. E
13. D	26. C	39. A	52. E

Guidelines for Using Chapter Sixteen

Case Illustration:
An Integrative Approach
In Working With Stan

in

Theory and Practice of
Counseling and Psychotherapy
and the *Student Manual*

Case Approach to
Counseling and Psychotherapy

and

The Art of Integrative Counseling

I make reference to Stan concurrently with the study of each system. After all the therapy models have been examined, I focus in more depth on Stan as an exercise in review, comparisons and contrasts, and integration of the approaches. Typically, I ask the students also to work with Stan using a *combination* of the various approaches. This gives the students a chance to think in concrete terms of what aspects of each theory they might incorporate into their personal style of counseling. In the essay test section, I have a question that can be used for this purpose.

One hope I have for my students is that, after they have studied and done some practice with the various theories of counseling, they will begin to find some basis for developing an integrative approach to counseling. While I know it will take many years of experience to refine and define their philosophy and approach to counseling, I do think that even beginning students will be critical of each theory as they study it and will think about the concepts they would most want to incorporate into their style of counseling.

I have tried to integrate these theories in a three-dimensional way by showing how I would work with Stan using something from each theory. I describe the following components and steps in my integrative approach, which focuses on thinking/feeling/doing:

- beginning with getting a sense of what it was like for Stan to come to the initial session

- clarifying the nature of our relationship

- clarifying the goals of therapy

- identifying the main currents of Stan's feelings

- challenging Stan to think about the decisions he has made and to put what he is learning about himself into some kind of cognitive perspective

- valuing Stan's past by looking at how it affects his feelings, thoughts, and behavior now

- encouraging Stan to act on the insights he is gaining by developing a plan for change – helping him translate what he is learning about himself in therapy into ways that he can apply this new learning in daily situations and thus bring about changes in the way he feels, the way he thinks about himself and others, and the ways that he behaves.

- encouraging Stan to work with his family of origin.

- incorporating a spiritual dimension in my counseling with Stan.

- encouraging Stan to join a therapy group.

- there is also a section illustrating approaches for dealing with Stan's alcoholism.

Suggested Activities and Exercises

Critique of Various Therapies: Working with Stan

Some suggestions for class activities are as follows:

Have one student who feels some identification with Stan volunteer to play the role of Stan. Alternatively, the instructor could play Stan (which I typically do in my classes). In either case, "Stan" acts out his or her role in a session with a "therapist," who is a volunteer from class also. Eleven students volunteer to play the role of the therapist, each student representing one of the eleven therapeutic approaches. Each "therapist" demonstrates how he or she, from the standpoint of a specific orientation, would counsel Stan. After the "therapist" has had about six to seven minutes in counseling the client, the entire class can participate in a critique and discussion of the sessions. Here are some specific suggestions.

a. It is best to get volunteers a week in advance so they can think about some aspects they want to focus on and can do some preparation in the particular therapy orientation.

b. In my classes, I prefer to have all the counselors work with Stan one after the other, without stopping to discuss each segment. We hold the processing session until all ten volunteers have had a chance to work with Stan for about seven minutes each.

c. During the time that each counselor is attempting to stay within a single therapeutic model, the other students are asked to write notes on their observations of *both* Stan and each counselor. They might comment about what they particularly like, about leads that were missed, and about alternative techniques in working with whatever material is present.

d. Each of the eleven volunteers is asked to assume that they were watching the prior counselor work with Stan through a one-way glass. In this way, each counselor does not have to start from scratch (except for the first counselor). The idea is to build upon previous sessions, and ideally, to demonstrate how a different theoretical perspective might attack the same theme from a different angle. Volunteers can use some imagination here, by saying something like:

"Well, Stan, with your last therapist you were role playing with your 'mother,' telling 'her' (the counselor) what you wanted from 'her.' Let's see if we can follow up on that work you did, only this time I have another approach I'd like to suggest."

e. After all "therapists" have had a chance to counsel Stan (this takes about one hour), then Stan can be given a chance to talk about his or her experience during this time. What was it like to be "Stan?" Any different reactions to different therapists and the variety of perspectives?

f. Then, the eleven students who functioned as separate therapists can sit together (form an inner circle in the class) and share their reactions to the time they spent with "Stan." What were they thinking and feeling? What were their reactions to Stan? And, more importantly, what impressions did they have of themselves as they counseled him?

g. Next, the class members have a chance to discuss what they saw and their reactions to the sessions. It might be better to systematically go through each of the therapies in the order in which they were demonstrated. This orderly progression allows for comparing and contrasting approaches. In this processing and sharing time it is good to be kind, sensitive, and constructive. The students who were courageous enough to volunteer deserve recognition for this alone. Rather than focus on "right" and "wrong" approaches, I tend to explore with students what it was like for them to function within a particular model and what they learned from the experience. It might also be helpful to comment about alternative strategies and other directions that might have been taken within each of the separate theoretical models. From my perspective, this is a learning experience for all involved, and hopefully even enjoyable. I strive to approach this exercise with a constructive spirit, rather than being on the lookout for "mistakes." I tell the students that the biggest mistake is to do nothing or to hold back on their hunches and reactions.

h. Of course, if time permitted, this entire process could be repeated, only this time with a new set of eleven volunteers. If the class meets in a three-hour block, this would be ideal for a full session. If not, it would need to be spread out over two or three class sessions.

Another interesting variation of the above exercise is to arrange for a case *conference* to discuss treatment plans for Stan. After everyone has observed the ten mini-sessions, one approach is for the eleven volunteer "therapists" to function for a time as a professional staff member at a case conference. Each "therapist" would stay within his or her theoretical orientation as the discussion focuses on Stan.

STUDY GUIDE FOR CHAPTER SIXTEEN

CASE ILLUSTRATION – STAN

1. In this chapter I show what I might draw from each of these approaches and then I illustrate how I might work with Stan by integrating therapeutic concepts and techniques from the various perspectives. At this point, strive to develop your own way of integrating the approaches and applying them to Stan.

2. In Chapter 13 of the *Case Approach* book, *Bringing the Approaches Together and Developing Your Own Therapeutic Style*, you will get further ideas and suggestions for looking for themes in a client's life and for working with these themes by integrating ideas from all of the approaches. I describe various ways that counseling strategies might be modified depending on the cultural background of Ruth. The implications for multicultural counseling are explored as they apply to the case of Ruth. I suggest that you read this chapter on working with Ruth from an integrative perspective very carefully, as doing so should assist you to develop your own basis for selecting what you consider to be the features that appeal to you from the eleven approaches.

Test Items

Chapter Sixteen

Theory and Practice of

Counseling and Psychotherapy

CASE OF STAN

1. How would a psychoanalytic therapist view Stan's drinking problem?
   a. as a manifestation of his failure identity
   b. as rooted in faulty development during the phallic stage
   c. as an oral fixation
   d. as a result of the ego-defense mechanism of introjection
   e. as a manifestation of his collective unconscious

2. Which of the following is not true when viewing Stan's problems from the standpoint of self-psychology and the object-relations theory?
   a. On some levels, he is stuck in the symbiotic phase.
   b. The focus would be on Stan's developmental sequences.
   c. He is unable to get confirmation of his worth from himself.
   d. He had accomplished the task of individuation.
   e. He is repeating patterns he formed with his mother during infancy.

3. Which of the following would not be part of an Adlerian approach to working with Stan?
   a. giving homework assignments to be carried out
   b. gathering data about his dreams
   c. examining his private logic
   d. gathering data about his family constellation
   e. confronting the ways he is seeking to escape his freedom through drugs and alcohol

4. An Adlerian therapist would interpret Stan's depression as:
   a. a sickness that needs to be cured.
   b. discouragement that can be helped by encouragement.
   c. a feeling that leads to his faulty thinking.
   d. related to unfinished business.
   e. internalized anger and guilt.

5. Which therapeutic approach is likely to use interventions with Stan such as pre-therapy change, exception questions, scaling questions, and the miracle question?
   a. Adlerian therapy
   b. rational emotive behavior therapy
   c. existential therapy
   d. solution-focused therapy
   e. none of the above

6. Which therapeutic approach would focus on gender-role analysis and gender-role socialization with Stan?
   a. strategic family therapy
   b. Adlerian therapy
   c. feminist therapy
   d. existential therapy
   e. narrative therapy

7. There are several issues in Stan's life that would interest an existential therapist. Which of the following is not one of these?
   a. his use of alcohol and drugs
   b. his suicidal thoughts
   c. his persistent feelings of guilt
   d. his feelings of isolation
   e. his positive experience with his summer camp supervisor

8. How might an existential therapist work with Stan's depression and suicidal thoughts?
   a. by examining his faulty belief system
   b. by confronting Stan with the issue of finding meaning and purpose in his life
   c. by using active listening and reflection as Stan talks about his feelings
   d. by determining the nature of his shadow
   e. both (a) and (b)

9. The therapy approach most likely to focus directly on helping Stan to stop using alcohol and drugs would be:
   a. person-centered therapy.
   b. Gestalt therapy.
   c. behavior therapy.
   d. existential therapy.
   e. psychoanalytic therapy.

10. Stan's person-centered therapist would see Stan as a man who:
    a. needs help in setting goals.
    b. has unresolved issues from his past.
    c. must face the fact that he is ultimately alone.
    d. needs to learn to live with his anxiety.
    e. possesses the necessary resources for personal growth.

11. According to a person-centered therapist, the most important aspect of therapy with Stan will be:
    a. the therapeutic relationship.
    b. the exploration of his past.
    c. putting insights into action.
    d. teaching him to think in new, positive ways.
    e. active listening.

12. Which therapeutic approach would place the *least* emphasis on having Stan explore his feelings about his ex-wife?
    a. psychoanalytic therapy
    b. behavior therapy
    c. Gestalt therapy
    d. person-centered therapy
    e. both (b) and (c)

13. Which therapeutic approach would work to help Stan recognize, claim, and embrace his personal power?
    a. narrative therapy
    b. rational emotive behavior therapy
    c. reality therapy
    d. feminist therapy
    e. existential therapy

14. What are some Gestalt techniques that would help Stan deal with the unfinished business concerning his ex-wife?
    a. having him "speak" to her in the present
    b. "staying with the feeling"
    c. the rehearsal experiment
    d. all of the above

15. The Gestalt approach to helping Stan resolve issues from his past would involve:
    a. asking him to bring these significant people to future therapy sessions.
    b. talking in detail about past experiences.
    c. interpreting his dreams by using universal symbolism.
    d. reliving and reexperiencing painful scenes.
    e. examining Stan's stages of development for fixations.

16. Which one of the following approaches to therapy would pay the least attention to Stan's thought processes?
    a. rational emotive behavior therapy
    b. Adlerian therapy
    c. Gestalt therapy
    d. reality therapy
    e. cognitive-behavioral therapies

17. Which of the following approaches would ask Stan to focus on systemic issues?
    a. family therapy
    b. Gestalt therapy
    c. psychoanalytic therapy
    d. person-centered therapy
    e. solution-focused therapy

18. What technique(s) from behavior therapy might help Stan with his fear of women?
    a. systematic desensitization
    b. assertion training
    c. modeling
    d. behavior rehearsal
    e. all of the above

19. What would a rational emotive behavior therapist say about Stan's difficulties in life?
    a. He will feel better if he learns to think more rationally.
    b. He continually reindoctrinates himself with self-defeating sentences.
    c. He will feel better when he simply gains insight into the past roots of his problems.
    d. all of the above
    e. all but (c)

20. According to rational emotive behavior therapy, what will bring about actual changes in Stan's life?
    a. doing the hard work of challenging and changing irrational beliefs
    b. recognizing ways his faulty beliefs affect what he does and how he feels
    c. understanding the A-B-C theory
    d. acknowledging the "shoulds" and "oughts" he has accepted
    e. all of the above

21. Stan's reality therapist would focus on all of the following, except:
    a. Stan's positive experiences with his camp supervisor.
    b. Stan's negative experiences during his childhood.
    c. Stan's wants and perceptions.
    d. Stan's future goals.
    e. Stan's evaluation pertaining to his drinking.

22. Stan's reality therapist would:
    a. explore Stan's quality world.
    b. ask him to engage in the process of self-evaluation of his behavior.
    c. encourage Stan explore past experiences that might have contributed to his present problems.
    d. none of the above
    e. both (a) and (b)

23. Which of the following therapeutic approaches would place some emphasis on helping Stan with the future?
    a. narrative therapy
    b. Adlerian therapy
    c. reality therapy
    d. solution-focused therapy
    e. all of the above

24. Stan has completed his experience in counseling. Which of the following approaches would be concerned with evaluating the outcomes of therapy?
    a. existential therapy
    b. behavior therapy
    c. Gestalt therapy
    d. rational emotive behavior therapy
    e. the postmodern therapies

25. Stan has a tendency to relate external events to himself, even when there is no basis for making this connection. He related the incident in which a female classmate did not show up for a lunch date. He agonized over this and convinced himself that she would have been humiliated to be seen in his presence. This is an example of which form of cognitive distortion?
    a. arbitrary inferences
    b. overgeneralization
    c. personalization
    d. labeling and mislabeling

26. Stan frequently engages in thinking and interpreting in all-or-nothing terms. Through this process of dichotomous thinking, Stan has self-defeating labels and boxes that keep him restricted. This is an example of which form of cognitive distortion?
    a. arbitrary inferences
    b. overgeneralization
    c. personalization
    d. labeling and mislabeling
    e. polarized thinking

27. Stan makes conclusions without supporting and relevant evidence. He often engages in catastrophizing, which involves thinking about the worst possible scenario and outcome for a given situation. This is an example of which form of cognitive distortion?
    a. arbitrary inferences
    b. overgeneralization
    c. personalization
    d. labeling and mislabeling
    e. polarized thinking

28. Stan presents himself in light of his imperfections and mistakes. He allows his past failures to define his total being. This is an example of which form of cognitive distortion?
    a. arbitrary inferences
    b. overgeneralization
    c. personalization
    d. labeling and mislabeling
    e. polarized thinking

29. Stan holds extreme beliefs arrived at on the basis of a single incident and applies them inappropriately to other dissimilar events or settings. This is an example of which form of cognitive distortion?
    a. arbitrary inferences
    b. overgeneralization
    c. personalization
    d. labeling and mislabeling
    e. polarized thinking

30. Which of the following therapists would accept Stan's drinking as the problem and help him deconstruct his alcohol-saturated story and reauthor a new life story?
    a. solution-oriented therapy
    b. reality therapy
    c. person-centered therapy
    d. narrative therapy
    e. rational emotive behavior therapy

31. Using an narrative approach to Stan's therapy, the therapist would have the general goal of:
    a. exploring the causes of his current problems with women.
    b. assisting Stan in the process of reauthoring his life story.
    c. uncovering Stan's basic mistakes in his thinking.
    d. focusing on eliminating the presenting problem and finding solutions.
    e. attempting to restructure the family dynamics.

32. In working with Stan, a solution-focused therapist would most likely utilize the following technique(s):
    a. bibliotherapy
    b. assertiveness training
    c. cognitive restructuring
    d. exception questions
    e. none of the above

ANSWER KEY FOR CHAPTER SIXTEEN – CASE OF STAN

MULTIPLE-CHOICE TEST QUESTIONS

1.	C	17.	A
2.	D	18.	E
3.	E	19.	E
4.	B	20.	E
5.	D	21.	B
6.	C	22.	E
7.	E	23.	E
8.	C	24.	B
9.	C	25.	C
10.	E	26.	E
11.	A	27.	A
12.	B	28.	D
13.	D	29.	B
14.	D	30.	D
15.	D	31.	B
16.	C	32.	D

III

FINAL EXAMINATION

QUESTIONS

for

Theory and Practice of

Counseling and Psychotherapy

These tests can be most conveniently scored if the answers are transmitted to a SCAN TRON sheet (Form 884), which contains 200 answer spaces. Using the SCAN TRON forms can be especially convenient during the pressures of the ending of a semester.

You'll notice that some of the items that appear on both of these finals also appear in the chapter quizzes listed in this *Instructor's Resource Manual* and the *Student Manual* (the *Pre-Chapter Self-Inventories*). I tell students this so that they'll be a bit more inclined to review the weekly quizzes that I've given them, as well as review their *Student Manual.*

FINAL EXAMINATION

Directions: Please use SCAN TRON (Form 884) and number 2 pencil. Answer all items, leaving no spaces blank. In the following multiple-choice items, read the sentence that describes one of the therapeutic systems. Characteristics, key concepts, assumptions, techniques, and so on are described in the statement. Your task is to identify the theory that best fits the description, or to select the best response.

1. The person has a need for *identity;* either a "success identity" or a "failure identity" can develop.
    a. Gestalt therapy
    b. behavior therapy
    c. reality therapy
    d. psychoanalytic therapy
    e. person-centered therapy

2. The client has a tendency toward becoming fully functioning and moves toward openness, trust in self, spontaneity, and inner directedness.
    a. psychoanalytic therapy
    b. cognitive-behavior therapy
    c. behavior therapy
    d. family systems therapy
    e. person-centered therapy

3. Humans are shaped and determined by sociocultural environment and conditioning, and all behavior is learned.
    a. psychoanalytic therapy
    b. existential therapy
    c. Gestalt therapy
    d. person-centered therapy
    e. none of the above

4. Behavior is determined by unconscious forces and earlier experiences, by psychic energy, and by sexual and aggressive impulses.
    a. psychoanalytic therapy
    b. behavior therapy
    c. REBT
    d. reality therapy
    e. social constructionism

5. Though humans are born with the potential for rational thinking, there is a tendency toward crooked and irrational thinking.
    a. psychoanalytic therapy
    b. behavior therapy
    c. REBT
    d. reality therapy
    e. family systems therapy

6. Faulty personality development is viewed as the result of inadequate resolution of some specific stage of psychosexual development.
    a. psychoanalytic therapy
    b. person-centered therapy
    c. Gestalt therapy
    d. existential therapy

7. Mental health is viewed as the congruence between the ideal self and the real self.
    a. psychoanalytic therapy
    b. person-centered therapy
    c. REBT
    d. reality therapy

8.   Emphasis is given to personal responsibility, unfinished business, avoidance, direct experiencing in the here-and-now, and awareness.
        a.   REBT
        b.   Adlerian therapy
        c.   social constructionism
        d.   Gestalt therapy
        e.   behavior therapy

9.   The focus is on overt behavior, precision in specifying treatment goals, developing specific treatment plans, and assessing results.
        a.   psychoanalytic thrapy
        b.   behavior therapy
        c.   person-centered therapy
        d.   existential therapy
        e.   Gestalt therapy

10.   It stresses evaluation of behavior, personal responsibility, total behavior, and commitment to change.
        a.   psychoanalytic therapy
        b.   person-centered therapy
        c.   family therapy
        d.   existential therapy
        e.   reality therapy

11.   Clients are viewed from a systemic perspective.
        a.   psychoanalytic therapy
        b.   behavior therapy
        c.   family therapy
        d.   REBT
        e.   none of the above

12.   The general goal is eliminating maladaptive behavior patterns and learning constructive patterns.
        a.   Gestalt therapy
        b.   person-centered therapy
        c.   behavior therapy
        d.   existential therapy
        e.   psychoanalytic therapy

13.   This therapeutic model stresses anonymity of the therapist, recognizing and working through the transference relationship, and interpretation.
        a.   Adlerian therapy
        b.   Gestalt therapy
        c.   REBT
        d.   existential therapy
        e.   none of the above

14.   This approach claims that emotional disturbance is the result of the client's self-indoctrination and reindoctrination of unrealistic ideas.
        a.   reality therapy
        b.   Gestalt therapy
        c.   family therapy
        d.   REBT
        e.   all of the above

15.   This theory places central importance on the psychosexual stages of development.
        a.   reality therapy
        b.   family systems therapy
        c.   Adlerian therapy
        d.   person-centered therapy
        e.   none of the above

16. The therapist is seen largely as a teacher, and therapy is a didactic process.
    a. psychoanalytic therapy
    b. REBT
    c. person-centered therapy
    d. Gestalt therapy
    e. existential therapy

17. The "homework assignment" method is most closely associated with:
    a. REBT.
    b. Gestalt therapy.
    c. psychoanalytic therapy.
    d. person-centered therapy.
    e. family systems therapy.

18. The concept of transference is important in:
    a. reality therapy.
    b. REBT.
    c. behavior therapy.
    d. psychoanalytic therapy.
    e. existential therapy.

19. Which theory stresses the role of self-evaluation of total behavior as a central issue?
    a. cognitive-behavior therapy
    b. Gestalt therapy
    c. person-centered therapy
    d. behavior therapy
    e. reality therapy

20. The concept that "unfinished business" from our past gets in the way of our current functioning is from:
    a. cognitive-behavioral approaches.
    b. person-centered therapy.
    c. Gestalt therapy.
    d. existential therapy.
    e. Adlerian therapy.

21. Insight is not considered essential in which therapy (ies)?
    a. reality therapy
    b. behavior therapy
    c. psychoanalytic therapy
    d. rational emotive behavior therapy
    e. both (a) and (b)

22. Diagnosis and assessment are considered important in which therapy(ies)?
    a. behavior therapy
    b. psychoanalytic therapy
    c. Gestalt therapy
    d. person-centered therapy
    e. both (a) and (b)

23. Diagnosis is considered as not essential in which therapy(ies)"
    a. feminist therapy.
    b. solution-focused therapy.
    c. narrative therapy therapy.
    d. person-centered therapy.
    e. all of the above

24. The concept of "therapist congruence" is stressed most in:
    a. behavior therapy.
    b. psychoanalytic therapy.
    c. cognitive-behavior therapy.
    d. Adlerian therapy.
    e. person-centered therapy.

25. The concept of resistance is most a part of:
    a. behavior therapy.
    b. psychoanalytic therapy.
    c. Adlerian therapy.
    d. REBT.
    e. reality therapy.

26. The notion that the person is not the problem, rather the problem is the problem is stress in:
    a. existential therapy.
    b. Gestalt therapy.
    c. family systems therapy.
    d. Adlerian therapy.
    e. narrative therapy.

27. Which of the following is not considered as a technique commonly used in solution-focused therapy:
    a. formula first session task
    b. scaling questions
    c. exception questions
    d. lifestyle assessment
    e. the miracle question

28. The ego-defense mechanisms as a way of coping with anxiety are given emphasis in:
    a. psychoanalytic therapy.
    b. person-centered therapy.
    c. REBT.
    d. reality therapy.
    e. both (c) and (d)

29. The approach that relies most heavily on objective data and research to support its practice is:
    a. psychoanalytic therapy.
    b. behavior therapy.
    c. Gestalt therapy.
    d. existential therapy.
    e. family systems therapy.

30. The approach that begins with a comprehensive lifestyle assessment, and which stresses family constellation and early memories, is:
    a. psychoanalytic therapy.
    b. existential therapy.
    c. Adlerian therapy.
    d. solution-focused therapy.
    e. narrative therapy.

31. Which of the following would not be considered an experiential therapy?
    a. Gestalt therapy
    b. person-centered therapy
    c. reality therapy
    d. existential therapy
    e. solution-focused therapy

32. Which of the following would least be considered as a "cognitively oriented" therapy?
   a. Adlerian therapy
   b. REBT
   c. reality therapy
   d. Gestalt therapy
   e. behavior therapy

33. Which therapy utilizes dreams by having clients become all the parts of the dream and making their own interpretations of the dream?
   a. psychoanalytic therapy
   b. Gestalt therapy
   c. Jungian therapy
   d. Adlerian therapy
   e. person-centered therapy

34. The concept of developing a unique style of life as a way of compensating for basic inferiority feelings is a part of:
   a. reality therapy.
   b. cognitive-behavior therapy.
   c. existential therapy.
   d. Adlerian therapy.
   e. person-centered therapy.

35. Rollo May and Viktor Frankl are associated with which approach to therapy?
   a. person-centered therapy
   b. Gestalt therapy
   c. psychoanalytic therapy
   d. existential therapy
   e. narrative therapy

36. Erik Erikson built a theory around:
   a. the role of the body in psychology.
   b. critical tasks at each stage of development.
   c. dealing with early recollections.
   d. birth order and the family constellation.

37. Which of the following therapies does *not* involve a phenomenological orientation?
   a. Adlerian therapy
   b. reality therapy
   c. existential therapy
   d. person-centered therapy
   e. All of the above involve a phenomenological orientation.

38. Which approach places emphasis on such concepts as freedom and responsibility, anxiety, death, confronting one's ultimate aloneness, and searching for meaning in life?
   a. Adlerian therapy
   b. reality therapy
   c. existential therapy
   d. Gestalt therapy

39. Logotherapy is associated with:
   a. REBT.
   b. Adlerian therapy.
   c. behavior therapy.
   d. existential therapy.
   e. family systems therapy.

40. Which of the following stresses choice theory?
   a. REBT
   b. reality therapy
   c. behavior therapy
   d. solution-focused therapy
   e. Gestalt therapy

41. Which theorist stressed the view that universal feelings of inferiority and a striving for power are basic to personality development?
   a. Carl Rogers
   b. Alfred Adler
   c. Albert Ellis
   d. A. T. Beck
   e. Salvador Minuchin

42. The role of working through transference in the therapeutic process is given emphasis in:
   a. solution-focused therapy.
   b. Adlerian therapy.
   c. reality therapy.
   d. behavior therapy.
   e. none of the above

43. The approach that emphasizes the importance of the client's making a value judgment concerning current behavior is:
   a. Gestalt therapy.
   b. behavior therapy.
   c. Adlerian therapy.
   d. reality therapy.
   e. family systems therapy.

44. A therapist with what orientation is most likely to take a break of 5 to 10 minutes toward the end of each session to formulate feedback for the client?
   a. solution-focused therapy
   b. family systems therapy
   c. narrative therapy
   d. Adlerian therapy
   e. rational emotive behavior therapy

45. Looking at the client from a subjective (rather than an objective) viewpoint is stressed in which therapy approach(es)?
   a. narrative
   b. existential
   c. person-centered
   d. Adlerian
   e. all of the above

46. Concepts such as freedom and responsibility, anxiety, aloneness, and expanding self-awareness are most associated with:
   a. person-centered therapy.
   b. Adlerian therapy.
   c. existential therapy.
   d. psychoanalytic therapy.
   e. cognitive-behavior therapy.

47. Existential therapy is basically:
    a. a cognitive approach.
    b. an experiential approach.
    c. a behavioral approach.
    d. an extension and adaptation of psychoanalytic therapy.
    e. a systems approach.

48. Modeling methods are most closely associated with what approach?
    a. existential
    b. Gestalt
    c. behavioral
    d. reality
    e. Adlerian

49. Which of the following is not associated with behavior therapy?
    a. focus on cognitive patterns
    b. focus on exploring repressed childhood feelings
    c. focus on specific target behaviors
    d. focus on learning responses
    e. focus on evaluation of the therapy process

50. Person-centered therapy is:
    a. a form of existential therapy.
    b. an experiential therapy.
    c. a therapy that focuses on the subjective meanings of a client.
    d. an approach to understanding of persons.
    e. all of the above

51. Which of the following is not a method in behavior therapy?
    a. relaxation procedures
    b. systematic desensitization
    c. assertion training
    d. pre-therapy change
    e. positive reinforcement

52. Which of the following is a recent trend in behavior therapy?
    a. increasing attention to the role of the past
    b. increasing attention to cognitive factors
    c. decreasing emphasis on specificity of goals
    d. decreasing emphasis on evaluation of the progress of therapy
    e. both (c) and (d)

53. Rational emotive behavior therapy shares an interest in working with faulty beliefs with what other therapy approach?
    a. person-centered therapy
    b. existential therapy
    c. reality therapy
    d. Adlerian therapy
    e. Gestalt therapy

54. Which of the following is not a key concept of Adlerian therapy?
    a. family constellation
    b. community feeling
    c. social interest
    d. triangulation
    e. striving for superiority

55. REBT makes use of which kind of technique(s)?
   a. cognitive procedures
   b. behavioral techniques
   c. reading and bibliotherapy
   d. homework outside of the sessions
   e. all of the above

56. Which of the following techniques would not likely be used by the person-centered therapist?
   a. active listening
   b. interpretation of dreams
   c. reflection
   d. clarification
   e. caring confrontations

57. According to Carl Rogers, therapy does not need to include _____.
   a. diagnosis.
   b. therapist interpretation.
   c. active intervention of a directive nature by the therapist.
   d. giving information or giving advice.
   e. all of the above

58. Which of the following statements is false?
   a. Existential therapy is primarily aimed at working through the transference relationship.
   b. Existential therapy is subjective in nature.
   c. Existential therapy encourages clients to act on what they know and learn about themselves in therapy.
   d. Existential therapy deals with such matters as anxiety, guilt, and freedom.
   e. Existential therapy is aimed at helping clients make a commitment in the face of uncertainty.

59. The most research in the area of studying the process and outcomes of therapy has (have) been done by which approach(es)?
   a. postmodern therapists
   b. reality therapists
   c. behavioral therapists
   d. person-centered therapists
   e. both (c) and (d)

60. Exploration of polarities is a technique used in _____.
   a. cognitive-behavior therapy.
   b. family systems therapy.
   c. Adlerian therapy.
   d. existential therapy.
   e. Gestalt therapy.

61. Which therapy approach holds that the stories people live by grow out of conversations in a social and cultural context?
   a. feminist therapy
   b. existential therapy
   c. Adlerian therapy
   d. solution-focused therapy
   e. narrative therapy

62. The reversal technique is most closely associated with:
   a. Adlerian therapy.
   b. existential therapy.
   c. Gestalt therapy.
   d. family systems therapy.
   e. none of the above

63. Systematic desensitization is a technique used in which approach?
    a. Adlerian therapy
    b. existential therapy
    c. Gestalt therapy
    d. behavior therapy
    e. reality therapy

64. The technique of exaggeration is used in which approach?
    a. person-centered
    b. Gestalt
    c. cognitive-behavioral
    d. reality therapy
    e. psychoanalytic

65. Which statement is false as it applies to reality therapy?
    a. The focus is on observable behavior.
    b. A commitment is an essential part of therapy.
    c. There is a focus on getting clients to re-author their stories.
    d. The therapist needs to establish an involvement with the client.
    e. The past is not explored in this approach.

66. Rational emotive behavior therapy does *not* contend that_____.
    a. people make themselves disturbed by the sentences they tell themselves.
    b. traumatic events themselves cause problems such as depression and anxiety.
    c. people must be willing to reindoctrinate themselves if they hope to change.
    d. therapy is hard work and requires practice outside of the sessions.
    e. therapy is a cognitive matter.

67. According to REBT, the core of emotional disturbance lies in:
    a. unfinished business from the past.
    b. blame of self and others.
    c. experiences during the first five years of life-
    d. early repressed pain.
    e. the stories that have been influenced by culture.

68. The "empty chair" technique is most often used in which approach?
    a. Gestalt
    b. REBT
    c. Adlerian
    d. psychoanalytic
    e. behavioral

69. REBT does not stress:
    a. official evaluation of one's thoughts and beliefs.
    b. dream analysis.
    c. dealing with transference feelings.
    d. logical analysis.
    e. both (b) and (c)

Select the best or most appropriate answer in the following multiple-choice questions. These items relate to major *contributions* or *limitations* of the various therapies.

70. A contribution of the psychoanalytic approach is:
    a. the focus on the human-to-human encounter.
    b. a comprehensive and detailed system of personality.
    c. a reliance on the scientific method to assess therapeutic outcomes.
    d. that it can be practiced by a wide range of professionals.

71. A contribution of the existential approach is:
   a. the freedom of both the client and therapist to be creative during the therapy sessions.
   b. specific ad precise goals of treatment.
   c. a systematic treatment plan.
   d. wide applicability for lower-functioning clients.
   e. that many techniques are generated from this approach.

72. A contribution of the person-centered approach is:
   a. its applicability to nonverbal clients.
   b. the active stance of the therapist.
   c. the wide variety of techniques generated.
   d. the emphasis on the interpersonal relationship and the attitudes of the therapist as crucial.
   e. the systematic description of past influences and how these are significant in current behavior.

73. A contribution of the Gestalt approach is:
   a. the interpretation of the therapist.
   b. the attention given to the role of irrational beliefs as a cause of emotional disturbances.
   c. focusing on unfinished business in the past in a way that is immediate and direct.
   d. attention given to the therapeutic contract.
   e. the emphasis on value judgments in therapy.

74. A contribution of behavior therapy is that:
   a. it gives a rationale for explaining self-defeating behavior.
   b. it focuses on insight.
   c. it emphasizes freedom, choice, and deciding.
   d. it is a pragmatic approach based on experimental validation of the results.

75. A contribution of REBT is:
   a. the "I-Thou" relationship between client and therapist.
   b. the emphasis on understanding the subjective world of the client.
   c. the emphasis on putting newly acquired insights into action via the "homework assignment" method.
   d. the emphasis on experiencing fully one's feelings.

76. A contribution of reality therapy is that:
   a. it provides insight into causes of problems.
   b. it changes attitudes.
   c. it focuses on assisting clients to relive past trauma.
   d. it explains childhood influences on present behavior.
   e. it consists of simple and clear concepts that can be easily understood by a variety of people in the helping professions.

77. A limitation of psychoanalysis is that:
   a. few techniques are generated by this approach.
   b. it does not account for the past.
   c. there is not enough emphasis on action and *doing* as requisites for change.
   d. it does not account for unconscious factors or for the effects of early learning.

78. A limitation of the existential approach is:
   a. few techniques are generated from this approach.
   b. it is a deterministic theory.
   c. it does not give the client enough responsibility for the therapy process.
   d. the systematic description of past influences and how these are significant in current behavior.

79. A limitation of the person-centered approach is that:
   a. it discounts the value of the therapeutic relationship.
   b. it focuses too much on the past.
   c. it requires a lengthy period of time.
   d. some practitioners give support to their clients without challenging them.

80. A limitation of the postmodern approaches is that:
   a. they are deterministic.
   b. they cannot be applied with a wide range of clients.
   c. they do not generate many techniques.
   d. they rely too heavily on the therapist as expert.
   e. there has been little empirical research to support the interventions used.

81. A limitation of behavior therapy is:
   a. the overemphasis on insight.
   b. the results of therapy cannot be objectively assessed.
   c. the treatment goals are too broad.
   d. the danger of manipulation and misuse of power, particularly in institutions.
   e. the necessity for long-term therapy to effect any behavior change.

82. A limitation of rational emotive behavior therapy is:
   a. it is not a confrontive approach.
   b. the danger of being an overly intellectual approach that could explain away feelings.
   c. the extreme focus on experiencing feelings to the exclusion of recognizing cognitive factors.
   d. it does not stress action and doing.

83. A limitation of reality therapy is:
   a. that it does not stress unconscious factors.
   b. the focus on a client's problems, not strengths.
   c. the many lofty and abstract concepts.
   d. that it ignores behavior change by overstressing attitude change.
   e. that it requires lengthy professional training to use many of the concepts in practice.

84. A limitation of Adlerian therapy is that:
   a. it does not deal adequately with cognitive factors.
   b. it does not take into account family patterns.
   c. it underemphasizes social factors in personality.
   d. it has not been extensively subjected to research.

85. A contribution of the Adlerian approach is:
   a. Adler's influence on most of the other therapy systems.
   b. the concept of redecision therapy.
   c. its methods of analysis of transference.
   d. its techniques which help clients relive past emotional events in the here-and-now.

86. A contribution of the self psychology and object-relations theory is that:
   a. it provides an extension of psychoanalytic concepts.
   b. it gives a new perspective of human development.
   c. it provides ways of working with borderline disorders and with narcissistic character disorders.
   d. it shows how earlier experiences with significant others are important in terms of present relationships.
   e. all of the above

PSYCHOANALYTIC THERAPY

87. In psychoanalytic therapy, dream analysis:
   a. reveals a client's unconscious wishes, needs, and fears.
   b. gives insight into some areas of unresolved problems.
   c. often involves free association.
   d. all of the above
   e. all but (c)

88. Who is not associated with the object-relations approach?
    a. Heinz Kohut
    b. Otto Kernberg
    c. Arnold Lazarus
    d. Margaret Mahler

89. Self psychology and object-relations theory stresses:
    a. the influence of critical factors in early development on later development.
    b. the differentiation between and integration of the self and others.
    c. the importance of the family constellation and early memories.
    d. the striving for superiority based on inferiority feelings.
    e. both (a) and (b)

90. Who developed the psychosocial perspective?
    a. Alfred Adler
    b. Erik Erikson
    c. Albert Ellis
    d. A. T. Beck
    e. Otto Kernberg

91. Human nature as seen by Freudian psychoanalysis is that:
    a. people are motivated by social interest.
    b. people have a tendency to adopt irrational modes of thinking.
    c. people are determined by early childhood experiences.
    d. people define themselves by the choices they make.
    e. people strive to discover meaning in life.

ADLERIAN THERAPY

92. The concept of "private logic" refers to:
    a. the person's search for meaning in life.
    b. concepts about self, others, and life that constitute the philosophy on which one's lifestyle is based.
    c. irrational ideas that lead to emotional upsets.
    d. catastrophic expectations that lead to anxiety..

93. Another term for Adlerian therapy is:
    a. psychosocial approach.
    b. control theory.
    c. humanistic psychology.
    d. individual psychology.

94. All of the following are key concepts of this approach except for:
    a. fictional finalism.
    b. *Gemeinschaftscefuhl.*
    c. striving for significance and superiority.
    d. positive addiction.
    e. social interest.

95. Adlerians would be least likely to use which of the following techniques?
    a. advice
    b. paradoxical intention
    c. empty-chair
    d. spitting in the client's soup
    e. push button

96. All of the following are a part of the therapeutic process except:
   a. encouragement.
   b. analysis and assessment.
   c. insight.
   d. developing a therapeutic contract.
   e. analysis and interpretation of transference.

EXISTENTIAL THERAPY

97. Which term or phrase is least likely to be used by an existential therapist?
   a. restricted existence
   b. personal responsibility
   c. systematic desensitization
   d. anxiety

98. With this approach, therapy is viewed as:
   a. a form of operant conditioning.
   b. a shared journey.
   c. a process of exploring unconscious dynamics.
   d. a process of counterindoctrination.
   e. an intellectual and emotional debate aimed at changing one's irrational beliefs.

99. Anxiety is viewed as:
   a. the result of stupid self-talk.
   b. accepting irrational notions.
   c. the conflict between the id and the superego.
   d. part and parcel of human existence.
   e. a slip of impulse control.

100. Which of the following is not an existential key concept?
   a. capacity for self-awareness
   b. total behavior
   c. freedom and responsibility
   d. search for meaning

PERSON-CENTERED THERAPY

101. The most important variable related to therapeutic progress is:
   a. the therapist's skills.
   b. the client/therapist relationship.
   c. objective assessment and diagnosis.
   d. the client's willingness to participate in exercises.

102. This approach to therapy has been applied to:
   a. encounter groups.
   b. international relations.
   c. management.
   d. family therapy.
   e. all of the above

103. Carl Rogers drew heavily from concepts, especially as they apply to the client/therapist relationship as the core of therapy.
   a. psychoanalytic
   b. existential
   c. Adlerian
   d. behavioral
   e. none of the above

104. Rogers describes people as having which characteristic(s) as they move toward self-actualization?
    a. openness to experience
    b. internal source of evaluation
    c. capacity to challenge transference relationship
    d. ability to undermine irrational thought patterns
    e. both (a) and (b)

105. The concept of congruence is most closely associated with:
    a. unconditional positive regard
    b. empathy
    c. genuineness
    d. acceptance of others
    e. personal warmth

GESTALT THERAPY

106. All of the following are a part of this therapy system except:
    a. unfinished business.
    b. striving for superiority.
    c. energy and blocks to energy.
    d. avoidance.

107. Gestalt is a form of which general orientation to therapy?
    a. existential
    b. cognitive
    c. behavioral
    d. social-learning

108. If a client were to indicate an interest in exploring some traumatic childhood experience, the Gestalt therapist would most likely ask the client to:
    a. look at the beliefs leading to certain feelings.
    b. tell a story about this past experience.
    c. set up specific goals aimed at behavior change.
    d. relive the experience as though it were taking place now.

109. The defense(s) that is (are) considered the major channel of resistance is (are):
    a. introjection.
    b. projection.
    c. retroflection.
    d. sublimation.
    e. all but (d)

110. Of the following, what would the Gestalt therapist be most likely to pay attention to in a therapy session?
    a. thought patterns
    b. nonverbal cues
    c. energy and blocks to energy
    d. evidences of irrational thinking and faulty assumptions
    e. both (b) and (c)

BEHAVIOR THERAPY

111. For people who experience difficulty in expressing what they think and feel, which behavioral technique would be most appropriate?
    a. relaxation training
    b. assertion training
    c. operant conditioning
    d. systematic desensitization
    e. modeling

112. Which of the following is not a behavioral technique?
    a. coaching
    b. modeling
    c. analysis of transference
    d. stress-management training
    e. systematic desensitization

113. Which of the following is not a part of a self-management program?
    a. lifestyle assessment and summary
    b. selection of specific goals
    c. self-monitoring
    d. self-reinforcement procedures

114. Multimodal therapy stresses:
    a. relying exclusively on learning theory.
    b. limiting practice to a few specific techniques.
    c. adherence to an existential framework for practice.
    d. technical eclecticism.
    e. the role of the therapist's values in therapeutic outcomes.

115. From the standpoint of ethical accountability, behavior therapy:
    a. provides a basis for responsible practice.
    b. does not address this issue.
    c. utilizes techniques that have questionable validity.
    d. utilizes techniques that present more ethical concerns than do most other approaches.
    e. both (c) and (d)

COGNITIVE-BEHAVIOR THERAPY

116. Multimodal therapy is associated with:
    a. A. T. Beck.
    b. Donald Meichenbaum.
    c. Arnold Lazarus.
    d. Albert Ellis.
    e. none of the above

117. The person who has specialized in cognitive therapy with depression is
    a. A. T. Beck.
    b. Donald Meichenbaum.
    c. Arnold Lazarus.
    d. Albert Bandura.
    e. none of the above

118. The person who has developed cognitive behavior modification techniques, including self-instruction, coping-skills programs, and stress inoculation, is:
    a. A. T. Beck.
    b. Donald Meichenbaum.
    c. Arnold Lazarus.
    d. B. F. Skinner.
    e. none of the above

119. Ellis contends that we develop emotional and behavioral problems because:
    a. we are not successful in finding projects that give us meaning in life.
    b. we live by the values that our parents taught us.
    c. we are unable to cope with unfinished business from childhood years.
    d. we think of simple preferences as dire needs.
    e. others reject us when we are struggling to be real.

120. REBT holds that anxiety:
    a. is part of the human condition.
    b. is the result of intense feelings of failure.
    c. is what occurs when others do not give us approval.
    d. all of the above
    e. none of the above

REALITY THERAPY

121. The first phase in the practice of reality therapy is:
    a. conducting a comprehensive assessment that leads to a diagnosis.
    b. assuring the client that you will never give up.
    c. getting involved with the client and making friends.
    d. urging the client to live in reality.

122. Current reality therapy is based on the notion that:
    a. our brain works as a control system.
    b. the therapist's job is to make value judgments of client behavior.
    c. positive addiction will lead to success identity.
    d. negative addiction will lead to failure identity.

123. Contemporary reality therapy is based on the assumption that:
    a. people are moved by inner forces.
    b. external forces have a major influence on how people decide and what they will do.
    c. behavior is caused by environmental factors.
    d. negative attitudes cause behavioral problems.
    e. both (c) and (d)

124. According to Glasser, change occurs when:
    a. we change our attitudes.
    b. we release pent-up feelings dating back from childhood.
    c. we acquire insight into why we are behaving the way we are.
    d. we recognize and act on the reality that our behavior is the result of our choices.
    e. none of the above

125. Reality therapists contend that "neurotic" and "psychotic" behavior is:
    a. the result of a chemical imbalance.
    b. strictly the result of living in irresponsible ways.
    c. the product of irrational thinking.
    d. the result of severe stress and not being understood.
    e. behavior we choose as a way of attempting to control our world.

FEMINIST THERAPY

126. What perspective calls for feminist theory to include an analysis of multiple identities and their relationship to oppression?
    a. postmodern feminism
    b. lesbian feminism
    c. radical feminism
    d. cultural feminism
    e. liberal feminism

127. Which of the following is considered to be a major contribution feminists have made to the field of counseling?
    a. pioneering research in the therapy process
    b. creation of a brief, solution-focused therapy approach
    c. integrating a diagnostic perspective in counseling practice
    d. paving the way for gender-sensitive practice
    e. all of the above

128. The principle of "the personal is political" implies that women's problems are
    a. primarily due to unresolved intrapsychic conflicts.
    b. mainly socially, culturally, and politically caused.
    c. due to the fact that women have traditionally been denied political power.
    d. best solved through adjustment to social and political norms and expectations.

129. All of the following are considered to be constructs of feminist theory except being
    a. gender-neutral.
    b. androcentric.
    c. life-span-oriented.
    d. interactionist.
    e. flexible.

130. All of the following are ways feminist therapy differs from traditional therapy except for
    a. viewing problems in a sociopolitical and cultural context.
    b. demystifying the therapeutic process.
    c. accepting the premise that diagnosis is a basic prerequisite for effective treatment.
    d. creating a therapeutic relationship that is egalitarian.
    e. recognition that clients know what is best for their life and are experts in their own life.

POSTMODERN APPROACHES

131. In social constructionism, which of the following would be least important in understanding how individuals construct their lives?
    a. gender awareness
    b. cultural perspectives
    c. developmental processes
    d. the impact of irrational beliefs
    e. dominant narratives

132. The techniques of externalization and developing unique events is associated with:
    a. solution-focused therapy.
    b. the linguistic approach.
    c. the narrative approach.
    d. the reflecting team.
    e. the social constructionist approach.

133. All of the following are associated with solution-focused therapy except:
    a. Insoo Kim Berg.
    b. Michelle Weiner-Davis.
    c. Steve de Shazer.
    d. Michael White.

134. In working with a client, a solution-focused therapist would be least likely to use which of the following techniques?
    a. co-create new solutions with the client
    b. explore problems transmitted from generation to generation
    c. miracle questions
    d. exception questions
    e. scaling questions

135. In which approach(es) does the therapist adopt a "not knowing" position to help clients develop alternative stories?
    a. feminist therapy
    b. strategic family therapy
    c. existential therapy
    d. the linguistic approach
    e. Gestalt therapy

FAMILY SYSTEMS THERAPY

136. The techniques of joining, accommodating, unbalancing, tracking, and boundary making are associated with which approach to family therapy?
    a. Bowenian family therapy
    b. human validation process model
    c. structural family therapy
    d. strategic family therapy

137. One of Satir's techniques is:
    a. externalizing the problem.
    b. family sculpting.
    c. paradoxical intervention.
    d. reauthoring life stories.

138. Which approach operates on the assumption that a family can best be understood when it is analyzed from at least a three-generational perspective?
    a. Bowenian family therapy
    b. human validation process model
    c. structural therapy
    d. strategic therapy
    e. experiential/symbolic family therapy

139. Which approach operates on the assumption that unresolved emotional fusion to one's family must be addressed if one hopes to achieve a mature and unique personality?
    a. Bowenian family therapy
    b. human validation process model
    c. structural therapy
    d. strategic therapy
    e. experiential/symbolic family therapy

140. What is the technique in family therapy that casts a new light on a problem and provides a different interpretation of a problematic situation?
    a. reorganization
    b. family mapping
    c. restructuring
    d. refraining
    e. joining

141. A couple direct the focus of their energy toward a problematic son as a way to avoid facing or dealing with their own conflicts. This is an example of
    a. enmeshment.
    b. triangulation.
    c. displacement.
    d. individuation.
    e. differentiation.

142. What lens deals with questions such as: Are the parents effective leaders of the family? How do the children respond to parental leadership? Is the process of leadership balanced or imbalanced? Does it lead to harmony or conflict?
   a. internal family systems
   b. the teleological lens
   c. sequences
   d. the organization lens
   e. the developmental lens

143. Which lens raises questions such as: How does a typical day go? Are there processes and patterns that characterize current or past transitions for the family? What routines support your daily living?
   a. internal family systems
   b. the teleological lens
   c. sequences
   d. the organization lens
   e. the developmental lens

144. All of the following are major general movements of the multilensed approach to family therapy except for:
   a. forming a relationship.
   b. conducting an assessment.
   c. hypothesizing and sharing meaning
   d. facilitating change
   e. conducting outcome research to evaluate techniques used

145. Which approach would be most interested in the appropriateness of hierarchical structure in the family?
   a. Bowenian family therapy
   b. human validation process model
   c. structural family therapy
   d. strategic family therapy
   e. experiential/symbolic family therapy

Directions for Conceptual Items:

Items 146 through 200 are conceptual items in which there is a series of related concepts and/or techniques pertaining to one therapeutic approach. *One item in the series of five does not fit with the other four items.* Identify the word or phrase that does not fit with the rest of the series.

146. (a) life stages, (b) developmental crises, (c) psychosocial stages,
   (d) relational cultural theory, (e) critical tasks

147. (a) fictional finalism, (b) basic mistakes, (c) power analysis, (d) social interest
   (e) style of life

148. (a) coaching, (b) modeling methods, (c) systematic desensitization, (d) reversal technique,
   (e) relaxation technique

149. (a) pre-therapy change, (b) exception questions, (c) the miracle question, (d) scaling questions,
   (e) problem-saturated stories

150. (a) object-relations, (b) strategic, (c) structural, (d) multigenerational, (e) experiential/symbolic

151. (a) the internal dialogue exercise, (b) the rehearsal experiment, (c) cognitive restructuring, (d) the exaggeration exercise, (e) making the rounds

152. (a) style of life, (b) openness to experience, (c) formative tendency, (d) internal source of evaluation,
   (e) willingness to continue growing

153. (a) behavior modification, (b) mistaken goals, (c) private logic, (d) early recollections, (e) family constellation

154. (a) ego-defense mechanism, (b) anxiety, (c) psychosexual development stages, (d) the unconscious, (e) social action

155. (a) search for self-awareness, (b) awareness of death, (c) courage to be, (d) striving for superiority, (e) search for meaning

156. (a) storied lives, (b) personal is political, (c) deconstruction, (d) search for unique outcomes, (e) re-authoring

157. (a) May, (b) Meichenbaum, (c) Ellis, (d) Beck, (e) Bandura

158. (a) differentiation of self, (b) triangulation, (c) enmeshment, (d) early recollections, (e) family life cycle

159. (a) Michael White, (b) Albert Ellis, (c) Insoo Kim Berg, (d) Steve de Shazer, (e) Harlene Anderson

160. (a) lifestyle assessment, (b) genograms, (c) family-life chronology, (d) accomodating, (e) joining

161. (a) self-evaluation, (b) plan for action, (c) commitment, (d) unconditional positive regard, (e) WDEP

162. (a) total behavior, (b) quality world, (c) confronting irrational beliefs, (d) cycle of counseling, (e) choice theory

163. (a) person-centered therapy, (b) feminist therapy, (c) Gestalt therapy, (d) existential therapy, (e) experiential therapies

164. (a) A-B-C theory, (b) irrational beliefs, (c) not-knowing position, (d) cognitive restructuring, (e) self-defeating thought patterns

165. (a) reflection, (b) clarification, (c) active listening, (d) empathic understanding, (e) miracle question

166. (a) holism, (b) field theory, (c) figure-formation process, (d) social constructionism, (e) organismic self-regulation

167. (a) exception questions, (b) the dialogue experiment, (c) staying with the feeling, (d) reversal technique, (e) present-centered dream work

168. (a) externalization and deconstruction, (b) metaframeworks, (c) narrative conversations, (d) reauthoring one's life, (e) collaborative partnership

169. (a) Arnold Lazarus, (b) Murray Bowen, (c) Virginia Satir, (d) Car; Whitaker, (e) Salvador Minuchin

170. (a) systematic desensitization, (b) cognitive restructuring, (c) modeling methods, (e) assertion training, (e) empty chair technique.

171. (a) dream analysis, (b) free association, (c) early recollection, (d) interpretation of transference, (e) analysis of resistance

172. (a) unconditional positive regard, (b) empathic understanding, (c) congruence, (d) active listening, (e) gender role interventions

173. (a) totalizing descriptions, (b) paradoxical directive, (c) problem-saturated story, (d) dominant story, (e) building an audience

174. (a) solution-focused therapy, (b) dialectical behavior therapy, (c) exception questions, (d) miracle question, (e) formula first session task

175. (a) quality world, (b) WDEP, (c) choice theory, (d) self-evaluation, (e) transference

176. (a) reexperiencing unfinished business in the here-and-now, (b) transference, (c) free association, (d) interpretation, (e) maintaining the analytic frame

177. (a) irrational ideas, (b) homework assignments, (c) shame-attacking exercises, (d) rational-emotive imagery, (e) dream interpretation

178. (a) polarized thinking, (b) labeling and mislabeling, (c) magnification and minimization, (d) selective abstraction, (e) externalization and deconstruction

179. (a) sequences, (b) internal family systems, (c) the developmental lens, (d) collaborative empiricism, (e) metaframeworks

180. (a) collective unconscious, (b) archetypes, (c) persona, (d) shadow, (e) narrative therapy

181. (a) object relations theory, (b) choice theory, (c) self psychology, (d) relational psychoanalysis, (e) interpersonal analysis

182. (a) Individual Psychology, (b) self psychology, (c) object-relations theory, (d) borderline personality, (e) narcissistic personality

183. (a) empowerment and egalitarianism, (b) power analysis and power intervention, (c) choice theory, (d) social action, (e) self in relation theory

184. (a) layers of neurosis, (b) unfinished business, (c) genograms, (d) contact and resistance to contact, (e) energy and blocks to energy

185. (a) positive orientation, (b) look for what is working, (c) exceptions to a problem, (d) small changes pave way for larger changes, (e) therapist as expert

186. (a) cognitive behavior modification, (b) cognitive therapy, (c) coping skills programs, (d) stress inoculation, (e) stress management training

187. (a) multimodal therapy, (b) BASIC ID, (c) technical eclecticism, (d) therapeutic flexibility and versatility, (e) cognitive behavior modification

188. (a) power analysis and power intervention, (b) assertion training, (c) stress-management training, (d) eye movement desensitization and reprocessing, (e) exposure therapies

189. (a) documenting the evidence, (b) re-authoring alternative stories, (c) flooding, (d) narrative letter writing, (e) mapping the influence of the problem

190. (a) total behavior, (b) choice theory, (c) existential-phenomenological orientation, (d) family systems therapy, (e) reality therapy

191. (a) establishing the relationship, (b) exploring the individual's dynamics, (c) working through transference neurosis, (d) encouraging insight, (e) helping with reorientation

192. (a) fictional finalism, (b) shame-attacking exercises, (c) acting "as if," (d) lifestyle assessment, (e) teleological approach

193. (a) shame-attacking exercises, (b) the internal dialogue exercise (c) the reversal technique, (d) the rehearsal experiment, (e) the exaggeration experiment

194. (a) experiential therapy, (b) existential therapy, (c) person-centered therapy, (d) Gestalt therapy, (e) postmodern approaches.

195. (a) change and the search for new possibilities, (b) the encouragement process, (c) family constellation, (d) gender role intervention, (e) personal priorities

196. (a) cognitive disputation, (b) cognitive homework, (c) rational-emotive imagery, (d) shame-attacking exercises, (e) solution-focused therapy

197. (a) listening from a "not-knowing" position, (b) paradoxical interventions, (c) enactments, (d) reframing, (e) issuing directives

198. (a) death and nonbeing, (b) search for meaning, (c) search for unique outcomes, (d) striving for identity, (e) anxiety as a condition of living

199. (a) joining and accommodation, (b), deconstructing problem-saturated stories, (c) family reconstruction, (d) tracking interactional sequences, (e) enhancing interpersonal communication

200. (a) reexperiencing one's past, (b) planning and commitment, (c) exploring a client's picture album, (d) refusing to accept excuses, (e) teaching clients self-evaluation

ANSWER KEY FOR FINAL EXAMINATION QUESTIONS

Questions 1 - 100

1.	C	21.	E	41.	B	61.	E	81.	D
2.	E	22.	E	42.	E	62.	C	82.	B
3.	E	23.	E	43.	D	63.	D	83.	A
4.	A	24.	E	44.	A	64.	B	84.	D
5.	C	25.	B	45.	E	65.	C	85.	A
6.	A	26.	E	46.	C	66.	B	86.	E
7.	B	27.	D	47.	B	67.	B	87.	D
8.	D	28.	A	48.	C	68.	A	88.	C
9.	B	29.	B	49.	B	69.	E	89.	E
10.	E	30.	C	50.	E	70.	B	90.	B
11.	C	31.	C	51.	D	71.	A	91.	C
12.	C	32.	D	52.	B	72.	D	92.	B
13.	E	33.	B	53.	D	73.	C	93.	D
14.	D	34.	D	54.	D	74.	D	94.	D
15.	E	35.	D	55.	E	75.	C	95.	C
16.	B	36.	B	56.	B	76.	E	96.	E

17.	A	37.	E	57.	E	77.	C	97.	C
18.	D	38.	C	58.	A	78.	A	98.	B
19.	E	39.	D	59.	E	79.	D	99.	D
20.	C	40.	B	60.	E	80.	E	100.	B

Questions 101 - 200

101.	B	121.	C	141.	B	161.	D	181.	B
102.	E	122.	A	142.	D	162.	C	182.	A
103.	B	123.	A	143.	C	163.	B	183.	C
104.	E	124.	D	144.	E	164.	C	184.	C
105.	C	125.	E	145.	C	165.	E	185.	E
106.	B	126.	B	146.	D	166.	D	186.	B
107.	A	127.	D	147.	C	167.	A	187.	E
108.	D	128.	B	148.	D	168.	B	188.	A
109.	E	129.	B	149.	E	169.	A	189.	C
110.	E	130.	C	150.	A	170.	E	190.	D
111.	B	131.	D	151.	C	171.	C	191.	C
112.	C	132.	C	152.	A	172.	E	192.	B
113.	A	133.	D	153.	A	173.	B	193.	A
114.	D	134.	B	154.	E	174.	B	194.	E
115.	A	135.	D	155.	D	175.	E	195.	D
116.	C	136.	C	156.	B	176.	A	196.	E
117.	A	137.	B	157.	A	177.	E	197.	A
118.	B	138.	A	158.	D	178.	E	198.	C
119.	D	139.	A	159.	B	179.	D	199.	B
120.	E	140.	D	160.	A	180.	E	200.	A

IV

<u>Test Items</u>

Case Approach to

Counseling and Psychotherapy

CHAPTER ONE

Introduction and Overview

1. Which of the following therapeutic approaches most places emphasis on an individual's competencies, avoiding defining a client by a problem, establishing a collaborative relationship where the client is the senior partner, and focusing on a client's strengths and resources?
    a.   cognitive behavior therapy
    b.   postmodern approaches
    c.   reality therapy
    d.   behavior therapy
    e.   psychoanalytic therapy

2. In what theoretical orientation is the therapist's job to confront clients with the restricted life they have chosen and to help them become aware of their own part in creating this condition?
    a.   psychoanalytic therapy
    b.   Adlerian therapy
    c.   existential therapy
    d.   person-centered therapy
    e.   reality therapy

3. Which of the following is not an aspect of Adlerian therapy:
    a.   People are primarily social beings.
    b.   Human nature is creative, active, and decisional.
    c.   Feelings of inferiority from childhood lead us to develop a style of life in which we become the master of our fate.
    d.   All people react out of the social unconscious.
    e.   Clients are not "sick" and needing to be "cured".

4. Which theory views people as being significantly influenced by unconscious motivation, conflicts between impulses and prohibitions, defense mechanisms, and early childhood experiences?
    a.   psychoanalytic therapy
    b.   Adlerian therapy
    c.   existential therapy
    d.   person-centered therapy
    e.   reality therapy

5. Which theory operates on the premises that all relationship problems are in the present and must be solved in the present, and that once the significant relationship is improved, the troubling symptom will disappear?
    a.   psychoanalytic therapy
    b.   Adlerian therapy
    c.   existential therapy
    d.   person-centered therapy
    e.   reality therapy

6. _____ assumes that people are basically shaped by learning and sociocultural conditioning.
    a.   feminist therapy
    b.   behavior therapy
    c.   Gestalt therapy
    d.   cognitive behavioral therapy
    e.   narrative therapy

7. The assumption that we have the capacity to understand our problems, we have the resources within us to resolve them and that clients can move toward growth and wholeness by looking within is central to:
    a.   feminist therapy.
    b.   person-centered therapy.
    c.   Gestalt therapy.
    d.   existential therapy.
    e.   Adlerian therapy.

8. Which theory states that the therapist's task is to support the client as they explore their present experience through an awareness of their internal (intrapersonal) world and the external environment?
   a. feminist therapy
   b. person-centered therapy
   c. Gestalt therapy
   d. existential therapy
   e. Adlerian therapy

9. Which theory assumes that people are prone to learning erroneous, self-defeating thoughts that perpetuate their difficulties and that these thoughts can be corrected to create a more fulfilling life?
   a. reality therapy
   b. behavioral therapy
   c. Gestalt therapy
   d. cognitive Behavioral therapy
   e. existential therapy

10. Feminist therapy includes:
    a. the influence of power inequalities and gender-role expectations.
    b. encouraging a genderless approach to life.
    c. the detrimental effects of gender socialization.
    d. both (a) and (b).
    e. both (a) and (c).

11. According to family systems therapy a client's behavior:
    a. may be the result of the system's inability to function effectively.
    b. may serve a function or a purpose for the family.
    c. may result from dysfunctional patterns that are passed on from generation to generation.
    d. both (b) and (c).
    e. all of the above.

12. Which theory(ies) is (are) *least* likely to use assessment and diagnosis in the therapeutic process?
    a. feminist therapy
    b narrative therapy
    c. behavior therapy
    d. psychoanalytic therapy
    e. both (a) and (b)

13. _____ consists of evaluating the relevant factors in a client's life to identify themes for further exploration in therapy, whereas _____ consists of identifying a specific category of psychological problem based on a pattern of symptoms.
    a. Diagnosis, assessment
    b. Life evaluation, assessment
    c. Assessment, life evaluation
    d. Assessment, diagnosis
    e. none of the above

14. All therapies share some common denominators. These are:
    a. identifying the dysfunctional thoughts of clients and correcting them.
    b. identifying what the client wants and then modifying the person's thoughts, feelings, and behaviors.
    c. identifying the client's weaknesses in order to cure them.
    d. facilitating the client's expression of emotion or catharsis.
    e. all of the above.

15. In working within a multicultural framework, what is especially important?
    a. having a thorough knowledge of the client's culture
    b. assisting the client in adapting to your theoretical orientation
    c. using techniques flexibly
    a. using appropriate referrals if the client is different than you

16. Although it is not bound by prescribed techniques, this theoretical perspective focuses on developing social interest, providing encouragement, and facilitating insight into client's mistaken ideas and their personal assets.
    a. feminist therapy
    b. behavioral therapy
    c. Gestalt therapy
    d. cognitive behavioral therapy
    e. Adlerian therapy

17. _____ have as main assumptions that people: are competent and healthy, have the capacity to find their own solutions to the difficulties they face; and that the client is the expert on his or her own life.
    a. Psychoanalytic approaches
    b. Behavior therapy
    c. Gestalt therapy
    d. Postmodern approaches
    e. Rational emotive behavior therapy

18. Which theoretical perspective is active, directive and didactic, assisting clients in making plans to change specific behaviors that they determine are not working for them?
    a. psychoanalytic therapy
    b. reality therapy
    c. existential therapy
    d. person-centered therapy
    e. Adlerian therapy

19. Which theoretical perspective is most likely to use techniques such as reframing and relabeling, bibliotherapy, advocacy, power intervention, social action, and gender-role analysis and intervention?
    a. cognitive behavioral therapy
    b. family systems therapy
    c. Gestalt therapy
    d. feminist therapy
    e. Adlerian therapy

20. Which theoretical perspective places primary emphasis on the client/therapist relationship and uses few techniques other than active listening, reflection, and clarification?
    a. psychoanalytic therapy
    b. reality therapy
    c. existential therapy
    d. person-centered therapy
    e. Adlerian therapy

21. In diagnosing a client, what is as important as deciding upon a specific diagnosis?
    a. making sure you do not pathologize a cultural trait or behavior
    b. determining whether or not their insurance covers that diagnosis
    c. ruling out other possible diagnoses
    d. both (a) and (c)
    e. all of the above

CHAPTER TWO

Case Approach to Psychoanalytic Therapy

22. What fundamental interest is a critical distinction between analytic therapy and other approaches?
    a. the individual client's thinking
    b. an interest in the client's childhood and family experiences
    c. the "whys" of an individual client's experience and behavior
    d. how the client's behavior helping or preventing them from getting what they want

23. Assessment of an individual client's need for analytic therapy would include:
    a. development of behaviors that express an unconscious desire.
    b. determining whether he/she wants and needs to understand the unconscious roots of his/her neurosis.
    c. identifying an early childhood trauma that resulted in becoming fixated at an early developmental stage.
    d. the client's ability to recall his/her dreams so that they may be analyzed.

24. A psychoanalytic perspective views _____ as active processes that give clues to the client's underlying psychodynamics.
    a. feelings
    b. impulses
    c. medical illnesses
    d. psychological symptoms
    e. interrelational problems

25. A headache might serve to keep a client sexually distant from her husband while also providing a pretext for avoiding social contacts that might threaten her marriage. This is an example of:
    a. double bind.
    b. multifaceted distinction.
    c. overt and covert behavior.
    d. secondary gain.
    e. an outcome of a triangulation.

26. Insight in analytic therapy typically requires the client to experience therapeutic regression and the "working through" of distortions in the context of the therapeutic relationship. These processes:
    a. require an immense amount of commitment from the client and are only for the strong willed.
    b. cannot be terminated prematurely without danger of psychological harm to the client.
    c. suggest the client has to be psychologically "reborn".
    d. are well-understood by managed care institutions and are usually financially supported.
    e. are resigned to the unconscious and will happen no matter what the client or therapist does.

27. Treatment techniques of psychoanalytic psychotherapy include all except:
    a. dreams, jokes, slips and symptoms.
    b. interpretations of resistance and content.
    c. transference and countertransference.
    d. paradoxical intention.
    e. the therapeutic contract.

28. Failure to resolve a conflict at a given stage of life is called:
    a. deadening.
    b. conflicted anhedonia.
    c. fixation.
    d. all but (b).
    e. none of the above.

29. Repeating interpretations of a client's behavior and overcoming his/her resistance, allowing the client to resolve his/her neurotic patterns is called:
    a. redundant interpretation.
    b. wearing down.
    c. working through.
    d. transference absorption.
    e. projective identification.

CHAPTER THREE

Case Approach to Adlerian Therapy

30. Adlerians tend to see counseling as a four-stage process. Which of the following is not one of the four stages?
    a. forming a relationship
    b. conducting a psychological investigation
    c. exploring the client's multigenerational family characteristics
    d. psychological disclosure
    e. reorientation and reeducation

31. After establishing and maintaining a good working relationship between Ruth and the therapist, what would be the next goal using the Adlerian approach?
    a. assist her in developing alternative ways of thinking, feeling and behaving by encouraging her to translate her insights into action
    b. provide a therapeutic climate in which she can come to understand her basic beliefs and feelings about herself and discover how she acquired these faulty beliefs
    c. help her achieve a balance between her "Parent", her "Child" and her "Adult"
    d. help her reach insight into her mistaken goals and self-defeating behaviors through a process of confrontation and interpretation

32. Adlerians believe that first comes _____, then _____, and then _____.
    a. feeling, behaving, thinking
    b. thinking, behaving, feeling
    c. thinking, feeling, behaving
    d. behaving, thinking, feeling

33. In doing a lifestyle assessment with Ruth, the therapist is likely to gather information about her life except for:
    a. her Oedipal strivings.
    b. family influences.
    c. early memories
    d. birth order
    e. early childhood experience

CHAPTER FOUR

Case Approach to Existential Therapy

34. The primary goal of existential therapy is:
    a. to make known the unconscious.
    b. to deal with unfinished business.
    c. for clients to lead more authentic lives.
    d. to establish well-defined goals and the means to achieve them.
    e. to understand the client's position in his or her family of origin.

35. The first step in existential therapy is:
    a. to conduct a thorough life history.
    b. to establish a therapeutic alliance whereby the therapist can understand the client's world.
    c. to ask the client to identify wants, needs, and perceptions.
    d. to examine past traumas from childhood.
    e. to assess for cognitive distortions.

36. The final phase of Ruth's existential therapy is:
    a. to arrange homework assignments for a follow-up session.
    b. to engage her in objectively evaluating what contributed to each of the changes that occurred during therapy.
    c. to use her self-talk as a way to maintain healthy thinking.
    d. to help her put into practice the behaviors that express the values she has chosen for her new self.
    e. to review what she has learned about how her family of origin still has a present impact in her daily life.

37. All of the following concepts are a part of existential therapy with Ruth except for
    a. reconstruction of the self
    b. being in the world
    c. total behavior
    d. existential anxiety
    e. finding new values

CHAPTER FIVE

Case Approach to Person-Centered Therapy

38. In person-centered therapy assessment occurs:
    a. during the first session.
    b. as an ongoing process throughout therapy.
    c. only after a solid therapeutic relationship has been built.
    d. only at the initial and termination phases of therapy.
    e. none of the above

39. A person-centered therapist's main role is to be a:
    a. coach.
    b. teacher of life skills.
    c. friend or confidant.
    d. facilitator of learning.
    e. both (a) and (b)

40. As basic assumption in counseling Ruth from a person-centered perspective is that counseling:
    a. should be directed at solving problems.
    b. is best aimed at teaching coping skills.
    c. works best when the therapist makes appropriate and timely interpretations.
    d. proceeds best if clients are provided with structure and direction.
    e. is aimed at helping clients tap their inner resources so she can better deal with her problems.

41. In person-centered therapy with Ruth, the essential purpose of assessment is:
    a. to enable her to develop relevant and meaningful personal knowledge.
    b. to develop a treatment plan.
    c. to figure out which therapeutic strategies will be most effective in dealing with specific problems.
    d. to have a framework for conducting research on the outcomes of therapy.
    e. both (b) and (c)

CHAPTER SIX

Case Approach to Gestalt Therapy

42. Gestalt therapy is practiced with a theoretical foundation grounded in:
    a. field theory.
    b. phenomenology.
    c. dialogue.
    d. all of the above.
    e. none of the above.

43. The main goal of Gestalt therapy is:
    a. teaching clients how to replace dysfunctional thinking with constructive thinking.
    b. the restoration of awareness.
    c. teaching clients how to make specific behavioral action plans.
    d. the elimination of disabling symptoms.
    e. both (c) and (d).

44. In Gestalt therapy, assessment is best conceived of as:
    a. something that is completed at the intake session.
    b. a behavioral description of what the client is doing.
    c. an ongoing process embedded in the dialogue between client and therapist.
    d. something that gets in the way of understanding the client's subjective world.
    e. a process that results in a traditional diagnosis that can be used for insurance purposes.

45. A Gestalt therapist would be interested in Ruth's:
    a. awareness of her moment-to-moment experiencing.
    b. contact with her therapist.
    c. ability to attribute meaning to what she is thinking, doing, and feeling.
    d. reactions to what is happening during the therapeutic hour.
    e. all of the above.

46. In Gestalt therapy there is an emphasis on drawing heavily on:
    a. cognitive techniques aimed at eliminating critical judgments of self.
    b. understanding and exploring ego states.
    c. behavioral strategies that are aimed at acquiring new interpersonal skills.
    d. experiential techniques aimed at intensifying here-and-now experiencing.
    e. both (a) and (b).

47. In Gestalt therapy, techniques are best considered as:
    a. experiments.
    b. strategies created by the therapist.
    c. planned exercises to elicit feelings.
    d. interventions designed to remove symptoms.
    e. ways to get the client past layers of resistance.

48. Which of the following would a Gestalt therapist be least likely to bring into a counseling session with Ruth?
    a. exploring polarities within Ruth.
    b. encouraging Ruth to create a dialogue in therapy as a way to work through unfinished business.
    c. asking Ruth to "become a conflict" rather than talk about the conflict.
    d. asking Ruth to pay attention to what she is experiencing in her body.
    e. asking Ruth to engage in free-association.

CHAPTER SEVEN

Case Approach to Behavior Therapy

49. Who is the founder of multimodal therapy?
    a. Frank Dattilio
    b. Albert Ellis
    c. William Glasser
    d. Arnold Lazarus
    e. Jon Frew

50. Multimodal therapy with Ruth begins with:
    a. a therapeutic contract.
    b. a formal DSM-IV-TR diagnosis.
    c. encouraging her to tell her story in great detail.
    d. a comprehensive assessment of her present functioning.
    e. teaching her how to identify and debate her faulty thinking.

51. Multimodal therapy is based on a principle of:
    a. theoretical eclecticism.
    b. technical eclecticism.
    c. I-Thou relating between client and therapist.
    d. understanding the client's existential anxiety.
    e. bringing all of the client's struggles into the here and now.

52. Which of the following is not a basic assumption of behavior therapy?
    a. Assessment is an ongoing process.
    b. Attention is directed toward observable behavior, although this can include not only actions but also feelings and thoughts.
    c. The therapeutic relationship is a powerful reinforcer and is very important if therapy is to succeed.
    d. The client is encouraged to try new behaviors both in the session and in daily life.
    e. Change will not take place until the client develops insight into the causes of his or her problems.

53. A behavior therapist is most likely to focus on _____ in counseling Ruth.
    a. the present
    b. the past
    c. the future
    d. whatever time period Ruth's wants to focus on
    e. both (b) and (c)

54. The behavior therapist believes that setting the stage for success is crucial to carrying out an action plan. This would most involve:
    a. exploring early childhood trauma.
    b. arriving at a traditional DSM-IV-TR diagnosis.
    c. analyzing antecedents and consequences.
    d. understanding the influence of the client's family of origin of present behavior.
    e. understanding the client's cultural background.

55. All of the following are examples of goals that would guide the behavior therapy process with Ruth except:
    a. learning and practicing methods of relaxation.
    b. learning stress management techniques.
    c. learning assertion training principles and skills.
    d. learning how unconscious factors are playing out in present interactions.
    e. learning and practicing new behavior.

56. Ruth informs her therapist that she does not know how to say no to people when they make a request of her. Which behavioral technique would be most appropriate in dealing with this problem?
    a. systematic desensitization
    b. operant conditioning
    c. eye movement desensitization reprocessesing
    d. flooding
    e. assertion training

CHAPTER EIGHT

Case Approach to Cognitive-Behavior Therapy

57. Albert Ellis views Ruth's problems primarily from the vantage point of:
    a. injunctions she accepted and early decisions she made.
    b. her clinging to dogmatic, rigid "musts" and commands that she continues to live by.
    c. the impact of early childhood experiences.
    d. negative conditioning from her parents.
    e. societal standards of what is acceptable for a woman.

58. REBT includes which therapeutic technique(s) in counseling Ruth?
    a. cognitive techniques
    b. emotive techniques
    c. behavioral techniques
    d. all of the above
    e. none of the above

59. When Albert Ellis gives Ruth homework assignments to be used between therapy sessions and then checks up during a following session, this is an example of a:
    a. cognitive technique.
    b. emotive technique.
    c. behavioral technique.
    d. spiritual technique.
    e. social and political action technique.

60. Which of the following would Albert Ellis be least likely to incorporate in his counseling sessions with Ruth?
    a. encouraging her to relive her early childhood traumatic experiences
    b. using *in vivo* desensitization
    c. exploring her irrational thinking
    d. teaching her how to debate self-defeating thinking patterns
    e. teaching her new and more functional beliefs

61. Which of the following is an example of an *emotive* technique of REBT?
    a. learning to dispute her demands and irrational "musts"
    b. reading books and other written material on REBT
    c. reinforcing herself after she has completed a difficult homework assignment
    d. writing down a specific plan aimed at change
    e. carrying out a shame-attacking exercise

62. Ruth closes her eyes and vividly imagines one of the worst things that could happen to her. This is a part of the technique known as:
    a. self-affirmation.
    b. assertion training.
    c. rational-emotive imagery.
    d. cognitive disputation.
    e. *in vivo* desensitization.

63. In using REBT techniques with Ruth, the therapist's main aim is to:
    a. ameliorate her presenting symptoms, such as panic or guilt.
    b. help her make a profound philosophical change.
    c. help her to feel better.
    d. uncover unconscious dynamics that are causing present problems.
    e. experience her feelings as intensely as possible.

CHAPTER NINE

Case Approach to Reality Therapy

64. The founder of reality therapy is:
    a. Robert Wubbolding.
    b. Albert Ellis.
    c. David Cain.
    d. William Glasser.
    e. William Blau.

65. From a reality therapy framework, psychological symptoms are viewed as:
    a. the problem to address in therapy.
    b. merely the underlying dynamic of a particular problem.
    c. a chosen behavior.
    d. unconscious patterns.
    e. feelings that need to be expressed.

66. A reality therapist would be most interested in learning how Ruth is:
    a. meeting her basic needs.
    b. expressing her social interest.
    c. gaining insight into the causes of her behavior.
    d. able to experience catharsis.
    e. all of the above.

67. A reality therapist would:
    a. explore what Ruth wants.
    b. help Ruth evaluate what she is doing.
    c. help Ruth formulate an action plan.
    d. all of the above.
    e. none of the above.

68. Reality therapy is:
    a. active.
    b. directive.
    c. practical.
    d. cognitive behavior in focus.
    e. all of the above.

69. A basic premise of reality therapy is that:
    a. behavior controls our perceptions.
    b. behavior is a manifestation of unconscious dynamics.
    c. behavior will not change until the client acquires insight.
    d. behavior will become healthy after the client experiences catharsis.
    e. both (c) and (d).

70. All of the following are elements in the process of reality therapy except:
    a. establishing a therapeutic relationship.
    b. encouraging her to re-author a problem-saturated story.
    c. challenging Ruth to evaluate her behavior.
    d. assisting Ruth in developing a realistic plan for change.
    e. getting Ruth to make a commitment to carry out her plan.

71. Which of the following is not a part of the WDEP system of reality therapy as applied to Ruth?
    a. determining Ruth's wants
    b. assisting Ruth in understanding the direction of what she is doing
    c. assisting Ruth to understanding how her family of origin issues are still present today
    d. assisting Ruth in making her own inner self-evaluation
    e. developing realistic plans aimed at fulfilling her needs

CHAPTER TEN

Case Approach to Feminist Therapy

72. Feminism holds that gender inequity exists and that this is a source of oppression. This inequality is based on:
    a. the natural differences between women and men.
    b. cultural factors.
    c. an imbalance of power in favor of men.
    d. the manner in which men are socialized.
    e. a matriarchal society.

73. _____ believe patriarchy is the source of women's oppression and that men's power over women in all spheres of life is so engrained that only a total restructuring of society will bring about lasting changes.
    a. Liberal feminism
    b. Cultural feminism
    c. Socialist feminism
    d. Radical feminism
    e. None of the above

74. _____ view the core of women's oppression as a complicated blend of economic philosophy and gender disparity.
    a. Liberal feminism
    b. Cultural feminism
    c. Socialist feminism
    d. Radical feminism
    e. None of the above

75. Which of the following is considered to be a basic tenet of feminist therapy?
    a. Gender-role socialization is healthy for women and men.
    b. Therapy needs to be based on a diagnostic framework.
    c. The main goal of therapy is to teach clients how to dispute faulty thinking.
    d. The personal is political.
    e. Patriarchy is good for human relationships.

76. Regarding the use of traditional diagnosis from a feminist perspective, which of the following statements is false?
    a. Without an accurate formal diagnosis, there is no basis for effective therapy.
    b. The DSM-IV-TR reflects the dominant culture's definition of pathology and health.
    c. Sexism, racism, and classism are embodied in traditional diagnosis.
    d. Diagnostic labels generally locate the source of a client's problems in the person, rather than in the environment.
    e. Many feminist therapists avoid using traditional diagnostic practices.

77. When the feminist therapist intervenes to increase Ruth's insight about how societal gender-role expectations adversely affect women, the therapist is using:
    a. reframing.
    b. cognitive restructuring.
    c. gender-role and power analysis.
    d. social action strategies.
    e. exploration of injunctions and early decisions.

78. Ruth makes it clear that she wants to work on her weight problem and her body image in her therapy. A feminist therapist is likely to:
    a. begin with developing a specific contract and behavioral plan aimed at helping her to lose weight.
    b. teach Ruth the value of dieting and exercises.
    c. explore with Ruth the unconscious dynamics of why she has a weight problem.
    d. explore societal standards that impose unrealistic views of body image and ideal weight.
    e. encourage Ruth to examine other issues that may be more pressing.

CHAPTER ELEVEN

Case Approach to Postmodern Approaches

79. Operating from a social constructionist's perspective, the therapist would likely take what stand on making a diagnosis in Ruth's case?
    a. It is essential to develop a treatment plan.
    b. It is useful to set the climate for therapy.
    c. The therapist would collaborate with Ruth on assigning an appropriate diagnosis.
    d. The therapist would develop a working diagnosis which would be firmed up by the third session.
    e. Both (a) and (b)

80. At the first session, the social constructionist therapist would primarily be interested in:
    a. establishing a DSM-IV-TR diagnosis.
    b. explaining to Ruth the theoretical orientation and techniques to be used.
    c. what Ruth wants for her future.
    d. Ruth's background pertaining to the development of the problem.
    e. giving Ruth a battery of psychological tests.

81. The social constructionist therapist working with Ruth:
    a. sees herself in a non-expert position in relation to what is the correct path for Ruth in her life.
    b. views her expertise in the area of language and meaning.
    c. proposes that reality is created in language between people.
    d. all of the above
    e. none of the above

82. Which of the following is something the solution-focused therapist tends to avoid in working with Ruth?
    a. There is a focus on looking for exceptions to the problems that Ruth brings up for discussion.
    b. Much of the therapeutic endeavor is devoted to talking about Ruth's symptoms and promoting insight on her part so that she can make changes.
    c. The emphasis is on Ruth's strengths, assets, accomplishments, abilities, competencies, skills, and successes.
    d. An attempt is made to keep the conversation non-pathological.
    e. Ruth is helped to view her problems as something external to herself and to her life.

83. The solution-focused therapist:
    a. asks questions about the "news of difference."
    b. attempts to get Ruth to shift from problem-talk to solution-talk.
    c. avoids giving Ruth compliments, since doing so can make her dependent on the therapist.
    d. makes a tentative diagnosis for treatment purposes before the end of the initial session.
    e. both (a) and (b)

84. A narrative therapist's work with Ruth would be based on the assumption that:
    a. change will occur more effectively if the therapist adopts a nondirective stance.
    b. mental health is best defined in terms of dominant cultural values.
    c. Ruth needs to become the senior partner in the collaborative relationship with the therapist.
    d. using techniques tends to undermine the client's self-direction.
    e. both (a) and (b)

85. Narrative therapists believe that "The person is not the problem, but the problem is the problem." This phrase illustrates which of the following interventions that is likely to be made with Ruth?
    a. mapping the effects
    b. deconstruction of a problem-saturated story
    c. co-authoring alternative stories
    d. externalizing conversation
    e. building an audience as a witness to an emerging preferred story

86. The narrative therapist will likely listen respectfully to Ruth's story, examine with her the problem influences in a systematic way, and will assist Ruth in moving away from the harmful effects of the problem. This intervention is best known as:
    a. making use of scaling questions.
    b. mapping the effects of the problem story.
    c. documenting the evidence.
    d. conducting a functional assessment.
    e. formulating a tentative diagnosis.

87. A narrative therapist would maintain that Ruth's problems can best be understood:
   a. by examining how she originally acquired a problem in the first place.
   b. analyzing the role of her parents in contributing to her present dysfunctions.
   c. through understanding the socio-cultural and relational contexts.
   d. by focusing on her cognitive distortions.
   e. exploring her feelings toward the therapist.

CHAPTER TWELVE

Case Approach to Family Therapy

88. Ruth appears to be unable to define herself separately from her husband and her children. Her struggle with identity leads the family therapist to examine her process of _____ as a central issue.
   a. boundary disturbance
   b. differentiation
   c. transference reactions
   d. maintaining homeostatis
   e. idealization

89. Ruth and John are often not able to discuss emotionally charged issues in their relationship. At different times, most of their discussions focus on one of their children. This illustrates:
   a. a triangular process.
   b. a struggle to achieve autonomy.
   c. a process of separation and individuation.
   d. a healthy way of dealing with problems.
   e. a process of working through transference.

90. A _____ is an organized map, or diagram, that demonstrates one's family over three generations.
   a. life style assessment
   b. behavioral assessment
   c. schema
   d. technique known as "The Miracle Question"
   e. genogram

CHAPTER THIRTEEN

An Integrative Approach to Working With Ruth

91. Which approach would most tend to focus on Ruth's internal dialogue?
   a. solution-focused brief therapy
   b. cognitive-behavior therapy
   c. person-centered therapy
   d. reality therapy
   e. Adlerian therapy

92. Which approach would be the least structured to provide the direction for Ruth's therapy?
   a. narrative therapy
   b. cognitive-behavior therapy
   c. person-centered therapy
   d. reality therapy
   e. Adlerian therapy

93. Which approach would begin with a thorough assessment of Ruth's current behavior?
    a. solution-focused brief therapy
    b. behavior therapy
    c. existential therapy
    d. narrative therapy
    e. person-centered therapy

94. Which approach would be guided by the principles of choice theory?
    a. family systems approach
    b. cognitive-behavior therapy
    c. person-centered therapy
    d. reality therapy
    e. Adlerian therapy

95. Which approach would focus on Ruth's lifestyle, examine her early recollections, and be interested in her family constellation?
    a. psychoanalytic therapy
    b. narrative therapy
    c. solution-focused brief therapy
    d. reality therapy
    e. Adlerian therapy

96. Which approach would provide the most techniques in helping Ruth manage stress, become more assertive, and learn to relax?
    a. psychoanalytic therapy
    b. behavior therapy
    c. existential therapy
    d. Adlerian therapy
    e. person-centered therapy

97. Which approach would focus on Ruth co-creating a preferred new story to replace her problem-saturated story?
    a. narrative therapy
    b. cognitive behavior therapy
    c. Gestalt therapy
    d. Adlerian therapy
    e. family systems therapy

98. Which approach would most likely be most appropriate in challenging Ruth to find meaning in her life?
    a. psychoanalytic therapy
    b. behavior therapy
    c. existential therapy
    d. cognitive-behavior therapy
    e. solution-focused brief therapy

99. Which approach would focus on the degree to which Ruth has become differentiated from her significant others?
    a. psychoanalytic therapy
    b. behavior therapy
    c. Adlerian therapy
    d. cognitive-behavior therapy
    e. family systems therapy

100. Which approach would most pay attention to signs of unfinished business in Ruth's life, as evidenced by ways in which she reaches impasses in her therapy?
    a. Gestalt therapy
    b. behavior therapy
    c. cognitive-behavior therapy
    d. solution-focused brief therapy
    e. narrative therapy

ANSWER KEY FOR MULTIPLE-CHOICE TEST ITEMS

CASE APPROACH TO COUNSELING AND PSYCHOTHERAPY

Chapter 1

1. B
2. C
3. D
4. A
5. E
6. B
7. B
8. C

9. D
10. E
11. E
12. E
13. D
14. B
15. C
16. E
17. D
18. B
19. D
20. D
21. D

Chapter 2

22. C
23. B
24. D
25. D
26. B
27. D
28. C

29. C

Chapter 3

30. C
31. B
32. C
33. A

Chapter 4

34. C
35. B
36. D
37. C

Chapter 5

38. B
39. D
40. E
41. A

Chapter 6

42. D
43. B
44. C
45. E
46. D
47. A
48. E

Chapter 7

49. D
50. D
51. B
52. E
53. A
54. C
55. D
56. E

Chapter 8

57. B
58. D
59. C
60. A
61. E
62. C
63. B

Chapter 9

64. D
65. C
66. A
67. C
68. E
69. A
70. B
71. C

Chapter 10

72. C
73. D
74. C

75. D
76. A
77. C
78. D

Chapter 11

79. C
80. C
81. D
82. B

83. E
84. C
85. D
86. B
87. C

Chapter 12

88. B
89. A

90. E

Chapter 13

91. B
92. C
93. B
94. D
95. E
96. B
97. A
98. C
99. E
100. A

V

Test Items

The Art of

Integrative Counseling

1. As a counselor:
    a. empathic understanding of your client is your best technique.
    b. you are your very best technique.
    c. utilizing one theory is your best technique.
    d. none of the above

2. A *holistic* approach:
    a. emphasizes one specific theory.
    b. emphasizes a thorough knowledge of all theories.
    c. is grounded on a variety of perspectives.
    d. none of the above

3. If the focus of the helping process is on what people are doing, there is a greater chance that they will also be able to change their:
    a. feeling.
    b. behavior.
    c. thinking
    d. (a) and (c) above

4. In developing your personal counseling perspective:
    a. you need to consider your own personality.
    b. you need to think about what concepts and techniques work best for a range of clients.
    c. it is essential that you be willing to take an honest look at your own life to determine if you are willing to do for yourself what you challenge clients to do.
    d. all of the above

5. According to the author, to be an effective counselor:
    a. your personality and style are sufficient core variables.
    b. you need a thorough grounding in counseling theory and technique.
    c. you need considerable supervised experience in counseling practice.
    d. (b) and (c) above

6. The value of the client/therapist relationship is:
    a. exclusive to the humanistic model.
    b. exclusive to the existential model.
    c. not a technique used in gestalt therapy.
    d. a common denominator among all approaches.

7. Techniques are designed to:
    a. stimulate clients to think, feel, or act in a certain manner.
    b. create a close client/therapist relationship.
    c. enhance some aspect of the client's experiencing.
    d. (a) and (b) above

8. Congruence implies:
    a. there is a deep and subjective understanding of the client.
    b. you are able to communicate to your clients a deep and genuine caring for them personally.
    c. that you are genuine, integrated and authentic during the therapy hour.
    d. all of the above

9. According to the author, the single most important element in becoming a competent counselor is:
    a. techniques.
    b. knowing who you are.
    c. being completely free of personal problems.
    d. a thorough knowledge of many counseling theories.

10. The main task of the first few sessions is:
    a. clarifying therapeutic goals.
    b. clarifying the client's problems.
    c. clarifying the client's values.
    d. defining boundaries.

11. The author sees the counseling process as:
    a. a mutual endeavor in which the client assumes the responsibility for making change happen.
    b. a mutual endeavor in which both the client and therapist share the responsibility for making change happen, with the final decision resting with the therapist.
    c. a mutual endeavor in which both the client and therapist share the responsibility for making change happen, with the final decision resting with the client.
    d. a mutual endeavor in which the therapist assumes the responsibility for making change happen.

12. Creating a collaborative partnership means that:
    a. the therapist can greatly assist the client by teaching him/her how to assess their own problems and search for their own solutions.
    b. the client assumes a fair share of the responsibility for what takes place both inside and outside the session.
    c. the therapist assumes a fair share of the responsibility for what takes place both inside and outside the session.
    d. (a) and (b) above.

13. The counselor assumes a variety of helping roles, which include:
    a. educator, advocate, social change agent, and influencer of policy making.
    b. leader, educator, problem solver, and decision maker.
    c. advocate, educator, decision maker, and problem solver.
    d. none of the above.

14. The systemic perspective holds that:
    a. individuals are best understood within the context of relationships and through assessing the interactions with their therapist.
    b. individuals are best understood within the context of relationships and through assessing the interactions within an entire family.
    c. individuals are best understood within the context of relationships and through assessing their values.
    d. all of the above

15. The one central principle agreed upon by therapists who utilize a family systems orientation is that:
    a. the client is connected to living systems and that change in one part of the unit reverberates throughout other parts.
    b. the client is connected to their feelings and that change in their thinking and behaving will change their feelings.
    c. the client is connected to their behavior and that change in their thinking and feeling will change their behavior.
    d. none of the above

16. The goals of bringing about change within systems is indicative of:
    a. Adlerian therapy and Gestalt therapy
    b. person-centered therapy and psychoanalytic therapy.
    a. reality therapy and cognitive-behavior therapy.
    b. feminist therapy and family systems therapy.

17. The Adlerian notion of goal-alignment means:
    a. the client's goals are coherent with his/her family of origin.
    b. goal setting involves a mutual, collaborative process between the client and therapist.
    c. the therapist's goals are preeminent in the therapeutic session.
    d. none of the above

18. The multimodal approach is a form of:
    a. psychodrama.
    b. Gestalt therapy.
    c. behavior therapy.
    d. existential therapy.

19. Behavioral change, better decision making, improving significant relationships, enhanced living, and more effective satisfaction of the psychological needs are goals of which approach?
    a. existential therapy
    b. reality therapy
    c. psychodrama
    d. none of the above

20. According to the author, therapy can hardly be complete without establishing _____.
    a. concrete cognitive goals.
    a. concrete behavioral goals.
    b. concrete emotive goals.
    c. concrete values.

21. Asking a client to examine his/her present level of physical and psychological well-being and having him/her decide what balance they want to achieve in areas such as rest, exercise, diet, and ways to spend time is an example of:
    a. a cognitive goal.
    a. a process goal.
    b. an action goal.
    c. an emotive goal.

22. The "socioteleological" approach of Adlerian therapy implies that:
    a. we are primarily motivated by social forces and are striving to achieve certain goals.
    b. we create goals, both short-term and long-term, that motivate our behavior and influence our personality development.
    c. we cannot see beyond our own core set of values and therefore need social resources to assist us with our problems.
    d. (a) and (b) above

23. The integrative perspective favors broadening the base of the contemporary theories to encompass:
    a. an emotional, cultural, and educational component.
    b. a social, spiritual, and even political dimension.
    c. a behavioral, spiritual, and cultural component.
    d. an emotional, spiritual, and political dimension.

24. Wubbolding believes that reality therapy needs to be modified to fit:
    a. the wide array of problems facing our nation.
    b. revisions in the DSM-IV.
    c. the cultural context of people other than North Americans.
    d. all of the above

25. Both feminist and multicultal therapists demand:
    a. conformity to the dominant culture.
    b. conformity to the dominant sex.
    c. direct action for social change as a part of the role of the therapist.
    d. the clients freedom from insecurities.

26. According to the author, addressing spiritual and religious values:
    a. should never be discussed in the therapeutic setting.
    b. can be beneficial to the client if he/she adopts the therapist's value system.
    c. can be integrated with many of the theoretical orientations and various therapeutic methods to enhance the therapy process.
    d. none of the above.

27. Which of the following statements are true?
    a. It is unethical to attempt to convert your client to a particular religious or spiritual set of values.
    b. The therapist's job is to assist his/her clients in exploring their values to determine to which they are living within the framework of this value system.
    c. There is empirical evidence that our spiritual values and behaviors can promote physical and psychological well-being.
    d. all of the above

28. Resistance, from the psychoanalytic perspective, is considered:
    a. a fundamental part of therapy and is something that needs to be recognized and explored.
    b. a sign that the therapist is not making a correct assessment or is inappropriately applying a treatment plan.
    c. the client's projection of a feeling on the therapist.
    d. a conscious desire to suppress a memory from early childhood.

29. The technique "staying with the feeling" is commonly used with which approach?
    a. person-centered
    b. Gestalt
    c. experiential
    d. Adlerian

30. One way in which the client can make the therapeutic setting safer is by:
    a. working in a familiar environment.
    b. talking about what their reluctance means to them.
    c. participating in both individual and group therapy.
    d. avoiding issues that make the client uncomfortable.

31. According to the author, courage means:
    a. being afraid, yet plunging ahead anyway.
    b. delineating boundaries about what can and cannot be discussed during the therapy hour.
    c. respecting resistance by discussing issues that are comfortable for the client.
    d. none of the above

32. When dealing with resistance, the author suggests that you:
    a. work with the resistance, rather than fight it.
    b. think of resistance as the lack of readiness to engage in therapeutic work.
    c. recognize that coming in for counseling may be a sign of weakness to the client, which may make them hesitant to be open.
    d. all of the above

33. When dealing with resistance, it is wise for you to:
    a. state your observations, hunches, and interpretations in a tentative way.
    b. distinguish between the phenomenon of resistance, which is occurring in your client, and your reactions to the client's resistance.
    c. meet resistance with resistance.
    d. (a) and (b) above

34. The therapist's role entails:
    a. educating clients about ways they can use the relationship with you to help themselves.
    b. letting clients know that counseling often entails some setbacks.
    c. helping your clients prepare for possible disruptions in the family that is triggered by changes clients make in their counseling.
    d. all of the above

35. Getting your client's involvement in formulating clear goals that will guide the counseling process is likely to:
    a. ensure that you avoid therapist burnout.
    b. ensure that insight is achieved.
    c. encourage the client to follow the plan.
    d. none of the above

36. An integrative approach to counseling requires dealing with:
    a. self-talk.
    b. faulty thinking.
    c. core beliefs.
    d. one's worldview
    e. all of the above

37. Two main forms of cognitive-behavioral approaches include:
    a. experiential therapy and reality therapy.
    b. rational emotive behavior therapy and cognitive therapy.
    c. Gestalt therapy and existential therapy.
    d. person-centered therapy and psychoanalytic therapy.

38. Both cognitive therapy and rational emotive behavior therapy are based on the assumption that:
    a. if we change the way we act, we can also change our feelings and thinking.
    b. if we change our feelings, we can change the way we think and act.
    c. if we change our thinking, we can change the way we act and behave.
    d. if we change our thinking, we can also change our feelings and the way we act.

39. The cognitive focus in counseling asserts that:
    a. the client and his/her family must be actively involved if change is to occur.
    b. the therapist must be actively involved if change is to occur.
    c. the client must be active if change is to occur.
    d. thinking is the only component necessary for change to occur.

40. Adlerian therapy, rational emotive behavior therapy, cognitive therapy, and choice theory/reality therapy share the basic assumption that:
    a. situational events have the power to determine you.
    b. your interpretation of events are insignificant in your life.
    c. situational events do not have the power to determine you; rather, it is your interpretation of these events that is crucial.
    d. the cognitive focus is irrelevant to the therapeutic outcome.

41. Cognition takes into account:
    a. attitudes and core beliefs.
    b. cultural and spiritual values.
    c. self-talk and faulty beliefs.
    d. all of the above

42. It is the author's view that much of the counseling endeavor will deal with:
    a. educating the client.
    b. teaching the client coping skills.
    c. enabling the client to see the connection to what they are learning in the therapy office to everyday living.
    d. all of the above

43. Cognitive-behavioral techniques include:
    a. paying attention to your thinking.
    b. homework assignments.
    c. the Adlerian concept of exploring "private logic."
    d. all of the above

44. The emotive focus emphasizes that:
    a. catharsis, or the release of emotions, is an end in itself.
    b. often the best route to get the client to examine their cognition is by encouraging them to identify, express, and deal with what they are feeling.
    c. it is essential to work with insights associated with an emotional situation and cognition underlying emotional patterns.
    d. (b) and (c) above

45. The Gestalt therapy approach is experiential in that the client:
    a. comes to grips with what and how they are thinking, feeling, and acting while interacting with the therapist.
    b. techniques are geared to the client's thoughts, feelings, and actions.
    c. experiments grow out of the phenomenological context of therapy.
    d. all of the above

46. Gestalt experiments are designed to:
    a. expand the client's awareness and helps the client try out new modes of behavior.
    b. promote catharsis and a release of emotions.
    c. promote an intimate client/therapist relationship.
    d. assist the client in establishing goals for their therapeutic hour.

47. Gestalt-oriented questions that promote "now" awareness include:
    a. "why" and "when" questions.
    b. "what" and "why" questions.
    c. "what" and "how" questions.
    d. "who" and "why" questions.

48. According to the author, for some clients, or in certain situations, expressing intense emotions:
    a. is the only means by which a client can achieve insight.
    b. may be contraindicated.
    c. will provide the client with a spiritual epiphany.
    d. is a goal in and of itself.

49. Insight, according to the author, is:
    a. the cognitive shift that connects the awareness of the various emotional experiences with some meaningful narrative or some growing understanding.
    b. not necessary following catharsis.
    c. contraindicated with certain clients.
    d. all of the above

50. "Behavioral focus" encompasses not only standard or traditional behavior therapy, but also action-oriented therapies. These action-oriented therapies include:
    a. multimodal therapy, cognitive-behavior therapy, rational emotive behavior therapy.
    b. cognitive therapy and reality therapy.
    c. person-centered therapy, Adlerian therapy, and psychoanalysis.
    d. (a) and (b) above

51. Behavior therapists operate on the premise that:
    a. changes in behavior cannot occur prior to understanding of oneself and that behavior changes alone may not lead to an increased level of self-understanding.
    b. changes in behavior can occur prior to understanding of oneself and that behavioral changes may well lead to an increased level of self-understanding.
    c. changes in behavior cannot occur without experiencing catharsis and insight.
    d. (a) and (c) above

52. Action-oriented therapies provide methods that are:
    a. cathartic, insightful, and revealing.
    b. non-specific and unrealistic.
    c. measurable, plan-specific, and realistic.
    e. none of the above

53. Techniques that are derived from social-learning theory include:
    a. reinforcement, modeling, shaping.
    b. cognitive restructuring, desensitization, relaxation training.
    c. coaching, behavioral rehearsal.
    d. all of the above

54. According to the author, both the assessment and treatment process of therapy are enhanced when:
    a.   the therapist establishes measurable, plan-specific goals for the client.
    b.   the client experiences catharsis.
    c.   the worldviews of the therapist are made a central part of the counseling process.
    d.   the worldviews of the client are made a central part of the counseling process.

55. According to the behavioral model, self-awareness is a crucial step in the change process, however:
    a.   insights alone can move your forward.
    b.   insights are not necessary for growth.
    c.   insights without action hardly will move your forward.
    d.   insights provide a framework for you to make decisions and to engage in translating what you know about yourself into plans for change.
    e.   (c) and (d) above

56. Arnold Lazarus's acronym for BASIC-ID stands for:
    a.   behavior, avoidance, sensations, insight, cognitions, interpersonal relationships, and doing.
    b.   behavior, affective responses, sensations, integration, caring, interpersonal relationships, and drugs.
    c.   behavior, affective responses, sensations, images, cognitions, interpersonal relationships, and drugs, biological functions, nutrition, and exercise.
    d.   none of the above

57. Wubbolding's WDEP formulation represents:
    a.   whining, drugs, eccentricities, and problems.
    b.   winning, doing, evaluation, and performance.
    c.   wants, needs, and perceptions; exploring the direction of your current behavior; evaluation; and planning.
    d.   none of the above

58. Behavioral contracts are important because:
    a.   they are a useful frame of reference for evaluating the outcomes of counseling.
    b.   they foster an active stance.
    c.   they ensure that the client is following through with the therapist's goals.
    d.   (a) and (b) above
    e.   all of the above

59. Two common pathways for achieving an integrative perspective include:
    a.   technical eclecticism and therapeutic integration.
    b.   technical eclecticism and theoretical insight.
    c.   technical eclecticism and theoretical integration.
    d.   none of the above

60. Technical eclecticism tends to:
    a.   focus on similarities, limits itself to a few approaches, and has a defined set of techniques.
    b.   focuses on similarities, has no basis for a theoretical foundation, has a defined set of techniques.
    c.   focuses on differences, chooses from many approaches, and doesn't use techniques.
    d.   focuses on differences, chooses from many approaches, and is a collection of techniques.

61. Theoretical integration, on the other hand:
    a.   refers to a conceptual or theoretical creation beyond a mere blending of techniques.
    b.   has the goal of producing a conceptual framework that synthesizes the best of two or more theoretical approaches under the assumption that the outcomes will be richer than operating from a single theory.
    c.   (a) and (b) above
    d.   none of the above

62. According to the author, an integrated system:
    a. offers the possibility to incorporate some key principles and concepts from the various theoretical orientations.
    b. offers the possibility to view counseling in the context of integrated human beings by focusing on thinking, feeling, and acting.
    c. limits you to techniques from one specific theory.
    d. (a) and (b) above

63. The author suggests that beginning counselors:
    a. select a primary theory that is closest to their basic beliefs; thoroughly learn that theory; be open to discovering ways of drawing on techniques from many different theories.
    b. thoroughly learn about as many theories as possible; incorporate as many techniques as possible from as many theories as possible to their clientele.
    c. adhere to a single theory.
    d. none of the above

64. For counseling to be effective, it is necessary to:
    a. utilize techniques and procedures in a manner that is consistent with the therapist's values, life experiences, and cultural background.
    b. utilize techniques and procedures in a manner that is consistent with the values of the dominant culture.
    c. utilize techniques and procedures in a manner that is consistent with the client's values, life experiences, and cultural background.
    d. none of the above

65. According to the existentialist view, we are capable of:
    a. awareness of others, which is the distinctive capacity that allows us to reflect and to decide.
    b. self-awareness, which is the distinctive capacity that allows us to reflect and to decide.
    c. (a) and (b) above
    d. none of the above

66. Gestalt therapy focuses on:
    a. making the unconscious conscious.
    b. establishing realistic, measurable goals.
    c. disequilibrium in the family of origin.
    d. whatever is in the client's awareness.

67. Psychodrama is an approach in which:
    a. the client acts out or dramatizes past, present, or anticipated life situations and roles.
    b. deep understanding, exploration of feelings, emotional release, and behavioral skills are experienced and developed.
    c. imagery, action, and direct interpersonal encounter is used.
    d. all of the above

68. The underlying assumption of the multimodal approach is that:
    a. because individuals are troubled by a variety of specific problems, it is appropriate that both a multitude of treatment strategies and different therapeutic styles are used in bringing about change.
    b. because individuals experience few problems, it is desirable to develop a single treatment strategy to bring about change.
    c. because individuals experience similar problems, it is desirable to develop a brief overview of as many theories as possible and experiment with techniques to bring about change.
    d. none of the above

69. The concept of "total behavior' teaches us that:
    a. all behavior is derived from early childhood memories.
    b. all behavior is a consolidation of experiences throughout our life.
    c. all behavior is made up of four inseparable but distinct components: acting, thinking, feeling, and physiology that must accompany all of our actions, thoughts, and feelings.
    d. all behavior is made up of six inseparable but distince components: acting, thinking, feeling, physiology, family, and society, that must accompany all of our actions, thoughts, and feelings.

70. Alfred Adler's theory assumes that people are:
    a. motivated by social factors.
    b. are responsible for their own thoughts, feelings, and actions.
    c. are the creators of their own lives, as opposed to helpless victims.
    d. are impelled by purposes and goals, looking more toward the future than to the past.
    e. all of the above

71. The basic goal of the Adlerian approach is to:
    a. help clients identify and change their mistaken beliefs about self, others, and life and thus participate more fully in a social world.
    b. help clients uncover unconscious or repressed material from early childhood trauma.
    c. work in the present and the future, as the past is insignificant to present behavior.
    d. none of the above

72. Contemporary social constructionist theories, or constructive therapies share the following common characteristics with the Adlerian approach:
    a. an emphasis on establishing a respectful client/therapist relationship.
    b. an emphasis on clients' strengths and resources.
    c. an optimistic and future orientation.
    d. all of the above

73. According to the psychodynamic approach, transference:
    a. is often an unconscious process whereby clients project onto you past feelings or attitudes they had toward significant people in their lives.
    b. typically has its origins in the client's early childhood.
    c. constitutes a repetition of past conflicts.
    d. because of unfinished business, the client perceives the counselor in a distorted way.
    e. all of the above

74. Psychoanalytic practitioners consider the transference situation to be valuable because:
    a. its manifestations provide clients with the opportunity to re-experience a variety of feelings that would otherwise be inaccessible.
    b. its manifestations provide therapists with the opportunity to recognize that this phenomenon is not to be taken personally.
    c. its manifestations provide therapists with the opportunity to examine their own countertransference issues.
    d. all of the above

75. Reality therapist William Glasser views transference and countertransference:
    a. the same as the psychoanalytic approach.
    b. as a phenomenon that must be addressed immediately so as not to interfere with the client/therapist relationship.
    c. as a way that people avoid taking personal responsibility in the present.
    d. none of the above

76. Rational emotive behavior therapist Albert Ellis views transference as:
    a. indulgence therapy.
    b. an irrational belief that the client must be liked and loved by the therapist (or parent figure).
    c. a necessary evil.
    d. (a) and (b) above

77. Countertransference refers to:
    a. the feelings aroused in the client by the therapist.
    b. the feelings aroused in the therapist by the client.
    c. a psychotic episode experienced by the client.
    d. an irrational belief that the client must be liked and loved by the therapist (or parent figure).

78. It is important for the therapist to recognize signs of countertransference because:
    a. the unconscious emotional responses to a client may result in a distorted perception of the client's behavior.
    b. the overt expressions of feelings toward the therapist may be a violation of the ACA code of ethics.
    c. the unconscious emotional response toward the therapist may hinder the therapeutic process.
    d. all of the above

79. Signs of transference include:
    a. clients who make you into something you are not.
    b. clients who are not able to accept boundaries.
    c. clients who displace anger onto you.
    d. clients who fall easily in love with you.
    e. all of the above

80. Which of the following is/are true:
    a. It is essential for the therapist to gain awareness of his/her own needs and motivations.
    b. It is a mistake to think that all feelings your clients have toward you are simply signs of transference.
    c. You can err both by being too willing to accept unconditionally whatever clients tell you and by interpreting everything they tell you as a sign of transference.
    d. Paying attention to your own feelings about a client who imposes on you and makes unreasonable demands of you will give you a sense of how significant people in this client's life are affected by this individual.
    e. all of the above

81. Countertransference is:
    a. unrealistic reactions you might have toward your clients that may interfere with your objectivity.
    b. unrealistic reactions that your clients have toward you that may interfere with the therapeutic relationship.
    c. a displacement of feelings from the client to the therapist.
    d. none of the above

82. Which of the following statements is/are true regarding countertransference?
    a. You do not have to be problem free, but it is crucial that you be aware of how your own problems or countertransference can affect the quality of your working relationship with clients.
    b. Countertransference can have both positive and negative effects on the counseling process.
    c. It behooves you to seek consultation, participate in supervision, or enter your own therapy for a time to work out unresolved personal issues that stand in the way of your clinical effectiveness.
    d. all of the above

83. The following theories do not include an exploration of the past as a key concept in therapy:
    a. person-centered therapy, Gestalt therapy, existential therapy, and behavior therapy
    b. Adlerian therapy, Gestalt therapy, reality therapy, and behavior therapy
    c. reality therapy, behavior therapy, rational emotive behavior therapy, and cognitive therapy
    d. none of the above

84. With regard to how the past influences the present, reality therapist, William Glasser argues:
    a. that individuals are presently disturbed because they presently believe in their self-defeating view of themselves and their world.
    b. early learning is not irreversible; but to change its effects, we must become aware of how certain early experiences have contributed to our present personality structure.
    c. therapy is largely based on the early relations of a child and mother and how this early relationship shapes the child's inner world and later adult relationships.
    d. since we are not able to change our past, we should not waste time in revisiting it.

85. With regard to how the past influences the present, rational emotive therapist, Albert Ellis argues:
    a. "Big deal! Where is it written that our parents must love us and that we are worthless if they don't love us the way we think they should love us!"
    b. individuals are presently disturbed because they presently believe in their self-defeating view of themselves and their world.
    c. therapy is largely based on early relations of a child and mother and how this early relationship shapes the child's inner world and later adult relationships.
    d. (a) and (b) above

86. "Redecision therapy" rests on the basic concepts of:
    a. injunctions, early decisions, and new decisions.
    b. decisions in the here and now, establishing realistic goals, and a new way of being.
    c. (a) and (b) above
    d. none of the above

87. Redecision therapy is a form of transactional analysis which is based on the assumption that:
    a. as an adult you make decisions on past premises that are still valid.
    b. as an adult you make decisions on past premises that at one time were appropriate to your survival needs, but may no longer be valid.
    c. as a child your family made decisions that were inappropriate for you.
    d. none of the above

88. An injunction is defined as:
    a. a message given to children by their siblings that tells children what they have to do and be in order to get recognition and acceptance.
    b. a message given to children by their teachers that tells children what they have to do and be in order to get recognition and acceptance.
    c. a message given to clients by their therapist that tells them what they have to do and be in order to be self-actualized.
    d. a message given to children by their parents that tells children what they have to do and be in order to get recognition and acceptance.

89. If you are participating in redecision therapy as a client:
    a. it is assumed that you cooperate in making early decisions that direct your life, so you can now make new decisions that are appropriate and will allow you to experience life anew.
    b. the premise is that awareness is an important first step in the process of changing your ways of thinking, feeling, and behaving.
    c. you enter the past and create fantasy scenes in which you can safely give up old and currently inappropriate early decisions, because you are armed with an understanding in the present that enables you to relive the scene in a new way.
    d. all of the above

90. Cognitive restructuring is a technique that:
    a. assists you to understand early decisions in the form of core beliefs and self-talk.
    b. assists you to understand present emotions via catharsis and insight.
    c. assists you to understand the importance of long-range goals.
    d. assists you to understand present decisions in the form of injunctions.

91. Cognitive techniques include:
    a. cognitive disputing, debating, Socratic questioning, reframing, and cognitive restructuring.
    b. cognitive disputing, Kantian questioning, doubting, and cognitive restructuring.
    c. decision making, planning, goal setting, and evaluation.
    d. none of the above

92. Action-oriented therapies stress the importance of moving beyond the insight and self-awarensss levels into the realm of taking action to bring about change. Therapies that are considered action-oriented include:
    a. person-centered therapy, Gestalt therapy, behavior therapy, and existential therapy.
    b. existential therapy, psychodrama, Gestalt therapy, and person-centered therapy.
    c. behavior therapy, rational emotive therapy, cognitive-behavior therapy, choice theory/reality therapy, and Adlerian therapy.
    d. none of the above

93. The Adlerian technique of acting "as if" encourages the client to:
    a. act as if the client grew with different family dynamics.
    b. act as if their therapy were to come to an end.
    c. act as if they are the person they want to be.
    d. all of the above

94. The goal of having the client act "as if" is to:
    a. challenge their self-limiting assumptions.
    b. have the client catch themselves in the process of repeating old patterns that have led to ineffective behavior.
    c. translate new insights and new decisions into concrete actions.
    d. all of the above

95. "Restricted existence" refers to:
    a. the client being traumatized during early childhood by frequently being placed on restriction.
    b. a psychodrama technique whereby the client is restricted from expressing their pent-up emotions.
    c. the client seeing few options of dealing with life situations.
    d. none of the above

96. Tasks of termination include:
    a. summarizing the counseling experience, consolidating gains, reviewing goals and progress, discussing future work and establishing contracts, suggesting referrals.
    b. reviewing informed consent, establishing a client/therapist relationship, understanding the problem.
    c. understanding the problem, exploring the past, developing a plan, establishing goals.
    d. none of the above

97. The following approaches are especially useful in providing methods for consolidation of learning and transfer of what was learned in therapy to daily living:
    a. Adlerian therapy, existential therapy, Gestalt therapy, behavior therapy
    b. narrative therapy, person-centered therapy, psychodrama, and behavior therapy
    c. Adlerian therapy, reality therapy, behavior therapy, and cognitive-behavior therapy
    d. none of the above

98. Some guidelines for the therapist to consider in effectively accomplishing the task of therapeutic endings include:
    a. reminding clients of the approaching ending.
    b. discussing fees for service.
    c. review the course of treatment.
    d. (a) and (c) above

99. Other guidelines for the therapist to consider in effectively accomplishing the task of therapeutic endings include:
    a. allowing clients to talk about their feelings of separation.
    b. letting clients know of the therapist's availability at a future time.
    c. assisting clients to translate their learning into action plans.
    d. all of the above

100. The final phase of counseling may be a difficult time. The author suggests that the client:
    a. have an opportunity to fully express their feelings about the termination or the therapeutic relationship.
    b. understand what they did to make the therapy experience meaningful.
    c. review what they learned, how they learned it, and what they will do with what they learned now that the counseling sessions are coming to an end.
    d. all of the above.

ANSWER KEY FOR MULTIPLE-CHOICE TEST QUESTIONS

THE ART OF INTEGRATIVE COUNSELING

1.	B	21.	B	41.	D	61.	C	81.	A
2.	C	22.	A	42.	D	62.	D	82.	D
3.	D	23.	A	43.	D	63.	A	83.	C
4.	D	24.	D	44.	D	64.	C	84.	D
5.	D	25.	C	45.	D	65.	B	85.	D
6.	D	26.	C	46.	A	66.	D	86.	A
7.	C	27.	D	47.	C	67.	D	87.	B
8.	C	28.	A	48.	B	68.	A	88.	D
9.	B	29.	B	49.	A	69.	C	89.	D
10.	B	30.	B	50.	D	70.	E	90.	A
11.	C	31.	A	51.	B	71.	A	91.	A
12.	D	32.	D	52.	C	72.	D	92.	C
13.	A	33.	D	53.	D	73.	E	93.	C
14.	B	34.	D	54.	D	74.	A	94.	D
15.	A	35.	C	55.	E	75.	C	95.	C
16.	D	36.	E	56.	C	76.	D	96.	A
17.	B	37.	B	57.	C	77.	B	97.	C
18.	C	38.	D	58.	D	78.	A	98.	D
19.	B	39.	C	59.	C	79.	E	99.	D
20.	B	40.	C	60.	D	80.	E	100.	D

VI

FACILITATOR'S RESOURCE GUIDE for CD-ROM for INTEGRATIVE COUNSELING

CD-ROM for Integrative Counseling

Program Segment
Opening
An Integrative Approach: An Overview
Introduction to the Case of Ruth

Session 1 The Beginning of Counseling
Lecture
Counseling with Ruth
Commentary

Session 2 The Therapeutic Relationship
Lecture
Counseling with Ruth
Commentary

Session 3 Establishing Therapeutic Goals
Lecture
Counseling with Ruth
Commentary

Session 4 Understanding and Dealing with Diversity
Lecture
Counseling with Ruth
Commentary

Session 5 Understanding and Dealing with Resistance
Lecture
Counseling with Ruth
Commentary

Session 6 Cognitive Focus in Counseling
Lecture
Counseling with Ruth
Commentary

Session 7 Emotive Focus in Counseling
Lecture
Counseling with Ruth
Commentary

Session 8 Behavioral Focus in Counseling
Lecture
Counseling with Ruth
Commentary

Session 9 An Integrative Perspective
Lecture
Counseling with Ruth
Commentary

Session 10 Working with Transference and Countertransference
Lecture
Counseling with Ruth
Second Lecture
Second Counseling
Commentary

Session 11 Understanding How the Past Influences the Present
Lecture
Counseling with Ruth
Commentary

Session 12 Working toward Decisions and Behavior Change
Lecture
Counseling with Ruth
Commentary

Session 13 Evaluation and Termination
Lecture
Counseling with Ruth
Commentary
Concluding Comments

INTRODUCTION

This Facilitator's Resource Guide is designed to provide the course instructor with information and a comprehension test for the classroom for students who are utilizing *CD-ROM for Integrative Counseling*. If you are using any of my books, (1) *The Art of Integrative Counseling*, or (2) *Case Approach to Counseling and Psychotherapy*, or (3) *Theory and Practice of Counseling and Psychotherapy,* you will find a test item bank for each of these books in this *Instructor's Resource Manual for Theory and Practice of Counseling and Psychotherapy*, *Case Approach to Counseling and Psychotherapy*, and *The Art of Integrative Counseling*.

The *CD-ROM for Integrative Counseling* program contains a great deal of useful information to promote interactive learning for each of the 13 sessions in the program. The self-study program includes a list of key points, exercises, and questions for students to complete at home after viewing a session, small-group activities that can be done in the classroom, and references to other Corey books that coordinate with the CD-ROM (with a focus on techniques). The combination of this instructor's manual and the *CD-ROM for Integrative Counseling* provide you with ample ideas and suggestions for how to make the best use of this unique learning package for both home-study and in-class use.

PROGRAM OVERVIEW

Students in counseling, psychology, social work, nursing and other helping professions often ask how they can develop a counseling approach that fits with their own personal style. Experienced practitioners as well struggle with this issue as they constantly assess their own approaches and incorporate new methods as a result of life experience and acquiring new knowledge. This unique video program addresses these issues for both new and experienced clinicians.
Student Video and Workbook for the Art of Integrative Counseling was originally a video/workbook package which has been converted into this program, entitled *CD-ROM for Integrative Counseling*. While most counseling film or video programs show a single counseling session, this CD-ROM program demonstrates how an integrative approach to counseling is applied from the first session through termination with each aspect of Gerald Corey's integrative approach being demonstrated and discussed.

SYNOPSIS OF THE CD-ROM PROGRAM

CD-ROM for Integrative Counseling

In this program, I (Gerald Corey) demonstrate my own integrative approach to counseling with a client named Ruth. Her presenting problems include tension in her neck and shoulders, and heart palpitations for which her physician can find no cause. She is a married mother of four teenagers who has dedicated her life to her family. As her children are now becoming independent, she is re-examining her life purpose as well as her relationship with her husband. In the program I rely on a variety of therapeutic approaches including person-centered, cognitive-behavioral, existential, Gestalt, reality, and psychodynamic. These theoretical models are integrated in a manner that fits my own personal style—one that is direct, supportive, genuine, lively, and stresses the importance of the therapeutic relationship.

Highlights from 13 counseling sessions are shown. Each session is introduced by a brief lecture that I present. This is followed by a counseling session with Ruth and my commentary discussing what specific approaches I was utilizing and what I was trying to accomplish with Ruth.

Resource Textbooks as Companions With the CD-ROM Program

An integrated package of materials is available as a resource to you. The core text, *Theory and Practice of Counseling and Psychotherapy* (TPCP), presents the various theories in detail. The *Student Manual for Theory and Practice of Counseling and Psychotherapy* provides readers with practical hints on studying and personalizing the material. *Case Approach to Counseling and Psychotherapy* is geared to the TPCP text (in that it covers the same eleven theories) and provides readers with vivid examples of how the various therapies work with a single client, Ruth. My book, *The Art of Integrative Counseling*, is designed to help students construct their personal orientation to counseling and describes in detail the case of Ruth. These textbooks mentioned above are ideal companions to the self-study CD-ROM program.

LEARNING OBJECTIVES

After viewing this CD-ROM program, viewers will be better able to:
1. Describe how one therapist incorporates a variety of counseling techniques and approaches in an integrative approach.

2. Work with clients with a clear understanding of how counseling proceeds from the first session to termination.

3. Discuss the concepts of resistance, transference, countertransference, and diversity perspectives and their importance in counseling clients.

4. Discuss the value of self-awareness for themselves as counselors.

A RATIONALE FOR AN INTEGRATED TEACHING/LEARNING PACKAGE

Some students learn best by listening to lectures and reading; others learn best by working on projects alone; others prefer collaborative learning approaches, such as working in study groups; some learn more when they are participants in experiential learning (such as role plays and group interaction); and some work best when they are presented with a problem situation and are challenged to figure out a solution

Recognizing the reality that there are multiple routes to learning, many instructors employ a diversity of teaching/learning strategies. There are certainly implications of the various styles of learning for the teaching of a counseling theory and practice course. The integrated teaching/learning package that can accompany *CD-ROM for Integrative Learning* is based on the assumption that your students will best learn if a combination of approaches are built into your course. Ideally, this integrated package consists of the main text, along with the CD-ROM program.

CD-ROM for Integrative Counseling provides a model for how your students can assume roles of both client and counselor, as they creatively act out problem situations. The CD-ROM program will bring to life a range of challenging situations that helps students to think about counseling interventions.

In addition to traditional teaching approaches—reading, lectures, discussion, small groups, guest speakers, field trips, writing papers, and taking tests—your class can include an experiential component where students enact counseling interventions.

The comprehension test found later in this manual may be duplicated and used in class. If your students are using the book, *The Art of Integrative Counseling*, or *Case Approach to Counseling and Psychotherapy*, they will have considerable exposure to the case of Ruth. Both of these books use Ruth as the central example. Test questions are also contained in this *Instructor's Resource Manual* for *Theory and Practice of Counseling and Psychotherapy*, *Case Approach to Counseling and Psychotherapy*, and *The Art of Integrative Counseling*.

Utilizing *CD-ROM for Integrative Counseling* for Self-Directed Home Study

1. Students use *CD-ROM for Integrative Counseling* as an interactive home-study program, to be used in conjunction with at least one textbook.

a. Engage the class in discussion utilizing the pre-viewing questions.

b. Students, as homework, might watch all 13 counseling sessions in one or two sittings to get an overview of the complete program.

c. As homework, ask students to watch one segment at a time, then do the exercises that are a part of the program. If they are using **The Art of Integrative Counseling**, ask them to read the related chapter immediately after viewing a particular session.

d. Students can then bring the their written responses to class and use them as a basis for the practical demonstrations and experiential work and for further discussion of the counseling sessions.

e. The CD-ROM program contains several small-group activities for classroom use. As much as possible, students can practice what they see being modeled in the counseling sessions in their small group.

Utilizing *CD-ROM for Integrative Counseling* in Class

1. Assign students to view the various counseling segments and complete related sections that follow each of the counseling session, and bring their written responses to class.

2. After the students review each segment at home, show the segment in class and discuss the activities found in the program—especially the exercises, questions, and small-group activities.

3. For each segment that illustrates a counseling session:

   a. Encourage the class to try to identify the various approaches that Gerald Corey is utilizing. Also, suggest that they think about how they would work with Ruth if they were her therapist. You might mention that therapy rarely proceeds as neatly as seen in the various counseling sessions. However, for purposes of demonstration, they will see the highlights of the sessions.

   b. Put the class to work in groups using the discussion questions, exercises, and small-group activities for each segment.

4. You might want to show all of the 13 counseling sessions again toward the end of the semester. Showing this again is a way for students to bring together what they are learning about integrative counseling.

GUIDE TO EXERCISES AND ACTIVITIES IN CLASS

In the CD-ROM program are discussion questions geared to each of the 13 counseling sessions that are a part of the program. For each session, students can review a list of Key Points. Following the key points are "Reflection and Responses" for students to complete at home. This provides an interactive learning format and insures that students do more than simply watch the counseling sessions and commentaries. Students are required to become active learners and are guided in reflecting about the personal implications of what they are viewing as well as thinking about how they would work with Ruth.

In the CD-ROM program each segment begins with a brief lecturette of specific theories and techniques that I draw from in my integrative perspective. The program contains a summary of the material in the lecturette in the form of Key Points. Discussion questions are designed to tap the reader's critical thinking about the counseling process. After students view the CD-ROM at home (segment by segment), and then complete the accompanying "Reflection and Responses" sections, this material can be used as the basis for classroom interaction and small group practice. These questions make a useful study guide and serve as a catalyst for discussion in class.

For each of the 13 sessions, there are *Small-Group Activities* that are ideally suited for use in the classroom. These activities tend to ask students to reflect on each session by applying to themselves personally what they see in the program. There are also questions pertaining to Ruth or to clients in general. Although these are useful catalysts for discussion, the best use of these activities is to encourage students to role-play a variety of situations. Rather than just talk about how they might intervene with Ruth at a particular point, one student can take on the role of Ruth and others in the group can demonstrate (by becoming the counselor) how they would intervene. After students have seen certain segments of the program and done the exercises at home, an ideal follow-up activity is to break them into small groups and give them opportunities to share and process how they answered the questions on their own. In addition to talking about Ruth as the client, students can be asked to think up other client situations that would fit for each of the 13 sessions.

Comprehension Test for *CD-ROM for Integrative Counseling*

1. An integrative approach to counseling is best described as one that:
    a. subscribes to one theory of counseling over others.
    b. relies on a variety of therapeutic approaches consistent with the therapist's style and the client's needs.
    c. includes the use of therapeutic methods from all of the major theories.
    d. all of the above

2. The advantage(s) of an integrated approach include(s):
    a. the ability to utilize a number of therapeutic tools depending on the client's needs.
    b. the ability to address the change process in the areas of thinking, feeling and behavior.
    c. allowing the counselor's values and personality to be consistent with the counseling approach utilized.
    d. all of the above

3. The best way to develop your own style of counseling is to:
    a. learn one theory in depth and branch out from there.
    b. immerse yourself in many approaches and see which fits best for you.
    c. utilize whatever therapeutic method that seems to work and learn about the theory behind it later.
    d. avoid doing any counseling until you have thoroughly developed your own approach.

4. Developing a personalized approach to counseling:
    a. should be accomplished early in your counselor training.
    b. is an ongoing process and your model will continuously undergo revision.
    c. can best be done with supervision from experienced counselors.
    d. can be accomplished only by blending two or more theories of counseling.
    e. b and c

Session 1: The Beginning of Counseling

5. The initial session is the foundation of the counseling relationship because:
    a. it involves teaching the client how she/he can benefit most from counseling.
    b. the structure for future sessions is established.
    c. the client is assessing whether counseling is a "safe" place in which she/he is able to trust the counselor.
    d. it is where the client talks about the reasons for coming to therapy.
    e. all of the above

6. Informed consent is defined as:
    a. parental approval for counseling.
    b. papers the client must sign to pay agreed upon fees.
    c. giving the client enough information about the therapy process so that she/he can make an informed choice about whether or not she or he wants to be a client.
    d. informing the client of the importance of the therapeutic relationship.

7. Dr. Corey utilizes which two of the following approaches in the early phase of counseling?
    a. existential therapy and person-centered
    b. behavioral approach and reality therapy
    c. rational emotive behavior therapy
    d. cognitive behavioral and Adlerian therapy

Session 2: The Therapeutic Relationship

8. Which therapeutic approaches place special emphasis on the quality of the client/therapist relationship?
    a. reality therapy and feminist therapy
    b. existential, person-centered and Gestalt approaches
    c. person-centered approaches only
    d. none of the above

9. According to the person-centered approach, what are the three main characteristics of the therapist which form the essence of the therapeutic relationship?
   a. trust, accurate assessment, and a collaborative relationship
   b. congruence, unconditional positive regard, empathic understanding
   c. respect, intuition, self-actualization
   d. unconditional positive regard, flexibility, interest
   e. empathic understanding, sympathy, insight

10. A working therapeutic relationship is essential:
   a. only in the initial session.
   b. only for person-centered therapy.
   c. for therapy to be productive.
   d. primarily in the early phases of therapy.

Session 3: Establishing Therapeutic Goals

11. Goal alignment, where counselor and client collaborate on developing goals for counseling is a term described in:
   a. Alderian approaches.
   b. behavioral approaches.
   c. psychodynamic approaches.
   d. family systems approaches.
   e. Gestalt therapy.

12. Goals are best determined by:
   a. the client.
   b. the counselor.
   c. the client and the counselor.
   d. the therapeutic approach being utilized.
   e. the client's insurance plan.

13. Developing goals is something that is done:
   a. in the first few counseling sessions.
   b. when the client is ready to talk about goals.
   c. throughout the course of therapy.
   d. in the later stages of therapy.

14. The approach which stresses breaking goals down into specific and operational terms is:
   a. systems approach.
   b. person-centered approach.
   c. existential approach.
   d. behavioral approach.
   e. psychodynamic therapy.

Session 4: Understanding and Dealing with Diversity

15. In understanding diversity, it is important for the counselor to:
   a. identify early on what the client's cultural issues are.
   b. let the client bring up his or her concern regarding differences.
   c. have considerable knowledge about the cultures of the clients with whom he/she works, and to be of the same culture as the client.
   d. attend to issues of diversity as prescribed by the therapeutic approach

16. The best source of information about differences between the counselor and the client is:
   a. the counselor.
   b. supervisors.
   c. books on culture.
   d. the client.
   e. both a and b

17. Knowledge of a client's culture is not enough. Each individual client must be seen in the context of:
    a. the backdrop of his or her cultural group.
    b. the degree to which he or she has become acculturated.
    c. the level of development of racial identity.
    d. all of the above
    e. none of the above

Session 5: Understanding and Dealing with Resistance

18. Psychoanalytic approaches view resistance as:
    a. a result of incorrect assessment techniques.
    b. something that is rarely discussed in therapy.
    c. rich material to work with in therapy.
    d. stubborn refusal of the client to cooperate.

19. The goal(s) in working with resistance is to:
    a. recognize it.
    b. work with it therapeutically.
    c. use it as a catalyst for exploration.
    d. all of the above
    e. none of the above

20. The therapeutic approach(es) that emphasize(s) working with resistance is/are:
    a. behavioral approaches.
    b. psychoanalytic approaches.
    c. existential approaches.
    d. systems approaches.
    e. b and c

Session 6: Cognitive Focus in Counseling

21. The major emphasis in the cognitive focus is on:
    a. behavior.
    b. feeling.
    c. thinking.
    d. catharsis and insight.

22. Two main forms of cognitive behavioral approaches were developed by:
    a. Ellis and Beck.
    b. Ellis and Adler.
    c. Glasser and Freud.
    d. Freud and Adler.

23. Which of the following is not a cognitive behavioral technique?
    a. self-talk
    b. socratic questioning
    c. exploring anxiety as a condition of living
    d. debating with internal dialog
    e. bibliotherapy

Session 7: Emotive Focus in Counseling

24. In counseling, emotions are expressed and released in a process referred to as:
    a. projecting.
    b. resistance.
    c. desensitizing.
    d. catharsis.
    e. acting out.

25. Rather than having clients talk about the emotion surrounding a situation or event, it is best to have them:
   a. try to identify those emotions through homework assignments.
   b. work experientially with the situation in the here-and-now.
   c. reserve such matters for discussion in a group setting.
   d. focus on their behavior in that situation.
   e. all of the above

26. Significant personal change is likely for clients only if they:
   a. transfer what they have learned in therapy to everyday situations.
   b. like their counselor.
   c. work through any resistance in therapy that might occur.
   d. can identify the cause of their problems.

27. Gestalt therapy is one approach that helps clients work with emotions via:
   a. here-and-now focus.
   b. awareness.
   c. role playing.
   d. contact.
   e. all of the above

Session 8: Behavioral Focus in Counseling

28. The main focus of behavioral approaches is on:
   a. thinking.
   b. homework activities.
   c. exploration.
   d. doing.
   e. catharsis.

29. The relationship of basic counseling skills, such as active listening and accurate empathy, to behavioral approaches is:
   a. they are diametrically opposed.
   b. they can and should be integrated into a behavioral approach.
   c. they neither help nor hinder behavioral approaches.
   d. none of the above

30. Which of the following is not one of the wide variety of behavioral techniques?
   a. emoting
   b. reinforcement
   c. modeling
   d. desensitization
   e. relaxation training

31. The WDEP system where W=wants, D=direction, E=evaluation and P=planning is a form of:
   a. cognitive restructuring.
   b. desensitization.
   c. reality therapy.
   d. self-talk.
   e. Adlerian therapy.

Session 9: An Integrative Perspective

32. The integrative approach which chooses techniques from many approaches is:
   a. person-centered approach.
   b. theoretical integration.
   c. technical eclecticism.
   d. rational-emotive approach.

33. The approach that has the goal of producing a conceptual framework that synthesizes two or more approaches is:
    a. person-centered approach.
    b. theoretical integration.
    c. technical eclecticism.
    d. rational-emotive approach.

34. An integrative approach has gained wide acceptance among counselors because:
    a. no one theory has universal application.
    b. clients are integrated beings where thinking, feeling, and behavior play major roles.
    c. the needs of the clients may require the therapist to be able to draw upon a number of various techniques.
    d. as a counselor, several theories may play an important role in one's own personal approach.
    e. all of the above

35. Which of the following approaches naturally lends itself to an integrative approach?
    a. Alderian
    b. rational-emotive therapy
    c. cognitive therapy
    d. Gestalt therapy
    e. psychodynamic therapy

**Session 10: Working with Transference
and Countertransference**

36. Transference, which refers to the client's experiencing with the therapist relationship issues from earlier situations, is at the heart of:
    a. reality therapy.
    b. rational-emotive therapy.
    c. existential approaches.
    d. psychodynamic approaches.
    e. cognitive approaches.

37. Countertransference is defined as:
    a. the client's expressing negative feelings toward the counselor.
    b. the counselor's unconscious emotional reaction to a client.
    c. the counselor's providing objective feedback to the client.
    d. the client's denial of any hostile feelings toward the counselor.
    e. the counselor's ability to enter the subjective world of the client.

38. The most basic tool to help the counselor with transference and countertransference is:
    a. self-knowledge.
    b. familiarity with various approaches in dealing with transference and countertransference.
    c. knowing the research.
    d. always questioning the client.
    e. taking more counseling classes.

**Session 11: Understanding How the Past
Influences the Present**

39. Which approach(es) place(s) little emphasis on the client's past?
    a. reality therapy
    b. behavior therapy
    c. cognitive therapy
    d. all of the above
    e. none of the above

40. One reason for exploring the client's past is that it may shed light on the:
    a. unconscious.
    b. present.
    d. resistance.
    d. approach to utilize.
    e. countertransference.

41. Understanding significant turning points in the client's developmental years:
    a. is generally useless.
    b. is generally useful in itself.
    c. may shed light on current key themes in the client's life.
    d. is essential for any significant therapy to occur.

Session 12: Working toward Decisions and Behavior Change

42. The approach that refers to the individual as the architect of his/her life is:
    a. existential therapy.
    b. behavior therapy.
    c. reality therapy.
    d. Adlerian therapy.
    e. psychoanalytic therapy.

43. Making behavioral changes is a central theme in which of the following therapies?
    a. existential therapy
    b. Gestalt therapy
    c. cognitive behavioral therapy
    d. behavioral therapy
    e. all of the above

44. Most therapies have as a basic assumption the notion that:
    a. the client is a victim of the past.
    b. change can occur only as directed by the counselor.
    c. with the proper tools, the client is able to make new decisions and change behavior patterns.
    d. the concept of free will is just a theoretical construct.

Session 13: Evaluation and Termination

45. Termination of therapy is often difficult for the:
    a. client.
    b. counselor.
    c. client and counselor.
    d. neither the client nor the counselor.

46. Which of the following is important to do in the last phase of counseling?
    a. Review the course of treatment.
    b. Discuss what about therapy was useful and what was not.
    c. Discuss feelings of separation.
    d. Help the client plan how she/he will proceed with implementing changes.
    e. all of the above

47. When ending therapy, it is probably best to:
    a. refer the client to another counselor for any future work.
    b. leave the door open so a client may return for counseling as needed.
    c. encourage the client to try to handle problems independently from that point forward.
    d. offer to have the client phone the counselor anytime he or she wishes to discuss issues.
    e. none of the above

General Questions

48. Which of the following are major categories of the therapeutic approaches?
    a. psychodynamic
    b. existential
    c. cognitive behavioral
    d. systems approaches
    e. all of the above

49. To assist in developing your integrative approach you can:
    a. practice with supervision.
    b. let yourself become your own client and think about what it would be like to experience your approach and therapy.
    c. attend workshops and courses.
    d. read about the theory.
    e. all of the above

50. Practicing reflectively refers to:
    a. being able to examine after a session why you counseled in a particular fashion and how that was for you and the client.
    b. using active listening techniques.
    c. a method used in existential therapies.
    d. being able to examine countertransference issues.
    e. thinking exclusively within the framework of a single theory.

Comprehension Test Answer Key

1. b	14. d	27. e	40. b
2. d	15. b	28. d	41. c
3. a	16. d	29. b	42. a
4. e	17. d	30. a	43. e
5. e	18. c	31. c	44. c
6. c	19. d	32. c	45. c
7. a	20. e	33. b	46. e
8. b	21. c	34. e	47. b
9. b	22. a	35. e	48. e
10. c	23. c	36. d	49. e
11. a	24. d	37. b	50. a
12. c	25. b	38. a	
13. c	26. a	39. d	

VII

On-Line Quiz Items

Theory and Practice

of Counseling

and Psychotherapy

Theory and Practice of Counseling and Psychotherapy

General Issues in Counseling

1. For counselors who work with culturally diverse client populations, it is especially important to:
    a. be aware of their own cultural heritage.
    b. have a broad base of counseling techniques that can be employed with flexibility.
    c. consider the cultural context of their clients in determining what interventions are appropriate.
    d. examine their assumptions pertaining to cultural values.
    e. all of the above

2. In the text, the main reason given for having counseling students receive some form of psychotherapy is to help them to:
    a. work through early childhood trauma.
    b. learn to deal with countertransference.
    c. recognize and resolve their co-dependent tendencies.
    d. become self-actualized individuals.
    e. learn technical skills needed to confront difficult clients.

3. With respect to the role of values in the counseling process, it is most accurate to state that:
    a. counseling can best be considered as teaching and persuading clients to act the right way.
    b. counselors would do well to maintain an indifferent, neutral, and passive role by simply listening to everything the client reports.
    c. counselors should avoid challenging the values of their clients.
    d. counselors avoid imposing their values, but they are likely to expose their values to clients.
    e. counselors should strictly keep their own values separate from their counseling practice.

4. Culturally encapsulated counselors would be most likely to:
    a. depend entirely on their own internalized value assumptions about what is good for people.
    b. have an appreciation for a multicultural perspective in their counseling practice.
    c. recognize the cultural dimensions their clients bring to therapy.
    d. accept clients who have a different set of assumptions about life.

5. Essential components of effective multicultural counseling practice include all of the following except for:
    a. counselors avoid becoming involved in out-of-office interventions.
    b. counselors feel comfortable with their clients' values and beliefs.
    c. counselors are aware of how their own biases could affect ethnic minority clients.
    d. counselors employ institutional intervention skills on behalf of their clients when necessary or appropriate.
    e. counselors are aware of how their culture experiences continue to influence them.

6. Because dual relationships are necessarily complex and multidimensional:
    a. there are few simple and absolute answers to neatly resolve them.
    b. they must always be avoided if you hope to be ethical.
    c. they are prohibited by most of the codes of ethics of the various professions.
    d. they are considered to be unethical, unprofessional, and illegal.
    e. all of the above.

7. Researchers have identified some traits of the effective counselor. What best captures the spirit of these studies?
    a. Effective counselors are emotionally healthy.
    b. Effective counselors are tolerant of divergent beliefs and lifestyles.
    c. Effective counselors have a deep interest in people.
    d. Effective counselors hold positive beliefs about people and see them as trustworthy and capable.
    e. all of the above

8. Personal therapy for the therapist can be instrumental in assisting them:
   a. to heal their own psychological wounds.
   b. to gain an experiential sense of what it is like to be a client.
   c. to understand their own needs and motives for choosing to become professional helpers.
   d. to work through their own personal conflicts.
   e. all of the above

9. Which of the following is not considered an essential skill of a culturally effective counselor?
   a. Being able to modify techniques to accommodate cultural differences.
   b. Being able to send and receive both verbal and nonverbal messages accurately.
   c. Being able to get clients to intensify their feelings by helping them to vividly reexperience early childhood events.
   d. Assuming the role of consultant and change agent.

10. According to the text, _____ includes taking responsibility and preventing burnout.
    a. becoming an effective multicultural counselor
    b. staying alive as a person and as a professional
    c. dealing with our anxieties
    d. tolerating ambiguity
    e. none of the above

Psychoanalytic Therapy

11. During psychoanalytic treatment, clients are typically asked:
    a. to monitor their behavioral changes by keeping a journal that describes what they do at home and at work.
    b. to make major changes in their lifestyle.
    c. not to make radical changes in their lifestyle.
    d. to give up their friendships.
    e. none of the above

12. Countertransference refers to the:
    a. irrational reactions clients have toward their therapists.
    b. irrational reactions therapists have toward their clients.
    c. projections of the client.
    d. client's need to be special in the therapist's eyes.
    e. the realistic perceptions a client has toward a counselor

13. Analysis of transference is central to psychoanalytic approaches because:
    a. it keeps the therapist hidden and thus feeling secure.
    b. it allows clients to relive their past in therapy.
    c. it helps clients formulate specific plans to change behavior.
    d. it is considered the *only* route to working with unconscious material.
    e. it helps clients examine their faulty beliefs and correct their logic.

14. Individuals who display exhibitionistic traits, who seek attention and admiration from others, and who are extremely self-absorbed might have which of the following personality disorders?
    a. narcissistic
    b. manic-depressive
    c. borderline
    d. psychotic

15. Which term refers to the repetition of interpretations and the overcoming of resistance so that clients can resolve neurotic patterns?
    a. working through
    b. transference neurosis
    c. family of origin work
    d. countertransference

16. How does the ego-defense mechanism of identification help a person cope with anxiety?
    a. It protects them from a sense of being a failure.
    b. It helps explain away a bruised ego.
    c. It swallows the values and standards of others.
    d. It enhances their feelings of self-worth.
    e. both (a) and (d)

17. Which of the following ego-defense mechanisms is a way of negating a disapproving thought or behavior?
    a. compensation
    b. repression
    c. identification
    d. displacement
    e. rationalization

18. If an infant's needs are not met, the infant will develop a sense of:
    a. shame and doubt.
    b. mistrust.
    c. isolation.
    d. despair.
    e. inferiority.

19. According to object-relations theory, the stage of development known as *normal infantile autism* involves:
    a. responding more to physical tension states than to psychological processes.
    b. perceiving parts rather than a unified self.
    c. inability to differentiate self from mother.
    d. all of the above
    e. all but (b)

20. The "fundamental rule" of psychoanalysis involves clients:
    a. recording their dreams.
    b. lying down on the couch.
    c. saying whatever comes to mind without censoring.
    d. writing down and discussing critical turning points in their early childhood.
    e. g willing to participate in at least three therapy sessions each week for at least five years.

Adlerian Therapy

21. Which of the following did Adler not stress?
    a. the unity of personality
    b. focus on reliving early childhood experiences
    c. the direction people are headed toward
    d. a unique style of life that is an expression of life goals
    e. feelings of inferiority

22. The phenomenological orientation pays attention to the:
    a. events that occur at various stages of life.
    b. manner in which biological and environmental forces limit us.
    c. the manner in which people interact with each other.
    d. internal dynamics that drive a person.
    e. way that individuals perceive their world.

23. The concept of fictional finalism refers to:
    a. an imagined central goal that guides a person's behavior.
    b. the hopeless stance that leads to personal defeat.
    c. the manner in which people express their need to belong.
    d. the process of assessing one's style of life.
    e. the interpretation that individuals give to life events.

24. Adlerians value early recollections as an important clue to understanding:
    a. one's sexual and aggressive instincts.
    b. the bonding process between mother and child.
    c. the individual's lifestyle.
    d. the unconscious dynamics that motivate behavior.
    e. the origin of psychological trauma in early childhood.

25. Which of the following is not an aspect of the therapeutic process in Adlerian counseling?
    a. identifying mistaken goals
    b. exploring faulty assumptions
    c. reeducation of the client toward constructive goals
    d. psychological testing
    e. offering encouragement

26. Which of the following is not a contribution of the Adlerian approach?
    a. the variety of cognitive, behavioral, and experiential techniques available
    b. therapist resourcefulness in drawing on many methods that can be applied to a diverse range of clients in various settings.
    c. that the approach is well suited to short-term formats
    d. the impact of Adler's ideas on other therapy approaches
    e. the evidence-based techniques that can be used in both individual and group counseling

27. _____ refers to an individual's basic orientation to life, or one's personality, and includes the themes that characterize the person's existence.
    a. Superiority
    b. Lifestyle
    c. Social interest and community feeling
    d. Self-acceptance

28. Four central objectives that correspond to the four phases of the Adlerian therapeutic process includes:
    a. informed consent; confidentiality; establishing rapport; unconditional positive regard.
    b. Establishing the relationship; exploring the individual's dynamics; encouraging self-understanding and insight; helping with reorientation.
    c. unconditional positive regard, empathy, congruence, genuineness
    d. none of the above

29. Which child tends to behave as if he or she were in a race and appears to be in training to surpass an older sibling?
    a. the oldest child
    b. the second child
    c. the middle child
    d. the youngest child
    e. the only child

30. Which child generally receives a good deal of attention, tends to be dependable and hard-working, and strives to keep ahead?
    a. the oldest child
    b. the second child
    c. the middle child
    d. the youngest child
    e. the only child

31. Existential therapy is best described as a:
    a. systematic approach to behavior modification.
    b. philosophy on which a therapist operates.
    c. set of techniques designed to change behavior.
    d. form of psychoanalytic therapy.
    e. separate school of therapy.

32. Which of the following is a limitation of the existential approach in working with culturally diverse client populations?
    a. the focus on understanding and accepting the client
    b. the focus on finding meaning in one's life
    c. the focus on death as a catalyst to living fully
    d. the focus on one's own responsibility rather than the focus on social conditions

33. Existential therapy places emphasis on:
    a. a systematic approach to changing behavior.
    b. the quality of the client/therapist relationship.
    c. teaching clients cognitive and behavioral coping skills.
    d. uncovering early childhood traumatic events.
    e. working through the transference relationship.

34. Which of the following is not true of the existential concept of aloneness?
    a. it is part of the human condition
    b. it is a source of strength
    c. it is the result of our neurotic fear of intimacy
    d. we must learn to stand alone before we can stand beside another
    e. aloneness can be a path to finding one's identity

35. In working with a client from an existential perspective, the goals of therapy would most likely be:
    a. reliving the client's early childhood through the transference relationship.
    b. increasing awareness and the potential for choice.
    c. to facilitate doing family of origin work.
    d. complete restructuring of his or her personality.

36. The existential therapist would probably agree that:
    a. aloneness is a sign of detachment.
    b. aloneness is a condition that needs to be cured.
    c. ultimately we are alone.
    d. we are alone unless we have a faith in religion.

37. Guilt and anxiety are viewed as:
    a. behaviors that are unrealistic.
    b. the result of traumatic situations in childhood.
    c. conditions that should be removed or cured.
    d. all of the above
    e. none of the above

38. Which of the following is *not* true about Frankl's logotherapy?
    a. It is designed to help the person find meaning in life.
    b. It involves working with a client's "will to meaning."
    c. The therapist points out that clients can find meaning in suffering.
    d. The more we seek meaning, the more we are likely to find it.
    e. In developing this approach, Frankl was influenced by writings of existential philosophers.

39. "Bad faith" refers to:
    a. failing to live in accordance with the Scriptures.
    b. ignoring the spiritual aspects of counseling.
    c. the inauthenticity of not accepting personal freedom.
    d. choosing to live in selfish ways.
    e. living with anxiety and guilt.

40. According to the existentialists, anxiety is generated by:
    a. the lack of guarantees in life.
    b. stress in interpersonal relationships.
    c. a neurotic striving to be better than others.
    d. The striving to overcome feelings of inadequacy.
    e. Both (c) and (d)

Person-Centered Therapy

41. Unconditional positive regard refers to:
    a. feeling a sense of liking for the client.
    b. accepting clients as worthy persons.
    c. approving of a client's behavior.
    d. agreeing with a client's values.
    e. accepting a client if they meet the therapist's expectations.

42. In person-centered therapy, transference is:
    a. seen as a necessary, but not a sufficient, condition of therapy.
    b. viewed as a core part of the therapeutic process.
    c. regarded as a neurotic distortion.
    d. a result of ineptness on the therapist's part.
    e. not an essential nor significant factor in the therapy process.

43. According to Rogers, the three core conditions that create a growth-promoting climate are:
    a. congruence, conditional acceptance, faith in a client.
    b. congruence, unconditional positive regard, empathic understanding.
    c. total love and caring, therapist transparency, and full empathy.
    d. objectivity, detachment, and warm regard.
    e. commitment, compassion, and confrontation.

44. Congruence refers to the therapist's:
    a. genuineness.
    b. empathy for clients.
    c. positive regard.
    d. respect for clients.
    e. judgmental attitude.

45. Accurate empathic understanding refers to the therapist's ability to:
    a. accurately diagnose the client's central problem.
    b. objectively understand the dynamics of a client.
    c. like and care for the client.
    d. sense the inner world of the client's subjective experience.

46. According to person-centered theory, a personal relationship between the client and therapist in which the therapist demonstrates attitudes of caring, empathy, positive regard, genuineness, and understanding is:
    a. a necessary and sufficient condition for therapy to occur.
    b. a necessary but not sufficient condition for therapy to occur.
    c. neither a necessary nor a sufficient condition of therapy.
    d. none of the above.

47. Person-centered therapy focuses on:
   a. the role that our belief system plays in creating emotions.
   b. past experiences with our parents as the determinant of the level of our present happiness.
   c. the need for clients to adopt the values of the dominant society.
   d. clients' willingness to accept their ultimate loneliness and the inevitability of their eventual nonbeing.
   e. none of the above

48. The current formulation of person-centered therapy:
   a. stresses the role of cognitive factors in therapy.
   b. encourages an eclectic spirit in using a wider variety of methods.
   c. allows the therapist greater freedom to participate more actively in the relationship.
   d. calls for therapists to challenge the belief system of clients.
   e. both (b) and (c)

49. Roger's basic assumptions were that people:
   a. are essentially trustworthy.
   b. have vast potential for self-understanding and resolving their own problems.
   c. are capable of self-directed growth.
   d. all of the above
   e. none of the above

50. In the last few years of his life, Rogers devoted much of his attention to:
   a. the facilitation of personal growth and encounter groups.
   b. integrating psychotherapy with religion.
   c. empirical research on the process and outcomes of therapy.
   d. the promotion of world peace.
   e. both (a) and (b)

Gestalt Therapy

51. Which of the following is not true of Gestalt therapy?
   a. The focus is on the what and how of behavior.
   b. The focus is on the here-and-now.
   c. The focus is on integrating fragmented parts of the personality.
   d. The focus is on unfinished business from the past.
   e. The focus is on the why of behavior.

52. According to the Gestalt approach:
   a. awareness is by and of itself therapeutic.
   b. awareness is not a critical factor in the change process.
   c. awareness without specific behavioral change is useless.
   d. awareness consists of understanding the origin of one's problems.

53. What is a limitation (or limitations) of Gestalt therapy as it is applied to working with culturally diverse populations?
   a. Clients who have been culturally conditioned to be emotionally reserved might not see value in experiential techniques.
   b. Clients may be "put off" by a focus on catharsis.
   c. Clients may be looking for specific advice of solving practical problems.
   d. Clients may believe that to show one's vulnerability is to be weak.
   e. All of the above.

54. Gestalt techniques are aimed at:
   a. integrating conflicting aspects within the person.
   b. having the client make new decisions from a cognitive stance.
   c. teaching clients the basics of rational thinking.
   d. teaching clients how to discover the causes of future problems.

55. Which of the following is not a key concept of Gestalt therapy?
    a. acceptance of personal responsibility
    b. intellectual understanding of one's problems
    c. awareness
    d. unfinished business
    e. dealing with the impasse

56. Gestalt techniques are aimed at:
    a. integrating conflicting aspects within the person.
    b. having the client understand how his or her family of origin impacts current behavior.
    c. teaching the client how to think rationally.
    d. teaching the client how to discover the causes of future problems.
    e. both (c) and (d)

57. The Gestalt approach can be applied to:
    a. individual counseling.
    b. group counseling.
    c. school and classroom situations.
    d. intensive workshops.
    e. all of the above

58. The therapeutic goals of Gestalt therapy include encouraging the client to:
    a. move toward greater self-awareness.
    b. gradually assume ownership of and responsibility for their experience.
    c. become more independent so that they no longer need to ask for help from others.
    d. all of the above
    e. (a) and (b) only

59. Gestalt therapies would not use which of the following type(s) of questions when working with a client?
    a. how
    b. what
    c. why
    d. all of the above
    e. both (a) and (b)

60. A Gestalt technique that involves having clients become aware of the many preparatory means they use in bolstering their social roles is:
    a. the exaggeration experiment.
    b. the reversal technique.
    c. the rehearsal experiment.
    d. the "I take responsibility for…"
    e. making the rounds.

Behavior Therapy

61. A behavior therapist working with a client would most likely:
    a. begin with a comprehensive assessment.
    b. put the focus on exploring the past.
    c. direct attention to the client's nonverbal expressions.
    d. be interested in exploring childhood trauma.
    e. ask the client to talk to an empty chair.

62. The person who is considered as a key pioneer of clinical behavior therapy because of his broadening of its conceptual bases and because of developing innovative clinical techniques is:
    a. Carl Rogers
    b. Alfred Adler
    c. B. F. Skinner
    d. Arnold Lazarus
    e. Robert Wubbolding

63. All of the following are characteristics of behavioral approaches except for:
    a. behavior therapy relies on the principles and procedures of the scientific method.
    b. behavior therapy specifies treatment goals in concrete and objective terms.
    c. behavior therapy focuses on the client's current problems and the factors influencing them.
    d. behavior therapy emphasizes observing overt behavior.
    e. behavior therapy employs the same procedures to every client with a particular dysfunctional behavior.

64. Which of the following is not a misconception about behavior therapy?
    a. the overall goal is to remove the client's symptoms
    b. new symptoms appear because underlying causes were not treated in sufficient depth
    c. client goals are generally determined and imposed by the therapist
    d. a good working relationship between the therapist and the client is seen as necessary, though not sufficient, in order for effective therapy to occur

65. If your client wanted to change a behavior such as learning to control smoking, drinking, or eating which behavioral technique would be most appropriate to employ?
    a. systematic desensitization
    b. self-management
    c. assertion training
    d. punishment
    e. relaxation training

66. What separates behavior therapy from other approaches?
    a. insistence on research supporting the efficacy of interventions with particular problems
    b. reliance on evidence-based treatment techniques
    c. commitment to applying experimental methods to the analysis of therapeutic practice
    d. all of the above
    e. the collaborative quality of the client/therapist relationship

67. Contemporary behavior therapy can be understood by considering which major area(s) of development?
    a. classical conditioning
    b. operant conditioning
    c. cognitive behavior therapy
    d. social learning theory
    e. all of the above

68. With respect to the goals of behavior therapy, it can be said that:
    a. they occupy a place of central importance in behavior therapy.
    b. the general goal of behavior therapy is to create new conditions for learning.
    c. the client usually formulates the goals.
    d. continual assessment occurs throughout therapy.
    e. all of the above

69. Examples of _____ include reading, writing, driving a car, and eating with utensils.
    a. classical conditioning
    b. social learning theory
    c. operant conditioning
    d. cognitive behavior therapy

70. Contemporary behavior therapy places emphasis on:
    a. the interplay between the individual and the environment.
    b. helping clients acquire insight into the causes of their problems.
    c. a phenomenological approach to understanding the person.
    d. encouraging clients to reexperience unfinished business with significant others by role playing with them in the present.
    e. creating solutions instead of talking about problems.

Cognitive Behavior Therapy

71. REBT stresses that human beings:
    a. think, emote, and behave simultaneously.
    b. think without emoting.
    c. emote without thinking.
    d. behave without emoting or thinking.

72. According to REBT, neurosis is the result of:
    a. inadequate mothering during infancy.
    b. failure to fulfill our existential needs.
    c. excessive feelings.
    d. irrational thinking.

73. In working with a client, Albert Ellis would likely use?
    a. behavioral techniques
    b. cognitive techniques
    c. emotive techniques
    d. all of the above
    e. none of the above

74. According to Albert Ellis, a warm and personal client/therapist relationship is:
    a. necessary, but not sufficient, for change to occur.
    b. necessary and sufficient for change to occur.
    c. neither necessary nor sufficient for change to occur.
    d. none of the above

75. REBT stresses:
    a. thinking, critically analyzing, and doing.
    b. subjectivity, existential anxiety, and striving for meaning.
    c. support, empathy, and personal warmth.
    d. narrative conversations and creating new stories.
    e. the I/Thou encounter between client and therapist.

76. What words would best describe REBT?
    a. nondirective and client-centered
    b. experiential
    c. highly didactic and very directive
    d. both (a) and (b)
    e. none of the above

77. REBT is based on the idea that we become emotionally disturbed because:
    a. others indoctrinate us with irrational ideas.
    b. we tend to keep reindoctrinating ourselves with irrational beliefs.
    c. others withdraw their love if we do not think as they do.
    d. both (a) and (c)

78. REBT methodology includes all of the following methods except for:
    a. shame-attacking exercises.
    b. homework assignments.
    c. use of force and vigor
    d. logical analysis.
    e. power analysis and power intervention.

79. Donald Meichenbaum's cognitive behavior modification is especially designed for:
    a. alleviating symptoms of depression.
    b. curing clients of phobias.
    c. coping skills programs.
    d. severely disturbed individuals.
    e. those with eating disorders.

80. In Beck's cognitive therapy, the therapist and client work together to uncover and examine faulty interpretations. This process is known as:
    a. automatic thinking.
    b. collaborative empiricism.
    c. technical empiricism.
    d. stress inoculation.
    e. therapeutic exploration of self-talk.

Reality Therapy

81. Reality therapy rests on the central idea that:
    a. thinking largely determines how we feel and behave.
    b. we choose our total behavior, and thus are responsible for what we do, think, and feel.
    c. environmental factors largely control how we feel and what we do.
    d. the way to change dysfunctional behavior is to re-experience a situation where we originally became psychologically stuck.

82. The core of reality therapy consists of:
    a. teaching clients how to acquire rational beliefs instead of irrational beliefs.
    b. helping clients to create a new preferred story.
    c. giving clients opportunities to cope with stress by using stress inoculation techniques.
    d. teaching clients to take effective control of their own lives.
    e. identifying their cognitive distortions by means of a Socratic dialogue.

83. All of the following are procedures that are commonly used by reality therapy, except for:
    a. exploring wants, needs, and perceptions.
    b. deconstructing problem-saturated narrative before attempting to co-create new stories.
    c. focusing on current behavior.
    d. planning and commitment.
    e. skillful questioning.

84. Which of the following statements is true as it applies to choice theory?
    a. Behavior is the result of external forces.
    b. We are controlled by the events that occur in our lives.
    c. We can control the behavior of others by learning to actively listen to them.
    d. We are motivated primarily by internal forces, and our behavior is our best attempt to get what we want.
    e. We can more easily control our feelings than our actions.

85. Choice theory tends to focus on:
    a. feeling and physiology.
    b. doing and thinking.
    c. coming to a fuller understanding of the past.
    d. the underlying causes for feeling depressed or anxious.
    e. how the family system controls our decisions.

86. Which of the following is not a characteristic of reality therapy?
    a. emphasis on the quality of one's relationships with significant others
    b. paying attention to "sparkling events" that contradict problem-saturated stories
    c. existential-phenomenological orientation
    d. keeping therapy in the present
    e. getting clients to evaluate what they are doing

87. The view of human nature underlying reality therapy is that:
    a. we have a need for survival.
    b. we have the need for love and belonging.
    c. we have a need for power.
    d. we have a need for freedom and fun.
    e. all of the above

88. Reality therapy was designed originally for working with:
    a. elementary school children.
    b. youthful offenders in detention facilities.
    c. alcoholics.
    d. drug addicts.

89. Once clients make an evaluation about their behavior and decide how they want to change, the reality therapist expects them to:
    a. express pent-up feelings.
    b. develop specific plans to change behavior.
    c. make a commitment to carry out plans in daily life.
    d. become self-critical if they do not carry out their plans.
    e. both (b) and (c)

90. Choice theory posits that we are born with five genetically encoded needs that drive us all of our lives. These five needs are:
    a. survival, love and belonging, power, freedom, and fun.
    b. shelter, food, affection, gratification, and self-actualization.
    c. shelter, food, intimacy, job satisfaction, and self-actualization.
    d. survival, intimacy, freedom, power, and success.
    e. none of the above

Feminist Therapy

91. Which of the following themes would clients in feminist therapy be least likely to explore?
    a. messages from society pertaining to gender-role socialization
    b. power structures
    c. transference reactions toward their therapist
    d. cultural forces influencing behavior

92. Which of the following techniques would a feminist therapist be least likely to employ?
    a. exception questions
    b. assertiveness training
    c. gender-role analysis
    d. power analysis and intervention

93. Of the following, which intervention would a feminist therapist probably consider most essential?
    a. challenging irrational beliefs
    b. maintaining an anonymous role as a therapist
    c. conducting a lifestyle analysis
    d. social action
    e. conducting a functional assessment of a specific problem area

94. All of the following are reasons many feminist therapists do not use diagnostic labels, or use them reluctantly, except for which one?
    a. Diagnostic labels reinforce gender role stereotypes.
    b. Diagnostic labels reflect the inappropriate application of power in the therapeutic relationship.
    c. Diagnostic labels focus on the social factors that cause dysfunctional behavior.
    d. Diagnostic labels encourage adjustment to the norms of the status quo.
    e. Diagnostic labels reduce one's respect for clients.

95. An alternative to traditional diagnosis and assessment that is preferred by feminist therapists is:
    a. power analysis.
    b. gender role analysis.
    c. lifestyle analysis.
    d. exploration of family constellation.
    e. exploration of basic mistakes.

96. The concept in which the individuals' personal problems have social and political causes refers to:
    a. the lifespan perspective.
    b. the personal is political.
    c. phenomenology
    d. object-relations
    e. none of the above

97. The idea that a woman's sense of self depends largely on how she connects with others refers to:
    a. lifestyle perspective.
    b. lifespan perspective.
    c. holism.
    d. self-in-relation theory.
    e. gendercentrism.

98. Ethnocentrism is the idea that:
    a. there are two separate paths of development for women and men.
    b. power should be balanced in a relationship.
    c. one's own cultural group is superior to others and that other groups should be judged based on one's own standards.
    d. a women's sense of self is dependent upon her ethnic identity.
    e. none of the above

99. A theory that uses male-oriented constructs to draw conclusions about human nature is:
    a. gendercentrism.
    b. power analysis.
    c. gender schema.
    d. androcentricism.
    e. egalitarianism.

100. A technique whereby the counselor changes the perspective on looking at an individual's behavior, shifting from an intrapersonal to an interpersonal definition of a client's problem is:
    a. schema restructuring.
    b. cognitive restructuring.
    c. relabeling.
    d. assertiveness training.
    e. reframing.

101. Which of the following is true of narrative therapy and solution-focused therapy?
   a. The client is an expert on his or her own life.
   b. Prior to selecting treatment strategies, it is essential to formulate a diagnosis.
   c. Because therapist is the expert on change, it is his or her role to offer advice to clients.
   d. Clients should adjust to social and cultural norms.
   e. For change to occur, clients must first acquire insight into their problems.

102. Of the following, a major goal of narrative therapy is to
   a. teach clients more effective self-talk they can use in coping with their problems.
   b. assist clients in exploring the feeling dimensions attached to their problems.
   c. invite clients to describe their experience in new and fresh language, and in doing this opening up new vistas of what is possible.
   d. uncover a client's self-defeating cognitions.
   e. enable clients to gain clarity about the ways their family of origin still impacts them today.

103. Which of the following interventions is least likely to be used by a narrative therapist?
   a. externalizing conversations
   b. mapping the influence of a problem
   c. power analysis and intervention
   d. the search for unique outcomes
   e. documenting the evidence

104. All of the following are techniques commonly used in solution-focused therapy except for
   a. exception questions.
   b. scaling questions.
   c. the miracle question.
   d. functional assessment.
   e. formula first session task.

105. Two of the major founders of solution-focused brief therapy are
   a. Michael White and David Epston.
   b. Insoo Kim Berg and Steve deShazer.
   c. Harlene Anderson and Harold Goolishian.
   d. Tom Andersen and Bill O'Hanlon.
   e. John Walter and Jane Peller

106. The therapeutic process in solution-focused brief therapy involves all of the following except for the notion
   a. that therapists are experts in assessment and diagnosis.
   b. of asking clients about those times when their problems were not present or when the problems were less severe.
   c. that clients are the experts on their own lives.
   d. that solutions evolve out of therapeutic conversations and dialogues.
   e. searching for what works and encouraging clients to do more of this.

107. Pre-therapy change is a solution-focused therapy technique that
   a. is arrived at by asking clients about exceptions to their problems.
   b. asks clients to address changes that have taken place from the time they made an appointment to the first therapy session.
   c. is based on a series of tests that the client takes prior to beginning therapy to get baseline data.
   d. involves comparing the use of both pre-test and post-test data from instruments that report client satisfaction of therapy.

108. Which of these solution-focused therapy techniques involves asking clients to describe life without the problem?
   a. pre-therapy change
   b. the miracle question
   c. exception questions
   d. scaling
   e. ormula first session task

109. The techniques of externalization and developing unique events are associated primarily with:
   a. solution-focused therapy.
   b. the linguistic approach.
   c. the narrative approach.
   d. the reflecting team.

110. From a social constructionist perspective, change begins with:
   a. deconstructing the power of cultural narratives.
   b. understanding the root causes of a problem and a client's developing insight.
   c. the therapist's skill in using confrontational techniques and directing the client.
   d. understanding and accepting objective reality.

Family Systems Therapy

111. Ruth seems unable to define herself separately from her husband and her children. In family systems
   a. terminology, Ruth needs to examine her process of:
   b. acculturation.
   c. differentiation.
   d. assimilation.
   e. internalizing conflicts.

112. Ruth and John are generally unable to discuss emotionally charged issues in their own relationship. They focus on their rebellious daughter, Jennifer, as the problem. This is known as:
   a. autonomous relationships.
   b. triangular relationships.
   c. boundary crossings.
   d. arbitrary inference.
   e. family schema.

113. The family therapist working with Ruth makes use of an organized map, or diagram, that demonstrates one's family over three generations. This technique is known as a:
   a. genogram.
   b. life script analysis.
   c. life style analysis.
   d. historical sketch.
   e. multimodal assessment.

114. Differentiation of self is the cornerstone of which theory?
   a. Bowenian family therapy
   b. human validation process model
   c. structural family therapy
   d. strategic family therapy
   e. experiential/symbolic family therapy

115. All of the following are goals of Bowen's multigenerational family therapy approach except for:
   a. bringing about structural change by creating an effective hierarchical structure.
   b. lessening anxiety and relieving symptoms.
   c. increasing the individual member's level of differentiation.
   d. changing individuals within the context of the system.
   e. ending generation-to-generation transmission of problems by resolving emotional attachments.

116. All of the following are phases of the multilensed approach to family systems therapy except for:
   a. forming a relationship.
   b. conducting an assessment.
   c. giving a client a lifestyle assessment, with emphasis on the family constellation.
   d. hypothesizing and sharing meaning.
   e. facilitating change.

117. Which of the following statements about family therapy is false?
   a. An individual is best understood by assessing the interactions between and among family members.
   b. Family therapists today tend to rely on a single theory and are moving away from integrative approaches.
   c. An individual's symptoms are best understood within the context of a dysfunctional system.
   d. Effective family therapy tends to be time-limited, focuses on solutions, and deals with present interactions within the family.
   e. It is essential for family therapists to include an examination of how one's culture has influenced each person in the family.

118. All of the following are goals of Whitaker's experiential family therapy approach except for:
   a. facilitating individual autonomy and a sense of belonging in the family.
   b. helping individuals achieve more intimacy by increasing their awareness and their experiencing.
   c. encouraging members to be themselves by freely expressing what they are thinking and feeling.
   d. supporting spontaneity, creativity, the ability to play, and the willingness to be crazy.
   e. resolving presenting problems by focusing on behavioral sequences.

119. Which of the following is least associated with experiential/symbolic family therapy?
   a. It is an interactive process between a therapist and a family.
   b. It focuses on the here and now.
   c. Techniques grow out of the spontaneous reactions to the present situation within the family therapy context.
   d. Focus is on the subjective needs of the individual in the family.
   e. It is the therapist's task to plan a strategy for solving the problems of each family member.

120. The central goal of _____ is to resolve a family's presenting problem (or symptoms) by focusing on changing its current behavioral sequences.
   a. Bowen's multigenerational approach
   b. Whitaker's experiential family therapy
   c. Haley's strategic family therapy.
   d. Minuchin's structural family therapy.
   e. Satir's human validation model of family therapy.

ANSWER KEY FOR ON-LINE QUIZ ITEMS

1.	E	29.	B	57.	E		
2.	C	30.	A	58.	E	85.	B
3.	D	31.	B	59.	E	86.	B
4.	A	32.	D	60.	C	87.	E
5.	A	33.	B	61.	A	88.	B
6.	A	34.	C	62.	B	89.	E
7.	D	35.	B	63.	E	90.	A
8.	E	36.	C	64.	D	91.	C
9.	C	37.	E	65.	B	92.	A

10.	B	38.	D	66.	D	93.	D
11.	C	39.	C	67.	E	94.	C
12.	B	40.	A	68.	E	95.	B
13.	B	41.	B	69.	C	96.	B
14.	A	42.	E	70.	A	97.	D
15.	A	43.	B	71.	A	98.	C
16.	E	44.	A	72.	D	99.	D
17.	B	45.	D	73.	D	100.	E
18.	B	46.	A	74.	C	101.	A
19.	D	47.	E	75.	A	102.	C
20.	C	48.	E	76.	C	103.	C
21.	B	49.	D	77.	B	104.	D
22.	E	50.	D	78.	E	105.	B
23.	A	51.	E	79.	C	106.	A
24.	C	52.	A	80.	B	107.	B
25.	D	53.	E	81.	B	108.	B
26.	E	54.	A	82.	D	109.	C
27.	B	55.	B	83.	B	110.	A
28.	B	56.	A	84.	D	111.	B
						112.	B
						113.	A
						114.	A
						115.	A
						116.	C
						117.	B
						118.	E
						119.	E
						120.	C

VIII

InfoTrac

Flow Chart

InfoTrac Flow Chart

Start Here

Go to
http://www.infotrac-college.com/wadsworth

Click

Enter *InfoTrac College*

Enter Your Passcode

Hang on to your passcode. You will
need it every time you log in.

First time user

After signing in, the search screen will appear.
Type in the topic you would like to research.
Select *"Subject Guide"* or *"Key Words"* and
click the *"Submit Search"* button.

Activate Your Account

Complete the registration form if you
are a first time user. You must complete
all items in bold type.

Error message

Occurs if registration
items are missing or
invalid.

Click the *"Back"* button
on your browser's
toolbar to return to the
registration form.

Confirm that all
information is accurate.
Click on the *"Submit"*
button to send your
completed registration
form.

Registration Complete

Subject Guide Search

If your search words do not match the
Subject Guide database, a list of similar
and related subjects will come up on the
screen. Simply select the subject that
most closely matches your topic.

Once a subject has been selected from the
database, a screen will appear with links
to *Periodical References, Subdivisions,*
and *Related Subjects*.

Periodical References will list the title,
author and publications for articles
available on your subject.

Subdivisions will list subcategories of
articles on your subject.

Related Subjects will list topics closely
associated to your subject.

Continue

$$\left(\begin{array}{c}\textit{Continue}\\\textit{Subject Guide}\\\textit{Search}\end{array}\right)$$

A list will appear on the screen containing
bibliographic information for each article in your
search up to a maximum of 20 articles per page.

To select an article check the *"Mark"* box by clicking on
it with your mouse.

To read your selected articles click on the *"View Text
and Retrieval Choices"* link.

To narrow your search click on the *"Limit Search"* link
located at the top of the list of articles screen.

The screen will narrow the search to reference articles
with the full text available, by date, journal or word(s).

Your marked articles will have the bibliographic
information at the top of the article followed by an
abstract (when available) and the full text of the
article. To browse through your articles, click on
the *"Previous"* or *"Next"* button.

Using PowerTrac

With **PowerTrac**, a more complex search can be
conducted. Click on the *"Down Arrow"* on the *"Select an
Index"* listbox, choose the criteria you want to use. The
code for your criteria will appear in the entry box. Type
your criteria in the entry box after the code.

If you want to search by multiple criterion, simply
repeat the process with an operator between them.

Logical operators (and/or/not) specify inclusive or
exclusive relationships between search terms or result sets.

Proximity operators (Wn, Nn) specify that two search
terms must be within a specified distance (in words) of
each other. Proximity operators work only with free text
indexes such as keywords, abstracts, text and titles.

Range operators (since, before, etc.) specify upper
bounds, lower bounds or both in searches for numeric
data. Numeric indexes include publication dates, number
of employees and annual sales.

Nesting operators determine the order in which operators
are evaluated.

IX

Overhead Transparency

Masters

Transparency Masters
for Gerald Corey's

THEORY AND PRACTICE OF COUNSELING AND PSYCHOTHERAPY
Seventh Edition

Keith Palmerton

Ashland University

Revisions by:

John Perry

Wadsworth Group

A division of

Thomson Learning, Inc.

CONTENTS

Introduction

- **The author's perspective:**
  - ◆ No single model can explain all the facets of human experience
    - • Eleven approaches to counseling and psychotherapy are discussed

- **The book assumes:**
  - ◆ Students can begin to acquire a counseling style tailored to their own personality
    - • The process will take years
    - • Different theories are not "right" or "wrong"

Where Corey Stands

- He is strongly influenced by the *existential* approach and so believes:
  - ◆ Clients can exercise freedom to choose their future
  - ◆ The quality of the client/therapist relationship is key

- He likes to use a variety of techniques:
  - ◆ Role playing and various techniques from cognitive and behavioral therapy approaches

Where Corey Stands (2)

■ He believes:

◆ "...*counseling entails far more than becoming a skilled technician*"

- Who you are as a therapist, is critical
- Students should experience being a "client" and feel anxiety over self disclosure, and learn to model courage and growth

◆ It is not "*sufficient to be merely a good person with good intentions*"

- Also essential are a knowledge of counseling theory and techniques, theories of personality, and supervised experiences

Suggestions for Using the Book

- Relate readings to your own experiences

  ◆ Reflect on your own needs, motivations, values, and life experiences

- Apply key concepts and techniques to your own personal growth

- Develop a personalized style of counseling that reflects your personality

- Early on, read chapter 16 and skim chapter 15

The Case of Stan (Chapter 16)

- As you read about Stan ask yourself:

  ◆ What themes in Stan's life merit special attention?

  ◆ What techniques and methods would best meet these goals?

  ◆ What characterizes the relationship between Stan and his therapist?

  ◆ How might the therapist precede?

The Effective Counselor

- The most important instrument you have is YOU
  - ◆ Your living example, of who you are and how you struggle to live up to your potential, is powerful
- Be authentic
  - ◆ The stereotyped, professional role can be shed
  - ◆ If you hide behind your role the client will also hide
- Be a therapeutic person and be clear about who you are
  - ◆ Be willing to grow, to risk, to care, and to be involved

Counseling for the Counselor

■ In your experience of being a client you can:

- ◆ Consider your motivation for wanting to be a counselor

- ◆ Find support as you struggle to be a professional

- ◆ Have help in dealing with personal issues that are opened through your interactions with clients

- ◆ Be assisted in managing your countertransferences

■ Corey believes " ...*that therapists cannot hope to open doors for clients that they have not opened for themselves.*"

The Counselor's Values

- Be aware of how your values influence your interventions
- Recognize that you are not value-neutral
- Your job is to assist clients in finding answers that are most congruent with their own values
- Find ways to manage value conflicts between you and your clients
- Begin therapy by exploring the client's goals

Multicultural Counseling

- Become aware of your biases and values

- Attempt to understand the world from your client's vantage point

- Gain a knowledge of the dynamics of oppression, racism, discrimination, and stereotyping

- Study the historical background, traditions, and values of your client

- Be open to learning from your client

Issues Faced by Beginning Therapists

- Achieving a sense of balance and well-being
- Managing difficult and unsatisfying relationships with clients
- Struggling with commitment and personal growth
- Developing healthy, helping relationships with clients

Staying Alive – It's a Prerequisite

- Take care of your single most important instrument – YOU

- Know what <u>causes</u> burnout

- Know how to <u>recognize</u> and <u>remedy</u> burnout

- Know how to <u>prevent</u> burnout

Ethical Decision Making

- **The principles that underlie our professional codes**
  - ◆ Benefit others, do no harm, respect other's autonomy, be just, fair and faithful

- **The role of ethical codes – they:**
  - ◆ Educate us about responsibilities, are a basis for accountability, protect clients, are a basis for improving professional practice

- **Making ethical decisions**
  - ◆ Identify the problem, review relevant codes, seek consultation, brainstorm, list consequences and decide

Client's Rights

- Clients need enough information about the counseling process to be able to make informed choices

- Educate clients about their rights and responsibilities

- Confidentiality is essential but not absolute

  - ◆ Exceptions:
    - The client poses a danger to others or self
    - A client under the age of 16 is the victim of abuse
    - The client needs to be hospitalized
    - The information is made an issue in a court action
    - The client requests a release of record

Multicultural Issues

- *Biases are reflected when we:*
  - ◆ Neglect social and community factors to focus unduly on individualism
  - ◆ Assess clients with instruments that have not been normed on the population they represent
  - ◆ Judge as psychopathological – behaviors, beliefs, or experiences that are normal for the client's culture

Dual Relationships

- **Some helpful questions:**

  ◆ Will my dual relationship keep me from confronting and challenging the client?

  ◆ Will my needs for the relationship become more important than therapeutic activities?

  ◆ Can my client manage the dual relationship?

  ◆ Whose needs are being met -- my client's or my own?

  ◆ Can I recognize and manage professionally my attraction to my client?

The Development of Personality

- **ORAL STAGE**   **First year**
  - ◆ Related to later mistrust and rejection issues
- **ANAL STAGE**   **Ages 1-3**
  - ◆ Related to later personal power issues
- **PHALLIC STAGE**   **Ages 3-6**
  - ◆ Related to later sexual attitudes
- **LATENCY STAGE**   **Ages 6-12**
  - ◆ A time of socialization
- **GENITAL STAGE**   **Ages 12-60**
  - ◆ Sexual energies are invested in life

Theory and Practice of Counseling and Psychotherapy - Chapter 4 (1)

The Structure of Personality

- **THE ID — The Demanding Child**
  - ◆ Ruled by the pleasure principle
- **THE EGO — The Traffic Cop**
  - ◆ Ruled by the reality principle
- **THE SUPEREGO — The Judge**
  - ◆ Ruled by the moral principle

The Unconscious

- **Clinical evidence for postulating the unconscious:**
  - ◆ Dreams
  - ◆ Slips of the tongue
  - ◆ Posthypnotic suggestions
  - ◆ Material derived from free-association
  - ◆ Material derived from projective techniques
  - ◆ Symbolic content of psychotic symptoms
    - • NOTE: consciousness is only a thin slice of the total mind

Ego-Defense Mechanisms

- **Ego-defense mechanisms:**
  - ◆ Are normal behaviors which operate on an unconscious level and tend to deny or distort reality
  - ◆ Help the individual cope with anxiety and prevent the ego from being overwhelmed
  - ◆ Have adaptive value if they do not become a style of life to avoid facing reality

Psychoanalytic Techniques

- **Free Association**
  - ◆ Client reports immediately without censoring any feelings or thoughts
- **Interpretation**
  - ◆ Therapist points out, explains, and teaches the meanings of whatever is revealed
- **Dream Analysis**
  - ◆ Therapist uses the "royal road to the unconscious" to bring unconscious material to light

Transference and Countertransference

- **Transference**
  - ◆ The client reacts to the therapist as he did to an earlier significant other
    - • This allows the client to experience feelings that would otherwise be inaccessible
    - • ANALYSIS OF TRANSFERENCE — allows the client to achieve insight into the influence of the past

- **Countertransference**
  - ◆ The reaction of the therapist toward the client that may interfere with objectivity

Theory and Practice of Counseling and Psychotherapy - Chapter 4 (6)

Resistance

- Resistance
  - ◆ Anything that works against the progress of therapy and prevents the production of unconscious material

- Analysis of Resistance
  - ◆ Helps the client to see that canceling appointments, fleeing from therapy prematurely, etc., are ways of defending against anxiety
    - • These acts interfere with the ability to accept changes which could lead to a more satisfying life

Alfred Adler's Individual Psychology

- A phenomenological approach
- Social interest is stressed
- Birth order and sibling relationships
- Therapy as teaching, informing and <u>encouraging</u>
- Basic mistakes in the client's private logic
- The therapeutic relationship — a collaborative partnership

The Phenomenological Approach

- **Adlerians attempt to view the world from the client's <u>subjective</u> frame of reference**

  - ◆ How life is in reality is less important than how the individual believes life to be

  - ◆ It is not the childhood experiences that are crucial – it is our present <u>interpretation</u> of these events

- **Unconscious instincts and our past do not determine our behavior**

Social Interest

- **Adler's most significant and distinctive concept**

    ◆ Refers to an individual's attitude toward and <u>awareness</u> of being a part of the human community

    ◆ <u>Mental health</u> is measured by the degree to which we successfully share with others and are concerned with their welfare

    ◆ Happiness and success are largely related to social connectedness

Birth Order

■ **Adler's five psychological positions:**

1) <u>Oldest child</u> – receives more attention, spoiled, center of attention

2) <u>Second of only two</u> – behaves as if in a race, often opposite to first child

3) <u>Middle</u> – often feels squeezed out

4) <u>Youngest</u> – the baby

5) <u>Only</u> – does not learn to share or cooperate with other children, learns to deal with adults

Encouragement

- **Encouragement is the most powerful method available for changing a person's beliefs**

  - ◆ Helps build self-confidence and stimulates courage

  - ◆ Discouragement is the basic condition that prevents people from functioning

  - ◆ Clients are encouraged to recognize that they have the power to choose and to act differently

Existential Therapy

A Philosophical/Intellectual Approach to Therapy

- **BASIC DIMENSIONS – OF THE HUMAN CONDITION**

    ◆ The capacity for self-awareness

    ◆ The tension between freedom & responsibility

    ◆ The creation of an identity & establishing meaningful relationships

    ◆ The search for meaning

    ◆ Accepting anxiety as a condition of living

    ◆ The awareness of death and nonbeing

The Capacity for Self-Awareness

- The greater our awareness, the greater our possibilities for freedom
- Awareness is realizing that:
  - ◆ We are finite - time is limited
  - ◆ We have the potential, the choice, to act or not to act
  - ◆ Meaning is not automatic - we must seek it
  - ◆ We are subject to loneliness, meaninglessness, emptiness, guilt, and isolation

Identity and Relationship

■ Identity is "the courage to be" – We must trust ourselves to search within and find our own answers

◆ Our great fear is that we will discover that there is no core, no self

■ Relatedness – At their best our relationships are based on our desire for fulfillment, not our deprivation

◆ Relationships that spring from our sense of deprivation are clinging, parasitic, and symbiotic

The Search for Meaning

- **Meaning – like pleasure, meaning must be pursued obliquely**
  - ◆ Finding meaning in life is a by-product of a commitment to creating, loving, and working
- **"The will to meaning" is our primary striving**
  - ◆ Life is not meaningful in itself; the individual must create and discover meaning

Anxiety – A Condition of Living

- *Existential anxiety is normal* - life cannot be lived, nor can death be faced, without anxiety

  ◆ Anxiety can be a stimulus for growth as we become aware of and accept our freedom

  ◆ We can blunt our anxiety by creating the illusion that there is security in life

  ◆ If we have the courage to face ourselves and life we may be frightened, but we will be able to change

Theory and Practice of Counseling and Psychotherapy - Chapter 6 (5)

Relationship Between Therapist and Client

- **Therapy is a journey taken by therapist and client**
  - ◆ **The person-to-person relationship is key**
  - ◆ **The relationship demands that therapists be in contact with their own phenomenological world**

- **The core of the therapeutic relationship**
  - ◆ **Respect and faith in the clients' potential to cope**
  - ◆ **Sharing reactions with genuine concern and empathy**

Person-Centered Therapy

(A reaction against the directive and psychoanalytic approaches)

■ **Challenges:**

◆ The assumption that "the counselor knows best"

◆ The validity of advice, suggestion, persuasion, teaching, diagnosis, and interpretation

◆ The belief that clients cannot understand and resolve their own problems without direct help

◆ The focus on problems over persons

Person-Centered Therapy

- **Emphasizes:**
  - ◆ Therapy as a journey shared by two fallible people
  - ◆ The person's innate striving for self-actualization
  - ◆ The personal characteristics of the therapist and the quality of the therapeutic relationship
  - ◆ The counselor's creation of a permissive, "growth promoting" climate
  - ◆ People are capable of self-directed growth if involved in a therapeutic relationship

A Growth-Promoting Climate

- Congruence - genuineness or realness
- Unconditional positive regard- acceptance and caring, but not approval of all behavior
- Accurate empathic understanding – an ability to deeply grasp the client's subjective world
  - ◆ Helper attitudes are more important than knowledge

Six Conditions

(necessary and sufficient for personality changes to occur)

1. Two persons are in psychological contact

2. The first, the client, is experiencing incongruency

3. The second person, the therapist, is congruent or integrated in the relationship

4. The therapist experiences unconditional positive regard or real caring for the client

5. The therapist experiences empathy for the client's internal frame of reference and endeavors to communicate this to the client

6. The communication to the client is, to a minimal degree, achieved

The Therapist

- Focuses on the quality of the therapeutic relationship
- Serves as a model of a human being struggling toward greater realness
- Is genuine, integrated, and authentic, without a false front
- Can openly express feelings and attitudes that are present in the relationship with the client

Gestalt Therapy

- *Existential & Phenomenological* – it is grounded in the client's "here and now"

- *Initial goal* is for clients to gain awareness of what they are experiencing and doing *now*

  ◆ Promotes direct experiencing *rather than* the abstractness of talking about situations

  ◆ Rather than talk about a childhood trauma the client is encouraged to become the hurt child

The Now

- Our "power is in the present"
  - ◆ Nothing exists except the "now"
  - ◆ The past is gone and the future has not yet arrived
- For many people the power of the present is lost
  - ◆ They may focus on their past mistakes or engage in endless resolutions and plans for the future

Unfinished Business

- **Feelings about the past are unexpressed**
  - ◆ These feelings are associated with distinct memories and fantasies
  - ◆ Feelings not fully experienced linger in the background and interfere with effective contact
- **Result:**
  - ◆ Preoccupation, compulsive behavior, wariness oppressive energy and self-defeating behavior

Contact and Resistances to Contact

- **CONTACT** – interacting with nature and with other people without losing one's individuality

- **RESISTANCE TO CONTACT** – the defenses we develop to prevent us from experiencing the present fully

  ◆ Five major channels of resistance:

  - Introjection
  - Projection
  - Retroflection
  - Deflection
  - Confluence

Therapeutic Techniques

- **The experiment in Gestalt Therapy**
- **Preparing clients for experiments**
- **Internal dialogue exercise**
- **Rehearsal exercise**
- **Reversal technique**
- **Exaggeration exercise**

Behavior Therapy

- A set of *clinical procedures* relying on experimental findings of psychological research

  ◆ Based on principles of learning that are systematically applied

    · Treatment goals are specific and measurable

  ◆ Focusing on the client's current problems

    · To help people change maladaptive to adaptive behaviors

  ◆ The therapy is largely educational - teaching clients skills of self-management

Exposure Therapies

- *In Vivo* Desensitization
  - ◆ Brief and graduated exposure to an actual fear situation or event
- Flooding
  - ◆ Prolonged & intensive *in vivo* or imaginal exposure to highly anxiety-evoking stimuli without the opportunity to avoid them
- Eye Movement Desensitization and Reprocessing (EMDR)
  - ◆ An exposure-based therapy that involves imaginal flooding, cognitive restructuring, and the use of rhythmic eye movements and other bilateral stimulation to treat traumatic stress disorders and fearful memories of clients

Four Aspects of Behavior Therapy

1. Classical Conditioning

- ◆ In classical conditioning certain respondent behaviors, such as knee jerks and salivation, are elicited from a passive organism

2. Operant Conditioning

- ◆ Focuses on actions that operate on the environment to produce consequences

  - If the environmental change brought about by the behavior is reinforcing, the chances are strengthened that the behavior will occur again. If the environmental changes produce no reinforcement, the chances are lessened that the behavior will recur

Four Aspects of Behavior Therapy

3. **Social Learning Approach**
   - ◆ Gives prominence to the reciprocal interactions between an individual's behavior and the environment

4. **Cognitive Behavior Therapy**
   - ◆ Emphasizes cognitive processes and private events (such as client's self-talk) as mediators of behavior change

Therapeutic Techniques

- **Relaxation Training** – to cope with stress
- **Systematic Desensitization** – for anxiety and avoidance reactions
- **Modeling** – observational learning
- **Assertion Training** – social-skills training
- **Self-Management Programs** – "giving psychology away"
- **Multimodal Therapy** – a technical eclecticism

Rational Emotive Behavioral Therapy (REBT)

- **Stresses thinking, judging, deciding, analyzing, and doing**

- **Assumes that cognitions, emotions, and behaviors interact and have a reciprocal cause-and-effect relationship**

- **Is highly didactic, very directive, and concerned as much with thinking as with feeling**

- **Teaches that our emotions stem mainly from our beliefs, evaluations, interpretations, and reactions to life situations**

The Therapeutic Process

- **Therapy is seen as an educational process**
- **Clients learn**
  - ◆ To identify and dispute irrational beliefs that are maintained by self-indoctrination
  - ◆ To replace ineffective ways of thinking with effective and rational cognitions
  - ◆ To stop absolutistic thinking, blaming, and repeating false beliefs

View of Human Nature

- We are born with a potential for both rational and irrational thinking

- We have the biological and cultural tendency to think crookedly and to needlessly disturb ourselves

- We learn and invent disturbing beliefs and keep ourselves disturbed through our self-talk

- We have the capacity to change our cognitive, emotive, and behavioral processes

The A-B-C theory

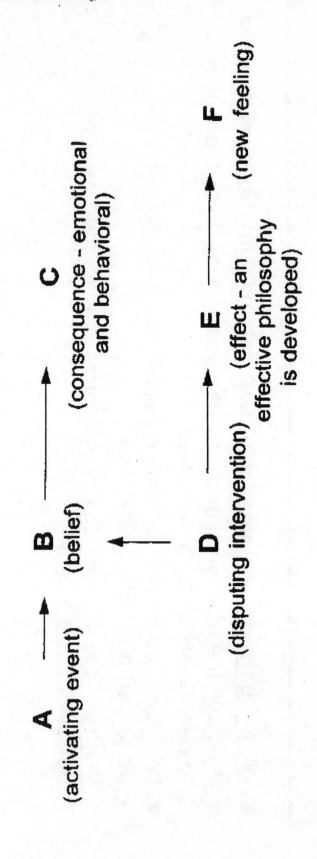

A ⟶ **B** ⟶ **C**
(activating event) (belief) (consequence - emotional and behavioral)

D ⟶ **E** ⟶ **F**
(disputing intervention) (effect - an effective philosophy is developed) (new feeling)

Theory and Practice of Counseling and Psychotherapy - Chapter 10 (4)

Irrational Ideas

- Irrational ideas lead to <u>self-defeating behavior</u>

- Some examples:

  ◆ "I must have love or approval from all the significant people in my life."

  ◆ "I must perform important tasks competently and perfectly."

  ◆ "If I don't get what I want, it's terrible, and I can't stand it."

Aaron Beck's Cognitive Therapy (CT)

- **Insight-focused therapy**
- **Emphasizes changing negative thoughts and maladaptive beliefs**
- **Theoretical Assumptions**
  - ◆ People's internal communication is accessible to introspection
  - ◆ Clients' beliefs have highly personal meanings
  - ◆ These meanings can be discovered by the client rather than being taught or interpreted by the therapist

Theory, Goals & Principles of CT

- **Basic theory:**
  - ◆ To understand the nature of an emotional episode or disturbance it is essential to focus on the cognitive content of an individual's reaction to the upsetting event or stream of thoughts

- **Goals:**
  - ◆ To change the way clients think by using their automatic thoughts to reach the core schemata and begin to introduce the idea of schema restructuring

- **Principles:**
  - ◆ Automatic thoughts: personalized notions that are triggered by particular stimuli that lead to emotional responses

CT's Cognitive Distortions

- **Arbitrary inferences**
- **Selective abstraction**
- **Overgeneralization**
- **Magnification and minimization**
- **Personalization**
- **Labeling and mislabeling**
- **Polarized thinking**

CT's Cognitive Triad

- **Pattern that triggers depression:**

  1. Client holds negative view of themselves

  2. Selective abstraction: Client has tendency to interpret experiences in a negative manner

  3. Client has a gloomy vision and projections about the future

Donald Meichenbaum's Cognitive Behavior Modification (CBM)

- **Focus:**
  - ◆ Client's self-verbalizations or self-statements

- **Premise:**
  - ◆ As a prerequisite to behavior change, clients must notice how they think, feel, and behave, and what impact they have on others

- **Basic assumption:**
  - ◆ Distressing emotions are typically the result of maladaptive thoughts

Meichenbaum's CBM

- **Self-instructional therapy focus:**
  - ◆ Trains clients to modify the instructions they give to themselves so that they can cope
  - ◆ Emphasis is on acquiring practical coping skills
- **Cognitive structure:**
  - ◆ The organizing aspect of thinking, which seems to monitor and direct the choice of thoughts
  - ◆ The "executive processor," which "holds the blueprints of thinking" that determine when to continue, interrupt, or change thinking

Behavior Change & Coping (CBM)

- **3 Phases of Behavior Change**
  1. Self-observation
  2. Starting a new internal dialogue
  3. Learning new skills

- **Coping skills programs – Stress inoculation training (3 phase model)**
  1. The conceptual phase
  2. Skills acquisition and rehearsal phase
  3. Application and follow-through phase

Theory and Practice of Counseling and Psychotherapy - Chapter 10 (12)

Reality Therapy Basic Beliefs

- Emphasis is on responsibility
- Therapist's function is to keep therapy focused on the present
- We often mistakenly choose misery in our best attempt to meet our needs
- We act responsibly when we meet our needs without keeping others from meeting their needs

Basic Needs

■ All internally motivated behavior is geared toward meeting one or more of our basic human needs

- ◆ Belonging
- ◆ Power
- ◆ Freedom
- ◆ Fun
- ◆ Survival (Physiological needs)

■ Our brain functions as a control system to get us what we want

Procedures That Lead to Change:
The "WDEP" System

W Wants - What do you want to be and do?

 Your "picture album"

D Doing and Direction - What are you doing?

 Where do you want to go?

E Evaluation - Does your present behavior have a reasonable
chance of getting you what you want?

P Planning – "SAMIC"

Planning For Change

S Simple - Easy to understand, specific and concrete

A Attainable - Within the capacities and motivation
of the client

M Measurable - Are the changes observable and helpful?

I Immediate and Involved - What can be done today?
What can you do?

C Controlled - Can you do this by yourself or will
you be dependent on others?

Total Behavior
Our Best Attempt to Satisfy Our Needs

- **DOING** – active behaviors
- **THINKING** – thoughts, self-statements
- **FEELINGS** – anger, joy, pain, anxiety
- **PHYSIOLOGY** – bodily reactions

Key Concepts of Feminist Therapy

- Problems are viewed in a sociopolitical and cultural context
- The client knows what is best for her life and is the expert on her own life
- Emphasis is on educating clients about the therapy process
- Traditional ways of assessing psychological health are challenged
- It is assumed that individual change will best occur through social change
- Clients are encouraged to take social action

Four Approaches to Feminist Therapy

1. Liberal Feminism

◆ **Focus**

- Helping individual women overcome the limits and constraints of their socialization patterns

◆ **Major goals**

- Personal empowerment of individual women
- Dignity
- Self-fulfillment
- Equality

Four Approaches to Feminist Therapy

2. Cultural Feminism

◆ Oppression stems from society's devaluation of women's strengths

◆ Emphasize the differences between women and men

◆ Believe the solution to oppression lies in feminization of the culture

  • Society becomes more nurturing, cooperative, and relational

◆ Major goal of therapy is the infusion of society with values based on cooperation

Four Approaches to Feminist Therapy

3. Radical Feminism

◆ Focus

- The oppression of women that is embedded in patriarchy
- Seek to change society through activism
- Therapy is viewed as a political enterprise with the goal of transformation of society

◆ Major goals

- Transform gender relationships
- Transform societal institutions
- Increase women's sexual and procreative self-determination.

Four Approaches to Feminist Therapy

4. Socialist Feminism

◆ Also have goal of societal change

◆ Emphasis on multiple oppressions

◆ Believe solutions to society's problems must include consideration of:

- Class
- Race
- Other forms of discrimination

◆ Major goal of therapy is to transform social relationships and institutions

Principles of Feminist Therapy

- The personal is political

- Personal and social identities are interdependent

- The counseling relationship is egalitarian

- Women's experiences are honored

- Definitions of distress and "mental illness" are reformulated

- There is an integrated analysis of oppression

Goals of Feminist Therapy

- To become aware of one's gender-role socialization process

- To identify internalized gender-role messages and replace them with functional beliefs

- To acquire skills to bring about change in the environment

- To develop a wide range of behaviors that are freely chosen

- To become personally empowered

Intervention Techniques in Feminist Therapy

- **Gender-role analysis and intervention**
  - ◆ To help clients understand the impact of gender-role expectations in their lives
  - ◆ Provides clients with insight into the ways social issues affect their problems

- **Power analysis and power intervention**
  - ◆ Emphasis on the power differences between men and women in society
  - ◆ Clients helped to recognize different kinds of power they possess and how they and others exercise power

Intervention Techniques in Feminist Therapy

- **Bibliotherapy**
  - ◆ Reading assignments that address issues such as
    - Coping skills
    - Gender-role stereotypes
    - Power differential between women and men
    - Gender inequality
    - Ways sexism is promoted
    - Society's obsession with thinness
- **Self-disclosure**
  - ◆ To help equalize the therapeutic relationship and provide modeling for the client
  - Values, beliefs about society, and therapeutic interventions discussed
    - Allows the client to make an informed choice

Intervention Techniques in Feminist Therapy

- **Assertiveness training**
  - ◆ Women become aware of their interpersonal rights
  - ◆ Transcends stereotypical sex roles
  - ◆ Changes negative beliefs
  - ◆ Implement changes in their daily lives
- **Reframing**
  - ◆ Changes the frame of reference for looking at an individual's behavior
    - • Shifting from an intrapersonal to an interpersonal definition of a client's problem

Intervention Techniques in Feminist Therapy

- **Relabeling**
  - ◆ Changes the label or evaluation applied to the client's behavioral characteristics
  - ◆ Generally, the focus is shifted from a negative to a positive evaluation

Third-Wave Feminist Approaches

- **Postmodern feminists** provide a model for critiquing both traditional and feminist approaches

- **Women of color feminists** assert that it is essential that feminist theory be broadened and be made more inclusive

- **Lesbian feminists** call for inclusion of an analysis of multiple identities and their relationship to oppression

- **Global/international feminists** take a world-wide perspective in examining women's experiences across national boundaries

Constructivist Narrative Perspective (CNP)

- **Focuses on the stories people tell about themselves and others about significant events in their lives**

- **Therapeutic task:**

  ◆ **Help clients appreciate how they construct their realities and how they author their own stories**

Social Constructionism

■ **The client, not the therapist, is the expert**

■ **Dialogue is used to elicit perspective, resources, and unique client experiences**

■ **Questions empower clients to speak and to express their diverse positions**

■ **The therapist supplies optimism and the process**

Social Constructionism Therapy Goals

- Generate new meaning in the lives of clients
- Co-develop, with clients, solutions that are unique to the situation
- Enhance awareness of the impact of various aspects of the dominant culture on the individual
- Help people develop alternative ways of being, acting, knowing, and living

Key Concepts of Social Constructionism

- Postmodernists assume there are multiple truths

- Reality is subjective and is based on the use of language

- Postmodernists strive for a collaborative and consultative stance

- Postmodern thought has an impact on the development of many theories

Key Concepts of
Solution-Focused Brief Therapy

- Therapy grounded on a positive orientation --- people are healthy and competent

- Past is downplayed, while present and future are highlighted

- Therapy is concerned with looking for what is working

- Therapists assist clients in finding exceptions to their problems

- There is a shift from "problem-orientation" to "solution-focus"

- Emphasis is on constructing solutions rather than problem solving

Basic Assumptions of Solution-Focused Therapy

- People can create their own solutions

- Small changes lead to large changes

- The client is the expert on his or her own life

- The best therapy involves a collaborative partnership

- A therapist's not knowing afford the client an opportunity to construct a solution

Questions in
Solution-Focused Brief Therapy

- Skillful questions allows people to utilize their resources

- Asking "how questions" that imply change can be useful

- Effective questions focus attention on solutions

- Questions can get clients to notice when things were better

- Useful questions assist people in paying attention to what they are doing

- Questions can open up possibilities for clients to do something different

Three Kinds of Relationships in Solution-Focused Therapy

- **Customer-type relationship:** client and therapist jointly identify a problem and a solution to work toward

- **Complainant relationship:** a client who describes a problem, but is not able or willing to take an active role in constructing a solution

- **Visitors:** clients who come to therapy because someone else thinks they have a problem

Techniques Used in
Solution-Focused Brief Therapy

■ **Pre-therapy change**

   ◆ (What have you done since you made the appointment that has made a
   difference in your problem?)

■ **Exception questions**

   ◆ (Direct clients to times in their lives when the problem did not exist)

■ **Miracle question**

   ◆ (If a miracle happened and the problem you have was solved while you
   were asleep, what would be different in your life?)

■ **Scaling questions**

   ◆ (On a scale of zero to 10, where zero is the worst you have been and 10
   represents the problem being solved, where are you with respect to
   _____?)

Key Concepts of Narrative Therapy

- Listen to clients with an open mind

- Encourage clients to share their stories

- Listen to a problem-saturated story of a client without getting stuck

- Therapists demonstrate respectful curiosity and persistence

- The person is not the problem, but the problem is the problem

The Therapeutic Process in Narrative Therapy

- Collaborate with the client in identifying (naming) the problem

- Separate the person from his or her problem

- Investigate how the problem has been disrupting or dominating the person

- Search for exceptions to the problem

- Ask clients to speculate about what kind of future they could expect from the competent person that is emerging

- Create an audience to support the new story

Theory and Practice of Counseling and Psychotherapy - Chapter 13 (11)

The Functions of the Narrative Therapist

- To become active facilitators

- To demonstrate care, interest, respectful curiosity, openness, empathy, contact, and fascination

- To adopt a not-knowing position that allows being guided by the client's story

- To help clients construct a preferred story line

- To create a collaborative relationship --- with the client being the senior partner

The Role of Questions in Narrative Therapy

- **Questions are used as a way to generate experience rather than to gather information**

- **Questions are always asked from a position of respect, curiosity, and openness**

- **Therapists ask questions from a not-knowing stance**

- **By asking questions, therapists assist clients in exploring dimensions of their life situations**

- **Questions can lead to taking apart problem-saturated stories**

Externalization

- Living life means relating to problems, not being fused with them

- Externalization is a process of separating the person from identifying with the problem

- Externalizing conversations help people in freeing themselves from being identifying with the problem

- Externalizing conversations can lead clients in recognizing times when they have dealt successfully with the problem

Deconstruction and Creating Alternative Stories

- Problem-saturated stories are deconstructed (taken apart) before new stories are co-created

- The assumption is that people can continually and actively re-author their lives

- Unique possibility questions enable clients to focus on their future

- An appreciative audience helps new stories to take root

The Family Systems Perspective

- **Individuals – are best understood through assessing the interactions within an entire family**

- **Symptoms – are viewed as an expression of a dysfunction within a family**

- **Problematic behaviors –**
  - ◆ Serve a purpose for the family
  - ◆ Are a function of the family's inability to operate productively
  - ◆ Are symptomatic patterns handed down across generations

- **A family – is an interactional unit and a change in one member effects all members**

Theory and Practice of Counseling and Psychotherapy - Chapter 14 (1)

Adlerian Family Therapy

- Adlerians use an educational model to counsel families

- Emphasis is on family atmosphere and family constellation

- Therapists function as collaborators who seek to join the family

- Parent interviews yield hunches about the purposes underlying children's misbehavior

Adlerian Family Therapy
Therapy Goals

- Unlock mistaken goals and interactional patterns

- Engage parents in a learning experience and a collaborative assessment

- Emphasis is on the family's motivational patterns

- Main aim is to initiate a reorientation of the family

Multigenerational Family Therapy

- **The application of rational thinking to emotionally saturated systems**
  - ◆ A well-articulated theory is considered to be essential
- **With the proper knowledge the individual can change**
  - ◆ Change occurs only <u>with</u> other family members
- **Differentiation of the self**
  - ◆ A psychological separation from others
- **Triangulation**
  - ◆ A third party is recruited to reduce anxiety and stabilize a couples' relationship

Multigenerational Family Therapy Therapy Goals

- To change the individuals within the context of the system
- To end generation-to-generation transmission of problems by resolving emotional attachments
- To lessen anxiety and relieve symptoms
- To increase the individual member's level of differentiation

Human Validation Process Model

- Enhancement and validation of self-esteem
- Family rules
- Congruence and openness in communications
- Sculpting
- Nurturing triads
- Family mapping and chronologies

Human Validation Process Model
Therapy Goals

- **Open communications**
  - ◆ Individuals are allowed to honestly report their perceptions
- **Enhancement of self-esteem**
  - ◆ Family decisions are based on individual needs
- **Encouragement of growth**
  - ◆ Differences are acknowledged and seen as opportunities for growth
- **Transform extreme rules into useful and functional rules**
  - ◆ Families have many spoken and unspoken rules

Experiential Family Therapy

- **A freewheeling, intuitive, sometimes outrageous approach aiming to:**
  - ◆ Unmask pretense, create new meaning, and liberate family members to be themselves
- **Techniques are secondary to the therapeutic relationship**
- **Pragmatic and atheoretical**
- **Interventions create turmoil and intensify what is going on here and now in the family**

Experiential Family Therapy
Therapy Goals

- Facilitate individual autonomy <u>and</u> a sense of belonging in the family

- Help individuals achieve more intimacy by increasing their awareness and their experiencing

- Encourage members to be themselves by freely expressing what they are thinking and feeling

- Support spontaneity, creativity, the ability to play, and the willingness to be "crazy"

Structural Family Therapy

- Focus is on family interactions to understand the structure, or organization of the family

- Symptoms are a by-product of structural failings

- Structural changes must occur in a family before an individual's symptoms can be reduced

- Techniques are active, directive, and well thought-out

Structural Family Therapy
Therapy Goals

- Reduce symptoms of dysfunction
- Bring about structural change by:
  - ◆ Modifying the family's transactional rules
  - ◆ Developing more appropriate boundaries
  - ◆ Creation of an effective hierarchical structure
    - It is assumed that faulty family structures have:
      - Boundaries that are rigid or diffuse
      - Subsystems that have inappropriate tasks and functions

Strategic Family Therapy

- Focuses on solving problems in the present

- Presenting problems are accepted as "real" and not a symptom of system dysfunction

- Therapy is brief, process-focused, and solution-oriented

- The therapist designs strategies for change

- Change results when the family follows the therapist's directions & change transactions

Strategic Family Therapy
Therapy Goals

- Resolve presenting problems by focusing on behavioral sequences

- Get people to behave differently

- Shift the family organization so that the presenting problem is no longer functional

- Move the family toward the appropriate stage of family development
  - Problems often arise during the transition from one developmental stage to the next